About Pfeiffer

Pfeiffer serves the professional development and hands-on resource needs of training and human resource practitioners and gives them products to do their jobs better. We deliver proven ideas and solutions from experts in HR development and HR management, and we offer effective and customizable tools to improve workplace performance. From novice to seasoned professional, Pfeiffer is the source you can trust to make yourself and your organization more successful.

Essential Knowledge   Pfeiffer produces insightful, practical, and comprehensive materials on topics that matter the most to training and HR professionals. Our Essential Knowledge resources translate the expertise of seasoned professionals into practical, how-to guidance on critical workplace issues and problems. These resources are supported by case studies, worksheets, and job aids and are frequently supplemented with CD-ROMs, websites, and other means of making the content easier to read, understand, and use.

Essential Tools   Pfeiffer's Essential Tools resources save time and expense by offering proven, ready-to-use materials—including exercises, activities, games, instruments, and assessments—for use during a training or team-learning event. These resources are frequently offered in looseleaf or CD-ROM format to facilitate copying and customization of the material.

Pfeiffer also recognizes the remarkable power of new technologies in expanding the reach and effectiveness of training. While e-hype has often created whizbang solutions in search of a problem, we are dedicated to bringing convenience and enhancements to proven training solutions. All our e-tools comply with rigorous functionality standards. The most appropriate technology wrapped around essential content yields the perfect solution for today's on-the-go trainers and human resource professionals.

Pfeiffer
www.pfeiffer.com

Essential resources for training and HR professionals

Rapid Instructional Design

Rapid Instructional Design

Learning ID Fast and Right

SECOND EDITION

George M. Piskurich

Pfeiffer

A Wiley Imprint
www.pfeiffer.com

For additional copies/bulk purchases of this book in the U.S. please contact 800-274-4434.

Pfeiffer books and products are available through most bookstores. To contact Pfeiffer directly call our Customer Care Department within the U.S. at 800-274-4434, outside the U.S. at 317-572-3985, fax 317-572-4002, or visit www.pfeiffer.com.

Pfeiffer also publishes its books in a variety of electronic formats. Some content that appears in print may not be available in electronic books.

Library of Congress Cataloging-in-Publication Data

Piskurich, George M.
Rapid instructional design: learning ID fast and right / George M. Piskurich.—2nd ed.
p. cm.
Includes index.
ISBN-13: 978-0-7879-8073-3 (alk. paper)
ISBN-10: 0-7879-8073-0 (alk. paper)
1. Instructional systems—Design. I. Title.
LB1028.38.P57   2006
371.33—dc22   2006008739

Acquiring Editor: Matthew Davis
Production Editor: Justin Frahm
Editor: Kristi Hein
Manufacturing Supervisor: Becky Carreño
Editorial Assistant: Leota Higgins

Printed in the United States of America
PB Printing   10 9 8 7 6 5 4 3

Contents

Preface to the Second Edition

Since the completion of the first edition of *Rapid Instructional Design*, very little has changed concerning *how* we do ID, but very much has changed concerning *what* we do with it. E-learning, which was in its infancy back then, has become a major delivery system, and both organizations and their instructional designers are still struggling with how to take advantage of all that it promises, not to mention all the promises that were made about it.

Thus we have added two chapters on e-learning to this edition: the first, Chapter Nine, deals with *asynchronous e-learning*, which is basically the design of self-instruction in a net-based delivery; the second, Chapter Ten, addresses *synchronous e-learning*, with an emphasis on preparing facilitators as well as designers for this new and inarguably different delivery process.

You'll also find a bit of information in Chapter Nine on asynchronous e-learning in general, particularly as it relates to the design decision and to creating an e-learning system for your organization, and a brief consideration in Chapter Ten on online learning, which we define here as an ID technique that combines what our academic colleagues do when they teach a class on line with what we know about ID to create a hybrid delivery that can make e-learning faster to design and more effective, while holding down the costs.

Beyond these major additions, this second edition explores some new concepts (which aren't necessarily new, but just weren't in the first edition)—such as learning analysis, one-on-one design, and blended designs—and augments the discussions of evaluation, particularly Levels 4 and 5, analysis, and working with subject matter experts (SMEs). Finally, this edition presents you with some new job aids to help make your instructional design even more rapid.

We hope all of these changes will help to make you an even better instructional designer than you already are.

A special thanks to Shaunda Paden for her incisive thoughts on how to make this edition better than the last.

—George

Introduction

The purpose of this book is to consider how to make both the learning and the doing of instructional design faster. Proper instructional design is an absolutely critical but very time-consuming aspect of any training process, so finding techniques to do it right—but rapidly—is important, and the benefits of employing these techniques are pretty obvious.

This book covers all the basics of instructional design, from analysis to evaluation, and perhaps just a little more, but does so without the theory, with plenty of practical checklists, and with many hints on how to design better and more quickly in this age of technology-based training.

Some might say that in dealing with basic instructional design this book is treading on much furrowed ground. Although this may be the case, we will be using a somewhat different type of plow; and perhaps it is time to revisit that ground, particularly from a new perspective.

Instructional design is a difficult topic to write about at best. It seems that no matter what you say or how you say it you'll miss the mark for someone. You'll be too theoretical for some, yet not theoretical enough for others; too simplistic in your explanations or not basic enough; too focused on the needs of the new designer or the needs of experienced practitioners—and what about the "sometimes designer"?—and so on.

Add to this quandary the concept of *rapid* instructional design, which presents questions such as What can you skip in the design process? What had you better *not* skip unless you truly know what you're doing? Can it be rapid and still be right?—and you're simply asking for more trouble. So what can I say, except, "We're asking."

AUDIENCES

The concept of rapid instructional design means different things to different people; therefore there are a number of intended audiences for this book.

The first and perhaps foremost is what I term *occasional* designers. These are individuals who, because of their subject-matter expertise, are called on to train others from time to time—and not just to "do" the training, but to create it. For you, this book will present a basic instructional design methodology that will help you to create effective training. By *effective* I mean training that meets the needs of your trainees and of those who assigned you this task. The process will be rapid because I've left out the theory and provided numerous checklists to help you through the process.

The second audience is those individuals who, without really planning it or in most cases being prepared for it, have become training professionals. I've met many of you in my wanderings. Sometimes you're assigned to a training position for a year or two as part of your career development or because the company needs you there. Others have been excellent occasional trainers who for one reason or another find themselves permanently assigned to a training function, or who become personally responsible for all the training for their work groups.

What you all have in common is that you want to do a good job, but you need the right tools. This book will provide you with those tools—everything from analyzing your work group or company for training needs to evaluating programs to make sure those needs have been met—and all the design and development required in between. Once again, we'll do it rapidly, with minimal theory and maximum practical information in the form of hints for doing what needs to be done better and faster.

The third audience comprises those who need to know about instructional design but are not, and probably never will be, practitioners. This includes managers and administrators who must make decisions about what training their work groups require and how to do it most efficiently, human resources professionals who need to understand a bit about instructional design as part of their job responsibilities, and sales colleagues in training and consulting organizations who are responsible for helping their clients understand what this instructional design "stuff" (particularly new technology training) is all about.

The final audience is seasoned practitioners who are looking for rapid methods for doing instructional design. We will not be exploring these concepts in detail in this book, but we will recognize and discuss them. We'll explore how they fit into the basic instructional design process, both as we encounter them and in the last chapter.

SPECIAL ELEMENTS

To deal with these various audiences and their varied needs, this book uses some special elements. One of the most obvious is the icons. There are two basic types of icons that you may see at the beginning of a section or subsection. The first is a ⊘. This means that this area is *not critical for an occasional designer.* If you are a reader who is basically a subject-matter expert asked to design and teach a specific course, when you see the ⊘ icon you can probably skip this section with no harm done. It's not that the concepts discussed in these sections are not important to instructional design, it's just that because you are designing a single course for which you are the expert, and the topic has been decided on, and no one will teach it but you, doing everything in these sections would be overkill or not particularly useful for you. Remember, we are effecting *rapid* instructional design here, so you should only do what you really need to do for your training situation.

This process is called *situational instructional design,* and we could fill the entire book with all the various instructional design situations and what you should do in each. However, for the sake of creating a book that might be read, instead of one that makes a great doorstop, we'll only deal with this one general situation as it relates to one of our chosen audiences. Once again, if you are a subject-matter expert, designing and instructing for a topic that has been assigned to you, you can skip the areas marked with a ⊘.

You'll also find areas marked with the ◖ icon without a slash. These are areas *of special interest to you as an occasional designer.* Most often they will indicate places where we'll tell you how you can shortcut the concept we are discussing, due to your particular situation.

The second type of icon is a ✥. A ✥ means that the information following is a rapid design *shortcut.* This is mainly for readers who are seasoned practitioners, to help them find the rapid design aspects of the book without reading through a lot of what they already know. It does not mean that those readers who are in other audiences should not read these pieces; there is almost always some useful information for everyone in any section. However, using the rapid techniques might not be the best approach for an inexperienced designer.

If you're part of the other audiences, you should be able to utilize just about everything in the book somewhere along the line in your instructional design processes.

A second special element, besides the icons, is the recommended resources. Each resource is what I consider to be the best book, magazine article, or website for further information on the topic. You'll find them in every chapter whenever I have a recommendation for a new topic or concept as it's introduced. These resources are mainly for those readers who need to know more, such as those of you who have just taken on full-time training or training management responsibilities. The full reference titles are provided at the end of the book, in sections and alphabetically by title.

Now I don't want to start a big controversy with my recommendations, so please note that these are only my opinions, and only in relation to the specific audiences we just discussed. Please don't call, write, or e-mail asking why I didn't choose such and such, or how could I have missed so and so. I'll be more than glad to hear from you concerning nearly anything else in the book, or instructional design, or training in general.

Another special element is the *hints* at the end of some of the chapters. One of the difficulties in talking about instructional design is that sooner or later you get off on tangents, particularly when you begin to discuss delivery systems. As we wanted to make the basic information in this book as simple and straightforward as possible for the new or occasional designer, we took many of these tangents and simply made bulleted lists for them, included in the hints area. Some of these lists get pretty extensive, particularly when discussing media formats, but don't forget that they are resources, not intended to be read as a list. Refer to them as required for your needs. Simply reading through them will not be particularly effective.

There is also a Glossary. The definitions there include ones that are more or less accepted and others that are simply practical. Some are mine; some are borrowed in part or whole from others. We'll note within a chapter when a certain usage might be more relevant for this book. However, the Glossary goes well beyond this to explore a number of possible terms and definitions. For example, we'll use *trainee* rather than *student* and *trainer* instead of *instructor* in most cases in this book, but you'll find all of these terms in the glossary.

The Suggested Readings at the end of the book are exactly that, not references or a bibliography. They are divided by topical area to make it easier for you to use, although some books tend to spill over into a number of topics. They are alphabetized, not prioritized.

The Other Resources listing at the end of the book contains mostly websites that have information on the various topics and some pointers to periodicals or groups that can help you if you need to explore a concept in greater detail or if you just like electronic communications better than print.

ORGANIZATION OF THE BOOK

The problem with organizing any instructional design book is that the instructional design process is not what it seems, or at least not what most people make it out to be. It is not a simple linear method that starts with analysis and moves on through stages to evaluation, even though that's what you see in most models. Instead, it's more like a connected circle, with the end feeding back into the beginning, or even like a web with all of the aspects interconnected and leading to parts of each other.

But because a book is linear, the organization of instructional design herein will be as well, using the tried-and-true five-component design model of analysis, design, development, implementation, and evaluation. We'll start in Chapter One with a basic introduction and some thoughts on why instructional design is important. Don't get this *why* confused with theory. I think it's important here and there to have a brief discussion of *why* you want to do certain aspects of instructional design, particularly the process as a whole, but we won't be looking at the theory behind the why, just the practical necessity.

 Believe it or not, this is a good place for the first of those rapid design hints we just discussed. Because instructional design is like a web, you don't have to complete all of one component before moving on to the next. For example, you may choose to begin developing some of your training material even as you're finishing the analysis component. You may need to do a little rewriting at the end, but the majority of what you do will be fine, and you won't have wasted time waiting for all the analysis data to be in before moving on.

Chapter Two deals with what we term *pre-instructional design* activities— that is, things that need to be done before you actually begin to design your program. These include concepts such as training needs assessments, performance assessments, and cost-benefit analysis. If you're an occasional designer, most of Chapter Two will be less important to you, whereas if you are newly in charge of a training function, the information here will be critical. Follow the icons and use your own situation as your guide.

Many experts would say that Chapter Three is the real beginning of instructional design, the component known as analysis. Of course, just as many would say that Chapter Two is the real beginning, as much of what we accomplish there feeds into analysis. Anyway, we'll look at the various types of analysis, what they are used for, and the methods for doing them. There are a number of them and all are important, although some will be more critical than others, depending on your particular situation.

Chapter Four is very long because it deals with a number of critical design issues. We start with another analysis that determines what delivery system will be most effective for your training tasks and your organization. This in itself is controversial, as some designers balk at deciding on a delivery system before writing objectives and content. However, with all the technology variations that are available for delivering training today, and their associated cost in both dollars and time, we feel that a delivery decision is a critical early step in the design component.

We'll move from there to objectives, design documents, test questions, and instructional plans to complete the design component. This is actually a more-or-less random stopping point for Chapter Four. Some of these concepts could just as easily fit into the delivery component; others interrelate so much that it is hard to tell where they go—but we had to stop somewhere.

Chapter Five is the delivery component, which is concerned with the actual development of the training materials. We follow a lesson plan format in this chapter. Even though lesson plans are basically a classroom delivery product, they make a good outline for on-the-job training (OJT) and for technology-based training (TBT) as well, which covers most of the other major delivery systems. We discuss openings, motivation, activities, summaries, and some evaluation aspects.

Because development is the component during which you add media, the hints section there is pretty formidable. We cover ideas on everything from flip charts to satellite mediated broadcasts, with plenty of attention on the technologies such as multimedia and net-based training. (*Note*: There is a lot of terminology flying around concerning the process of internet-, intranet-, and web-based training. In this book, we will use the term *net-based training* to mean any type of training for which a computer network is the delivery system. This might include intranets, internets, and webs. If there is a particular reason for focusing on one of these processes over the others, it will be called out specifically.)

Chapter Six is concerned with program implementation. However, it begins with information on pilots and beta testing. Some would say that this material belongs with evaluation (Chapter Seven) or even development, as—like many instructional design activities—it has a lot of connections to both. We chose the implementation connection, as this is the first time you'll actually see your training implemented. Chapter Six continues with some general concerns, and the hints section contains ideas for various types of implementations.

Chapter Seven deals with evaluation: both of the trainees, which is discussed in various other chapters as well, and of the training program itself. We cover reasons for doing evaluations, what might be evaluated, and how to evaluate, as well as evaluation of self-instructional programs, which requires a somewhat different approach. Thoughts on revising programs and program materials end the chapter and bring us back full circle to analysis, which is the end product of evaluation.

The purpose of Chapter Eight is to provide you with a little more detail on a number of rapid design techniques. This chapter is more for the experienced designer, but the concepts may be interesting to all readers. These short discussions are not meant to make you an expert on these methods, but rather to supply you with enough information to decide whether they are useful for you and, with the suggested readings, to send you on your way to learning more about them.

Chapters Nine and Ten consider the design of two newer and widely used delivery systems: asynchronous and synchronous e-learning.

As we noted earlier, instructional design, particularly rapid instructional design, is not an easy concept to discuss. It is highly situational, often depending on the level of knowledge of the designer, the organizational environment, the needs of the trainees, the responsibilities of the trainers, and other even less tangible things. I hope that this book will help you deal with these complexities and make your instructional designing the best, and fastest, it can be.

Rapid Instructional Design

Chapter 1

What Is This Instructional Design Stuff Anyway?

This chapter will help you to:

- Discover why you need instructional design
- Begin to see what instructional design is
- Consider the advantages and disadvantages of instructional design

*T*here is an old saying that if you don't know where you are going, any road will get you there. This is a fine philosophy if you are spending the summer between your junior and senior year "experiencing" Europe or if you have embarked on an Australian "walk-about," but when you are developing training programs it leaves a lot to be desired.

One purpose of instructional design is to provide both an appropriate destination and the right road to get you there, whenever you are responsible for creating a training program. Your destination is usually some form of learning that your trainees will accomplish; the road is one of the many paths that instruction can follow to facilitate that learning.

Instructional design, stripped to its basics, is simply a process for helping you to create effective training in an efficient manner. It is a system—perhaps more accurately a number of systems—that helps you ask the right questions, make the right decisions, and produce a product that is as useful and useable as your situation requires and allows.

Some people refer to instructional design as the "science" of instruction because it follows a set of theories and methods and is concerned with inputs and outputs. Other people see instructional design as an "art" because the best designs usually have a direct relationship to the creativity and talent of the designer. Still others see it as "a good thing to do if we have the time," but stress that it can't get in the way of producing the training.

How you see instructional design is up to you. In this book we will not champion one view over another, or even one definition as the most correct. What we will do is try to convince you that creating a training program without using instructional design principles is inviting failure. Once you are (we hope) convinced, we will explore the most basic of those principles, not from a theoretical point of view but rather from the direction of how to apply them, rapidly and successfully. In fact, if you are seeking instructional design theory you've probably come to the wrong source; you may want to read Dick and Carey's *The Systematic Design of Instruction* (2004).

One of those basic instructional design principles we will explore is to *know your target audience.* This book's target audiences were described in the introduction. Primarily, they are individuals with little to no instructional design experience who need to learn to do it right, but fast. For the most part you are not permanent training professionals planning to make a career out of instructional design, so the theory is not as important as the actual practice.

Our audience analysis (we'll be talking a lot more about analysis in the next couple of chapters) tells us that you are much more preoccupied with *how* it is done than with what is behind the doing. Not that you aren't interested in the theory, but you just don't have the time to explore these aspects when everyone is expecting your training program yesterday. So terms such as *adult learning theory, learning styles,* and even *cognitive science* may appear here from time to time, but we won't be discussing them in any detail. We will spend most of our time considering how to apply good instructional design principles, specifically to the various ways you can deliver training, such as classroom training, on-the-job training, self-instruction, and technology-based training.

However, for the more experienced practitioner, we'll also discuss ways to speed up the instructional design process through simple hints and larger-scale methods, such as instructional design software, learning object-based design, rapid prototyping, and performance-support-based design. If you are an experienced instructional designer, or plan to be one someday, you might want to at least check out the shortcut icons and hang around for Chapter Eight to pick up some new ideas and shortcuts.

WHY INSTRUCTIONAL DESIGN?

So why should you concern yourself with instructional design? Perhaps the best reason I can give is one we've all experienced: the course, class, seminar, or other training event that sounded good on paper, but that you left (and that left you) wondering why you ever came. There are a number of reasons for this universal phenomena, but in the end they all boil down to one cause: *poor instructional design.* Did the class not meet the objectives stated in the course description? Poor instructional design. Did the test at the end of the program not make any sense? Poor instructional design. Did the instructor meander from topic to topic with no clear pattern to what was being discussed? Poor instructional design. Was the material over your head, or too basic? Blame it on poor instructional design. (OK, I admit there may be other reasons as well, but poor instructional design is often the most critical reason, and because this is a book on how to become a better instructional designer, allow me just a little overstatement.)

On an individual basis, these ineffective learning experiences are annoying, but when considered for a company-wide training course they are rather painful, particularly to the bottom line. Multiplied by five or a dozen or fifty training courses, they are appalling. Hundreds of thousands of precious training hours are wasted every year telling participants what they already know or things they cannot use. The cost in wasted time, wasted money, and wasted opportunities is staggering—all because the person responsible for the program did not know, or did not take advantage of, a few mostly commonsense rules for creating good training.

What instructional design will do for you, the training course developer, is help you guard against making such mistakes. It will help you create good, clear objectives for your program that can be understood and mastered by your trainees. It will help you develop evaluations that truly test for the knowledge and skills that your objectives are based on. It will help you or whoever instructs the course to facilitate the participants' learning effectively and efficiently, and, most important, it will help you make sure that what is in your program is what your trainees need to learn. This reduces wasted time, wasted money, and wasted opportunities for helping to develop more effective employees who, through their knowledge and skills, increase corporate profitability.

WHAT IS INSTRUCTIONAL DESIGN?

Earlier we discussed instructional design in generalities: a science, an art, a way to create training. These are all fine concepts, and perhaps good definitions, but instructional design is really a *set of rules*—or *procedures,* you could say—for creating training that does what it is supposed to do. Some of those procedures have to do with finding out *what* the training is supposed to do (you might call it determining the goals of the training); other procedures deal with letting the participant know what those goals are. Still other procedures ensure that everything in the training focuses on those goals, and one more set monitors how we know that the goals have been achieved.

Instructional design is a way to plan your training program from the moment you have the idea for it (or the idea is given to you) until the moment you complete your revisions of your first effort and get ready to run the program again. It is a working model that you can use to manage the concepts and tasks that are part of a successful training process.

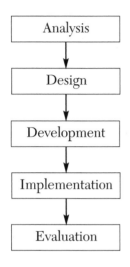

There are many ways to do instructional design—probably about as many as there are good instructional designers—but each way follows the same basic principles, and it's those principles that we will explore here. No matter whether you are training technicians, service workers, or managers, or if you will be utilizing classes, on-the-job training, e-learning, or satellites, you will need to use these principles in one form or another to make your training a success.

Those principles were developed by the military in the 1940s, and set down as a method of instructional design called Instructional Systems Design or ISD. The following graphic depicts the straight-line ISD model with its five phases: analysis, design, development, implementation, and evaluation.

As time went on, designers began to realize that although the phases were a pretty good representation of how instructional design worked, the straight-line model with a beginning and an end was not realistic. Evaluation usually led to more analysis, which created the need for redesign, and so on. So we began to look at an cyclic ISD model, like this:

Instructional Systems Design Straight-Line Model.

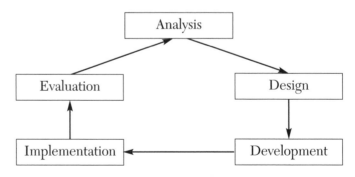

Instructional Systems Design Cyclic Model.

However, to confuse you a bit, and because it mirrors the reality of ISD as an iterative process in which we keep making and remaking decisions all through the five phases as we create our design, I offer you my rendition of the ISD model.

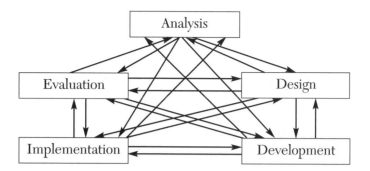

Instructional Systems Design Spiderweb Model.

I affectionately refer to this as the ISD spiderweb model, and I challenge you that if you can recite an instance for each of the arrows in which you would move from one phase to the other, then you probably don't need to continue reading this book.

In the final analysis, instructional design requires only specific behavioral outcomes, a way to measure them, and reviews and revision to make sure the training effectively covers the outcomes. Everything else is just icing on the cake—though as all of us with a sweet tooth know, the icing is what makes the cake.

A FEW DEFINITIONS

Before we get into the advantages of instructional design, we'd better take some time to develop a couple of definitions. An *instructor* (as we'll use the term in this book) is the person who stands up in front of a class or a person and performs the main role of disseminator of content information. There is obviously a lot more to training than just that, and—as we all know from sad experience—there are instructors, and then there are INSTRUCTORS, but for now let's just leave it there.

The term *facilitator* is also meant to describe an individual who stands up before others in a training setting, but one whose main role is to assist in helping them to learn rather than to disseminate content information. This is not to say that an instructor doesn't assist in learning, or that facilitators don't provide content information at times, but these aren't their main responsibilities. Lectures are given by instructors; classroom simulation or role-play activities are expedited by facilitators. Instructors almost always have to be content experts; facilitators do not.

We'll use the term facilitator often in this book, as this is the role a good designer tries to design for, even if he or she throws some instruction into the mix. We'll use the term *trainer* to mean a facilitator as well. For example, an on-the-job training (OJT) trainer for our purposes will be basically a facilitator, even though he or she may occasionally provide some content information.

A *designer* is the person who puts the training together for the instructor, facilitator, trainer, or whomever. Often the designer is also the trainer; just as often he or she is not. If the designer is the trainer, this makes instructional design simpler and more treacherous, as trainer-designers tend to take a lot of liberties with the instructional design process, knowing they can deal with any shortcomings on the fly during the class. If the trainer and designer are not the same person, then instructional design is more difficult, but normally less inconsistent, as the designer needs to spell everything out in detail for the trainer if the training is to be done right.

The designer's function can be broken down into lots of subfunctions—such as material developer, evaluator, writer, artist, and so on—many of which theorists would argue have nothing to do with "true" design. However, as I mentioned earlier, we will not deal much with theory in this book, so for simplicity's sake we'll group all these functions under the designer role.

Another role is that of *subject-matter expert* or SME. As the name suggests, an SME is a person who, mainly through experience, knows a lot about the content to be taught. A designer will team with an SME to help in the development of content and for review purposes. A trainer or facilitator may consult an SME concerning thorny issues in the content, or just to get some good ideas to use during the class, some "examples from the trenches."

In far too many cases in training, people who are SMEs are given the role of designer or trainer or both, simply because they are SMEs. They may know little about how to put a training together—and even less about how to run an effective training class—but because they have expertise in how to do the job, they're elected, appointed, or volunteered. They usually teach what they think is important (and it often is, although it may not be everything needed or important for this particular audience). They tend to teach it the way they have been taught, or the way they are most comfortable learning (which may be wrong, or at least not effective, for the content or the audience). In other words, they are very often not practitioners of good instructional design.

If you find yourself in this predicament, please don't feel that we are criticizing you. We are definitely criticizing the people who put you there, but it certainly isn't your fault that you've been told to do something you have not been trained to do. No one would ask you to drive a bulldozer or fly an airplane without the proper training, but this does not hold true for training. Books such as this one can help SMEs become good designers, and there are other books that will make them better facilitators. (See Bob Pike's *Creative Training Techniques,* 1994.) But SMEs are *subject-matter experts*, and that does not make them facilitators or designers.

If you are in this circumstance, take heart. As the old saying goes (slightly paraphrased), "The fact that you are here and recognize that you have a problem means the situation is not beyond hope." An advantage of instructional design is that it can help make SMEs good designers.

ADVANTAGES OF INSTRUCTIONAL DESIGN

Now, on to advantages. The main advantage of instructional design is simple: it assists you in correctly doing what you need to do. In the case of developing a training program, this means creating training that helps your trainees learn the things they need to know. This sounds pretty obvious, but that doesn't mean it always happens.

When developing training, the trainer—who is often charged with designing the training as well—frequently makes the decisions as to what the trainees need to know, based on the trainer's experience and the amount of time the trainer has been given to deliver the training. These may be accurate guesses or not, but invariably in such an approach some aspects—at times critical ones—are missed or deleted due to time constraints. The advantage of instructional design is that it does not rely on one person's concept of what the trainees need to know, so it is more likely that the final product will be the right one.

We can take this advantage even further when we consider not just what is in a program (often called the *content*), but also the program itself and the other programs that make up a training curriculum. Someone must decide who needs to take what courses and how many of them. Instructional design procedures make this overall decision more systematic and thus more accurate.

 ### Cost Effectiveness

Ensuring cost-effective training is another advantage of using instructional design. One way it does this is obvious. If you are training people in what they really need to know, and not just what someone thinks they need to know, then you are wasting less training time—and in this case time truly is money.

It costs a lot of money to run training programs. Some estimates put the cost of private training in the United States alone at over $58 billion a year! You need money to pay trainers, for classroom space, and for materials and equipment. You also need to pay trainees to be at the training, and often you must hire other people to replace them while they are away. There are travel costs, food costs, and a number of other specific cost issues, depending on your particular company. If following proper instructional design principles can save even 10 percent of these expenditures (and often the savings are much, much more dramatic), the effect on the bottom line of an organization can be quite significant.

And you can add on to all of these direct costs what I consider to be a major hidden cost of poor training: *lost productivity.* Workers who are poorly trained make mistakes, create scrap, lose customers, and get in accidents. Workers who are not well trained seldom reach their potential, costing the company untold dollars in possible profits.

Instructional design won't solve all your cost, productivity, and profitability problems, but it will give you a fighting chance by helping to ensure that the workforce at least knows what it is supposed to do and how to do it.

Time Effectiveness

Instructional design can also help your training become more time effective. We've already mentioned the main way it does this—simply through providing training that meets the right needs of the right people, thus not wasting their time or the trainer's. But it can do more than that. Instructional design also helps you provide training when it is needed and in a way that the trainees can best use it.

The antithesis of this aspect of instructional design is the old "Everyone needs training on this, so we'll run a class on it every Tuesday and Friday" training plan. Instructional design helps you to ask questions such as, "Is a class the best approach, or should we use on-the-job training or computer-based training for this material?" and "Are Tuesdays and Fridays the right days, or should it be Mondays, or should it be available when the trainees need it no matter what the day?" (a concept called *just-in-time training*).

Instructional design can also be time effective for the designer. This statement may seem to be in conflict with its major disadvantage—taking more time to do, as discussed in the next section—but we are talking absolutes here. If you absolutely do not care how effective the training is as long as it gets done, then instructional design takes longer than just having someone get up before a group and talk. However, if you want absolutely the best training possible, then instructional design is a time-effective method for achieving this, and the more you use its procedures, the better you will become at them and the faster you will become at creating not just training, but the *right* training.

Instructional design also includes various shortcuts to make the designer even more time effective once he or she has mastered the basics. One of these, often termed *object-oriented learning*, allows you to create a segment of training once, but use it over and over again in a number of different programs and training situations. This may sound pretty simple, but unless you follow good instructional design procedures you will find that this concept will not work well, if at all.

Another shortcut is the use of template-based instructional design software to help you design. Knowing instructional design to begin with makes the use of these programs easier and more effective. We will discuss both of these concepts, as well as some other instructional design shortcuts, in Chapter Eight.

Learning Effectiveness

Now I know that this sounds like some of that theory we said we weren't getting into, but it really isn't. Learning effectiveness relates to some of the time-effectiveness processes we discussed earlier. An advantage of using instructional design is that it helps you choose the most effective way to present your content, which can be translated as the easiest way for the trainees to learn it.

We've all attended training during which the instructor delivered hour after hour of content on a process that, if they had just let us sit down and work, we could have learned in half the time. Instructional design helps you look at what is to be learned and decide the best method for learning it. Instead of a classroom, it might be a laboratory, or a simulation, or even a piece of virtual reality training—or no training at all, but simply a job aid that can be used back on the job when the trainee is actually performing the task.

This is what learning effectiveness is about: determining the best way for the trainee to learn, based on what content needs to be learned and what the trainee will be doing with the new knowledge after the learning is done.

Training Effectiveness Evaluation

We've been discussing the advantages of instructional design based on its various types of effectiveness: cost, time, and learning. Another advantage is that you can use instructional design to create a valid and useful evaluation of the training itself and therefore determine whether your training was truly effective. Most training evaluations, particularly those that are not based on instructional design, consider evaluation to be limited to finding out whether the trainees liked the course. A few even go so far as to ask the trainees if they feel they "got something" from it.

Through the use of instructional design procedures, you will create objectives for the course that you can use as the basis of evaluation, determining which objectives the trainees have met. Because instructional design bases these objectives on job tasks or competencies, you can relate your training to the job requirements and then evaluate whether the trainees are using what they've learned. Another set of instructional design procedures helps you consider whether the training is worth doing at all—that is, whether the benefits of the training outweigh the costs. Using this information, you can evaluate your training even further, analyzing whether it lived up to its cost-benefit expectations. However, if proper instructional design procedures are not used when the training is created, all of these processes are less useful, harder to measure, and often not particularly valid.

Competitive Advantage

Other advantages of instructional design are related to the fact that some organizations consider good training to be a competitive advantage. An industry in which this seems to be a golden rule is information technology. The best companies, often characterized as those with exemplary training, are constantly having their trained people "pirated" by other companies. These top companies will use the promise of more training, leading to further job skill development and possible promotion, to keep their people in-house and to attract new employees as well.

I know of one old-line manufacturing company that began a franchising venture. When asked why they felt their franchise was more valuable than their competitor's, they replied, "Our name recognition, our reputation for quality, and our training system, which will guarantee that both of these other advantages remain intact for the franchisee." Did someone say, "Sounds like instructional design at work?" Good!

Business Integration

Using instructional design also creates training that is related to the goals and objectives of the organization. This is begun early in the instructional design process and follows through to how the training is evaluated. It means that the training received by your trainees not only will help them, but also will help your company achieve its vision and the goals related to it.

Consistency

The last set of advantages in using instructional design relate to consistency. With instructional design, the quality of your training is consistent. All of your programs will be at the level of quality that your instructional design procedures dictate.

Your programs will also be consistent over time and place. No longer will one trainer teach one set of content for a program while another, six months later or six thousand miles away, teaches something different. This consistency will create even greater quality, not only in your training, but in whatever the training helps your company to do.

 ## DISADVANTAGES OF INSTRUCTIONAL DESIGN

We've already mentioned the major disadvantage of instructional design: that it takes time. It takes time to learn how to follow the instructional design procedures and time to implement them when you create training. However, if you consider the alternative of producing possibly (perhaps probably) ineffective training if you don't use instructional design, then this disadvantage may be less critical than it first appears.

Sure, that's easy for me to say, sitting here writing this book. I'm not out there with you, being told by your supervisor that the training is needed yesterday, being asked by the department manager why you need to talk to all those busy people before the "classes start," being second-guessed as to why you can't simply use the company's "all-knowing" SME by putting him in front of a classroom. Well, nobody said the job was easy—or if they did, it's because they never tried it themselves. Remember the old saying: You can only have two of these three: fast, cheap, good.

I have no magic answer to the problem of time. Let's face it, if it wasn't more difficult and time-consuming to use instructional design, we'd all be using it already, and I'd have to find a new topic for this book. Who can argue with what instructional design does, except from the point of view that it takes so long to do it? I'm reminded of a boss I had early in my career who really believed in instructional design, but became so frustrated one day that he looked at me and said, "It really does take too long to do things right."

There are days when I think he may have been right, but then I remember that it is better to spend one person's time now than to waste ten people's time later. Yes, it does take longer to use instructional design to do it right, but it's worth it.

Resources

A much less significant disadvantage of instructional design is that it takes more and varied resources to accomplish. Unlike what we might call *SME-based training*, in which only one person is involved in construction, delivery, evaluation, and everything else that may need doing, good instructional design requires a number of resources. These might include a designer; an instructor who may be different from the designer; an SME, if the designer is not the one to provide content and review; other reviewers; target audience members to analyze; job incumbents to talk to; and the list goes on and on. Fortunately, none of these resources, with the exception of the first two or three, are required to contribute a lot of their time to the instructional design process. For them it may be an hour or two—or at most a day. Yet what they do contribute, when used properly, can multiply the effectiveness of the training considerably.

Another consideration in balancing this disadvantage around resource utilization is that instructional design can often save your resources. For example, if your best manager spends three days a month every month teaching his or her management specialty to new managers, those are days the manager is not doing what he or she does best: managing. One process of instructional design is to look at situations like this and ask whether there isn't a way to make more effective use of that manager's time. One answer might be to put him or her on video or in a multimedia program, or to possibly cut back the classes to once a month through the use of a distance-learning technology. This is the type of thing instructional design helps you do.

You may not find an efficiency in every situation, and the use of resources may far outweigh the little you save, but don't lose track of what instructional design provides in the end for the use of resources: the most effective and efficient training you can create, and savings that can be extraordinary.

Overcoming Disadvantages

I mentioned earlier that I don't have a magic answer to the disadvantages of instructional design; and notwithstanding the claims of "true believers" concerning the virtues of their pet technologies, from the days of film strips to today's web-based training, I don't think there is one magic answer. What this book *will* do for you is twofold. First, to decrease your learning time, it will present instructional design with practically none of the theory at its foundation. That's not to say that the theory isn't important (it is) or that you wouldn't be a better designer if you knew it (you would). It is simply a response to the fact that you are pressed for time, particularly if designing training is not your main job function, and that you can be a good—even an excellent—designer without the theory. This will mitigate that first disadvantage: the amount of time needed to learn instructional design.

Second, also to deal with the disadvantage of the time needed to do instructional design, this book provides you with a number of helpful hints and shortcuts to use. Some of these are contained within the chapter content; others are found at the end of the chapters in the form of checklists and ideas. Still others, of a more general nature, make up the entire last chapter (Chapter Ten). To start you off, here's a checklist that can help you determine whether you need instructional design at all.

	CHECKLIST: DO I NEED INSTRUCTIONAL DESIGN?

Instructions: Answer each of the following questions with Yes, No, or Not Sure.

☐ Yes ☐ No ☐ NS   I know who my trainees are and what their specific needs are.

☐ Yes ☐ No ☐ NS   I know all the content that the trainees require from my programs.

☐ Yes ☐ No ☐ NS   My trainees always know what is expected of them.

☐ Yes ☐ No ☐ NS   The materials I create are exactly what the content and trainees require.

☐ Yes ☐ No ☐ NS   I always know and use the most effective approach when delivering the required training.

☐ Yes ☐ No ☐ NS   I know whether my trainees learned what they needed to learn.

☐ Yes ☐ No ☐ NS   I know whether my training is being used back on the job.

☐ Yes ☐ No ☐ NS   I always create the most cost-effective training.

☐ Yes ☐ No ☐ NS   The training I create is always the most time effective for me and the trainees.

☐ Yes ☐ No ☐ NS   My training is meeting the needs of my organization.

If you answered "No" or "Not sure" to any of these questions, you can probably use some aspect of instructional design. If you answered "No" or "Not sure" to several of them, you need the whole instructional design approach. Read on, *s'il vous plaît,* and remember:

> *Give a man a fish and he'll eat for a day. Teach him how to fish and he'll eat as long as there are fish in the pool. But design a training program that helps him learn how to stock and manage his pool, and there is no telling how far he might go.*

Chapter 2

Before You Do Anything: Pre-Instructional Design Activities

This chapter will help you to:

- Differentiate the various kinds of assessments that you can do
- Determine company needs through an organizational needs assessment
- Find out what a performance assessment does and what human performance technology is
- Determine your organization's training needs
- Create a needs analysis report
- Do a "quick and dirty" training cost-benefit analysis

Well, if you're reading this it should mean that we've achieved at least part of the first objective of this book: convincing you that instructional design is important. In this chapter it's possible that we'll convince you it's also not worth the effort, simply because it seems to take so much time to do it right. I say this only slightly with tongue in cheek. You are probably anxious to start creating some training, but by the end of this chapter you are likely to feel as if you are no further along toward this goal than you were when you started. However, that is a misconception.

This chapter may not give you the information you need to jump right in and start putting training stuff together, but it will provide you with a workable blueprint for your training. Some of the things we'll discuss here will help you ensure that when your training is implemented it won't fail due to a lack of interest on the part of your organization. Other concepts will help you determine what your final training should look like in relation to what your company wants and needs it to look like. You don't want to build a fifty-room mansion when what your company needs is a two-story colonial.

 If you are an occasional designer, as we defined this role in the introduction, most of the work that this chapter covers has been (or should have been) done for you. If you don't foresee this current responsibility leading to further involvement in training, you may want to scan through this chapter, stopping only at those areas that have the ⊘ icon. However, if your training responsibility goes beyond one single-topic course with you as the only instructor, you'll want to consider this chapter in detail. What we'll discuss may be the deciding factor in making your training recognized as a successful, need-fulfilling process in your organization.

 ## ORGANIZATIONAL NEEDS

And that brings up the first question you ask in the pre-design phase of instructional design: "What *does* your organization need?" There are a number of terms for this process, though the two most commonly used are *needs analysis* and *needs assessment.* There have been entire books written on the difference between these two concepts, but for our purpose of rapid instructional design we will consider them to be the same. (Chapter Two: Business Analysis, in *HPI Essentials* edited by George M. Piskurich, 2002.)

Determining your organizational needs will help you to determine what training you need to do. More important, it will help you determine what training you *don't* need to do, either because the organizational need cannot be addressed by training or because the organization cannot support the training that is needed. Let's look at an example.

Suppose your manager comes to you and says that the company has to increase its production by 5 percent to meet the new customer orders that have come in. He feels that you should run a training program to bring some of the new people up to speed on the way you do your work, as you are the most productive member of the department. You tell him that you and your colleagues are having problems getting enough material to work with from other groups as it is, and that making them more efficient won't necessarily make the group more productive. Instead, material flow needs to be looked at and somehow enhanced.

What you've done on a very small scale is an organizational needs assessment. You've discovered an organizational need (or at least your supervisor has told you of it) and considered ways to meet it, this time rejecting training as a possible solution.

Of course, it's usually a lot more complicated than this example, but the basics are the same. Anyone who's in charge of a training function or given responsibility for some aspect of a training process should analyze what organizational needs exist and how these needs can best be met.

To Whom to Talk and What to Ask

The place to start an organizational needs assessment is at the top, or at least as close to the top as you can get. Ask the highest level of management that you can reach for their thoughts on organizational needs. However, don't make the mistake that many assessors make of beginning these conversations with the question: "What training needs do you have?" This seems like a pertinent question, but it is often too limiting and not really what you are looking for in this type of assessment. A better question is something along the lines of: "What organizational (or departmental, or group) business problems are critical to you and your staff at the moment?" Or, from a different focus: "What opportunities exist in your business unit that you would like to take advantage of?" Focus in even more by asking about customers and what their needs are, or about competitors and what they do well that your company doesn't quite match.

If you are in a product-centered environment, one possible approach is to discuss plans for new products. Will there be changes on the manufacturing side, on the sales side, in distribution, in customer service, or for the customers and their employees? What will these changes mean as far as organizational, training, or individual performance needs are concerned?

Your goal is to develop as complete a list as possible of organizational needs (not necessarily training needs—we'll determine those later) from multiple levels in the company. The more often you hear a particular one mentioned, the more critical it probably is and the more attention should be paid to it.

This list is the beginning of your training blueprint. It will help you to sketch out general areas of need in the organization and to take a first look at what needs may be most critical. It will become a plan that you can follow as you build your training process and make decisions on how big and how complex it will be and what it will look like.

 ### Organizational Needs and the Occasional Designer

This organizational needs assessment process is all well and good, but what if you have already been assigned to develop a particular training program? How does an assessment of organizational needs relate to your responsibility? Well, there are two possible answers. First, perhaps someone has done an assessment and decided that what you've been charged with doing is in reaction to a valid organizational need. From that assessment, you can find out more about the need and why training was chosen as a solution. This information will provide you with background, help you to outline your program, and allow you to create the proper blueprint, so you won't build the wrong kind of training structure, even if it's only for a single program.

The second answer is a bit less concrete, but just as important. If your research (asking a few questions such as "What need are we addressing?") seems to indicate that there is no connection between what you've been asked to do and an organizational need, you can do a sort of retro-assessment to determine whether the program you will be creating has a worthwhile purpose. As in our previous example, your assessment may indicate that a training program is not what is needed at all, or that the program you've been asked to develop will not meet an organizational need. Alternatives to conducting training might include

- Creating feedback mechanisms
- Developing job aids
- Implementing incentive and recognition systems
- Revising employee selection systems
- Redesigning the organization

Determining whether training is or is not the right response to a need and bringing it to the attention of the right people can save your company a lot of time and money (remember, this was one of the main advantages of using instructional design—or in this case, pre-instructional design) and will save you a lot of the frustration inherent in developing a training program that no one can actually benefit from.

Here is a real-life example of what happens when you don't take the time to do even a quick organizational assessment of an already stated training need. (Some of the following examples have been adapted from case studies in *Leading Organizational Change* by Elwood Holton III, 1997.)

> Because the senior management at a large bank was adding an entire new line of business to their offerings, they requested that their training department provide project management training to their branch managers. The department selected a proven project management consultant to do a two-day classroom training program.
>
> The senior vice president for marketing sat in on the first day, and halfway through called the training manager aside to criticize the length of the pro-

gram, the approach the consultant was using, and the lack of computer-based training as an alternative to the classroom. She canceled the training.

In this case, if a representative from training had spent a little time doing an organizational needs assessment or even a retro-assessment, he or she would have found out that what was really needed was product knowledge training with a bit of project management thrown in. This would have saved the company a lot of misspent resources and the training group a lot of headaches.

 ## How to Do an Organizational Needs Assessment

So how do you do an organizational needs assessment? Basically, there are about as many ways as there are people doing them. The simplest way is to ask the right people the right questions. The most complicated, but often the most complete, is to develop a survey form that can be distributed, collected, analyzed, and followed up on. In between these extremes are oral surveys, focus groups, observations, and a whole raft of variations and combinations of these basic methods. Here are some examples of how other companies have done and used an organizational needs assessment:

> The training director for a customer-service-based organization performed a high-level organizational needs assessment by meeting individually with the organization's top eight officers, which covered the major divisions of the company. In the meetings, he asked for their understanding of the organization's basic philosophy, culture, and strategic goals. He also requested information on whom they saw as the organization's customers and their work group's customers. He created a series of customer-service needs using the officers' comments and information gathered from the front line on how the customers were being served. This led to a redefinition of customer service for the organization and a training session related to a customer identification model that helped each division redefine its role in the customer-satisfaction process.
>
> An HRD department did an analysis of its own training programs by performing an organizational needs analysis and then comparing what was being done to the results of the survey instrument that was used that asked questions such as:
>
> - How does the organization perform in relation to the expectations of our shareholders?
> - How do we react to these expectations?
> - What is our core mission?
> - What would be our ideal future?
> - What is our realistic future?
> - How can we reduce the difference between the two?

Outcomes of this organizational analysis included changes in quality inspection techniques, increased safety and maintenance training, expansion of the corporate intranet to an extranet, and development of a team-based problem-solving methodology.

Retro-Assessment

If you are doing what we've termed a retro-assessment to fill in the background on a program you've been asked to create, you'll probably want to stay with the "ask the right questions" approach to assessment, as it is quick and relatively simple. Of course, the first question is: "What corporate need is this program going to address?" Add follow-up questions based on the answer. Who you ask is often dependent on who is available to you, but try to get as far up the line as you can, at least to the person who requested the training in the first place (often termed the *stakeholder*). If your corporate structure won't allow you to talk directly to people at some levels, ask your supervisor to set things up or to act as a surrogate.

A rapid-design shortcut for an organizational assessment is to interview the top people most and first. If you can get to the CEO and his or her direct reports, and if they seem in agreement on what the organizational needs are, then you've probably got what you want. You might validate your findings with a person or two from other levels, but basically you should be there.

PERFORMANCE ASSESSMENT

Another method for determining organizational needs is termed *performance assessment*. (*First Things Fast: A Handbook for Performance Analysis* by Allison Rossett, 1997.) The difference between an organizational assessment and a performance assessment is not large, but can be very significant depending on the type of training you are considering. In a performance assessment, instead of trying to determine the somewhat general concept of organizational needs, your focus is on performance itself. This might be the performance of the organization, a department, a work group, a job classification, or individual contributors.

Another word on terminology here. This process is called *performance analysis* or *front-end analysis* just as often as it is called performance assessment. We are using the term *assessment* simply to differentiate what we are discussing here from the analysis processes that are described in Chapter Three. So if you hear someone discussing performance analysis, don't be confused; it's the same thing.

Performance Gap Assessment

One type of performance assessment is the performance gap assessment ("What Is Your Problem? Seven Steps to Analyze and Define Performance Problems" by Anne Marrelli, in *Performance & Instruction,* August 1993). The key aspect here is to look for the *difference* between what the performance should be and what it is now. This performance gap will help you determine what training needs (if any) there are. Let's look at a couple of examples:

> A telecommunications company was having problems keeping up with orders for its new cellular phone. The analysis indicated that the reason was not the number of phones coming off the line, but rather the number of rejects when the products went through final testing. A performance analysis was done in which the analyst first discussed the proper assembly technique with in-plant experts and then observed what was happening on the line. Later he discussed what he had observed with both supervisors and line employees. The performance gap was that when the circuit board supply was used up it was taking too long for new boards to be delivered; thus the employees were only spot-welding two of the four contact points in order to catch up with the demand that was created when they didn't have a circuit board supply—assuming two would be enough, which was not true. A combination of better materials management and retraining was used to bridge the performance gap.
>
> A finance company was finding that the number of companion products sold to current customers was well below the industry average. The company conducted a performance analysis by developing a survey in which customer service representatives were asked a number of questions concerning their work, including items such as the following:

I. Directions

- Can you find information related to how to perform your job?
- Is the information simple and not buried in unneeded data?
- Is the information up-to-date?

II. Feedback

- Do you understand the standards you are expected to meet?
- Is the feedback you receive related to these standards?
- Is it timely?
- Is it specific enough?
- Is it constructive?

III. Tools and Equipment

- Do you have the right tools to do your job?
- Do they work properly?

IV. Resources

- Do you have adequate materials and supplies to do your job?
- Are they the right materials and supplies?
- Are there any environmental problems that reduce your efficiency?

V. Incentives

- Is your pay competitive?
- Are your bonuses and raises based on performance?
- Are there meaningful nonmonetary incentives?
- Are there negative consequences for poor performance?

VI. Knowledge

- Do you have the knowledge you need to do your job well?
- Have you mastered the skills you need to perform your job?
- Do you have the right job aids?
- Do you understand the big picture for the company and how your job fits in?

VII. Motivation

- When you first began work for the company, did you want to do your job properly?
- Do you still desire to do so?

The analysis discovered that the performance gap was a combination of lack of knowledge and lack of motivation due to lack of incentive. A revised bonus program, retraining, and a performance support system were used to close the gap.

 If you are an occasional designer and want a quick approach to a performance gap assessment, try this list of steps:

1. Identify the problem.

2. Analyze the tasks and conditions of the job.

3. Analyze the current performance levels.

4. Identify the causes of the problem.

5. Identify the desired performance outcome.

6. Identify the expectations of your training as related to the outcome.

 This quick performance assessment method can also be a rapid design technique if you find that you don't have time to do a full performance analysis or don't really need one, but want to assess a specific performance gap.

After you have determined that a performance gap exists, you'll need to do some cause analysis. (Chapter Five, *HPI Essentials* edited by George M. Piskurich, 2002.) There are any number of ways to do this, from the somewhat famous root cause analysis methodology to affinity diagrams and the ever popular "Five Whys." We won't go into a how-to discussion here; there are resources in the Suggested Readings section or you can go to your QC group for what will almost certainly be a very detailed explanation of these processes. The important point is that without this next level of analysis you will be making a number of assumptions concerning the causes of the performance gap, which may or may not be true and may or may not send you down the entirely wrong path to closing the gap.

 ## Performance Opportunity Assessment

There are other performance assessments that do not deal with performance gaps, but rather look for "areas of opportunity"—that is, places where the work group being analyzed can improve on what is already good performance. ("Transforming Organizations Through Human Performance Technology" by Geary Rummler, in H. Stolovitch (Ed.), *Handbook of Human Performance Technology*, 1992.) Aspects that often fall under this heading include obtaining market leadership or greater market share, increasing customer satisfaction, reducing time to market, increasing quality, and obtaining new or better competitive advantages. These areas of opportunity assessments often include a training component as part of the solution, but are seldom purely training, so we won't go into detail on them here. A quick and effective way to do a mini-opportunity analysis is simply to find out what your top performers do that is different from what your average performers do. The data you collect from this simple concept should provide you with a number of performance opportunity possibilities at a level that can be affected by training.

An example of this type of performance analysis was performed by the finance division of a major car manufacturer that had just been congratulated for reducing the number of days needed for closing its books and for being a pioneer in voice response technology for accounts payable. Even with these accolades, division members felt there was potential for improved performance and so undertook a performance analysis process. It led them to a new structure in which the employees became more proactive instead of reactive; various bottlenecks were eliminated; and finance delays, particularly related to sales initiatives, were significantly reduced. This was accomplished through a combination of procedural changes and retraining of a significant number of the division's staff.

Sources of Performance Information

Information on performance can come from a number of sources:

- Your company's business information systems can provide a lot of information. Examples are weekly, monthly, and quarterly reports, budget documents, staffing and scheduling reports, profit-and-loss statements, weekly sales figures, quality control documents, and so forth.

- You can ask supervisors where they see weaknesses in their people who have recently completed any current training.

- You can talk to employees who have been on the job for a time and ask them what they feel was missing from their training or what they wish they had known when they started that they had to learn "the hard way."

- There might also be some good data on maintenance problems, causes of down time, and failure rates at the work group or departmental level that can help you determine whether performance issues exist.

- Test scores from evaluations that company employees take as part of training or a certification program can be illuminating.

- Reengineering and industrial engineering studies, if they have been done, are a valuable source of information.

- Performance appraisals can provide still more performance information. These documents are often difficult to obtain, as performance appraisals are usually considered confidential. Work with your human resources (HR) department to see whether they can provide you with a synopsis of certain areas or copies of the appraisals with the names removed. This may sound like a lot of trouble, but it can be very useful, not only in considering common problems, but also in seeing performance trends.

- If your company has some type of customer complaint or employee suggestion system, these are also good sources of performance information. The important thing to remember as you analyze these systems is that one comment is not a trend. It's easy to get carried away by focusing in on one or two items that are pretty obvious and easy to deal with. What you really want to do is to look for common suggestions or comments that seem to have a common reference. This doesn't mean you should ignore singular or somewhat off-the-wall comments, as there may be some real insights there. Just don't assume that they are necessarily keys to performance issues.

Performance Data Collection and Measurement

In a gap-based performance assessment, a key issue is objective measurement. Performance can be measured in a number of ways, four of the most common being outputs, quality, time, and costs. To find a performance gap, you will need to measure both required and actual performance, and you should use the same type of measurement for both aspects.

Data-collection methods for a performance assessment are, for the most part, the same as any analysis process (see Chapter Three for details), but there is often a stronger emphasis placed on observation. You can see why this might be the case. You want to know how the actual performance is different from the required performance, and there is no better way (once you understand what the required performance should be) than to observe what is actually going on. This shouldn't be your only data-collection tool, but it is an important one for a performance analysis. Once again, a consideration of top performers and what they do, this time compared with below-average performers via observation, can be one of your most effective data collection and measurement methods.

Benefits of Improved Performance

As part of your performance assessment, you'll also want to determine the benefit of the improved performance to the organization. If the solution to the performance problems you find requires training, you'll use this benefit information first to help you make a first-cut decision on whether the training should be done, and later as part of your cost-benefit analysis to make the final decision on whether you will follow through with the design of a particular training program. If you use the same measurements for the benefit as you used for the required and actual performance, it will make your job a lot easier.

For example, if your required performance was the handling of fifteen calls per hour, although the actual was twelve, use the difference between the two as your benefit to be gained for improved performance, with the appropriate cost values attached.

Performance gap evaluation is usually much simpler than performance opportunity evaluation. However, even these more abstract performances can be broken down to simpler issues, and benefits can be applied to them in most cases. In the example above, if you were considering a performance opportunity of increasing customer satisfaction, you might break it down to creating three repeat customers a day, each of whom buys $12 in product on a repeat visit. Many of the benefits of improved performance are very specific to your particular environment, but they are still there if you look for them ("Rapid

Analysis: Matching Solutions to Changing Situations" by Dale Brethower, in *Performance Improvement*, November/December 1997).

Performance Interventions

The data from your performance information sources should help you to determine the causes of the performance gap. Like organizational assessments, a performance assessment isolates causes or needs that may or may not be training related. When using a performance assessment to determine whether a training need exists, you must ask yourself (or those who would know) a simple question: Can the performance gap be bridged through training? In other words, will a training program change your trainees' current performance to what it should be?

Often the answer is either "No" or "Only in part." "No" means what it says: training won't make the difference, so don't implement it. (For more on the "Only in part" answer, see the section "Training's Relationship to Other Performance Interventions.") In fact, various studies have suggested that less than 20 percent of performance problems are due to a lack of the knowledge or skills necessary to do the job; that is, the things that training affects. On the other hand, over 60 percent of performance gaps are caused by lack of feedback to the employee or poorly designed work processes. These are just two of the many other performance interventions that you might apply to bridging the performance gap instead of training, so consider those possibilities instead of a training program. If your charge was to create a training program, then this conclusion may be the end point of your work, as long as you can convince those who charged you with creating training that your performance assessment is accurate—and that training is not the answer.

Nontraining Performance Interventions

On the other hand, if your responsibility was to solve a problem, then you are going to need to use one or more of those other performance interventions, which in most cases means more analysis.(*Performance Improvement Maps* by Ethan Sanders and Sivasailam Thiagarajan, 2001.) Here is a partial list of other types of performance interventions. They are listed here to give you the flavor of what we're talking about.

- Career development systems, such as job rotation, mentoring, and assessment centers

- Communications systems, such as bulletin boards, e-mail, and newsletters

- Documentation and standards, including reference manuals, certifications, and standardization practices

- Ergonomic and human factors, such as human-machine interfaces, color coding, interior design, and furniture

- Feedback systems, such as performance appraisal, performance management, peer appraisal, and customer appraisal

- Human development systems, such as literacy programs, retirement programs, and tuition reimbursement

- Training systems, such as computer-based instruction, distance learning, and on-the-job training

- Management practices, such as goal setting, supervisory and management philosophy, and strategic planning

- Measurement and evaluation systems, including competency testing, performance standards, and quality systems

- Resource systems, such as benefits programs, budgeting systems, and resource allocation

- Reward and recognition systems, such as bonus systems, commission systems, compensation processes, and incentive systems (Chapter Seven, *HPI Essentials* edited by George M. Piskurich, 2002)

As you can see from the list of performance interventions, there are a number of possible reasons for poor performance that go well beyond training. It may simply be that an employee is missing a tool or that a procedure is no longer adequate. The performer may have all the right skills, knowledge, and experience, but cannot do the task consistently because a key item is missing or does not function properly. These facts would further indicate that training is not the answer.

If your analysis indicates that training is not the answer, call in a specialist in these interventions, often known as a *human performance technologist* (HPT). The HPT can help you and your organization continue with the analysis and design interventions that speak to these nontraining issues.

Categories and Causes of Poor Performance

Generally, reasons for poor performance—and subsequent performance interventions—will be found in one of three major categories: *organizational/environmental causes, motivational/attitude problems,* or *skills/knowledge deficits.* Of these three categories, instructional design is mostly concerned with the third, which can be directly affected by training.

That's not to say that the other categories are not important. For example, the various environmental issues that can affect performance are often overlooked, yet they can affect not only performance but also the effectiveness of your training. These issues can sometimes be determined by observing your competitors. If their people seem to be able to perform better and are not from a different labor pool or trained any differently, then the problem may be in the environment your company has created in which they perform. You'll need to look for bottlenecks in the work-flow process, lack of responsiveness to issues, or basic inefficiencies that seem to crop up at the actual site where the work is being performed.

One indicator of motivational reasons for a performance gap is employee morale. A poor attitude usually leads to poor performance. High turnover can be an indicator of low morale, as can difficulties in hiring quality people. Look for policies and procedures that create attitude problems. Check on absence and tardiness records. Are they higher than your competitors' and those of the industry as a whole?

Other questions you can ask as part of your performance assessment include the following:

- What are the rewards and recognition for good performance?
- What are the personal consequences of poor performance?
- Is there sufficient time to complete this job?
- Does the work provide challenges to the employees?
- Are there sufficient people to complete this job?
- Is there commitment to the job?

This brief discussion is not meant to make you a human performance technologist—or even to help you analyze performance problems. We've included it to help you think about these nontraining issues so you can more clearly come to a decision on whether the need or performance gap can be affected by a training program.

Training's Relationship to Other Performance Interventions

We noted previously that another answer to your performance analysis question, "Can the performance gap be bridged by training?" might be "Only in part." This answer means that training is part of the solution but that one or more of the other performance interventions may be needed as well. In fact, this is most commonly the case. It is rare that a performance gap can be bridged without the use of some training. In fact, most of the performance interventions listed earlier require training as part of their implementation.

This makes it more difficult for you as an instructional designer, because you'll need to work with human performance technology specialists and others when designing the training that will augment other performance interventions. However, because the goal is performance improvement (or meeting an organizational need) and not just developing a training program and offering it, the product will be well worth your time and effort.

Following is a list of questions that you can use in making performance assessments. These are a mixed bag, with some aimed at managers, others at performers, some better for gap analysis and others for performance opportunity analysis. Use the ones that work best for your situation or rewrite them to meet your needs. Add your own questions to them and create a customized performance assessment for your organization.

PERFORMANCE ASSESSMENT QUESTIONS

- What should the employees be doing now that they are not doing?
- What are the employees doing now that they should not be doing?
- When the employees are working most effectively, what does it look like?
- What is preventing them from reaching the goal you have envisioned?
- Do they know the standards that are expected of them?
- Are the standards reasonable and achievable?
- Do they have the proper job aids and other performance tools to work to standard?
- What would you like to see changed that would help you to work more effectively?
- What would you like to see invented that would help you work more effectively?
- What are your competitors doing better than you are?
- What do your customers want that you are not providing?

Here is another way to do a quick but effective performance gap analysis from inception to evaluation.

For a simple but useful performance gap analysis, answer the following questions:

- What is it now?
- Why is it a problem?
- Do we want to fix what is or create something new?
- Either way, what change in performance are we looking for, and from whom or what?
- Did we get the change we were looking for?

ASSESSING TRAINING NEEDS

Another type of assessment deals specifically with training needs. This is the assessment that most people think of when they talk about a needs assessment, usually calling it a *training needs assessment* or *analysis*. In a nutshell, it basically asks: "What kind of training do you need?" You can guess from the question that it is most often asked (or should be) of possible trainees or at least of individual performers. It is also often asked of management, although we have already discussed the danger of this question: missing too much during our exploration of organizational and performance assessments. This does not mean that it is invalid or that you should not do it—only that you should realize its limitations.

The following are the three basic purposes of a training needs analysis; although they are not mutually exclusive by any means, it is important to know which one your analysis is focusing on:

- To determine what the organization's training needs are

- To determine what needs of the organization can be met by training

- To determine what training an individual or work group of learners needs

A specific training needs assessment is most useful when your charge for training has already been limited to a certain audience, or even a certain area of the company. For example, if you are an SME who has been charged with developing a specific course or group of courses, you may want to use this type of assessment to find out a little more about what the needs of your trainees might be. Here are two sets of questions you might ask when doing a specific training needs assessment.

TRAINING NEEDS ASSESSMENT QUESTIONS FOR MANAGEMENT

1. Describe the most important business opportunity currently facing your work group.

2. Explain the roadblocks that are keeping you from taking advantage of that opportunity.

3. Describe the most critical business problem currently facing your work group and the roadblocks that may keep you from solving it.

4. In what areas within your work group does there seem to be a gap between expected performance and actual performance?

   Why do you think this is so?

5. Does your work group have any current or anticipated time-critical training needs that you will require assistance in meeting?

6. What training delivery technologies are available for your work group?

7. What is the current training budget for your work group?

8. What training resources do you employ?

   Staff

   Vendors

   Facilities

9. Do you feel the individual contributors in your work group will be capable of and comfortable with using computers for their training?

   Why or why not?

10. What do you consider to be the most important general characteristics of the individual contributors in your work group in relation to training?

    Do they like to attend training? Dislike it?

    Like to learn on their own?

    Feel training is important? A necessary evil?

    Learn new things slowly? Quickly?

    Think that if they don't already know it, they probably don't need it?

11. How do you currently design and deliver training in your work group?

    Are you satisfied with this approach? If not, why not?

TRAINING NEEDS ASSESSMENT QUESTIONS
FOR INDIVIDUAL CONTRIBUTORS

- What do you think about the existing training programs?

- How well did the training you received prepare you for the job?

- How could we improve existing training?

- In what way do you like to be trained?
  - Classroom
  - On the job
  - Videotapes
  - Self-instruction
  - Computer instruction
  - Job aids
  - Team training
  - Observing others
  - Working with a mentor

- What are the most common problems you have when doing your job?

- What about your job changes often?

- What about your job always stays the same?

- What do you need to know to excel at your job?

- Who do you think excels at your job now? Why?

- What do you need to have to be more productive?

- When new employees begin working with you, what knowledge or skills do you often find they are lacking?

These two lists contain relatively general questions because training needs assessment is a more general type of analysis. If you want to get more specific, be sure to ask the learners or would-be learners questions related to

- Work directions

- Supervisory feedback

- Job tools and equipment

- Specialized resources

- Incentives

- Knowledge

- Motivation

Usually these assessments are done as interviews or focus groups (see Chapter Three) and with job incumbents. As you will also see in Chapter Three, it is difficult to say where this type of assessment ends and the various other aspects of instructional design analysis begin.

Here is a template I have used that takes some of the above questions down to the bare bones for a quick but effective training needs analysis.

TRAINING NEEDS ANALYSIS TEMPLATE FOR MANAGERS

1. Please describe the current situation as you see it.

2. What indicators do you have that this might require a training solution?

3. How is this impacting organizational or work group goals?

4. Are there specific tasks that are not being performed adequately?

5. How often is this occurring?

6. How many performers are exhibiting the negative behavior?

7. What is the desired performance?

8. What would you like a training solution to accomplish?

A rapid design shortcut is to forgo the time-intensive interviews and focus groups of a training needs assessment and simply read the various reports and statistics generated by the company, such as customer satisfaction surveys, supervisory comments, performance appraisals, developmental plans, lost-time accident reports, repair reports, and so on. Choose the right documents (if they are available) and analyze them well; then you'll have a good shot at doing a valid training needs assessment.

CHOOSING NEEDS TO ADDRESS

No matter what road you go down to get there, sooner or later you will be at the point at which you know what all the training needs for your particular situation are, and you will need to decide which ones you will address.

Validation

The first step in this process is to validate the needs you have discovered through your organizational, performance, or training assessments. This can be a fairly simple process. In its basic form you send your possible needs list to SMEs and managers and ask for their opinions. The major challenge is in determining who the SMEs might be. In most cases you will not want to use the individuals who helped you with your assessment. Their respected colleagues, however, could be of value, so ask them who they respect. You might also ask supervisors and managers for their recommendations of possible SMEs.

Here is a form you could use to help determine who might be an SME for this purpose, or any other for that matter.

SUBJECT-MATTER EXPERT SELECTION FORM

Name of candidate: _____

Date: _____

Position and/or title: _____

1. Years of experience in field: _____

2. Years of experience in current position: _____

3. Years of experience with company: _____

4. What do you think makes you an expert in your field?

5. What path did you follow to become an expert?

6. When you find that you do not understand something, where do you go for an answer?

7. What common mistakes do new people make at your job?

8. Could training help them? If so, how?

9. What do you like and dislike about training?

10. What would you change in our current training programs?

11. What advice would you give to someone starting out in your field?

SME Analysis: (Completed by assessor after reviewing data)

1. Experience	1	2	3	4	5
2. Knowledge of job	1	2	3	4	5
3. Attitude toward helping people	1	2	3	4	5
4. Commitment to training	1	2	3	4	5
5. Assessor's comfort in working with	1	2	3	4	5

Whoever you use as a subject-matter expert, ask that person to look over the needs and prioritize them for you, and if the SME sees missing needs, to jot these down. Request notations on why the top two or three are most important. There is a lot more discussion on working with SMEs in Chapter Three. You can go there now if you are looking a needs analysis in the face and need help on the topic.

Questions to Ask Yourself

Your next assignment is to choose the need (or needs) that you will actually deal with from your validated list. This is more art than science, as it is based on a number of variables related to your company and its structure. Your two most important parameters should be: "Where will I get the most return for my expenditure of resources?" and "What can or will the company support?"

Normally the data you gather for your needs assessments *does not* give you an obvious answer to these questions. There may be a number of needs, some big and some small, some with easy solutions and some much more difficult to fulfill. Your problem will be to pick and choose the ones that you can work on without overreaching your capabilities, your time, or your budget.

Look for needs that were common in all your data-collection processes. These will probably lead you to critical needs. Relate these to organizational goals, particularly those that are not being met. Carefully consider complaints you have uncovered concerning the inadequacy of existing training.

Here is a series of more formalized questions that can help you determine whether a need is worth considering:

NEEDS CONSIDERATION QUESTIONS

- Will fulfilling this need help employees accomplish more in assisting the organization to reach its business goals?

- What will happen if this need is not met?

- Is this need related to providing a solution to a performance problem?

- Is the need related to workers not knowing what to do, how to do it, or when to do it?

- Will your organization's culture support the necessary training?

- Will your organization's policies allow for the application of the training?

- Will you be able to obtain valid feedback on the outcome of the training?

- Are physical facilities, equipment, and supplies available to support both the training and the transfer of skills to the job?

- Will monetary and nonmonetary incentives be provided when necessary?

- Will your trainees be interested in learning and applying the information presented in the training?

- Do you have or can you find the resources to produce an effective training program for this need?

A final aspect of choosing training needs that you must consider is your own capabilities and environment. Be sure to pick needs that you can work on without overreaching your capabilities for creating and implementing training programs, going over your allotted design and development time, or over-spending your budget.

THE NEEDS ANALYSIS REPORT

You may want to develop an analysis report of some type to help you choose the right needs and report your findings (*Be a Better Needs Analyst, Info-Line,* 8502). This report can literally be a narrative of what you did and what you found out. It might also be a simple bulleted list of discoveries and decisions. The format you use should be based on what your boss and the organization prefer.

Here are some of the items you would normally find in a good analysis report:

- The task(s) not being performed to standard

- The required performance(s) and the actual performance(s)

- A summary of the causes of the performance deficiency

- How the causes were determined

- The recommended training solution(s)

- A detailed cost-benefit analysis used to determine the projected return-on-investment (ROI). (See the next section for more discussion of ROI.)

What you are creating through this process is often called a *training needs statement.* You will use this statement to formulate objectives for your program. Later, the objectives will be used to create the evaluation tools that will tell you whether the needs you have chosen have been met.

Here is an example of an analysis report:

Training Needs Analysis Report for Call Center Employees

This analysis was accomplished by interviews with twelve call center employees and three of their supervisors. We also observed the call center operations on three occasions during both peak and off peak times.

There were three sets of tasks not being performed to standard:

- Handling of non–English speaking customers
- Referring of type-two claims to higher-level adjusters
- Basic customer courtesy responses

Of these, we see only the third item as a training issue. The first item can only be addressed by training if the call center employees are taught Spanish, which would be cost prohibitive. To resolve this issue, we recommend a hiring change to recruit more Spanish-speaking employees. The second item is simply a procedural issue that can be addressed through management reinforcement of the proper procedure.

For basic customer courtesy responses, the required performance is that each call be answered with a time-based greeting ("Good morning"), that the representative identify him- or herself by name, that the client's name be used as often as possible, and that a "Thank you," a contact number, and a repeating of the representative's name conclude the interaction.

We found that this formula is followed in about 60 percent of the interactions, with the names of both customers and representatives being the items most often missed. The reasons for the performance deficiency seem to be a lack of orientation to the courtesy formula and a lack of supervisory follow-up.

The recommended training solution is a revised piece in the orientation program in which the representatives participate in a simulation to practice the formula and discuss its importance. Particular emphasis should be placed on how our customers will feel toward the company when the formula is used and when it is not used.

For current employees, a refresher course taught by their supervisors is the recommended solution. This process will involve the supervisors, and the train-the-trainer piece that will be needed can be used to discuss monitoring issues as well. The employee program is estimated at one hour; the supervisor preparation program will take approximately one-half day.

The cost-benefit analysis for the programs is included. Basically, it indicates design and development costs at $14,000 and implementation costs at $42,000. Using our normal repeat business profit add-on of $4.00 and assuming that each call center employee will enable two repeat customers a day through being more courteous, we will amortize the training cost in approximately five months and show a benefit of approximately $122,000 per year afterward.

Your final recommendations on your analysis report might also include consideration of aspects such as

- How critical the need is to the organization
- How many performers are affected by the need

- Safety issues related to the need

- Legal, accreditation, or other mandates related to the need

- How the need affects actual operations (particularly customer service)

- The relationship of the need to other needs (is it basic to other need fulfillment?)

Following is an outline template for a more formal analysis report.

OUTLINE TEMPLATE FOR AN ANALYSIS REPORT

I. Overview
  A. General comments
  B. Strategic importance of what was analyzed
  C. Purpose and goals of analysis

II. Data Collection
  A. Methods employed
  B. Constraints (decisions made on what to do and what not to do)
  C. Instruments used

III. Sources of Data
  A. Human sources (internal and external)
  B. Data sources (reports, procedures, etc.)
  C. Customer sources

IV. Conclusions
  A. Performance standards
  B. Performance deficiencies
  C. Causes of deficiencies
  D. Consequences of deficiencies

V. Recommendations
  A. Training recommendations
     goals
     target audience
     description
     benefits
     anticipated problems
  B. Nontraining recommendations
     rationale

description
audience
benefits
anticipated problems
C. Other recommendations and commentary

If you find all of this too time consuming—and to tell you the truth, often there is simply not that much time available—here is a six-step approach for a fast training needs analysis.

1. Identify the problem.
2. Analyze the tasks and conditions of the job.
3. Analyze the current performance levels.
4. Identify the causes of the problem.
5. Identify the desired performance outcome.
6. Identify the expectations of your training as related to the outcome.

By using this approach you can quickly determine whether training is the solution and generally what training needs to be done.

Reporting Your Findings

The analysis report, in one form or another, is a good tool for you to use when reporting your assessment findings to upper management. Basically, there are two paths to follow in this reporting process. Use the first when a performance gap or some other training need is fairly obvious and obtaining agreement that this should be addressed is a relatively simple matter. You can quickly go from here to defining your training process.

However, if the need is not as obvious, you will need to use the second path: going into more detail on the performance aspects and specific areas, such as customer satisfaction increases, time-to-market advantages, quality enhancements, and whatever other parameters fit your assessment—particularly cost, which brings up our last, but definitely not least, topic in this chapter.

QUICK AND DIRTY COST-BENEFIT ANALYSIS

We've mentioned cost-benefit analysis (CBA) a couple of times so far, so let's take a look at how to do one (*Costs, Benefits, and Productivity in Training Systems* by Greg Kearsley, 1981.) There are any number of ways to do a cost-benefit analysis. The approach we'll discuss here is a bit more traditional than some, but should help you in most circumstances and is relatively easy to do.

Basically, what you are trying to do by using a cost-benefit analysis is to figure out the projected cost of the training, which is not too difficult, and then compare it to the benefits of improved task performance or the meeting of an organizational need—which is often very difficult indeed, as hard data are not always available. It is usually a good idea to enlist the aid of an SME or the manager who helped you with your needs assessment to assist you with the development of some realistic numbers.

Sometimes a return-on-investment (ROI) ratio is created from the projected costs and benefits numbers to make them easier to understand. The ROI ratios also make it easier to compare your program plan with cost-benefit analysis processes for other programs ("The Three Rs of ROI" by Kim Ruyle, in *Technical Training,* May/June 1998), and even for nontraining methods such as those we discussed in the area on performance analysis. These comparisons will help you to decide which possible intervention makes the most sense for your situation. Remember, the basic purpose of your cost-benefit analysis is to determine whether the training solution you are considering should be implemented.

Costs

The steps involved in determining costs ("Where Have All the Dollars Gone?" by Bob Schriver, in *Technical Training,* July/August 1998) for your cost-benefit analysis are as follows:

1. *Salary costs:* Multiply the daily salary of the employees attending the class by the number of employees who will attend, and this result by the number of days the class will run. If you have employees at different salary levels, you can use an average or multiply out each of the various levels singularly. For non-classroom training (OJT, mentoring, self-instructional programs) you may need to calculate on an hourly basis, depending on the number of hours you anticipate the average trainee will need to master the program.

Example: Suppose you are considering a two-day class for twenty employees, all of whom are making $70 per day. The total salary cost for this class will be $2,800. On the other hand, if your training is a self-instructional program that you have designed to take the average individual eight hours to do, and your thirty trainees earn $22 per hour, the salary cost for your course will be $5,280.

2. *Benefits cost:* Add in the benefits cost for all employees using the same method. A benefits percentage of salary should be available from your HR department.

3. *Lost production:* Depending on the situation, you may need to add in the *anticipated value of lost production* while the employees are in training or *employee replacement costs* that will be incurred while the participants are away from the job if their work must be covered. A good rule of thumb here is 1.25 times the salary value, although this depends to a great extent on the employee's position.

Example: Your trainees are assembly-line workers who will need someone to cover their jobs while they are gone. You should consider the salary of their replacements as a cost here. If they are highly skilled workers and there will be an obvious productivity drop while they are away, use the 1.5 times salary formula.

Example: Your trainees are salaried or management employees who can cover their own work as needed. You may not want to add this aspect to your costs. However, you may want to use a factor for lost productivity, such as one-half or one-fourth of salary cost.

4. *Program development:* Compute the time and associated cost necessary to design, deliver, and evaluate the program. This should include your time as the designer and possibly the trainer, the trainer's time if you are not instructing (don't forget preparation time), and the cost of all materials, media, classroom rentals, and so on.

Time. There is no hard-and-fast rule for the time calculations, and many people will give you estimated numbers. I often work with a 10:1 ratio for instructor-led classes—that is, ten hours of design for each hour of delivered training; a 25:1 ratio for self-instructional print-based programs; and even higher ratios for programs requiring more technology support, like CBT, multimedia, and e-learning. It's likely you won't want to do any of these high-tech designs alone, so talk to some of the experts you might use to help you with them, and get their bids as part of your cost-benefit analysis.

Hard Costs. Actual costs for things like overheads, slides, videos, and other media are easier to determine. Don't forget the cost of your print materials, such as participant packages, trainer guides, certificates, and so forth. Costs for things like word processing, printing, or even binders can add up rapidly. And don't forget your trainer's travel costs.

Some things that are often forgotten in this area include the cost of doing a pilot (both trainer and participant costs, including travel), the time you've spent and will spend in analysis, the time of SMEs with whom you will need to talk, and duplication of materials. If you will be teaching a public class, the cost of tuition for the class covers all of these items.

Here are a few thoughts on more detailed items that might go into a cost estimate and some average costs for training resources (current at the time of publication) to help you with your estimating.

ITEMS TO CONSIDER WHEN CALCULATING TRAINING COSTS

Direct Costs

  Salaries and Benefits

    Full-time training personnel

    Part-time training personnel

    Occasional trainers or training developers

  Program Design Costs

    Travel costs for analysis meetings

    Salary and benefits costs for SMEs

    Cost of materials used in designing course

  Program Implementation Costs

    Cost of materials for course (including participant manuals, trainer manuals, media, special materials, etc.)

    Costs associated with train-the-trainer courses

    Travel costs for trainers

    Travel costs for trainees

    Salary and benefits cost for trainees

    Cost of training facility

  Administrative Costs

    Salary and benefits for record keeping personnel

    Record keeping hardware and/or software

  Evaluation Costs

    Travel costs associated with evaluation

    Salary and benefits costs of personnel involved in evaluation

Miscellaneous and Indirect Costs

  Tuition and Travel Costs for Seminars and College Courses

  Cost of Purchased Off-the-Shelf Programs

  Cost of Training Consultants and/or Out-of-House Trainers

  Cost of Training Hardware and Software (Computers, Overhead Machines, Authoring Programs, etc.)

  Cost of In-House Trainer Development (Seminars, Books, etc.)

  Cost of Other Purchased Training Resources

  Replacement or Lost Productivity Cost for Trainees

  Training Management Costs

SOME AVERAGE COSTS FOR TRAINING RESOURCES
AND TIME FOR DEVELOPMENT

Basic Overhead Transparencies	$3 to $15
Computer-Generated Overhead Transparencies	$12 to $75
Custom Produced Slides	$15 to $50 (depending on complexity)
Commercial Slides	$2 to $10
Audio	$25 to $150 per minute
PowerPoint Slides	$3 to $30 (depending on who is creating)
Participant Manuals (development)	$30 to $75 per page (with limited graphics)
Desktop Publishing	$25 to $50 per hour
Graphic Designer	$30 to $75 per hour
Writer	$40 to $60 per hour
Programmer	$80 to $150 per hour
Custom Video	$1,000 to $3,000 per edited minute
Commercial Videotapes	$15 to $20 per minute
Classroom Facilitators	$40 to $50 per hour
Instructional Designers	$85 to $100 per hour
Consultants	$500 to $1,500 per day
Standard Training Classroom (hotel or facility)	$150 to $200 per day
Technology Training Classroom	$300 to $500 per day
Enhanced Delivery Classroom (satellite, etc.)	$35 to $75 per day per student
Design and Delivery of Facilitated Instruction	7 to 15 hours per hour of instruction
Design and Delivery of Self-Instructional Programs	20 to 35 hours per hour of instruction
Low-Level Technology Graphics-Based Programs (CBT)	200 to 300 hours per hour of instruction $20,000 to $30,000 per hour of instruction
Higher-Level TBT Programs (Multimedia)	200 to 600 hours per hour of instruction
Asynchronous E-Learning (Low to High Interactivity)	$10,000 to $100,000 per hour of instruction

5. *Travel expenses:* Calculate all participant travel expenses, including hotels, meals, transportation, and miscellaneous.

Daily salary/employee × # of employees × # of days   = _____
+ Benefit percentage × # of employees × # of days   = _____
+ Lost production value (1.25 × salary) × # of employees × # of days   = _____
+ Design and development and delivery or tuition costs   = _____
+ Travel expenses × # of employees   = _____
And your total cost for the program is   _____

Here are a few examples of the process in operation:

Example 1: You want to design a three-day class for twenty trainees. Their daily salary average is $90 per day:

Salary costs	$90 × 20 × 3 =	$5,400
Benefits costs	(33 percent of $90) × 20 × 3 =	$1,782
Lost production	(1.25 × $90) × 20 × 3 =	$6,750
Development costs	(@10:1 and $50/hour) =	$12,000
Travel expenses average	$1500 × 20 =	$30,000
	Total =	$55,932

Example 2: You look at that $30,000 travel cost and decide to try a computer-based self-instructional package that no one has to travel to use. You figure that in this format it will take the average employee only sixteen hours to master the material:

Salary costs	$90 × 20 × 2 =	$3,600
Benefits costs	(33 percent of $90) × 20 × 2 =	$1,188
Lost production	(1.25 × $90) × 20 × 2 =	$4,500
Development costs	(@45:1 and $50/hour) =	$36,000
Travel expenses	=	0
	Total =	$45,288

Example 3: Now you try to see whether it would cost less to use a public course offering from a vendor. You find one that is also three days in length and that covers *most* of your needs.

Salary costs	$90 × 20 × 3 =	$5,400
Benefits costs	(33 percent of $90) × 20 × 3 =	$1,782
Lost production	(1.25 × $90) × 20 × 3 =	$6,750
Tuition costs	$2175 × 20 =	$43,500
Travel expenses average	$1,500 × 20 =	$30,000
	Total =	$103,432

Benefits

Now let's look at the benefits side of the equation. This is the more difficult part of the process and will require some detective work on your part—and a little guessing as well. Start with the task(s) or performance(s) to be taught.

Determine the benefit of improved performance, or the ability to do the task, or the meeting of an organizational need, or whatever. You may want to start with a verbal description of what this means and ask for a number of opinions from various interested parties as to what the dollar value might be.

Whatever you decide on as the benefit dollar amount should then be multiplied by the number of employees who will attend your program.

Depending on how you calculated the benefit, you may also need to multiply by the number of days an employee works each year (usually around 220).

This should give you something close to a yearly dollar benefit that will be realized from the program.

Other Benefits Associated with Training

As we've noted, it is difficult to determine the true benefit of training or look at it from the point of view of the costs associated with poor training. What we've done in the preceding discussion is based mainly on increases in productivity, but here is a list of other factors that might be taken into account and weighed in on the side of training benefit dollars:

Less overtime	Decreased turnover
Fewer injuries	Fewer penalties from noncompliance
Fewer correcting errors	Less equipment breakage
Less absenteeism	Lower loss of sales
Fewer lawsuits	Decreased inventory size
Decreased recruiting costs	Decreased set-up time

ROI

Again, return on investment or ROI is a ratio of your costs to your benefits. Ratios make it easier to compare various types of programs. Basically, positive ROIs are good, and the more positive the better. A negative ROI means that, as far as can be calculated, the company does not get enough of a benefit to justify the expenditure required for a program.

ROI numbers are not of much use by themselves, unless your company has an ROI goal that the training program must meet before it is considered worth doing. For example, if your company has an ROI goal of four, your training plan must achieve this number or it should not be undertaken. ROI numbers are more useful if you are comparing possible training programs or delivery systems.

Examples: An example here might be comparing the ROI for a computer-based training plan with that of a classroom-based plan, as we did in the cost example. You remember that the cost was higher for the classroom program, but an ROI will tell you how the cost stacks up to the benefit for each program. The higher ROI would be the more likely candidate for implementation.

Or you might use the ROI ratio to compare a program for training one group of employees to a program for training another, when you only have the resources at the time for one. The higher ROI gives the company the most benefit.

Calculate the ROI by subtracting the cost number from the benefit number, and then dividing the result by the cost number, as shown below.

$$\frac{\text{Benefits} - \text{Cost}}{\text{Cost}}$$

For example, from our previous cost estimations we found that the cost for a three-day classroom program was $55,932. If we added up all the improved productivity values that would be gained from all the trainees every day for a year, we might have a number of around $106,000.

$$\frac{\$106,000 - \$55,932}{\$55,932} = .89 \text{ ROI}$$

The cost of $45,288 for the CBT program would result in an ROI of 1.34. Both of these are positive, which means the company will benefit from either, but one is higher than the other. Which one would you choose? We'll discuss ROI in more detail in Chapter Seven, but this is the basis of how you calculate it.

 A somewhat facetious rapid-design hint for cost-benefit analysis is to simply use the following technique: "Let's just find out what this problem is costing us and whether it is worth putting up the money we'd need to use to solve it." This assumes that you know what the problem is, that you can calculate the cost of the problem and the cost required to solve it, and that it is a problem for which training is a solution. If you can do all this without the formal process we've just described, you will know what you need to know, and it is a shortcut. In the final analysis, answering the facetious question is really what cost-benefit analysis is all about.

So now you know what the various types of assessments are and how to do them. You have a list of corporate needs and possible training needs, and perhaps a cost-benefit breakdown for meeting some of those training needs. This is all done in what we've termed the pre-design stage. In the next chapter we'll take what you've done so far and manipulate it further until we find the most critical issues, and then we'll look even deeper into these issues to determine what really needs to go into your training program. Chapter Three is basically a continuation of what we've begun here in Chapter Two, and that can be said of the entire process of instructional design, as each aspect feeds into the next. Chapter Three deals more or less with analyzing work that you've already accomplished.

To finish up this chapter, here is a short list of questions that you can use to determine whether your training is as valuable to the organization as it should be.

HOW VALUABLE IS YOUR TRAINING?

- Does the training help management further its goals?

- Are the training materials useful back on the job?

- Are the trainees learning what they need to learn?

- Are the newly learned skills being applied back on the job?

- Are the right people being sent to training?

- Are there other barriers that are preventing the training from being used?

- Is additional training necessary to move the organization to where it wants to be?

- Does our CBA say that doing this training is worth it?

Chapter 3

Do You Know What You Need to Do? Analysis

This chapter will help you to:

- Master the most common analysis data-collection methods
- Differentiate among the various types of analysis
- Perform a job analysis
- Create a criticality analysis
- Determine whether you need to do a task analysis and learn how to do one
- Do an audience analysis
- Discover what a competency analysis is

Chapter Two helped to provide a blueprint for your training; this chapter creates the foundation upon which it will rest. Analysis will tell you what needs to be taught in your training program—and what does not.

Both of these aspects are important. You want your trainees to learn everything they require to do their job, but you don't want them to waste their time learning things they don't have to know. For example, if one of the needs that you isolated doing the processes in Chapter Two is for new employees to learn how to make a tire properly, there are a lot of things you can teach them. In public school the teacher would probably start with the history of tires, or even the history of the wheel. You may not want to go that far back, but you may think it's important for the trainees to learn about how the company has been making tires; then again, you may not. If "Joe" were teaching the class, he might want to tell the trainees about the problems they had installing and running the X45-B tread machine when it first came on line, whereas "June" might want to discuss her technique for moving those heavy truck tires without straining herself. And then again. . . .

By now you should be getting a clearer picture of what analysis does. As we said, at its simplest it helps you decide both what you want to teach and what you do not want to teach.

It's difficult to say where analysis really begins. Some designers would contend that what we labeled as pre-design in Chapter Two is actually part of analysis. Some even use the terms *assessment* and *analysis* interchangeably, as in *training needs analysis* and *audience assessment*. Others say that analysis is strictly job and task analysis, with everything else being part of the design component. For our purpose of rapid instructional design, this slicing and dicing really doesn't matter. Our delineations throughout this book are fluid. If you want to consider needs assessment as part of analysis, that's fine. If you want to move delivery analysis (which we'll discuss in Chapter Four) back to this chapter, that's good too. The important thing is that you know what these concepts are—and use them when your situation so dictates.

 ## DATA-COLLECTION METHODS

There are a number of different types of analysis and a number of ways of doing each. Which type(s) of analysis you choose and which data-collection method(s) you use will depend on your topic (or need), your business environment, and the type of training you are considering. For example, if you are involved in our tire building example from above, you will probably want to do an analysis that tells you what exact knowledge and skills a person must have to build a tire. These skills and knowledge are what your program will teach and, more important, what your trainees should learn. For this purpose, you will probably need to do a task analysis (more about task analysis later).

As far as data-collection methods are concerned, you already know that the best tire builder in the company is Sam down at the Knoxville plant. So you might want to go there and interview Sam, ask how he does it, and see what his tricks and shortcuts are. You might then want to observe him for a bit and see whether he practices what he preaches. Or you may not know who the best is, or even if there is a best. In that case you might want to interview a number of builders or to bring them together to talk about what they do.

There are specific names for each of these data-collection methods, and you can find them and others in the following list. (*Figuring Things Out* by Ron Zemke, 1982.)

Analysis Data-Collection Methods

- Focus groups
- Interviews
- Questionnaire or survey
- Observation
- Document collection and verification
- Job duties categorizing
- Delphi studies
- Job diaries
- Examination of performance and productivity measures
- Nominal group technique
- Critical incident method

The first four of these methods are the most commonly used, so we'll discuss them in some detail. Descriptions for the others can be found in the various analysis resources listed in the Suggested Readings.

Focus Groups

When using a focus group, you invite individuals who are experts on the information you want to gather to meet and discuss what they know. I like to keep the focus group to around four to five participants, as this is a manageable number, but you might want more or fewer participants depending on the material and your company's environment and politics.

A Focus Group Example

There are a number of methods for handling a focus group. One that works well is to start out with a brainstorming session in which the group simply states everything they think is important to the subject at hand. Don't worry about right or wrong, and don't let the participants get into a discussion. That will come later. Use a flip chart (or a lot of flip charts) to capture and post all the ideas. You might want an assistant to help you with the recording aspect.

If you have a large focus group, break the people into smaller groups for the brainstorming, each group with its own recorder. Then bring them together and rerecord the information onto general flip charts.

The next step is to categorize the information into groupings of some type, depending on what your main topic is. By categorizing you will be able to eliminate duplications and help your experts recognize concepts or whole areas that they might have missed.

Take a break, then have them look through your general groupings once more and make final changes and comments. This is where the discussion really gets going, so save about half your focus group time for this aspect. Generally, that about does it for a focus group. You may want to send typed lists back to the group for validation or further explanation, but this is done after the group meeting.

There are other activities you might want to do in focus groups that deal with specific types of analysis, such as task analysis, audience analysis, or performance analysis, but we'll discuss these augmentations when we look at each type of analysis.

Participants

There are many possible approaches for choosing focus group members. You may want a mix of seasoned performers, individuals with a year or two of experience, and one or two who have been on the job only a couple of months. Some designers like to hold more than one focus group, with a single level of experience in each.

You may want top performers, particularly if you are doing a competency analysis. These individuals can be found by comparing their years of experience to their ranking in the organization. Those with a great deal of experience and high rankings should be top performers. To obtain such rankings, do an informal poll of coworkers and supervisors, asking simply, "Who's the best at this?" or "Who do you go to when you have a problem?"

Make sure the experience is the right kind—that is, experience in what you are analyzing. The generalist who knows a little about a lot might not be the person you want for your specialized focus group.

There is great deal of debate as to whether you should mix supervisors and performers in a focus group. You need supervisory and even management input, but if you feel the supervisors will inhibit the discussion, you may not want to mix them in. If you think this may be a problem, talk to them later or use their expertise as part of the validation process. Each company and even each department has its own culture, and you will need to know yours before you decide whether to include or exclude supervisors from your focus group.

One other shortcut that works well with focus groups is the use of Post-it® Notes or what's commonly referred to as the "sticky" method. Instead of using flip charts, have your small groups write their tasks on *large* stickies and post them. Then during categorizing, just move the stickies around and combine them as required.

Another way to get a wide variety of participants for your focus groups is to use the telephone instead of face-to-face meetings. This method is a little cumbersome—think two degrees worse than a telephone conference call—but it may be the only way to collect data from some of your critical sources.

When using this method, you need to prepare the participants in advance even more than for a face-to-face focus group, with a strong objective and good questions that they can think about. A list of participants that they can refer to is also a good idea. During the phone focus group make sure the participants identify themselves before each submission (also cumbersome, but very necessary if you want to get good interaction), and monitor to make sure one or two don't take over. Having a scribe to write down the responses while you facilitate the group is also a good idea.

One thing I've learned from sad experience: never mix a face-to-face and a telephone focus group. The participants on the phone often feel left out as discussions get going among the face-to-face people, and many times they just can't hear what is going on. They end up paying little attention except when they want to speak, which is the opposite of what you want. Instead, run two focus groups, one for the face-to-face and one over the phone. It takes more of your time but will really be worth it.

Facilitating a Focus Group

One key to the success of a focus group is how well you do your job as facilitator. This means planning the process, communicating well, and listening a lot while talking as little as possible during the actual group process. Here is a list of activities a successful focus group facilitator performs, as adapted from material contained in Allen Communication's *Designer's Edge* instructional design software:

- Defines the scope of the process
- Develops the objectives to be accomplished
- Determines what strategies (activities) will be used
- Creates an agenda that effectively communicates the above
- Chooses the right participants and mix of participants
- Prepares the room
- Makes sure everyone knows everyone at the start of the meeting
- Reviews and clarifies the agenda
- Explains the procedures to be followed
- Keeps the meeting on track

- Records data and pushes for clarification where needed
- Communicates the results

 A somewhat different type of focus group, and a rapid design shortcut, is to use an electronic bulletin board instead of a live meeting. Focus group members can react to comments made by others and post their own responses to your questions when they have the time. You need to manage this process carefully so that neither the time nor the amount of data gets out of hand, but this method can be very time effective.

You can also run a chat-room focus group in which everyone is connected by computer synchronously. I've not found that these are much better than a telephone-mediated process, but in this age of computer everything, many participants—particularly younger ones—are very comfortable with this technique.

Interviews

Another data-collection technique is the one-on-one interview. For this process you talk to your experts individually, asking a series of questions. Or you may allow the interview to be free-form, listen to whatever the experts have to say, and ask questions as they come up.

If you are using predetermined questions, you may want to send them out to the interviewees in advance. This gives them time to consider what you are looking for and perhaps even to ask colleagues for their opinions. The interview itself can be spent discussing the expert's answers and delving into follow-up questions.

One of the problems with individual interviews is that the individuals bring their own biases into the situation, and because you can't expect a person to be completely objective, you have to interview several experts from the target population. This can be time-consuming for the interviewer.

 A rapid design shortcut for interviewing is to try to interview people two at a time. Not only does this cut down the amount of time you spend interviewing, but it gives the interviewees a chance to react to one another's comments, which can give you new and different insights.

Phone Interviews
Interviews are often done over the phone in lieu of meeting face to face in large or highly distributed companies, or when there are a number of SMEs that you need to talk to. This obviously saves travel cost and a lot of the interviewer's time as well.

What is lost is the feeling for the environment in which the work is being done. It's hard to put an objective measure on this, but I've found that it is important. Just looking around can also lead to follow-up questions that would never have occurred to you over the phone. My advice is to use the telephone and other high-tech methods as you need them and when you can. However, don't use them exclusively for your interviewing. Be sure to make at least one or two trips to the work site to see for yourself what's going on.

Advantages

The advantages of using interviews as a data-collection technique include the following:

- Can be used for almost any type of analysis
- Builds supporters for training
- Can easily be done at various organizational levels
- Is good for eliciting feelings and opinions
- Can be made more efficient through technology such as the telephone

A Last Question

One other thought on interviews. The last question I always ask is: "Is there anything that you are surprised that I did not ask about?" I use this question or a variation of it no matter what the purpose of the interview is. I've even used it at job interviews. Try it yourself sometime. You may be surprised at some of the things you learn.

Surveys or Questionnaires

A survey or questionnaire is simply a list of questions concerning the topic you are analyzing (Surveys from Start to Finish, Info-Line, 612). Use them when you need a lot of responses or when your training audience is widely dispersed. Surveys are a good tool for doing an audience analysis, as we will see later.

Disadvantages

The problem with surveys is that it is difficult to write really good questions that aren't subject to interpretation. The more interpretation, the less usable your data will be and the harder it will be to collect it into meaningful group-ings. With surveys the respondents cannot ask you to clarify what you meant, unless they go thorough the trouble of picking up the phone and finding you available. You cannot ask follow-up questions either, unless you go through the same process. This means that your respondents will be guessing at what you are asking for, and you will be doing some guessing at what they are really trying to say. This guesswork leads to misconceptions at worst, and at best, to a lot of extraneous data that you may or may not need.

Also, you normally receive pretty poor returns on a survey. Fifteen percent is a good return; 10 and even 5 percent returns are not unusual. So if you are using surveys, send out plenty more than you need, because you won't get back as many as you'd like.

Advantages

The advantages of using questionnaires as a data-collection technique include the following:

- Can be anonymous
- Can reach a large group in a short time
- Data is uniform
- Allows respondents time to think about answers and even to do research
- Is often the cheapest method
- Is usually the most time-effective method for respondents

Net Surveys

A lot of survey data collection is now being done through net-based survey instruments (www.astd.org). These high-tech programs make data collection and manipulation easier, but do not really solve the problems of item development and follow-up questions. Some of the best have a bulletin-board facility for posting questions, but this is not a lot better than the telephone and assumes that your respondents will check back in to read your explanations or questions. This can be a pretty large assumption when your respondents are busily engaged in their own jobs and you were lucky if they took the time to do your survey in the first place.

Experience seems to indicate that returns of net-based surveys are no higher than they are for the paper-and-pencil variety.

 Although net-based surveys have their pros and cons, using electronic methods for receiving feedback to any analysis process is another rapid design shortcut. This could be by computer disk or e-mail, but the key is to receive as much analysis information as possible electronically, which makes it easier to manipulate and place into other types of documents.

Observations

Observations are basically what the term indicates: you collect data by watching the expert at work. You might also want to watch those who are not quite as expert—and even those who are just beginning. This will give you a range of how the work should be done and how it actually is done.

A period set aside for questioning is important with any observation. This is usually done after the observation, but may be continuous during the observation if this does not bother the person being observed or somehow change the process as you are observing it.

I've always found it best to observe without questions first, then observe the process again with questions, if possible. If the individual I'm observing is giving a running commentary I might use a tape recorder; otherwise I try to take good notes.

I try to observe at least two "experts" and one or two "average" contributors for each data gathering process. The problem with observing only the experts is that they often use shortcuts that your trainees will be unable to master, as they will be new to the process. In other words, experts may make it look too easy and you will miss some key points. I've never had good results observing new contributors, although other folks who do analysis say that this should be part of any observation. Your choice.

Another observation method is to have a person who wants to develop the job skills observe the expert and document what he or she sees. Usually you will need to have two or three separate observations with different observers and experts to act as a control on this process. You might bring the observers together as a kind of mini focus group to finalize the process.

Disadvantages

The problem with observations is that they take a lot of time and may not necessarily catch all the needed information, as some things are done by an expert only on certain occasions and may not occur during the observation.

Advantages

The advantages of using observations as a data-collection technique include the following:

- Provides information on actual performance
- Gives a context for the training
- Allows you to be flexible through the asking of questions

- Often indicates other issues that you need to explore
- Is great for giving you an initial picture

Here is a template you can use for observations:

OBSERVATION FORM

Observer: _____

Date: _____

Location: _____

Individual observed: _____

Job or task observed: _____

Purpose of observation: _____

Behavior Observed	Training Required?	Priority (1–5)
1.		
2.		
3.		
4.		
5.		
6.		
7.		
8.		
9.		
10.		

Comments:

Hybrids

The best data-collection techniques are probably a combination of these processes and others. For example, you might do a questionnaire to gain an overall view of the topic and then focus in with a focus group. Or you might start by observing and then hold formal interviews based on the observations. Depending on how much time you are given, you might combine three or more techniques, or you may only have the time for one. Whatever you choose, let your topic, your corporate environment, and what it (and you) can support be the deciding factors.

Here are some questions to ask yourself when deciding on an analysis method:

- How much contributor involvement will be required, and can I get them to give their time?
- How much management involvement will be required, and will management support the analysis?
- How long will it take to collect and correlate the data, and do I have that much time?
- How much will it cost, and do I have the budget?
- How relevant will the data be from using this technique?

As you might guess, the last question is the most important. Nothing else matters if the data do not help you create the training. However, all five of these questions should be considered when planning your data collection.

WHY ANALYZE?

By now you might be saying: "But why do I have to ask anybody? I know how to build tires; in fact, I'm the best at it. That's why they chose me to do the training." Well, that may be, but did you ever hear the saying about the fool who has himself as his lawyer? The same goes for analysis. You may be a subject-matter expert—even *the* subject-matter expert—but it never hurts to ask a few others for their opinions. You may have mastered the job so thoroughly that you've forgotten some of the things that will puzzle a new person, or one of your colleagues may have a better way to do one of the tasks associated with the process.

Whatever the reason, don't analyze only your own expertise. Be sure that you have the total picture of what your trainees will need to learn. One of my favorite reasons for analysis is this dialogue between Alice and the Cheshire Cat:

"Would you tell me, please,
*   which way I ought to go from here?"*
"That depends a good deal
*   on where you want to go to."*

—LEWIS CARROLL, *ALICE'S ADVENTURES IN WONDERLAND*

TYPES OF ANALYSIS

There are many types of analysis associated with the instructional design process, and it seems new ones appear every few years. We discussed a couple of them already in the previous chapter—where we talked about organizational analysis, performance analysis, and training needs analysis—but let's look at a few of the other major types that you will almost certainly need to employ when developing a good training program. Here is a list of most of them. You may notice that the ones we've already discussed are on the left side, so we'll be on the right side for the rest of this chapter.

Types of Analysis

Organizational	Job
Performance	Criticality
Gap	Task
Opportunity	Learning
Training Needs (assessment)	Audience
Cost-Benefit	Delivery

 Job Analysis

The most common type of analysis is job analysis ("Be a Better Job Analyst," *Info-Line*, 903). The main purpose of a job analysis is to find out what tasks are necessary to do a job—that is, to break down a complex job into its component parts. If you are an SME who has been assigned the responsibility of creating a training program, this is where you will most likely start with your analysis.

Begin by recording your training need and the problem, issue, or opportunity that is related to it from the pre-design processes discussed in Chapter Two. Now record all the tasks associated with that need, paying special attention to any tasks that were not being performed properly according to your needs assessment.

Task Characteristics

If you are not sure what is a task and what is not, here are some task characteristics:

• Tasks have a definite beginning and end

- Tasks are of short duration—minutes or a few hours at the most
- A task can be observed so you know whether it has been completed
- Tasks are independent of other actions
- Tasks start with a verb or highly specific action

If this list of task characteristics helps you, then by all means use it, but be aware that many new designers spend a lot of time trying to fit things into these definitions. I find that the best approach to use is if you think it's a task, then write it down; you can always revise it later. The only one of these five characteristics that I really hold to is the last: your task should have a verb or action associated with it. For example, going back to our tire manufacturing scenario, you may find that the job tasks include:

- Choosing the correct tread size
- Reversing the interior matrix
- Laying on the steel belt
- Sequencing the assembly machine
- Trimming excess rubber
- Inspecting for proper seal

Notice that each of these tasks has an action associated with it; some have more than one. They may not all meet the characteristics listed earlier and so may need further analysis, but this list is a good start.

Action verbs are used to describe job tasks and steps. Here is a list of some action verbs you might use when recording tasks:

If the person's job or task includes the following actions . . .	*. . . then these action verbs are appropriate*
• Appraise conclusions	Argue
• Compare and contrast	Assess
• Critique materials	Attach
• Judge the logical consistency of written material or ideas	Choose
• Judge the adequacy with which conclusions are supported by data	Criticize
• Judge the value of a work, using internal criteria	Defend

If the person's job or task *includes the following actions . . .*	*. . . then these action* *verbs are appropriate*
• Judge the value of a work, using external standards of excellence	Estimate
	Evaluate
	Justify
	Predict
	Rate
	Score
	Select
	Support
	Value
• Assemble parts	Arrange
• Compose or compile a report	Assemble
• Create a new process	Collect
• Design a new machine	Combine
• Integrate learning from different areas into a plan for solving problems	Construct
• Propose a plan for an experiment	Devise
• Write a computer program or creative story	Formulate
	Generate
	Manage
	Modify
	Organize
	Plan
	Prepare
	Propose
	Rearrange
	Reconstruct
	Set up
• Assess the relevance of data	Analyze
• Break down a whole into parts	Appraise

If the person's job or task includes the following actions . . .	*. . . then these action verbs are appropriate*
• Diagram a workflow	Calculate
• Differentiate functions	Categorize
• Distinguish between facts and inferences	Compare
• Illustrate relationships	Contrast
• Recognize unstated assumptions	Criticize
• Recognize logical fallacies in reasoning	Discriminate
	Examine
	Experiment
	Question
	Separate
	Subdivide
	Test
• Apply concepts and principles to new situations	Change
• Apply laws and theories to practical situations	Choose
• Compute or solve equations	Construct
• Demonstrate correct usage of a method, process or procedure	Dramatize
• Manipulate objects	Employ
• Modify a process	Illustrate
• Operate equipment	Interpret
• Use in a new situation	Practice
	Prepare
	Produce
	Relate
	Schedule
	Show
	Sketch
	Solve
• Convert numbers	Classify
• Estimate future consequences implied in data	Describe

If the person's job or task includes the following actions . . .	*. . . then these action verbs are appropriate*
• Estimate outcomes	Discuss
• Explain concepts, facts and principles	Distinguish
• Interpret verbal material	Explain
• Interpret charts and graphs	Express
• Summarize information	Generalize
• Translate verbal material to mathematical formulas	Give examples
• Translate languages	Identify
	Indicate
	Infer
	Locate
	Paraphrase
	Predict
	Recognize
	Report
	Restate
	Review
	Rewrite
	Select
• Define basic terms or concepts	Arrange
• Describe basic processes	Duplicate
• Identify methods and procedures	Match
• Label parts	Memorize
• List or name key components	Name
• Recall specific facts	Order
• State principles	Recognize
• Select items from a list	Relate
	Repeat
	Reproduce

This list is not all-inclusive. Use the verb that best describes the actual work (performance) on the job.

Doing a Job Analysis

If you are not an SME, or even if you are one but you want to do this right, you will need to do data collection to make sure you have recorded all possible tasks. Focus groups are an excellent data-collection method for a job analysis, particularly when combined with observation. Interviews with job incumbents are also a good data-collection technique here. You might obtain information from any existing training courses already being used by your company and from company documents as well.

Here are a few questions you might ask yourself or your SMEs as part of a job analysis:

- What do you need to know to do your job well?
- What do you think you do well that a new employee at your job would not?
- What are the most common problems you encounter in your job?
- What changes often on your job?
- What tricks have you learned that help you do your job better?
- What do you like most and least about your job?
- What makes you most productive on your job?
- What prepared you best to do your job?

And here are a few ideas on where you might get information for your job analysis. Find out as much as possible about the job you are analyzing by

- Looking at job descriptions
- Listing all tasks involved in the job
- Noting prerequisite learnings
- Getting copies of existing courses
- Interviewing new hires
- Interviewing veterans

 A rapid design technique for job analysis, or any place where you are using SMEs, is to choose as your subjects individuals who are not overly experienced. You don't want new employees, but you also don't want those who have so much experience that they waste your time with information that is beyond the needs of your audience. Look for SMEs who know their stuff, but are capable of telling you what is needed without going too far beyond that.

REQUIREMENT	TASK STATEMENT	EXAMPLE
Clarity	Use wording that is easily understood.	"Compare written description to actual performance," but not "Relate results to needs of field."
	Be precise so words mean the same thing to all personnel in the job classification.	Use words such as check, co-ordinate, or assist with caution, as they are vague.
	Write separate, specific statements for each task. Avoid combining vague items of skill, knowledge, or responsibility.	Use "Supervise files" or "Maintain files," but not "Have responsibility for maintaining files."
Completeness	Use abbreviations only after spelling out the term.	"Closed Cycle Cooling System (CCCS)" may be followed by "Start Up the CCCS."
	When the task is to complete a standard form, include both form and title number, unless all that is needed is a general type of form.	"Complete Task Description Worksheet (Form Number 2243)."
Conciseness	Be brief. Short phrases are preferred to long expressions.	"Write production and control reports," not "Accomplish necessary reports involved in the process of maintaining production and control procedures."
	Begin with a present-tense action word (subject "I" or "you" is understood).	"Clean" or "Write."
	Indicate an object of the action to be performed.	"Clean engine" or "Write report."
	Use terminology that is currently used on the job.	"Use most recent NRC documentation."
Consistency	Avoid stating a person's qualifica-tions, such as intelligence, experi-ence, or education.	"Load computer tape," but not "Has one year of computer training" is not a task.
	Omit items on receiving instruction, unless actual work is performed during training.	"Give instruction," but "Attend lecture" is not a task.

Product of a Job Analysis

The product of your job analysis should be an exhaustive list of all the tasks that go into the performance of a job. Some of these tasks may require training and some may not, but you need to know what all of them are before you can make a decision. One thing you will know for sure: if you did a proper job analysis and something is not on your task list, then it *does not* require training. This is a key step in making sure you do not waste time instructing your trainees on things they do not need to know.

Use the following chart as an aid to produce a task list that you can use effectively.

Here is a simple job analysis template you might use for your job analysis:

JOB ANALYSIS TEMPLATE

Job Title: _____

Job Description: _____

_____

_____

_____

Tasks:

1. _____

2. _____

3. _____

4. _____

5. _____

Possible Prerequisite Learnings:

Important Audience Characteristics:

If your company has well-executed, very complete position descriptions, you may be able to employ them as a rapid design shortcut for job analysis. Use them as a framework for your interview or focus groups to make them more efficient or, if they are really complete, use them in lieu of these processes. Make sure that they are up-to-date and as accurate as possible by having a SME job incumbent validate them before their use.

Criticality Analysis

You make the decision for which tasks require training by doing what is called a *criticality analysis.* Basically, this type of analysis looks at four factors:

- How often is the task done?
- How difficult is it to do?
- How important it is to the job?
- How much training will be required to become proficient at the task?

Once again, you'll want to gather opinions on these factors from experts. This is one of those items we mentioned earlier that you can easily attach to your focus group process if you are using it as part of a job analysis.

A good tool for doing a criticality analysis is a criticality matrix, on which you list all of your tasks in one column and the four factors in others. Assign number values or descriptions, such as "extremely frequent," "moderately difficult," or "low importance," for each factor for each task. Then choose those tasks for training that meet your criteria. This is not terribly scientific, nor statistically sound, but it will work well for your job analysis. Here's an example of a completed criticality matrix:

Rate each task as 1 through 5

Task #	Task*	Frequency	Difficulty	Importance	Training Difficulty	Total
1	Choosing the correct tread size	5	3	5	1	14
2	Reversing the interior matrix	1	5	5	2	13
3	Laying on the steel belt	3	1	4	2	10
4	Sequencing the assembly machine	5	1	5	5	16
5	Trimming excess rubber	3	1	2	1	7
6	Inspecting for proper seal	5	1	4	2	11

*All tasks scoring 12 or higher, or with a 5 in the training column, should be considered for training for this analysis.

If your company captures performance data, it can help you make decisions about the need for training on various tasks as well, as can error analysis that is done by your quality group. Reviewing any current training evaluations or any standardized test that the company gives can also be useful for making decisions about which tasks need to be trained on.

Other Questions to Determine Task Criticality

Here are some other questions you might ask when considering whether or not a task should be trained on. Note that some of them are closely related to, or exact repeats of, assessment questions from Chapter Two.

- Is there some mandate from governmental or accrediting organizations for the training?

- Is the training required for legal or human resources (equal employment opportunity, wage and hour) reasons?

- What happens if the task is not performed correctly or not performed at all?

- What level of proficiency is necessary?

- How does the task relate to organizational goals?

- How much time is required to perform the task?

- What does the trainee need to know or be able to do before he or she can be trained on the task?

- If we do not train, how will the employees learn the task?

In the final analysis, what you are really seeking are the essential tasks related to doing the job that require training in order to be effectively mastered. Any task that is not essential or that cannot be addressed by training should not be found in your final cut.

Here is another form you can use, which combines both a job and a criticality analysis. Note the directions that follow it on how to use the form.

JOB ANALYSIS FORM

Need: _____

Job: _____ Date: _____

Task	*Frequency* 4 3 2 1	*Importance* 4 3 2 1	*Learning* 4 3 2 1	*Risk* 4 3 2 1
Subtasks	*Frequency* 4 3 2 1	*Importance* 4 3 2 1	*Learning* 4 3 2 1	*Risk* 4 3 2 1

Date: The date when this form is completed.

Tasks: The list of tasks is a breakdown of the broad activities to be performed on the job. The tasks statements should include a concise description of what the employee will do on the job.

Begin with an action verb.

Use a noun following the action verb.

Avoid overlap with other tasks.

Subtasks: Any part of a task not at the level of knowledge, skills, and attitudes (KSAs)

Frequency: How frequently is the individual task performed on the job? Each task should be rated as daily, weekly, once a month, or less than once a month.

4 = daily

3 = weekly

2 = once a month

1 = less than once a month

Importance: How important is the individual task to overall job effectiveness? Each task should be rated as critical, moderately critical, not critical, or could be omitted.

4 = critical

3 = moderately critical

2 = not critical

1 = could be omitted

Learning: How difficult is the task to learn? Each task should be rated as very difficult, moderately difficult, somewhat difficult, or not difficult.

4 = very difficult

3 = moderately difficult

2 = somewhat difficult

1 = not difficult

Risk: What is the degree of risk associated with performing the task incorrectly? For instance, could the employee be injured or could the mistake cost the company a lot of money? Each task should be rated as high risk, moderate risk, minimal risk, or no risk.

4 = high risk

3 = moderate risk

2 = minimal risk

1 = no risk

Task Analysis

In many cases you will need to go deeper than a job analysis to determine what you need to train on or what the training will comprise. To do this, you analyze the specific skills and knowledge that make up a task from your job analysis. This is termed a *task analysis* ("Be a Better Task Analyst," *Info-Line,* 503).

A task analysis is simply a job analysis at a deeper level. You try and find the basic skills and knowledge that make up your task. You may find that your task can be divided into subtasks and even sub-subtasks before you get to these basics. You may also find that you can stop at one of the subtask levels, as this is where you will need to train.

A rapid design shortcut for task or job analysis is simply to spend a day observing an SME at work and ask questions. This is not perfect, but it will be pretty close.

Example

Let's use some of our examples of tire building tasks again:

> For the task "choosing the correct tread size," you realize that the trainees will need to know what the various tread sizes are and how to differentiate them. This is the knowledge that they need for the task, and there does not seem to be a deeper level than this, so your task analysis is complete for this task.
>
> For the task "reversing the interior matrix," you find that the knowledge is simply to know when the matrix needs to be reversed and that the skill is to reverse it correctly—simply a matter of turning it inside out.
>
> However, for "sequencing the assembly machine," you find that there are a number of subtasks, such as setting up the machine, moving the matrix to the correct position on the machine, creating the proper air pressure environment, laminating the sidewall layers, and so on. Each of these subtasks needs to be analyzed for what the trainee will be required to learn in the way of new knowledge and skills.

Depth of Task Analysis

Figuring out which tasks need to be further analyzed is another one of those skills in instructional design that come only with practice. The best advice I can give you is to overanalyze and then reduce as necessary. If you do your program development properly, there will be a number of checkpoints later on in the process that will tell you whether you have the right content to the right degree, and these will help you eliminate unnecessary detail. However, the checks (or *reviews,* as they are most often called) will not be as effective at finding anything that you did not include, so err on the side of too much at this point, if you can.

Of course, how much analysis you do and how deep you go is also dependent on the amount of time you have to do analysis. In the real world, where most of us work, you often have to shortchange your analysis simply to get the program done on time. If this is the case for your program, spend the time doing the job and criticality analysis and trust yourself or your SMEs as content experts for the more basic skills and knowledge. If you have a good foundation—that is, a valid task list—you should be OK in most circumstances.

And don't forget that one of the most important skills of a good instructional designer is the ability to revise based on the input of others. Many people get into the "pride of authorship" thing and don't want to take anything out of their program, particularly things they've spent a lot of time analyzing and getting right. Good instructional design requires constant revision, elimination, and addition as new aspects present themselves. Your program is not written in stone until the day it is taught, and even then only for that day; you should begin making revisions for the next class based on what you learn in this one.

Data Gathering for Task Analysis

You can use the same data gathering methods for task analysis as you did for your job analysis, sometimes doing both at the same time. This is normally not the best approach, as the burden of doing both types of analysis at the same time may cause you to miss important items in your push to finish. It can also be inefficient, as you may analyze tasks that you find out later don't need to be trained on, and thus do not have to be analyzed. However, corporate needs may dictate that you have only a limited amount of time or availability of analysis resources, so you must do the best you can.

Other places to gather data on skills and knowledge associated with tasks include textbooks or reference books dealing with the subject matter, technical manuals, drawings, and working models used by your organization.

Your output for all this analysis is a list of the tasks that you will train on to meet the need identified by your assessments in Chapter Two. Where necessary, lists of subtasks and the skills and knowledge related to each task or subtask will also be included.

Here is an example of a questionnaire that I've found useful when doing a task analysis.

TASK ANALYSIS QUESTIONNAIRE

Task: _____

Subtasks	**Skills and Knowledge**
List any subtasks related to each task.	List skills and knowledge required to perform each subtask.

1. _____   skills

knowledge

2. _____   skills

knowledge

3. _____   skills

knowledge

Questions related to the task (may be completed by the SME or asked of him or her as follow-up):

- What is the expected output of the task?
- What indicates that the task is done correctly or incorrectly?
- What is the outcome if the task is done incorrectly?
- What do you do if it is done incorrectly?
- How often do you do the task?
- How do you know it is time to do the task?
- What tools and references do you use to do the task?

If your company has well-written and complete procedures for various tasks, a rapid design shortcut is to use these for your task analysis in lieu of focus groups or interviews. Be sure that these procedures are complete. In fact, it's a good idea to have an SME look them over before you use them for your analysis; have the SME look over your analysis as well.

Another task or job analysis rapid design shortcut is to videotape experts doing their jobs and analyze the videotape for the component parts. This will save you time over multiple focus groups and interviews, but don't forget that you will be spending time taping and reviewing, so be sure it's worth the effort.

The following is a list of various types of data you might collect during a job and task analysis:

   ### DATA THAT MAY BE COLLECTED DURING A JOB AND TASK ANALYSIS

- Task listings for a given job
- Frequency of task performance
- Difficulty of task performance
- Task importance (consequence of inadequate performance)
- Conditions under which task is performed
- Cues for task initiation and termination
- Steps (elements) required for task performance (subtasks)
- Standards of task performance
- References utilized in task performance
- Tools and equipment utilized in task performance
- Outputs (results) of task performance
- Problems that may result from poor task performance and their resolution
- Human interfaces during task performance
- System interfaces during task performance
- Personnel safety considerations
- Required skills and knowledge for adequate task performance
- Required skills and knowledge for exemplary task performance
- Organization (sequencing) of skills and knowledge

Here is another form you might want to use for your task analysis. It follows the format of the previous combined Job and Criticality Analysis form, and also has directions after.

TASK ANALYSIS FORM

Task or Subtask: _____

Date: _____

| Element Description: | Inputs
Steps
Tools
Standards
Circumstances
Outputs
KSAs |

Inputs: What events, cues, orders, materials, or symptoms indicate that the task must be performed? In other words, what do employees need to get or receive before they can begin their subtasks?

Steps: Each task may be broken down into its component steps (processes.) The task statements should include a concise description of what the employee will do on the job.

Begin with an action verb.

Use a noun following the action verb.

Refer to the action verb table as needed (see separate sheet).

Tools: What tools, references, equipment or materials are used to complete the sub-tasks? Where appropriate, identify system software (screens and application functions).

Standards: How well must the task be performed? Standards include accuracy, time, quantity, cost, error rate, and customer satisfaction.

Circumstances: What circumstances influence task performance? For example, what physical locations, situations, adverse conditions, assistance, level of supervision, and obstacles or barriers exist when the task is being performed?

Outputs: What events, cues, orders, materials, or symptoms indicate that the task has been completed? What has been produced? What is passed on to another group or customer?

Feedback: What feedback does the employee receive when performing the task or after delivering the outputs? Feedback can be informal or formal.

KSAs: What are the knowledge, skills, and attitudes that make up this task or subtask as related to the other information found on this form? These elements are used to write your objectives.

Learning Analysis

Very often an instructional designer simply does not have enough time to do a complete job and task analysis (JTA). In these situations you may want to do a shorter process termed a *learning analysis*. A learning analysis is not as thorough as a JTA, and will probably mean that you'll do more bouncing back and forth across the ID web as we discussed in Chapter One, but if you have limited time it is a good place to start.

A learning analysis consists of two parts. In the first part you sit down—either alone or, ideally, with an SME, a manager, or both—and simply define the training need or program that is required.

Next you gather whatever data you can concerning what the program might cover, using whatever data collection methods you have the time to employ.

Now you create a list of all possible learnings that the course participants might achieve. You do this with no consideration for course time constraints or structure. You're basically working in a black box during this time.

The final step is to analyze the possible learnings to decide which of them the program must cover. You do this using something like the following methodology:

- Group the learnings into topics
- Prioritize the topics
- Prioritize the learnings within each topic
- Remove all redundant topics or learnings
- Combine learnings or topics where possible
- Indicate critical learnings that must be taught
- Remove all noncritical learnings
- Estimate instructional time for each topic

When you've finished, you will have a list of critical learnings that must be achieved by the course participants. From these you can begin to write your objectives, although because you have not gotten down to the knowledge, skills, and attitude (KSA) level this will be a bit more difficult.

 ### Trainee (Audience) Analysis

Either after, at the same time that, or even before you analyze what your trainees need to learn, you should also analyze the trainees themselves. This is called a *trainee* (or *learner* or *audience*) *analysis* (*Mastering the Instructional Design Process,* by Bill Rothwell and H. C. Kazanas, Chapter 5, 1992).

The more you can find out about your target audience, the more likely it is that your training will meet its needs. Aspects such as age, gender, educational experience, past training experiences, interests, and many other less obvious characteristics can help you design a better program, as you'll know what tone to use in your writing, what kind of examples to use, and how to populate your role-plays and other activities.

You'll use your trainee analysis for completing other types of analysis, to design your training program so it is most effective, to develop your materials properly, and to evaluate both your learners and the program. Basically you'll use it for just about everything you do from here on in; that should give you some idea of its importance and the amount of time you may want to spend on it.

Remember that you are finding out these things to help motivate your trainees and make them more comfortable in whatever learning environment you create.

Data Gathering Methods for a Trainee Analysis

Your first task is to figure out generally who your audience is and then to gather all the information you think you may need about them. You can use many of the data gathering methods we've already discussed. Here are some thoughts on their particular use for audience analysis.

Focus groups are not the best data gathering method, unless you have a very small audience or they are all very much alike. You might need to use this method if you cannot get around to a larger audience or if you are really pressed for time. Be sure that you pick people for your focus group who reflect the mix that you will have in your class. Random choice is seldom a good idea for any type of focus group, but particularly not for one that is involved in an audience analysis.

In your focus group you might ask questions such as these, adapted from Allen Communication's Designer's Edge instructional design software:

- What do you like most about training?

- What do you dislike about training?

- What can we do to make training better?

- Which of these training methods do you like/dislike?

  - Classroom

  - On-the-job

  - With a mentor

- Totally on my own with no direction
- On my own, but with self-instructional materials to direct me
- Using videotapes
- Using computers
- Training in teams
- By observing others
- By doing role plays and simulations

- What tricks do you use to remember important things?
- How do you and your colleagues feel about your jobs?
- What do you like most about your work?
- What do you like least about your work?
- If you were the supervisor, what would you change in how your work is done?
- What motivates you to do your best work?
- What would make you more productive?

Interviews are usually a better method than focus groups, but not much better. You receive a lot of interaction and can really feel the likes and dislikes of those you interview, but it is a time-consuming method. Unless you interview enough of each possible category of trainees, you might obtain some erroneous or skewed results. One advantage of using interviews for audience analysis is that this usually gives you a core of individuals who will be very supportive of the program because you asked their opinions. The same can also be said for focus groups. Many of the questions noted in the preceding focus group discussion are also valid for audience analysis interviews—and for surveys as well.

You might also want to interview your participants' managers or the initiators of the training to find out their thoughts on the audience. Here is a form I like to use when interviewing or surveying managers and initiators about the audience for a training program.

AUDIENCE ANALYSIS QUESTIONS
(FOR MANAGERS/INITIATORS)

Note to the interviewer: Begin by explaining prerequisites and showing the curriculum chart.

1. Who do you see as the primary audience for the intervention?

    Job functions

    Number

2. Who do you see as the continuing audience?

    Job functions

    Number

3. Are there other later audiences who need to be considered?

    External customers

    Others

    Number

4. What type of background should members of the primary audience possess?

    Education and/or training

        Academic

        Other

    Job experiences

    Company-specific experience

5. What skills and knowledge important to this process should they already possess?

    Any specialized equipment knowledge (hardware) required?

6. Other comments:

Surveys are the most often used method for collecting data when doing an audience analysis. It is an efficient use of time for collecting a wide range of opinions or covering a very diverse audience, but it can be less than effective if your questions are not well thought out, if your return rate is too low, or if people just don't take the time to answer your questions accurately or candidly. The interview form for managers and initiators that we have already seen makes a good survey form as well, and you can change the wording to make it applicable for just about anyone. In addition, here is another survey form I've used often:

AUDIENCE ANALYSIS TEMPLATE

1. How many participants will attend? _____
   In each session?_____

2. What are the job responsibilities and functions of the participants?

3. How well do the participants know each other?

4. Are there specific or special potential diversity issues to be aware of within the group?

5. Are there key individuals within the group? (Explain)

6. Is the training voluntary or mandatory? What have the participants been told?

7. What are the attitudes and beliefs of the participants, sponsor and managers toward the training topic?

8. What successes and difficulties have the participants encountered with the training topic?

9. What is the skill level of the participants in the training subject matter?

10. What are the barriers the participant might encounter in applying the training back on the job?

11. Have the participants taken other in-house classes?

12. Levels of evaluation to be used: ☐ 1 ☐ 2 ☐ 3

Observation is a fairly inefficient way to do audience analysis, particularly for large, diverse groups. You have to be patient and take a lot of time with each observation to make sure you cover all the possibilities. If you choose this method, you may want to enlist some other observers and then compare notes.

By now you might be saying, "Wait a minute, you've not said that any of these methods is particularly good for audience analysis," and you're right. Audience analysis is a very specialized analysis process, and the best method for data collection is usually a combination of methods. For example, a questionnaire with follow-up phone interviews works well—as does a focus group followed by observation.

Another good source of information for your audience analysis is personnel records. These records are kept by every company and can contain useful information, including educational level, age, gender, job skills, and so on. They are normally confidential, but you may be able to look at them by signing a nondisclosure agreement. Or you may be able to have someone who is officially allowed to access them tabulate some data for you. Check with your human resources department to find out about their policies and what is kept in the files that might be useful.

Additional Data

Here are some other thoughts on the kinds of data you may want to gather about your audience during an audience analysis:

- Knowing your audience's reading level is important in all training, but particularly in self-paced print-based programs. Be sure that you write to a level that will be both understandable and not boring.

- We mentioned current knowledge level before, but let's consider it again. In your job and task analysis, you probably chose a level at which you stopped analyzing because you expected all your trainees to have a basic (or what is often termed *prerequisite*) amount of knowledge.

  Now, in your audience analysis you need to make certain that these assumptions are valid. Do you expect all your trainees to know certain company-specific terms or acronyms? Should they be able to use certain measuring devices or drive a piece of equipment? Must they be able to recall various formulas or manipulate mathematical equations?

  You can see that a list like this can go on and on. You made some assumptions when doing your job and task analysis, but it is here in the audience analysis that you must make sure they were accurate, so take some time to develop and ask the right questions concerning prerequisite knowledge.

- If you're using higher technology, such as computer-based or CD-ROM training, you'll need to know your audience's computer abilities. Once again, the average and the extremes are important. You may need to design some remedial computer training to bring your trainees to the level at which they can use your new training system.

- Think about your audience from the point of view of their background and interests. Are they more technical or "arty"? Scientists or mechanics? Are they continuing their education, do they have advanced degrees, do they share common hobbies or interests? All of this knowledge may seem somewhat trivial, but using it can make the difference between a world-class training program and one that simply gets by.

  For example, at a management skills development program I heard about, at the very beginning of the program the designer played a twenty-minute silent video that used miming techniques to illustrate leadership skills. The audience was a group of power plant managers and supervisors, fresh from the production floor. Not only did they not relate to this rather artsy video, they literally walked out on it. A little consideration of the audience's background and preferences might have gone a long way here.

- Knowing characteristics such as job titles or levels in the company might tell you that you need to split your training into more than one class, each tailored for a particular group with specific characteristics and needs.

- Your trainees' level of job satisfaction is a good indicator of how motivated they will be to do your training. Find out what they like and do not like about their jobs and use this to help lead discussions.

To sum it all up, here is a shortcut list of the main audience characteristics you'll want to analyze for, followed by a template for an audience analysis report.

TOP AUDIENCE CHARACTERISTICS

- Age
- Gender
- Reading level
- Life background
- Experience in current or related jobs
- Performance in current job
- Language or cultural differences
- Motivation (or lack thereof)
- Formal schooling
- Company training programs attended
- Geographic location
- Prerequisite knowledge and skills

AUDIENCE ANALYSIS REPORT

Number of trainees eligible for this program:

Trainee location(s):

Organizational level(s):

Minimum/maximum and average level of education:

Minimum/maximum and average number of years in position:

Minimum/maximum and average number of years with company:

Expected entry-level knowledge and skill background:

Previous training related to this training:

Average reading level:

Language or cultural differences among trainees:

Trainee motivation and job satisfaction:

Attitude toward training:

Special physical characteristics of trainees relevant to training:

Special interests of trainees relevant to training:

Specific biases of trainees relevant to training:

Computer skills and confidence (if applicable):

 Your audience analysis can also provide you with another rapid design shortcut. It takes much more time to create training that meets the needs of a disparate audience, as you will have to add material to meet them all. Instead, design only for your majority audience; use some type of individualized instruction, prescriptive learning, or coaching for the others.

 One of the key issues in any audience analysis is literacy. If your audience analysis identifies literacy problems, a rapid design hint is to seriously consider a multimedia approach to the training. You can design multimedia with very little text, substituting visuals and an audio track for just about all text. This will make it easier for your trainees. On the other hand, because asynchronous e-learning is normally very text-oriented, you might want to delete this delivery system from your considerations early on if you've found literacy issues. This hint can also be expanded to multiple language issues as well. Multimedia with limited text and plenty of soundtrack can be easily translated into other languages. Heavily text-based deliveries, such as asynchronous e-learning and print-based self-instruction, are much more time-consuming to translate.

 ## Competency Analysis

To end our discussion on analysis, let's look at one last type of broad-spectrum analysis that is receiving a lot of play recently: the *competency analysis* ("An Introduction to Competency Analysis and Modeling" by Anne Marrelli, in *Performance Improvement*, 1998). The purpose of a competency analysis is to identify not just the tasks that are performed, but also the *way* they are performed or the level at which they are performed. This is most often done at the top performer level; that is, by analyzing the best people at the job or position.

Definition and Method

In a phrase, competencies can be defined as *the behaviors necessary for superior performance at a job.* You do a competency analysis by observing those top performers and trying to determine three things:

- What they are more likely than the average performer to do
- What they do more often than the average performer
- What they do more completely than the average performer

Of course, you will also have to observe some average performers to see the difference.

Next, you need to interview the top performers to find out why they do things differently. This should help you to develop a list of standards for the job based on what those who do it best actually do.

Questions to Ask

Questions you might ask of top performers in a competency analysis include the following:

- What do you think makes you a top performer?
- What was the path you followed to gain this status?
- What are your main responsibilities and work outputs?
- How do you determine when you have done a quality piece of work?
- What do you do to make sure your work is at the quality standard you've set?
- What background tasks or activities do you need to know or do?
- What do you think are the differences between yourself and someone who has been on the job only a couple of years?
- What are the problems you face most frequently in doing your job?
- What tricks have you learned to do your job faster and better?

Categories of Standards

In one of the more common methods, the standards are categorized as follows:

- Administrative competencies: those things that the top performers do simply to keep the work progressing. (Example: "Communicates with all members of a team in advance to prepare for day's work or new assignment.")

- Technical competencies: the actual skills used to produce the product or service. (Example: "Always describes both the minimum and maximum benefits to the customers before asking for their decision.")

- Personal competencies: how top performers feel and how they interact with others while doing the job. (Example: "Volunteers to be a mentor for new employees.")

These standards need to be validated by the top performers and then recorded as a competency model, which is basically a list of competencies and the behaviors associated with them for the job. From the competency list, you can develop informational, performance support, or training processes for the average and below-average performers.

Competency analysis is often used for (1) very complex jobs; (2) those positions for which it is critical that each person function at the highest possible level; (3) positions for which the actual performance of the job tasks is somewhat abstract and requires a lot of discretionary decision making, such as supervision or customer service; and (4) those jobs for which even a small upgrading in the ability of the performer can make a large difference to the company.

Competency Analysis Versus Job and Task Analysis

You may be thinking, "Well, this is not a heck of a lot different from the job and task analysis we've already covered," and once again you'd be right. A *well done* job and task analysis looks at the same things as a competency analysis: how the work is done, how it's done right, what the work environment is or should be, and what behaviors are most critical to the job. The major differences are that a competency analysis usually centers on top performers (though some experts wonder whether this is too narrow an assumption) and is structured to develop not just a list of tasks, skills, and knowledge, but also the behaviors that indicate success at mastering the tasks. A poor or too shallow task analysis often misses these key points.

A competency analysis has many other uses than just the development of training. The output is often used for creating job descriptions, for selection purposes, as a personal development guide for job incumbents, and even as a performance indicator.

 A competency analysis is rather time-consuming for a rapid instructional design process, but if you consider how you might use the products of this type of analysis in other ways, such as for hiring decisions or employee development, you might find that a competency analysis becomes more time-effective.

Here is a partial example of a competency model created from a competency analysis:

Job: Manager

Competency Area: Judgment/Decision Making

Competency: Develops alternative options based on reliable information and takes action at a level of risk appropriate to the situation

Top Performer Behaviors:

- Acknowledges own poor decisions and implements corrective actions
- Considers the people impacted by the decision
- Judges with a view to the organization's stated course of action

Competency Area: Oral Communications

Competency: Expresses information and ideas in one-on-one and group situations

Top Performer Behaviors:

- Establishes positive outcomes, even with hostile audiences
- Expresses ideas effectively, regardless of group size
- Communicates in a calm and confident manner, even in impromptu situations
- Handles objections skillfully

COMPUTER-AIDED ANALYSIS

A shortcut for doing any analysis is the use of analysis software. There are a number of different products on the market, ranging from very simple databases that help you compile tasks to much more complex programs that take you step by step through the analysis process, even going as far as helping you create questionnaires and other data-collection tools.

These programs can be very useful and save you a lot of time once you learn how to use them, but to learn them and to take the best advantage of them you still need to understand the basics of what analysis is all about, and why and how to do it.

Unless you do a lot of analysis, you probably will not be able to justify the amount of time you'll spend learning how the programs work, but look them over if you think you have the need. Most providers will send you an evaluation copy if you call and ask. We've listed a few of the most popular in the Resources section; new ones are coming along every month. Check with the ASTD or ISPI websites for an up-to-date list of who is supplying this type of software.

Most important, be suspicious of any software that states it will do the analysis for you and that you don't need any knowledge base to start with. These claims seldom prove out. The software is usually only as good as you are at analysis; it just makes you faster.

There's another series of computer-aided analysis tools: the net-based surveys we mentioned earlier. These are good data-collection tools if you have a highly dispersed audience or plan to obtain a lot of analysis data, as they are efficient at data manipulation. However, as we already noted, they have pretty much the same disadvantages as paper-and-pencil questionnaires. We've include a few of these in the resource list as well.

To sum up our journey through analysis, here is a job aid you can use to help you keep them all straight:

ANALYSIS JOB AID				
Type	*Purpose*	*Sequence*	*Best Methods*	*Product*
Learning Needs Analysis	To discover the learning needs of the organization, a work group within the organization, or individual contributors.	This is usually the first type of analysis done by the instructional designer. Look at documentation.	Talk to individuals and groups.	A list of training needs for the targeted level of the analysis, and a determination of which of those needs might be addressed.
Job Analysis	To discover what tasks make up the job or organizational aspect that requires training according to the needs analysis.	Done after the needs analysis for the components of each need that is to be trained on.	Interviews with SMEs, possibly focus groups	A list of tasks that comprise the job or organizational aspect that requires training.
Criticality Analysis	To determine which tasks are most critical and thus require the most training resources.	Done during the job analysis to each task.	Continued work with SMEs	A prioritized list of the tasks that will be trained on.
Task Analysis	To determine the knowledge, skills, and attitudes that make up each task that is to be trained on.	Completed after the job analysis	Continued work with SMEs	A list of the knowledge, skills, and attitudes that make up each task that will be trained on. This list will be used to write the training objectives.

Type	Purpose	Sequence	Best Methods	Product
Learning Analysis	To determine the critical learnings necessary to meet a training need.	Done in lieu of a job and task analysis.	Interviews with SMEs or focus groups	A prioritized list of critical learnings that must be mastered to meet the training need.
Audience Analysis	To determine the characteristics of the target learners that will be critical for program development.	Might be done any time during the design process, but always before developing program materials.	Questionnaires and interviews with learners and others who know the characteristics of the learners.	A list of general learner characteristics that the instructional designer needs to consider when creating course materials.
Delivery Analysis	To determine the best training delivery method for the course content, the organization, and the learners.	Might be done any time during the design process, but always before developing program materials.	This is done by the instructional designer, possibly with help from the training manager and other resources in theorganization such as IT.	A decision on the most effective and efficient delivery method that takes into account the requirements of the content, the capabilities of the organization, and the needs of the learners.

You might have noticed that we've not discussed the last type of analysis yet. In the next chapter, we'll begin by determining the best way to cover what your analysis has provided you with in the way of content and audience, then create the right structure to help your trainees learn most effectively. This is termed the *design component* of instructional design.

Chapter 4

How to Do It: Design

This chapter will help you to:

- Choose the right delivery system for your training
- Create useful objectives based on your job and task analysis
- Discover what a design document is and how it can be used
- Develop an instructional plan to guide you as you produce training materials
- Create test questions that will effectively measure your trainees' learning

---

By now you are probably pretty much "analyzed out"; you may be thinking, "This has all been very informative, but are we ready to start putting together a training program yet?" The answer is yes, but not quite yet. You have one more decision to make first, and it is probably the most important decision you will make in your instructional design. As a question, it might be "What will be the setting for my training?" or, put slightly less formally, "How will my training program be delivered?" If this book were about building a house, this would be the chapter that takes us though framing; that is, developing the skeleton structure for what our training will actually look like when it is done. Determining your delivery method is the first step you will need to take. If you are so inclined, you might call this delivery analysis.

 MAKE THE RIGHT DECISION NOW

Often—perhaps too often—this decision is seen as a no-brainer. It's training, so it's done in a classroom! This may be the correct decision; it could also be the first step down the road to an inefficient and even ineffective training program. The problem is, how do you know?

As usual, there is no easy answer. However, if you've done your analysis well you do have some data to work with. For example, you know who your target audience is and where they are located. This will give you some indication as to how efficient a classroom approach will be. Too many people in too many locations makes a classroom a less desirable delivery option.

You also know your training need(s) and the tasks, skills, competencies, and so on related to these needs. This knowledge will help you determine your program's requirements for special equipment or particular environments. Then you'll have a link with corporate goals and objectives. The strength of this link will help you determine funding possibilities and relationships with other training processes in the company that deal with the same goals as your program.

On the other hand, you have not yet learned very much about your resource or design limitations. You don't want to diminish the instructional integrity of your course, but at the same time you don't want to choose a delivery process that you don't have the time or money to design and develop fully. Or, if you have the time and budget, you don't want to sacrifice effectiveness by choosing a delivery process that is more than your training requires simply because it is "neat" and you've always wanted to try it.

Basically, what you need to do (and do right now) is consider all of the possible delivery systems—often referred to as *training settings*—and choose the one that will work best for your training need, your trainees, and your company. Everything else you do in designing and developing your training package will be affected by this decision.

 ## DELIVERY DECISION (TRAINING SETTING)

Your delivery decision can be very simple or quite complex, depending on your particular situation. As mentioned earlier, if you are charged with creating a training program, and training in your organization means bringing people to a classroom, then most of your decision is made. You only have to figure out how many classrooms, where they will be, and when, and who will be the trainers, and how you will train the trainers, and. . . .

Get the picture? Even the simplest delivery decision is not all that simple. And one hopes your organization is not mired in the "training means classrooms" scenario, so you will need to decide which of a number of possible training settings will work best for your needs and your trainees.

There are any number of variables to be considered, and these too can be at different levels of complexity depending on the material in your program and your corporate environment, but let's try to keep this simple by discussing the most common aspects of this decision-making process (*Effective Training Delivery*, 1989).

General Training Delivery Methods

First, you can make a general choice as to the delivery method based on what you already know or can easily find out. There are only half a dozen or so general training delivery methods to choose from, including these:

- *Instructor-Led Classrooms:* These are still the most common setting (*Instructing for Results* by Margolis and Bell, 1986).

- *On-the-Job Training (OJT):* This method does not require a classroom or training facility, but does demand a good trainer and some solid structure to be effective ("On-the-Job Training" by David Gallup, 1999).

- *Self-Instruction:* This means there is no instructor and possibly not even a facility for training, but there is a very structured program that is followed by the trainee (*Self-Directed Learning* by George Piskurich, 1993).

- *Technology-Based Training (TBT):* This used to be just a fancy way of doing self-instruction, but now it might include an instructor or an instructor-self-instruction combination and may employ delivery technologies anywhere from a simple computer program to internets and satellites (*Distance Learning* by Karen Mantyla & J. Richard Gividen, 1997).

- *Job Performance Aids:* Performance aids not are actually training; rather, the term refers to development of specialized materials that employees can use on the job to help them do the tasks properly in lieu of formal training. These are often called *job aids* and sometimes called *performance support systems* or, if found on a computer, *electronic performance support systems* ("Performance Support Systems and Job Aids" by Saundra Williams, 1999).

 Job aids themselves can be a rapid design shortcut. Because they are used in lieu of training, when you employ them you have automatically saved design and development time. Under the right circumstances you might be able to base your entire training program on job aids, in which case the only training you need to do is on how to use them. The time savings here are pretty obvious.

- *Training by Documentation:* This is also not training, but it is often called that by those who do not understand what training really means. In this setting the trainees are given technical manuals, flow charts, procedure documents, operating instructions, or other items and told to read them. Sometimes this occurs in a classroom with a trainer (usually an SME) present to answer questions, sometimes not.

This process combines some aspects of self-instruction and job performance aids and a little OJT, as the trainees are expected to return to the job and implement what they've learned. However, there is not enough of any of these deliveries, nor are they structured well enough, to be considered true training. It is usually ineffective, always wastes time, and most often leads to very frustrated employees, who must learn by trial and error or seek help elsewhere when they are actually on the job.

On the other hand, training by documentation can be developed very quickly, because you use materials that have been designed for other purposes. We've included it here because it is used so often (unfortunately) and because with a little effort you can take the general concept, add some proper training structure to it, and create good, fast, inexpensive training for certain needs and in specific situations.

Here is a chart of the major training settings and what they are best used for. (The more dots, the better the learning activity setting will be.)

	Classroom	OJT	Self-Instruction	TBT	Job Aids	Documentation
Knowledge Acquisition	••	•	••	••		•
Problem Solving	••	•	•	••	••	
Changing Attitudes	••	•		•		
Interpersonal Skills	••			•		
Knowledge Retention		••	••	••	••	

Making a Delivery Choice

From this list, make a general training delivery choice based on what you already know about your situation. For example, if your training need will require your trainees to practice on actual machines, you might choose OJT as the setting. On the other hand, if you have a large number to train and very few trainers to do the training, you may want to attempt a self-instructional approach. Be realistic here; if you don't have enough computers in your organization, a technology-based training setting will probably not work for you.

Here are some checklists to help you make a good training delivery decision:

CLASSROOM TRAINING

Use classroom-based training when:

☐ Interaction with the trainer or other participants is important

☐ Guided discussion will lead to more learning

☐ Questions will come up that need immediate answers

☐ You have qualified facilitators in the right numbers to match the training load

☐ The trainees can afford to be away from their jobs for long periods of time

☐ The facilitators will do the traveling instead of the trainees

☐ Individualization is not critical

☐ You want more control over the training outcome

ON-THE-JOB TRAINING

Use OJT when:

☐ Skills need to be mastered in the actual environment

☐ Training time is limited

☐ Design time is limited

☐ Non-moveable equipment is involved

☐ Trainee motivation is poor

☐ The tasks to be learned change frequently

☐ Qualified classroom trainers are not available

☐ Work flow must be learned as part of the training

☐ A lot of monitored practice is necessary

☐ The number of trainees is small

SELF-INSTRUCTION

Use self-instruction when:

☐ There are a number of highly distributed training sites

☐ You have a shortage of qualified classroom or OJT trainers

☐ Turnover is high

☐ Training must be delivered "just in time"

☐ Training must be consistent

☐ The content is relatively stable

☐ The content is known only by one or a few SMEs

☐ The training will be repeated often

☐ You want to decrease travel costs

☐ The training must be done on multiple shifts

☐ You have the time to develop the programs properly

TECHNOLOGY-BASED TRAINING

Use TBT when:

☐ Self-instruction is needed (see self-instruction checklist)

☐ Complex simulations are needed

☐ The content requires a lot of practice that can be simulated

☐ The trainees are comfortable or can be made to feel comfortable using computers

☐ Training is difficult to schedule or classes are hard to fill

☐ There is plenty of development time and money available

☐ The hardware is in place or can be bought easily

☐ Tracking of the training is critical and time intensive due to a large number of trainees

☐ Management is comfortable with TBT or can be sold on the concept

☐ Updates to the program will be minimal

☐ The use of multiple media formats will enhance the learning

NET-BASED TRAINING (INSTRUCTOR LED OR SELF-INSTRUCTION)

Use Net-based training when your environment requires a distributed delivery and:

☐ You need TBT (see TBT checklist) but revisions to content are frequent

☐ Video is not a critical element in the training

☐ Live interaction with an instructor is important

☐ Other content is already available that can be easily linked

☐ Content is more soft-skill oriented (instructor led)

☐ Heavy feedback (immediate or time sensitive) is required

☐ Trainees are comfortable with e-learning technology

☐ Your internal systems can support the usage

☐ Time and budget are available to produce and implement the training

☐ You have a large number of training programs that need to be delivered and re-delivered at various times

JOB PERFORMANCE AIDS

Consider creating job performance aids in lieu of training when:

☐ The task(s) are performed infrequently

☐ It is critical that the task(s) be performed exactly

☐ The task(s) are very complex

☐ Sequencing of the task(s) is critical

☐ Turnover is high

☐ Training cannot be done in a timely manner

☐ The consequence of performing the task(s) incorrectly is severe

☐ Tasks change frequently

☐ The body of knowledge is great

☐ Practice and feedback are not critical

Blended Delivery Systems

One other thought on delivery systems. There is no rule that says you cannot use more than one delivery system for a single training event. In fact, many of the most successful training processes combine delivery systems. This concept, often termed blended learning, has received a lot of publicity as of late due to the popularity of e-learning.

One of the most common examples of blending is the use of a self-instructional package (particularly an e-learning package) that covers the basic knowledge on a topic with a facilitated classroom that discusses the issues and applies what has been presented in the self-instruction. The self-instructional package is completed by the trainees before the class. The facilitator spends a very short time reviewing the main concepts at the start of class, then gets into simulations and other group activities, which is a major strength of a classroom approach. This hybrid delivery plays to the strengths of both formats and creates an effective and efficient training process.

Blended delivery is particularly useful when you are using technology-based training processes. Many people (good designers usually not among them) seem to tout each new technology that comes along for its ability to "take over training." This is seldom the case, much to the dismay of organizations that invest heavily in the technology. As a good designer yourself, think of technology as a reductive process, rather than a replacement process. It won't replace the interaction of a classroom or the hands-on of OJT, but it can be used in conjunction with these deliveries to reduce the amount of time trainees spend in these forms of training and to make that time more effective.

We'll discuss one of these technology blends—the integration of synchronous and asynchronous e-learning—a bit later.

There are many other examples of blending delivery methods, such as classroom with OJT or e-learning programs with embedded performance support systems. This does increase the complexity of the design, and you'll have to do an even more intensive analysis of the pros and cons of both delivery processes, but it is often worth the extra effort and expense.

An example of a very well-conceived blended delivery is the approach of a car manufacturer who uses OJT to do the basic training for new hires on the assembly line and a multimedia simulation of the line in a type of virtual-reality format for practice. The simulation allows the trainees to spend time practicing the machine sequencing and troubleshooting problems that may arise on the floor, all without actually slowing down the assembly line itself ("Virtual Reality: Is It for You?" by Carol Gunther-Mohr, 1999). One trainer notes that the simulation allows the trainee to practice a particular series of steps within the assembly process without continuously going through the entire assembly: "Without the simulation it would be like running a washing machine through the entire wash process just to look time and again at the rinse cycle."

One of the newest methods of blended learning is to combine asynchronous and synchronous e-learning segments. The learner receives an asynchronous assignment, which is followed up by a synchronous classroom in which the concepts detailed in the asynchronous aspect are discussed and interactions based on them are done. Of course, to use this blend you need both the technology and learners who are comfortable with it and with this type of learning, but it can be very effective.

Good designers also use a blended approach for remedial training or enrichment activities. A good example of this that I like to use is the assigning of web searches during a multiday stand-up classroom or as a post-classroom activity. The learners either come back to the class for the next session with new information based on their own explorations or, in the case of an after-class activity, post their findings on a bulletin board.

Blending delivery processes isn't really all that new. We were doing it back in the 1970s with classrooms that followed self-directed slide tape presentations. Even videos or the old 16-mm movies that were shown in classrooms can be considered a blended approach, though I'm afraid that often they were not blended too well.

In the end, blended learning is simply another instructional design decision, based on what's right for the content, the learners, the time available for both design and implementation, and the cultural and technology environment of the company. In other words, delivery analysis.

Constraints*

Once you've made a preliminary training delivery decision, you can run with it and start your design work, or you can do a little more thinking and consider the existing constraints to your training. We suggest the latter, as it will help you validate your delivery decision and provide you with some of the information you will need to create a design document, which is a critical step in the instructional design process. However, if you have limited time and are pretty sure you've made the right delivery decision, move on to objectives.

For everyone else, let's start this discussion by noting that there are many kinds of constraints to any training program, but that we've discussed a lot of them already. Here are some categories of constraints:

Logistical: Related to the number of trainees, the facilities, and the budget

Stakeholder: Who is sponsoring the program and their characteristics and expectations

Design: Aspects such as time to create and available materials

Training Methods: What you can and can't do in your current corporate training environment

Resources: What is and is not available in the way of instructors and content experts

Questions for Constraint Categories

Here are a few questions you might ask about your training for each category:

Logistical

- What will be the total number of trainees?
- What is your preliminary decision on a training setting(s)?
- If you are using a classroom approach, what is the optimum number of participants in a class?
- What are the necessary classroom size dimensions?
- What are the needs for delivery hardware?
- What other technology needs exist?

---

*Information in this section has been adapted from material contained in Langevin Learning Services' Langevin Instructional Designware software.

- What other facility needs exist?
- What type of trainee travel needs are there?
- What is the budget for the program?

Stakeholder
- Who is the main sponsor of the program?
- What type of input does the sponsor expect to provide?
- Who will be the contact person for the sponsor?
- How will managers and supervisors be brought into the program?
- What will it take to satisfy the sponsor?

Design
- Has analysis been done for the program?
- Are there any similar courses or courses that address the same need?
- When must the course be ready for piloting?
- When must the course be ready for distribution?
- Is there any current course material that can be used?
- What other documents are available?
- How available are subject-matter experts?

Training Methods
- What is the anticipated length of the course?
- What delivery methods are available in the corporate environment?
- What constraints exist as to training methods or media?
- Are performance aids a viable option for augmentation?
- What audiovisual material must be produced and distributed?
- Is there a need for job equipment to be used during the training?
- Is pre-work a possibility?
- Can work be done off the job?
- Is post-work a possibility?

Resources
- Are trainers available?
- Are possible trainers knowledgeable about the training content?

- Do possible trainers possess adequate training skills?
- Are there other resources available to help with design and material development?
- Are subject-matter experts needed, and does the expertise exist?
- Are clerical and production assistance available if needed?
- Are outside resources available if needed?

Depending on your particular situation, many of these questions may not apply, but it is a good idea to at least run through them as a check of your delivery decision. If the answers to these questions match your preliminary delivery decision, you are in good shape. If not, you may need to revise or augment your decision to make it work.

Selecting Delivery Method by Project Constraints
Here is another tool to help in your delivery analysis.
Use it to identify the project constraints and rank them from 1 (a minor constraint that most likely can be removed) to 5 (a major obstacle that most likely will not change).

Impact of Constraints	Considerations	Strategy Suggestions
1 2 3 4 5 Content requires interactivity (computer).	Does the content involve computer software, simulation, or practice?	Consider the following deliveries: • Computer-based training • E-learning
1 2 3 4 5 Content requires interactivity (human).	• Will participants gain interpersonal and communication skills by getting immediate feedback from an observer about their performance? • To what extent does the learner need to use or demonstrate interpersonal or communication skills, such as presentation, teamwork, leadership, or facilitation?	Consider the following deliveries: • Classroom • Synchronous e-learning • Coaching and mentoring

Impact of Constraints	*Considerations*	*Strategy Suggestions*
1 2 3 4 5 Incidental learning or collaborative learning is required.	• How important is incidental learning? • Can group learning occur, including opportunities to build relationships or share information?	Consider deliveries that allow personal interaction: • Classroom • Synchronous e-learning • Video teleconferencing • Web chat room
1 2 3 4 5 Audience requires motivation.	How motivated are the learners? *Note: Self-paced instruction or e-learning requires higher intrinsic motivation for successful learning.*	Consider • Classroom • Video • On-line learning • Various blends
1 2 3 4 5 Audience requires convenience, such as training at or near the worksite.	• Is time away from work not possible because of work schedules, project requirements, variable shifts, or time-sensitive performance? • Are participants dispersed and do they therefore require decentralized training?	Consider self-paced or flexible media: • Computer-based training • Computer-based teleconferencing • Mentoring or coaching • Performance support • Asynchronous e-learning • OJT • Self-paced workbook
1 2 3 4 5 Audience has limited access to technology.	• What technology is available? • Is there a barrier to technology?	Consider the following: • Audio teleconference • Classroom • Self-paced workbook

Impact of Constraints	Considerations	Strategy Suggestions
1 2 3 4 5 Audience has limited access to expertise.	• Is there limited expertise that must be shared across the organization?	Consider the following: • Computer-based training • Asynchronous e-learning • Synchronous e-learning • TBT • Video • Web chat room • Video teleconferencing
1 2 3 4 5 Content has a short life cycle or is changing rapidly.	• Is the content stable? Is it still under construction or development? • How does the stability of the content affect the frequency of revisions? How difficult is it to make revisions using this medium? *Note: Revisions to audiotapes, videotapes, CBT, and interactive video instruction are time-consuming and expensive.*	Consider: • Synchronous e-learning • Audio teleconferencing • Web page or database • Classroom • OJT
1 2 3 4 5 The audience spans multiple cultures or languages.	• Will reading, hearing, or understanding English be difficult for audience members? • Are varying levels and types of information needed?	Consider learner-controlled and self-paced deliveries: • Narrated asynchronous e-learning • TBT • Video • Text (easy to translate)

Impact of Constraints	Considerations	Strategy Suggestions
1 2 3 4 5 Materials must be available in a variety of formats.	• Do you need to adapt materials? • Are various hardware platforms used? • Do audience preferences vary? • Does technology differ in different geographic locations? *Note: Consider how the product could be distributed in a variety of formats.*	Consider the following media: • Video • TBT • Synchronous e-learning *Note: Video can be reused in a variety of media.*
1 2 3 4 5 There is an immediate need for application of expertise to the job. Employees must review the information frequently.	How critical is the knowledge or skill to the performance of job-related tasks?	Consider the following options: • Performance support • Mentoring or on-the-job training • Job aids • OJT
1 2 3 4 5 Employees use the information infrequently (once a month or less).	• How complex is the task? • How often will performers need to use the information or perform the task?	Consider the following options: • Electronic performance support • Job aids
1 2 3 4 5 Entry-level background knowledge varies widely within the audience.	How wide is the range of entry-level knowledge? *Note: Asynchronous e-learning provides the ability to branch users to different levels of training.*	Consider the following: • TBT • Asynchronous e-learning

Impact of Constraints	Considerations	Strategy Suggestions
1 2 3 4 5 Fewer than 200 employees per year need training or support.	• How many learners are in the target audience? • What is the size of the audience over the expected life cycle of the training?	Consider the following options: • On-the-job training • Performance support or job aids • Mentoring • Classroom • Synchronous e-learning • Audio teleconferencing
1 2 3 4 5 A large number of employees (500 or more) will need the training within a four-year time frame.	Are there 2000 or more people in the target audience?	Consider the following: • TBT • Asynchronous e-learning • Video • Audiotapes
1 2 3 4 5 Large numbers of employees must be trained quickly.	How much time is available to build, buy, or revise products? *Note: For shortened time frames, consider buying or revising existing products.*	Consider the following deliveries: • Asynchronous e-learning • Audio teleconferencing • Audiotapes • Print materials
1 2 3 4 5 Participants must spend the minimum possible time in training.	Is it important to reduce the time participants spend in training? *Note: Asynchronous e-learning has typical training compression ratios of 50% to 70%.*	Consider the following options: • Performance support • Asynchronous e-learning • TBT

Impact of Constraints	Considerations	Strategy Suggestions
1 2 3 4 5 Development cost per hour of instruction must be kept low.	What is the cost per learner for developing or acquiring this medium?	Consider the following: • Text • Classroom • Synchronous e-learning • Audio teleconferencing
1 2 3 4 5 Travel expenses must be kept low.	*Note: Self-paced media or performance support will reduce travel expenses.*	Consider the following: • Performance support • Asynchronous e-learning • Synchronous e-learning • Text • Self-paced workbooks • Audio teleconferencing
1 2 3 4 5 Implementation, delivery, and maintenance costs must be kept low.	Will resources and budget be limited or unavailable following development?	Consider the following options: • Performance support • Synchronous e-learning • Asynchronous e-learning • Audio teleconferencing • Self-paced workbook
1 2 3 4 5 Testing, evaluation, or tracking of student performance is necessary.	• Can the assessment be self-scored? • Is certification necessary? *Note: Assessment of interpersonal and communication skills requires observation. Some observation requires a trained expert.*	Consider the following media: • Workbook • Asynchronous e-learning • Classroom or OJT if human observation is necessary

Facilitator Assessment

There is one other constraint aspect that you may need to consider, depending on your delivery decision. That is the availability of facilitators. Facilitators come in many guises in training, ranging from the classroom facilitator (who looks like an instructor but most often doesn't act like one) to the self-instruction facilitator (which seems like a contradiction in terms). The availability of the right facilitators can often make or break your training, so here are some thoughts on facilitators, categorized by training setting.

Classroom

Facilitators in classrooms are not instructors. They are not even necessarily SMEs, and they do very little in the way of providing actual content. Rather, they lead the trainees through the training, help to facilitate discussions, and clarify main points. They lead activities and summaries, question the trainees about concepts, and examine their knowledge through test proctoring.

If your training program is simply an information dump, you need an instructor (actually you could be better off with a book) to deliver the content and ask questions. These individuals need a lot of content expertise and a little bit of knowledge on how to train. However, if your class is meant to help your trainees learn, master skills, and be able to use those skills and knowledge back on the job, you need a facilitator who has the training expertise to guide, to counsel, and to lead. The two sets of skills are very different, and you need to know whether you have people with the right skills available before you make your final delivery decision. Nothing will fail quite as dramatically as a facilitated classroom design with an SME who has content knowledge but is not trained in how to lead a class, rather than a skilled facilitator who knows how to properly conduct classroom activities—except perhaps a class that has been designed to be taught by a trainer who is an SME that is taught by a facilitator who is not an SME.

Self-Instruction

As the purpose of self-instruction is to have the trainees learn on their own, there would seem to be no need for a facilitator. However, someone is usually required to get the trainees started, to provide materials where necessary, and often to evaluate the learning. In this type of setting, facilitators don't guide, lead, or counsel the way they would in a classroom setting, nor do they provide content like an instructor. Often they are not even SMEs. If you are using self-instruction as your delivery system, you will need to determine what specific skills your facilitators will need (this will be dependent on your self-instructional design) and then find out whether people with these skills are available and have the time.

Following are two specific instances of self-instruction that require a facilitator:

Learning Center: If you are using a learning center delivery for your self-instruction, a facilitator should be available in the center. You will need to find out what the facilitator is and is not capable of doing and design your self-instruction appropriately.

Electronic (Distributed): Much self-instruction today is done through the higher technology delivery systems, such as CD-ROM or the Internet, and distributed to any number of training sites. If you decide to use these delivery systems, you will still need to consider what a facilitator might do for your training. Often it is little more than orienting the trainees to a new system of learning. Sometimes it may include observing the mastery of trained tasks and recording them on a performance checklist. Whatever it is, be sure you have people with the time and commitment to be your facilitators. You will also need a mechanism for letting them know what they need to do and for following up to make sure they did it. (More on this in Chapter Seven.)

On-the-Job Training

In an OJT setting, the facilitator is usually the trainer. Again, the person needs specific skills; being a job expert is not enough. If personnel who can handle the role of OJT trainer are not available, cannot be trained, or do not have the time do the training properly, you may want to reconsider your decision to implement an OJT delivery.

Mentoring

We have not discussed mentoring as a training delivery system, as many types of mentoring are so unstructured that they really cannot be considered training (unfortunately, the same can be said of much OJT). However, a mentor is often used in conjunction with performance-support tools and with documentation-based training to make it more systematic. If you are thinking of using a mentoring system, you will again need to determine what skills and attributes are required of your mentors and then find out whether such individuals can be found and utilized.

Here is a tool you can use when considering the general advantages and disadvantages of various delivery systems:

FINAL CRITERIA FOR DELIVERY SELECTION

Delivery	Description	Advantages	Limitations	Development Notes
Asynchronous e-learning	• Color graphics • Complex two-dimensional animation • Sound • Custom graphics • Testing or record keeping • Video • Branching • One platform • Feedback	• Offers consistent delivery • Enables training at or away from the work site • Provides possible graphic and multiple-sensory capability • Adapts to learner performance • Is self-paced and learner-controlled • Normally reduces training time • Offers reliable testing and record keeping • Includes extensive feedback opportunities • Provides realistic simulation or emulation of computer environment	• Requires highly skilled specialists to develop • Is inappropriate for large textual presentations • Can become monotonous • Is costly if hardware has to be dedicated to training	• Development involves a ratio of 300 to 450-plus development hours to 1 hour of training. • Average vendor development costs are $15,000 to $25,000 per student hour or $65 to $100 per development hour. • The typical course life cycle is unlimited people trained per year over two years.

Delivery	Description	Advantages	Limitations	Development Notes
Computer- and noncomputer-based performance support	Tools for individual use, such as the following: • Just-in-time training • On-line reference systems • Help lines • Expert systems • Employee support system • Job aids	• Supports performance at the time the task is performed • Provides consistent delivery • Enables training when performance is needed • Provides some graphic and multisensory capability • Adapts to performer's level of expertise • Is self-paced and learner-controlled • Reduces training time • Can provide realistic simulation or emulation of computer environment • Uses small expert systems to help users analyze relatively small but difficult problems by providing specific expert advice • Can be used effectively as job aids to reduce training time, minimize memorization, maximize accurate responses, and allow less-trained employees to do higher-level tasks	• Requires an available SME to assist with development • Is effective only for narrowly defined tasks	• Applications that are linked to software applications or are context-sensitive require extensive development efforts. • Applications that use reference systems or user-controlled help files are less time-consuming to create and maintain. • New or additional hardware and software may not be required.

Delivery	Description	Advantages	Limitations	Development Notes
Synchronous e-learning	• Use of regular computer networks to converse with several participants via a conference call and software • May use regular telephones or speaker phones	• Can transcend geographical and facilities limitations • Is interactive, with extensive opportunities for questions and feedback • Enables a single instructor to provide instruction to many groups without travel • Is highly effective when used with other media • Provides cost-effective decentralized training for large, dispersed audiences • Can train large numbers of students quickly • Reduces travel-related expenses by allowing students and instructors to participate from any location	• Can be time-consuming if the number of participants becomes high • Requires skilled facilitators • Requires proper redesign or repurposing	• Prior planning helps ensure the most effective use of time. • Send out agendas in advance. • Review facilitation techniques.

Delivery	Description	Advantages	Limitations	Development Notes
Paper self-paced	• Reference books and manuals • Job aids • Reference charts • Study guides • Workbooks	• Enables learner to control time, place, and pace of learning • Is inexpensive to develop • Is easy to edit and revise • Is easy to distribute • Provides consistent delivery	• Does not provide feedback • Involves only one sense; adapts to only one learning style	• A typical development product is Microsoft Word. Templates, style guides, and publishing support are available for development.
Linear video	Examples include the following: • Stories and documentaries • Vignettes and scenarios • Videotaped lessons • Both direct-to-video and tapes of IDLN broadcasts	• Can be delivered at or away from the work site • Offers full-color, full-motion visual presentations • Can transcend geographical limitations • Provides a standardized presentation • Enables unlimited opportunities for review	• Involves high production costs • Has limited interaction and evaluation • Involves a long development time • Lacks student-controlled branching • Has limited sequencing capability • Limits capability to revise or update	• The cost is prohibitive for local development ($2,000 to $10,0000 per minute of finished video).

Delivery	Description	Advantages	Limitations	Development Notes
Lecture, lab, or classroom	Classroom instruction led by an instructor or facilitator	• Is a familiar environment to most students; provides social interaction adaptable to any subject • Is useful with various sizes of audiences • Offers individualized feedback • Can include a variety of media and instructional methods • Can be tailored to the group • Requires less development time • Is a traditional teaching method that is comfortable for student and instructors • Gets students away from their offices so they can, ideally, focus exclusively on the class rather than on work • Is easier and less expensive to revise or update than most other media • Enables incidental learning	• May be difficult to schedule large blocks of time • May be boring, because trainee interest and involvement depend on instructor's skill • May transfer poorly to work situations • Is heavily reliant on instructor knowledge • Has potential for inconsistent delivery • Uses measurement and evaluation methods that can be inconsistent • Requires skilled specialists to develop and deliver • Requires expensive and time-consuming travel for both students and instructors • Reaches a limited number of students at any one time • Typically teaches to the mid-range performance level.	• Templates, style guides, and publishing support are available for development. • Typical development products are Microsoft Word and PowerPoint. • Labs and workshops may require special equipment.

Delivery	Description	Advantages	Limitations	Development Notes
Mentoring, coaching, or on-the-job training	• Working one-on-one with actual job tasks • Receiving training and support when it's needed to perform the task	• Involves a high degree of interaction • Provides immediate feedback • Meets the learner's immediate needs • Is an ongoing experience integrated with work	• Lacks consistency and uniformity • Is difficult to accommodate group learning • May interfere with regular equipment usage	• Needs must be anticipated and planned for. • It makes use of available resources instead of requiring special resources.

Audio	• Audiotapes
	• Audio teleconference
	• Telephone help lines
		• All audio options
		  • Are typically inexpensive
		  • Are typically available at numerous sites, including home
		• Teleconferencing or help line
		  • Provides social interaction
		  • Provides immediate feedback
		• Audiotape
		  • Can be used any time, at learner's pace
		  • Can be repeated for reinforcement and review
			• All audio options
			  • lack visual presentation
			• Teleconferencing or help line
			  • Requires complex logistics and scheduling
			  • Depends on the group dynamics
			• Audio tape does not provide feedback
				• Teleconferencing requires special equipment (which is generally available).

In the final analysis (so to speak) delivery analysis is concerned with three aspects: what will work best for the content, what will be most effective for the learner, and what is most efficient for the learning environment. When you determine a delivery system that meets these three needs, you have the right one.

OBJECTIVES

As we noted at the start of this discussion, the result of all this thinking and looking around is a simple decision on what training delivery system you will employ for your training. You should now see that it is not as simple a decision as it at first appeared to be. Don't worry about all the time you spent gathering data for this "simple" decision; you'll be using a lot of that data in your design document (what some people call a *course plan*).

However, we promised you that we would get into some real training design, so let's do that now by working on your program's objectives. We'll go to the design document after that. Purists might contend that the design document should be done before you write objectives, but this is another chicken-or-the-egg controversy. I like to include objectives in my design document, so I think this is a good time to work on them. If you don't, that's OK; in the end we'll all get to the same place: a training program that does its job.

What Are Objectives?

You've probably heard the term *objectives* somewhere before you picked up this book. You might even have seen some objectives associated with an educational or training program that you were participating in, although unfortunately the majority of training programs do not have much in the way of objectives, at least not ones that the trainee ever sees. This is a shame, because objectives—particularly well-written objectives that are shared with the trainees and can be used by them to guide their learning—are one of the essential foundations of good instructional design.

Uses of Objectives

Objectives have a number of uses. The most important use is to give the trainees a clear understanding of what they will be covering in the course and what they will be expected to know or do when the course is completed. Wouldn't it have been nice if every course you took in high school and beyond did that? Well, they would have if the designer had taken the time to do the job correctly and create proper objectives for the course.

A second use for objectives is to help the designer make sure that (1) all the content that is needed is there, (2) there are no gaps or time-wasting duplications in the material, and (3) there is no content that simply is not needed by the trainees. Objectives help you focus on "need to know" content and avoid—or at least limit—"nice to know" information. This saves your time in material development and your trainees' time in learning.

A third use of objectives is to describe to anyone who is interested, in a short, succinct fashion, what the course will teach. This is important for the trainees, but also for their managers. By looking at the objectives, they will know whether the course is covering what they think is important. Objectives also help your boss see that you are on the right track with the program you are creating and that what you are working on fits into the master training plan (if there is one).

Fourth, objectives can help you organize your course. They are the essence of your course; by dividing them into smaller groupings that have similar aspects, you divide your course into modules, lessons, sections, or whatever you want to call them. The term for this is *chunking,* and we'll discuss this process a bit later in more detail.

Fifth, objectives are also the basis for trainee evaluation within a course. If, as we said, they tell the trainees what they need to know and do at the end of the course, then it seems logical that they should be tied into how the trainees are evaluated. We'll talk a lot more about this aspect later in this chapter as well, but for now just keep in mind that objectives are the focus of your test questions and test development. Objectives will even help you decide on the type of test questions to write.

Finally, objectives set the criteria for how the course itself will be evaluated. Because we have created them to be statements of how the trainees should be able to perform by the end of the course, if the trainees have achieved them (a goal often referred to as *mastery*) then the course was successful; if not, the course flopped. This is rather a harsh way of looking at things, as there are lots of other variables—such as trainee ability, retention, and organizational environment—to take into account. But in the final analysis a course is only as successful as its participants are—as the saying goes, "You haven't taught if they haven't learned." In our case this means that they have learned what they needed to know based on your analysis.

Here's an example of what can go wrong if objectives are not well defined:

> A clothing manufacturer invests in new cutting machines that are supposed to reduce waste by 20 percent. The company hires a consultant to design a training program on how to use the new machines. At the end of six months, it is found that not only did waste not decrease, it actually increased. The training consultant and her poor training are blamed.

In the postmortem the company realizes the problem: the consultant's objective for the program was to teach the trainees how to use the new cutters, whereas the client's was to reduce waste by using the cutters in such a way that less fabric was lost. The two needs were not the same, and the training did not address the client's need. Good objectives, developed and reviewed early in the process, would have saved a lot of time and corporate resources—and the trainer her job.

Summarizing the Uses of Objectives

So let's go over this again. Objectives let the trainees know what they need to do, tell the designer and the trainer what they need to do, let higher management know what's going on, and are the criteria for trainee and course success. I would say that makes them pretty important.

Then why aren't they a required aspect of every course? Good question! They should be if the course is designed well. The reasons they are not are legion. Course designers don't understand how valuable they are. Course designers don't know how to create them. Course designers think they are developing them when they are not. Course designers construct them poorly, so they are not useful. Get the picture? It's your job as an effective course designer to create good, usable objectives for your trainees, your trainers, and your management—and for yourself to make your job easier.

I've found from experience that you never truly understand the importance of objectives until you are given the task of developing content and training activities for a training program when you're not an SME and the designer has not supplied you with objectives, or until you see a trainer mishandle a program you developed because he or she did not understand or ignored the objectives.

I hope by now we've sold you on the importance of objectives, so let's move on to discuss how to construct good ones. We'll start by considering common mistakes that occur in writing objectives.

Mistakes in Writing Objectives

Many things can go wrong in your quest to write a good objective. Following are two of the more important ones.

Objectives Versus Goals

The first mistake new designers (and a lot of old ones) tend to make is to confuse objectives with course goals. Course goals are statements developed to explain what the course will cover. We said earlier that objectives do this as well, but course goals are usually written from the course's perspective, whereas objectives are written from the trainees' perspective.

For example, a course goal might look like this:

The purpose of this course is to teach the trainees how to assemble a composite tire using the XB-45 tire-making machine.

An objective might be something more like this:

At the end of this course, the trainee will be able to effectively utilize the XB-45 tire-making machine to assemble a composite tire that will pass the company's inspection criteria.

They both say the same thing, but the goal refers to the course, whereas the objective refers to the trainee. In the final analysis you aren't really worried about what the course can do, but you are very concerned with what the trainee can (and cannot) do—so why spend time making statements about the course?

You might also say that the goal focuses more on the expectations of the organization (from Chapter Two), whereas the objective is more focused on the trainee performance.

Now, I'm not implying that course goals are useless. They have their place for curriculum design and some other administrative aspects. However, too often they are confused with real objectives. If you are designing a course, write it from the start for the most important person: the trainee. Everything else will follow.

You may have noticed other differences between our course goal and trainee objective: mainly, that statement about passing the company's inspection criteria. In objective writing this is called a *standard.* Standards are important because they form the basis for trainee evaluation. In our example the trainees will not have completed the course if they merely know how to run the machine; only if they can assemble a tire—and not just any tire, but one that passes inspection—will they have achieved the objective. This is important for the trainee to know and for you to know as the instructional designer, as it will help you to develop the trainee evaluation measures.

Standards are a key part of every objective. Sometimes they are so obvious that they are understood and not formally expressed, but they are always there. We'll get back to standards and the other parts of a good objective in a bit.

Levels of Objectives

Another common mistake that designers make when developing objectives is to stop after they have a statement, or even a number of statements like the objective above, and think that they have written the objectives for the course. What they have done is to develop the *primary level objectives* for the course.

The primary objectives, as a group, can also be called the *course objectives, program objectives,* or *terminal objectives.*

Call them what you like; if you develop them properly, they are a good beginning—but only a beginning. To make your objectives really useful for your trainees, you have to develop a second level, often called *supporting* or *enabling objectives.* We're not interested in terminology here, so let's call the first-level objectives *first-level objectives* and the next level down *second-level objectives.* Your company may use some of the other terms we've mentioned, so translate as needed.

First-level objectives give the trainees an overall guide to what they will accomplish in the course, but it is the second-level objectives that tell them exactly what they need to know and do. If you stop with first-level objectives, you will not have gone far enough to be able to use the objectives in most of the ways we discussed earlier.

Constructing Useful Objectives

So, how do you write good first- and second-level objectives? Well, you start with a good analysis. If this is a surprise to you, you weren't paying attention in the previous chapter and you probably need to go back and review it. The job and task statements, the skills and knowledge that you ferreted out during your analysis are the basis for your objectives.

For example, in our tire-making training analysis in Chapter Three we found six job tasks involved:

- Choosing the correct tread size
- Reversing the interior matrix
- Laying on the steel belt
- Sequencing the assembly machine
- Trimming excess rubber
- Inspecting for proper seal

If we were to construct a first-level objective based on the first task, it might read something like this:

> At the end of the training the trainee will be able to choose the correct tread size for the three major tire runs, on the assembly line, 90 percent of the time.

This is a somewhat cumbersome statement, but let's take it apart and look at the pieces.

Time Frames

The first part, "At the end of the training," is there to give a time frame. Almost all objectives relate to the end of the training, so this statement makes sense. There are cases, however, in which "the end of the training" may not be the time frame. For example, some designers write daily objectives for a long course, or even monthly ones. Some use the statement "at the end of this class," or module, or even section. If the learning goes beyond the actual training class and into post-class activities, your objective may start with something like this:

> At the completion of the post-class activity

or

> After working on the job for six months

Use whichever statement works best for your situation, or mix statements as needed, but note, somewhere in your objective, what the time frame is for objective mastery.

For the Trainee

The second part, "the trainee will be able to," is there for no other reason than to remind you, the instructional designer, for whom you are writing this objective. If you think this is silly, I can tell you from long experience that even the best designers sometimes forget. This statement acts as a check so that when you read the completed objective you will know immediately whether it makes sense from the trainee's point of view.

It becomes very cumbersome to write these two types of introductory parts for each objective, so most designers make a blanket statement at the beginning of a list of objectives, something like this:

> At the end of this program the trainees will be able to:

They then list the objectives that fit under this heading. So a list of objectives might look something like this:

> After completing this program the participants will be able to:
>
> 1. Relate the company's strategic objectives to the concept of cross functionality
> 2. Differentiate between monitoring and compliance
> 3. Propose possible methods for leveraging resources to achieve company monitoring and compliance goals

    4. Identify appropriate criteria for monitoring all programs

    5. Employ company information systems in their monitoring procedures

    6. Design and implement a plan for communicating monitoring results

Notice that we used a slightly different general opening for the list, but the process remains the same.

Behaviors

The next part of the objective, "choose the correct tread size," may be the most important aspect of this or any objective. This is the behavior—the thing the trainee must do or learn in the small piece of the training that this objective relates to. The behavior is often called the *action* or the *performance,* and objectives written with these verbs are termed *behavioral objectives, performance objectives,* or *action objectives.* As usual, we aren't interested in what you call it, as long as you do it. I'll call them *behaviors,* because that is what I was first taught to call them, and it's hard to break away from your initiation terminology.

    The behavior signals the trainees as to what must be done or learned in very specific terms. It also signals the designer in the same way. Look at some of the behaviors in the list of objectives for the monitoring program that we reviewed a bit earlier: differentiate, propose, identify, implement, design. These are all very specific things for the trainee to do.

    There are comprehensive lists of behaviors that have been developed to which the instructional designer can refer when constructing objectives. New instructional designers often keep one of these lists handy when constructing objectives. In fact, some experienced instructional designers (we won't mention any names) have been known to refer to a behavior list when working on objectives. Here is an example of such a list according to a hierarchy, from simple to more complex behaviors. I seldom create objectives without it. *(over)*

PERFORMANCE VERBS

Knowledge		Comprehension		Application	Analysis	Synthesis	Evaluation
Count	Recall	Associate	Interpret	Apply	Order	Arrange	Appraise
Define	Recite	Compare	Interpolate	Calculate	Group	Combine	Assess
Draw	Read	Compute	Predict	Classify	Translate	Construct	Critique
Identify	Record	Contrast	Translate	Complete	Transform	Create	Determine
Indicate	Repeat	Describe		Demonstrate	Analyze	Design	Evaluate
List	State	Differentiate		Employ	Detect	Develop	Grade
Name	Tabulate	Discuss		Examine	Explain	Formulate	Judge
Point	Trace	Distinguish		Illustrate	Infer	Generalize	Measure
Quote	Write	Estimate		Practice	Separate	Integrate	Rank
Recognize		Extrapolate		Relate	Summarize	Organize	Rate
				Solve	Construct	Plan	Select
				Use		Prepare	Test
				Utilize		Prescribe	Recommend
						Produce	
						Propose	
						Specify	

Your Behaviors Must Be Observable. The most important aspect to this list, or any other good one, is that all the behaviors mentioned are observable. The trainee can "do" something that someone else can see or hear, and something can be recorded as having been observed. You can listen to trainees proposing a solution; you can watch them differentiate between this and that; you can observe them implementing something; or you can read what they construct as an answer to a problem. This is the key to making objectives work: stating behaviors for the trainees to master that are observable to them and to others.

You can usually tell whether an instructional designer has grasped this key to objectives simply by looking at what he or she considers to be an objective. A telltale sign of misunderstanding is the use of two very common but worthless (at least as far as objectives are concerned) words: *know* and *understand.* I can't begin to count the number of times I've seen objectives with one of these words as the behavior. The trainee will "know how to" or the trainee will "understand the way that." If you've been following this discussion up to now, you will know and understand what is wrong with these "behaviors": they are not observable. How do you know when a trainee knows something or, more important, how do the trainees know when they know? How do you, or the trainees, measure their understanding of something?

When I ask these questions of new instructional designers who have used words like *know* and *understand*, they usually reply by saying something like, "They'll know it when they can list the ten steps to. . . ." and I say, "So why doesn't your objective tell the trainees and you that they need to list the ten steps?" Or they say, "When they can design a new widget right, then they understand the basics," and I say, "Why not have an objective that states the trainee will be able to design a new widget properly?"

This difference is pretty easy to see, and at the same time very difficult to put into practice. I'm not sure why this is so, but using your list of behavioral verbs rather than using words that have no observable behavioral meaning will help you write usable, useful objectives.

Reviews. It's also good to have someone who knows how to write objectives review yours for instructional design quality. Even the best designers construct objectives from time to time that seem perfect to them but make less sense to those who do not have the background to interpret what the objective is requiring. This means that in all probability it will not make sense to the trainee. This is particularly a problem if you are an SME for the content of your program. Your reviewer will see things that you took for granted but perhaps should not have and will help make your objectives even more usable for your trainees.

Picking the Right Verbs. Another common mistake that you need to watch out for is randomly picking behavioral verbs from your list simply because they sound good. Remember that what you choose in the form of a behavior is what the trainee must exhibit to master the objective, so don't pick just any verb— pick the right one. If you choose *list*, then that's what the trainee will be doing, not *compare* or *create*. If your behavioral objective is that the trainees will *summarize*, don't expect them to *differentiate* or *predict*.

This is particularly important when it comes to developing evaluation questions. *Recognize,* which is a good multiple-choice behavior, is a whole lot different from *discuss,* which usually means an essay or verbal type question. Your tasks will help you decide on the correct behaviors, as in our example, in which the task was choosing correct tread sizes and the objective reflected this by using the same behavior. Most often it is not this simple, but it is always doable if you've analyzed well and take the time to think it through carefully.

Standards and Conditions

Let's go back to our example and finish off this discussion on constructing good objectives. The rest of the objective reads like this:

. . . . choose the correct tread size for the three major tire runs, on the assembly line, 90 percent of the time.

This portion presents us with the other two main parts of an objective: the standard, often termed the *criteria,* and the condition, which is sometimes referred to as the *given.* Again, the first main part of the objective was the behavior, making a total of three. Some folks like to add an introduction ("At the end of this class the trainee will be able to. . . .") as a fourth part; others feel this is simply a piece of the condition or the criteria. Define it as you like, but don't forget to get all the parts in there somewhere.

Standards. The standard or criteria is sort of the basic measurement aspect of the objective. In our example, there are actually two parts to the criteria: "for the three major tire runs" and "90 percent of the time." I have to admit that I overcomplicated the objective in the example just to illustrate the idea of standards. In most cases, for this type of on-the-job performance you would not expect 90 percent accuracy, but 100 percent. If such is the case, the standard is more or less understood, and you may choose not to call it out in the objective. You might even omit the phrase "for the three major tire runs" if it is obvious that this is the way the work is always done.

If you look back at my earlier list of five objectives from the monitoring program, you won't see much in the way of standards. For these objectives, considering their scope, the content, and the audience, the standards are pretty much understood. I could have written: "Identify the nine appropriate criteria for monitoring all programs" if that's how many there were (there were literally hundreds, which is why the verb was *identify* and not *list*), or "Design and implement a plan for communicating monitoring results that is 95 percent effective" (which is probably more than we could ever hope for), but such criteria are really neither needed nor logical in this circumstance.

The important issue for objective writing is for you to remember that standards are a critical part of your objective, and that if they are not totally understood by everyone, then you need to state them specifically in your objective, such as "score an 85 percent on a written test" or "produce a salable tire 93 percent of the time," or whatever. If in doubt, write it in; you can always remove it later.

Conditions. The condition or *given* is a bit more difficult to understand, as it often slips into the standard—and even more often is understood and not written in the objective at all. The condition is basically the environment in which the behavior will be performed. I added a simple condition to our sample tire building objective: "on the assembly line." It's simple, but it says to the trainee and to you the designer that the objective is not mastered until the behavior is done "on the assembly line"—not in a classroom, but on the job. This determines how you will write evaluation measures, as well as where the trainee needs to spend some time practicing.

This is very few words for such large ramifications, but I wanted to show you what conditions are for and what they can do. In this case, because I wrote in this condition, I felt that practice and evaluation needed to be done in the work environment. There must have been a good reason for this, as shown by my analysis, such as the fact that this was a much more difficult task to perform when the line was running, the noise was high, and there were other distractions.

Anyway, that's what conditions do. If I hadn't added this condition to my objective, then the trainee could have practiced anywhere and been evaluated in a lab or in the classroom. Conditions tell you where, when, and how the behavior must be performed, if such things are important. Like standards, they are often assumed to be understood, but if your analysis indicates a need for certain specialized conditions then these should be noted as part of your objective. Some old pros, particularly when working with new instructional designers, require that all three parts of the objective (behavior, conditions, and criteria) appear in each objective that is written. This really isn't a bad idea, although you often end up with objectives like these:

> At the end of this program the trainee will be able to recognize the sixteen major uses of the clip shifter by scoring a grade of 95 percent or better on a written multiple choice test given in a classroom and pointing out at least nine uses during a trip to the factory floor where the clip shifter is in operation.

Believe it or not, this is actually a pretty good objective. It has an observable behavior, criteria, and conditions. Its major problem is that it is kind of long-winded. If you have thirty or forty of these as second-level objectives, they become difficult for both the trainee and the trainer to deal with, which means they are often ignored. The best rule of thumb is to put into the objective what needs to be there to help everyone use it effectively.

Here are some examples of objectives that are—well, less than adequate:

On the Dim Side . . .

Change a light bulb within one minute.

Without the use of notes or reference materials, write a two-hundred-word essay on "Why I Hate Emergency Planning."

Run the hundred-yard dash (or, make a pizza) (or, change a tire).

Perform and document a general area radiation survey.

Be familiar with safety precautions related to a 16-gauge shotgun.

And here are the same objectives written with enough information to make them useful for the learners; that is, with standards and conditions. Can you find them?

On the Bright Side . . .

Given a ladder of sufficient height and a new light bulb, replace a burned-out ceiling bulb of the same size within one minute and without breaking your neck.

Without the use of notes or reference materials, write a two-hundred-word essay on "Why I Like Emergency Planning." Essays must be written in five minutes or less, and must contain no more than two grammatical or spelling errors.

Run the hundred-yard dash on a dry track within twenty seconds.

In the plant or lab containing radiation check source, perform and document a general area radiation survey in accordance with PNPP procedures and determine any posting requirements.

State all of the safety precautions that must be followed when loading a Remington 16-gauge shotgun on an indoor range.

The large majority of objectives that you write will not include conditions or criteria as visible parts of the objective statement. However, they are always there, even if only implied, and you will use them—and the objective as a whole—continuously as you go through the rest of the aspects of your instructional design.

More Levels?

Did your eyes widen when I said thirty or forty objectives? Were you thinking, "Where did that number come from? In our tire-making example, we only seem to need six or so, one for each task." Well, maybe—and then again, maybe not. Remember when we talked about levels of objectives? We said that you may have a course or program objective (or objectives) and then a level below that related to a task or group of tasks. We called these first-level and second-level objectives. However, you may need another level; let's call them *third-level objectives.*

In the case of our tire-making example, our first-level objective was something like this:

At the end of this course, the trainee will be able to effectively utilize the XB-45 tire-making machine to assemble a composite tire that will pass the company's inspection criteria.

Whereas the objective for the first task, which is a second-level objective, was

At the end of the training the trainee will be able to choose the correct tread size for the three major tire runs, on the assembly line, 90 percent of the time.

But remember, when we did the task analysis (see Chapter Three) we found that the trainees will need to "know what the various tread sizes are and how to differentiate them." We may need to state both this piece of knowledge and this simple skill as objectives if we are going to help the trainees as much as possible with their learning. So we might construct the following:

At the end of this section of the course, the trainees will be able to (1) list the various tread sizes that are worked on the XB-45 machine and (2) utilize the tread caliper gauge to differentiate between tread sizes.

Now we have two third-level objectives. This is probably as far down as we need to go for this particular task. How do I know that? Experience! This is where the science of objective writing becomes art, or perhaps educated guessing. This feels right to me. If the trainees can master these two objectives, then they can master the second-level objective and the task. I may be wrong, and I may find out that I'm wrong when the SME reviews my objectives, or when I do my pilot, or possibly not until after I actually implement the course—but remember our rule, "Everything can change."

This is my first swing at the objectives, and we've got a way to go yet before the trainees see them. Many will change a little, some a lot; I may add another level and even another for some tasks, based on what happens during reviews and content development. But that's part of what the instructional design process is for: to catch the mistakes before the trainee ever sees them.

Reviews Again

Because we mentioned it, let's talk a little more about reviews. I just said that the objectives may change when the SME reviews them. This is not the same review that we discussed earlier, done by another instructional designer. This review is done by your SME, who does not look at behavioral levels or parts of the objective. He or she is interested in the width and depth of content that your objectives cover. Do they make sense? Do they cover all that needs to be covered? Do they cover too much? Do they ask the trainees to know and do what they need to know and do on the job? As with the instructional designer's review, it is not imperative that a special SME review be done for the objectives, but it is a great idea and will probably save you a lot of rewriting later.

Make sure the SME knows what you are looking for in the review; otherwise you will probably get a review of your grammar. This is a good rule to follow for all reviews and reviewers. Give them specific instructions as to what type of review you want and need from them. Just a couple of bullet points are usually all that is necessary. I often turn the bullet points into a form by simply putting space in between them. The SMEs make their comments on each review point in these spaces, thus making it easier for me to understand what they are getting at.

We've spent a lot of time here on objectives and given you a number of possibilities for their creation and use. It may seem difficult to grasp aspects such as how many levels you need, when criteria are understood, and when to add conditions—and it is. As a new instructional designer you will need to construct objectives, review them, ideally have other designers review them, change them, and often start over again, and maybe even again, to get them right—then still change them up to the day your material goes to print. It gets easier as you gain experience, but not even the best get their objectives right the first time. However, by constructing proper objectives and using them throughout the rest of your instructional design process, you will help to ensure that what the trainees get from your training is what they and your company need them to have so they can do the job.

Just in case you haven't heard enough about reviews, or you are working on your own without colleagues to lend a hand in the review process, here is one more method by which I always review my objectives.

Start by thinking as your learners think; put yourself in their place. Now, as a learner, ask yourself these three questions for each objective:

1. Do I know what I need to do?

2. Do I know how I need to do it?

3. Do I know how I will be evaluated on it?

If you've been following our discussion of objectives closely, you've probably noticed that these three questions ask for the behavior, the conditions, and the criteria, but in a way that, if you can answer yes to all three, will ensure that your learners can use your objectives effectively—and that's what it's all about.

Examples of Objectives

Here are some more objectives for you to consider; each begins with "The trainees will be able to . . ." See if you can decide which ones are good and which ones need help.

. . . utilize their knowledge of the techniques and theory of good management communications to implement an action plan for communicating effectively with fellow employees at all levels of the organization.

. . . list the four basic tasks of a router.

. . . differentiate between flat rate and usage lines.

. . . formulate a personal plan for applying the common-knowledge aspects of real estate processes to the practices of their program area.

. . . employ electronic information systems for learning about and dealing with real estate issues.

. . . correctly perform the steps necessary to troubleshoot a failing circuit board so that it passes a level II inspection.

. . . given a reference manual and template, cut and paste a sentence from one document to another.

. . . list the nodes of a DC-3 multi-switch without referring to the reference manual.

. . . properly send a fax on the FAXator AM-1 machine using the provided job aid,.

. . . demonstrate interest in staff by talking with them about non-job-related topics.

How did you do? Actually, all of the above are what I consider to be well-written objectives. Notice that they do not all have every one of the parts we discussed, but each one is clear, specific in its behavior, and trainee centered.

 ### Smart and Smarter Objectives

It goes without saying that objectives are a smart thing to have—and SMART is also an acronym that can help you to write good objectives:

- Specific
- Measurable
- Action Oriented (some like to use instead Aligned with Corporate Goals)
- Reasonable
- Timely

You can even make a SMARTER objective:

- Specific
- Measurable
- Action Oriented (or Aligned with Corporate Goals)
- Reasonable
- Timely
- Evaluate Consistently
- Recognize Mastery

SMARTER tends to go a bit beyond basic instructional design, but I thought I'd throw it in to help you remember the importance of objectives and to remind you, no matter how you do them—do them!

 As a rapid instructional design shortcut, take your completed objectives and distribute them to your trainees, along with a listing of resources (procedures, books, manuals, videos, CD-ROMS, people, and so on) they can use to master the objectives. Then leave them on their own to do so. This is actually a form of self-directed learning.

Using this shortcut means you will not need to develop comprehensive instructional plans, lesson plans, or training materials. You will probably want to develop criterion testing (discussed later in this chapter), but even that is not absolutely necessary. The two main problems with this shortcut are (1) the availability of resources and (2) the inconsistency in what the trainees pull from the resources.

 ## DESIGN DOCUMENTS

Earlier in this chapter we mentioned the need for a design document. These constructs are known by a number of different names, including *course plans*, *course treatments*, and others. In a more formal instructional design process, each of these is a separate document with its own characteristics, and it is developed in its own time. Because we are talking rapid instructional design here, we'll lump them all together and call the report a *design document*.

The purpose of a design document is to put all the decisions you've made up to this point concerning your training into one place and add a couple more. The design document then becomes your guide as you continue to develop your training. You can also use it to explain to others (colleagues, SMEs, reviewers, stakeholders, management, your boss) what you are doing.

Here is a template for a pretty complete design document:

DESIGN DOCUMENT TEMPLATE

1. Scope of Project (Focus)

    Goal

    Audience

    Design Time and Milestones

2. Delivery

    Content

    Method

    Training Time

    Problems and Opportunities

3. Objectives

4. Materials

5. Who Is Involved

6. Topical Outline

7. Administration and Evaluation

8. Links

You may not want or need to go into this level of detail with your design document, or you may want to add even more information. Of the following two other design document templates, one is a bit simpler, the other more complex.

SIMPLE DESIGN DOCUMENT TEMPLATE

1. We need this course because. . . .

2. The participants will be. . . .

3. The course content will be. . . .

4. The course will cost _____ to design and _____ to deliver.

5. Design and implementation staff will include. . . .

6. The course will be delivered. . . .

COMPLEX DESIGN DOCUMENT TEMPLATE

Requesting department:

Requesting supervisor or manager:

Job:

Analyst:

Course title:

Participants:

Identified skills to be taught:

Identified concepts to be taught:

Objectives:

Course description:

Techniques to be used:

☐ Lecture   ☐ Discussion   ☐ Q and A

☐ Hands-On   ☐ Demonstration   ☐ Video

☐ CBT   ☐ Role Plays   ☐ Pre-Work

☐ WBT   ☐ Self-Instruction   ☐ Games

☐ Other:

Follow-up activities:

Other departments that might benefit:

Location for training:

Trainers:

Course duration:

Proposed dates:

Number of employees per class:

Development costs:

Delivery costs:

Cost per trainee:

Travel costs:

Cost responsibilities:

Evaluation plan:

A Design Document in Detail

Because the first design document template we looked at is more or less middle-of-the-road in complexity (and just happens to be the one I like to use), let's go over it in some detail.

1. Scope of Project

By now you should have a pretty good idea of what the scope or focus of your training is going to be. Here is the place to write it down in statement form. At its simplest, a training project scope usually has two parts: the goal and the audience. I normally add a third aspect: the amount of time the design will take and significant milestones in that time period.

Goal. Your goal should be a clear general statement of what the outcomes of the program will be; that is, what the trainees will achieve. As such, it should relate directly back to the need you identified in your assessment process. Keep it fairly general; you'll have a chance to add detail later with your objectives. This is sort of a mission statement for your training.

If you cannot identify a single goal, but seem to have multiple ones, you probably need multiple courses or modules. One advantage of stating the training goal is that it will indicate to you if this is the case. Don't make the mistake of eliminating the detail you know your trainees will need simply because it seems the goal is too complex; create a series of courses with more focused goals instead. And don't err by covering material that may be too advanced for your trainees before giving them the basics because your goal requires a lot of content and your time is short. Create a basic course and an advanced one, each with separate but related goals. To do anything less is to handicap your training program before it's ever used.

This is another of the many points in a good instructional design process at which you might rethink some of your basic decisions about your training program. In this case you may decide that you really do need more than one course, or a basic and an advanced course. Stating your goal can help you decide.

Let's use our tire manufacturing scenario again and develop a design document, starting with the project scope. We know from our assessment and analysis that the goal of the program is "to train employees to make tires." You can make this statement fancier by putting in words like "effectively" or "properly," or by adding condition statements, as we've discussed. However, in the end, making tires it what this particular program is all about.

Audience. You should know your audience pretty well by now if you did a good audience analysis. You don't need to put much detail here, just a short statement on who will and possibly who will not be trained. For our example we might state the following:

> The audience will be all employees newly assigned to a tire assembly line station. This will include new employees and those transferred from other areas.

Uh-oh—did we consider these transfers in our analysis?

One of the very good reasons for doing a design document is to check on your own planning. If you forgot something, like a particular portion of your audience, you may need to go back a step and catch up.

Design Time and Milestones. These are exactly what they appear to be. You know your delivery method from your delivery analysis, so you should have a good idea of how long it is going to take you to put the course together and the checkpoints along the way that will tell you, and your stakeholders, how it's going.

In our example, we have determined from our delivery consideration that we will use OJT, and we estimate that it will take us around four weeks to develop the OJT material for the objectives we've written. Milestones will be

- Completion and review of objectives: end of week one
- Content completed for first two modules: end of week two
- Content for second two modules completed and first two reviewed: end of week three
- Trainer's guide and evaluations completed: end of week four
- Pilot and revisions done: end of week five

If you are really sharp you may have noticed that it took us five weeks, rather than the planned four weeks, to complete the program. I did this to stress the importance of piloting your program. We'll talk about this concept in detail a bit later, but don't forget to leave room for it in your plan. A good reason for going to this level of detail with your milestones is, again, to check the accuracy of the amount of time you thought it would take to get your program ready. If you find you have more milestones than will fit in the planned time, something's got to give.

Length of Course. How long should your course be? A key to helping you determine how much design time you need is the actual course presentation time. How long the course should be is usually one of the first things everyone thinks about when developing training. The right answer to this question is based on a number of factors, including

- Your target audience and their abilities and availability
- The availability of resources such as classrooms trainers or, as in our tire-making example, the actual machines
- The content that you know must be taught, based on your analysis and prioritization, as well as what content can be held for another session
- Organizational needs that tell you whether this piece of training must stand alone or is part of a larger curriculum and can therefore draw on what comes before and after
- Instructional needs, such as the importance of breaking the program into modules with time in between for the trainees to practice or to digest the information

There is no easy answer to the question of how long the course should be. If you want some additional guidelines, consider what the experts say:

- It is best to do the training all in one sitting if possible
- Lessons (often defined as a session that addresses one first-level objective) should be no longer than twenty minutes without a change in activity
- Courses should be no longer than three hours
- For self-instructional training, break the course into as many smaller pieces as possible and always be aware that trainees tire easily with this type of training, particularly if it involves using a computer

Once you know (or think you know) the length of your course, you need to figure out how long it will take to design and develop it. This depends to a great extent on your delivery method. There seem to be as many ways to calculate design and development time as there are instructional designers, but here are a few very rough ratios I use, based on delivery time:

Delivery Process	Hours of Development/1 Hour Instruction
Lecture	2–3
Activity-based classroom	5–10
Print-based self-instructional	15–30
Low-level computer-based	25–50
Multimedia-based	40–150
Satellite-based	50–100
E-learning (synchronous)	25–40
E-learning (asynchronous)	45–100

Delivery Process	Hours of Development/1 Hour Instruction
OJT	10–20
Training by documentation	1
Job performance aids	3–300

You can see that these ranges are not very specific, but you can use them to help gauge delivery time, which can change as you get deeper into content development. This is an ongoing process, and you will need to refine your timing as you go. My best advice to you is to guess (estimate) on the high side. No one ever got in trouble for finishing a project too soon or under budget. The opposite is certainly not true.

2. Delivery

Part two of the design document is delivery. By now you should have a pretty good idea of what these items entail. You simply need to put them down on paper.

Content. A concise statement of what the course will cover is enough. Use your task statements from your job analysis to write this. For our tire-building program it might read something like this:

> This program will cover the knowledge and skills practice needed for the participant to build tires at our company

or

> The content of this program will consist of the six tasks necessary to build a tire using the X45-B tire-making machine.

The first content statement is pretty general; it allows you to add in company history, tire-making theory, and whatever else you might want. The second is very specific and requires that all your content speak directly to the six tasks. If written with a little forethought, your content statement can help you stay on track and tell others what your program will accomplish.

Method. You've already decided on your delivery method, so put it down on paper here. Note any special aspects, such as follow-up activities, job aids, or preprogram activities. You might also do a bit of editorializing concerning the advantages and disadvantages of your chosen method.

> The method for this program will be on-the-job training. A pre-reading of the X45-B manual will be part of the process. This will be a mastery learning, with

a criterion performance checklist used by the OJT trainer to determine mastery. Due to compliance problems with pre-reading processes, a pretest will be given by the trainer to check knowledge before OJT begins.

Training Time. This is still an estimate, but put it down anyway.

The average new employee will spend twenty contact hours with the OJT trainer and sixty monitored or observed practice hours to prepare for the criterion evaluation.

Problems and Opportunities. This is a place to note anything special that may affect the course.

There could be a problem with getting enough practice time on the machine during peak production runs. We may need to schedule most training during third shift.

Capturing the knowledge of our expert operators for the course will give us an opportunity to rewrite the operating manual at a later date.

3. Objectives

In part three of the design document, you need to state the course objectives. Your program objective and your first-level objectives are probably enough here, with possibly an occasional second-level objective if you feel something needs more explanation.

4. Materials

For the materials aspect, note any special materials that you plan on creating or using as part of the course, such as videos, CD-ROMS, models, lesson plans, and participant guides.

This program will include a participant's guide that explains the training process to the trainees and provides both reference material and background reading, an OJT trainer's guide that provides a training schedule, day-by-day instructions, evaluations for the trainer, and two videotapes that explain the functioning of the machine. These tapes have been supplied by the manufacturer.

5. Who Is Involved

This area is usually a simple list of those individuals who will be part of design, delivery, and evaluation and their functions in the program.

Ray Johnson	Training Specialist	Designer of program
Dana Wagner	Operator	SME/OJT trainer
Mike Colcott	Operator	OJT trainer
Harry Lark	Operator	OJT trainer
Lan Winston	Manager	Final approval

6. Topical Outline

Part six of your design document is a short outline of the topics your program will address. Keep this at the Roman numeral level, with just enough detail so that anyone who needs to can see what the course will be covering. Use your objectives and tasks to help you with this aspect. It will be another useful guide as you develop the course material. Note that this is a topic outline, not an instructional plan or a lesson plan. We'll get to those later.

Topical Outline

    I. Tread sizes and their importance

   II. Identifying proper tread size

  III. Reversing the tire matrix

  IV. Types of belts

    V. Laying belt layers

  VI. Operating the assembly machine

 VII. Trimming

VIII. Checking the seal

  IX. Final inspection

   X. Troubleshooting

You may have noticed that items IX and X have suddenly appeared, though there was no indication of them in the objectives or tasks. This often happens; it's just another one of those instances when you have to perform a check to decide whether something does or does not belong in your course. A little retro-thought tells us that we simply missed the final inspection, so we need to go back and write an objective for it—and possibly even a task.

As for troubleshooting, this really was not part of the plan for this course, and although it is important, we decide it will have to wait, so we note this in the "problems and opportunities" area and remove it from our outline. Don't be afraid to make changes. Nothing is written in stone—not your task list, not your objectives. In fact, if you never make any changes as you go through the design process, be afraid. No one is that good!

7. Administration and Evaluation

Note how the course will meet these two important aspects. Who will be in charge of scheduling, signing up trainees, reviewing, and updating the course? How will they do this? What evaluations will be done on the trainees and the course in general? You may have noted some of this in the other areas, but pull it together here.

> This is a mandatory course for all new tire-assembly-line hires. As such, it will be administered through our general training administration system. The designer will be responsible for reviewing evaluation data and updating as needed.
>
> Evaluations will include our general reaction evaluation instrument, a pre-OJT knowledge test as described above, a criterion checklist-based performance evaluation as described above, and a ninety-day assessment of job application, using the company's observation and interview format.

8. Links

The last area of the design document is a catchall that I like to call *links*. This is a place to put anything that doesn't fit anywhere else but that needs to be said—particularly relationships to other training. For example, if you're going to need a train-the-trainer program or if a management overview will be needed, you might note that here.

> A train-the-trainer program will be needed for the three OJT trainers involved in this program. The training should take around two days and include information on one-on-one training as well as how to use the trainer's guide.

The following is a completed example of a design document using the above template.

Team Production Process Design Document

1. Project Scope

Goal: To train all processing staff in the policies and procedures that relate to the Team Production Process initiative.

Audience: The audience will be all employees involved in production at both the field and regional levels, their managers up to and including the division managers, and appropriate members of the sales force.

Design Time/Milestones: The complete design will take approximately two months. Analysis will be completed in two weeks from the decision to go ahead with the project. Objectives will be completed the following week and test questions the next. Material development will last two weeks, followed by a beta test and pilot to round out the two-month schedule.

2. Delivery

Content: The content will be based on the policies and procedures developed by the Team Production Process project team, which in turn are based on the best practices from all of the company in the task areas of receipt and distribution, processing, producing, and closing. It will consist of selling the concept of the Team Production Process to the participants, familiarizing them with policy and procedure, and practicing skills based on job aids.

Method: The core delivery will be a two-day facilitated classroom taught by an experienced facilitator with the assistance of an SME from the company. These experts will be drawn from the project team and the field manager levels of the organization. The SME will lead question-and-answer discussions and be on hand to answer collateral questions related to the organization. The class work will consist of a segment on "What's in it for me?" and for the company, discussion of policies and procedures, explanation of the integrated job aids, and application of the job aids in various simulations and practices. The participants will be asked to create their own personalized job aids after they have mastered the various processes.

The core delivery will be preceded by a test-based pre-work that introduces the policies and procedures and the job aids.

The core delivery will be followed by a post-work activity in which the participants answer a series of simulation-based questions concerning the Team Production Process and then discuss their answers with their manager, who has been provided with the correct answers.

Training Time: This training will be completed in approximately six months in the time period from late January to June 2006. Actual learning time per participant will be: (1) two hours of self-instructional pre-work, (2) two eight-hour facilitated classes, and (3) two hours of follow-up work.

To achieve this timetable, we recommend that two corporate regions with eight to ten training locations in each region be trained every two weeks.

Problems and Opportunities: (1) There is some question as to whether all participants should be trained in the entire process or whether the training should be compartmentalized according to participants' job function; (2) a problem may exist in that all sites will not have received New Production training before the January rollout date; this may mean that some background knowledge will not be available at some sites; and (3) a "permanent" Team Production Process trainer could be chosen from the involved SMEs for each area or region to handle the training of new hires.

3. Objectives

Program: At the end of this program, the participants will be able to properly implement the procedures of the company's Team Production Process when processing all data.

Supporting: At the end of this program the trainees will be able to (1) discuss the overall purpose of the Team Production Process, (2) describe the overall receiving and distribution flow, (3) effectively implement the team receiving and distribution process, (4) discuss the decision-making aspect of the Team Production Process, (5) differentiate among the various level decisions related to the Team Production Process, (6) effectively use the Team Production Process procedures to make decisions, (7) overview the data-processing aspect of the Team Production Process, (8) correctly employ the procedures of the Team Production Process when processing data, (9) list the tasks associated with completion of a data stream using the Team Production Process, and (10) properly close a data stream using the procedures of the Team Production Process.

4. Training Materials

Training materials to be developed for the program include

- Print-based booklet for pre-work
- Facilitator guide for classroom portion
- Participant guide for classroom portion
- SME guide for SMEs participating in classroom portion
- Job aids as required
- Post-work material for both participants and managers

5. Involvement

Personnel will be responsible for the program as follows:

- Consultant instructional design team: Perform analysis, create design document and training materials, observe pilot and revise as needed, train facilitators and SMEs
- Consultant desktop publisher: Finalize material format
- Consultant facilitators: Facilitate all classes
- Company project team: Supply policies and procedures, review training materials, act as SMEs at classes, support training of facilitators and other SMEs

- Company SME: Work with course developers to create job aids and other performance-based materials as needed

- Company field managers: Act as classroom SMEs

6. Topical Outline

    I.   Introduction

        A. What the Team Production Process is

        B. Why it is good for the company

        C. How it will affect me

    II. Receiving and distribution

        A. Sales rep responsibilities

        B. Data receiving tasks

        C. Data logging and distribution tasks

        D. Manager responsibilities

    III. Decisions

        A. Data specialist decision flow

        B. Senior data specialist decision flow

        C. Decision differentiation

        D. Logging tasks

        E. Documentation needs

        F. Decisions (data specialist)

        G. Decisions (senior data specialist)

        H. Post-decision form and screen completion

    IV. Processing

        A. Type determination

        B. Document requirements

        C. Initial review tasks

        D. Decision path determination

        E. Letters

        F. File setup tasks

    V. Completion

        A. Completion flow

        B. Responsibilities for completion

C. Verification tasks

D. Completion document preparation

E. Completion documents

F. Validation tasks

G. Streaming tasks

7. Evaluation

Level-one evaluation will be achieved through the use of the company's current instrument or a general instrument. Level-two evaluation will be achieved informally through the classroom-based activities. Level-three evaluation will be a combination of management observation (informal or formalized with a criterion checklist and other documentation) and analysis of the metrics that are part of the project's post-implementation review.

8. Links

Train-the-Trainer Training: There will be two types of train-the-trainer training in the program. The first, for the core facilitators, will consist of familiarization with the lesson plan and content, plus basic information concerning the company. This should be led by a member of the instructional design team and be supported by a member of the internal project team and possibly another company person qualified to discuss the company in detail. The second will be for the SMEs who will help instruct the core classes. This class will cover their part in the training and give them background information on the entire project. It is suggested that members of the project team take on the SME responsibility at first, bringing others into the process when necessary. The new SMEs should go through the actual training first, then the train-the-trainer session. This should be followed by an observation of a training session before they take over the process on their own.

This system will probably necessitate more than one iteration of the SME train-the-trainer. However, it is likely that as the consultant facilitators become more knowledgeable about the company, the need for an SME will disappear and these individuals can get on with their regular duties.

Training time for the train-the-trainer program should be approximately two days for the core facilitators and one day for the SMEs.

Management Overview: There is a need for an executive summary type of program for the various levels of management from the divisional level on down. This program should discuss the project in general, the aspects that affect the various levels of management, and management's responsibilities in making the process successful.

As the numbers here are relatively small, this could be handled through a classroom approach in less than half a day. The class would be best facilitated by a member of the project team, and it will probably be necessary to give it at least once in each region.

Sales Force Training: There is also a need for training members of the sales force about the purpose of the project and their role in starting it properly. We suggest a possible CD-ROM distribution of a minimal training package that discusses these two aspects and possibly supplies a job aid.

 ## COURSE DESCRIPTIONS

Your design document should serve you well as a preliminary explanation of your training. However, some designers prefer a more formal course description as part of their design process. The course description might be done in lieu of the design document, it might be the next step in your design, or you might not do one at all. In case you feel you want to or need to do one, here is a template for creating a formal course description:

    I. Title of course

    II. Designer

    III. Scope

    IV. Audience

    V. Training time

    VI. Delivery method

    (Up to this point, this model is a lot like our design document, but things change with the next item as the course description gets into a lot more detail.)

    VII. The task(s) that will be trained on

    VIII. The objectives related to each task

    IX. An overview of how the content of the course fits into the job structure

        A. Where the task is done

        B. Who does it

        C. Why the task is important

        D. Problems associated with poor performance

    X. Prerequisite knowledge necessary before beginning the course

    XI. Lesson overview

        A. Subtasks

        B. Exercises

        C. Practices

XII. Instructional materials

XIII. Visuals and/or other media

XIV. Reviews

XV. Testing

XVI. Performance monitoring

Neither design documents nor course descriptions are a mandatory part of an instructional design, but I suggest you use one or the other in some form to help you think through your course and to keep you on track as you continue with design and material development.

Design documents, course descriptions, analysis reports of every kind—we've talked about a lot of paper so far, and there is plenty more to come. A rapid design shortcut is to keep your reports to a minimum. All the things we've discussed are important, but unless someone is going to read them you don't need to write reports about them. Just jot down what you need for your own use. Keep your formal reporting to a minimum and even those reports minimal. Try for one page whenever possible. We've given you much longer templates, for sure, but that's only if you need them.

GATHERING CONTENT

No matter what method you use to create a skeleton for your course, your next activity is to gather the content that you will need to present. You have actually been doing this all along, as you did your analysis and as you developed objectives, but its important to formalize the process now.

If you are the SME—particularly if you are the only SME—your process is simple. You sit down in a quiet place with your objectives and write down what the trainees need to know to master each of them. This is not the recommended method (although it is the fastest), but if it's all you have the time or resources to do, now is the time to do it.

If you are not the SME, or if there are others you can call on to help, you'll need to select the right people and then meet with them to determine the content.

Selecting Subject-Matter Experts

We discussed how to select SMEs for analysis in Chapter Two. The process is pretty much the same for selecting content SMEs ("Getting Inside an Expert's Brain" by D. Gayeski, 1992). Look for experienced people who have a good attitude concerning training and with whom you feel it will be easy to work. Ask them about their experience and how they became experts at the job.

Check on how they deal with problems and mistakes. Now pick those people you are most comfortable with and who will be most comfortable with you. This choosing is not a formal science and your comfort is a key issue, as you are going to be working very closely with one another.

Working with Your Subject-Matter Experts

When working with your SME(s) to develop content, you can use the same type of data-collection tools that you used for analysis. Many designers like questionnaires and surveys for this process, as these are more to the point and less time-consuming, but I prefer face-to-face interviews.

Give your SMEs a copy of your analysis and your design document or whatever you have used as a planning tool. Discuss it together so they know where the course is coming from and where it is trying to go. Now give them the whole list of objectives. If you did not use their input in developing the objectives (or in reviewing them), ask for it now and make changes where needed. Explain the importance of their using the objectives as a guide. I often leave the objectives with the SME and ask him or her to write content based on each, although you may want to stay with the person, listen as he or she talks, and do the writing yourself.

Be sure to explain the importance of "need to know" versus "nice to know" content. I ask SMEs to label each thought as "need" or "nice" to remind them and to help me later. Don't be afraid to question their decisions on this aspect, as it is the key to efficient content.

Also remind SMEs that the content is not for them, but for people who do not have the knowledge that they do. Therefore they need to keep it simple and at the proper level. Without this warning, SMEs often forget to include the basics, as these are so second nature to them that they skip right over this important content.

Be sure that you ask for any job aids, shortcuts, or other physical materials that your SMEs use to help them do their jobs. These will be invaluable to your trainees if presented in the right context.

Here are some hints that may help you when working with SMEs:

- When requesting an SME from a department, provide the manager with a list of the characteristics you are looking for.
- Prepare your SME with a list of topics or concepts you want to cover, and even objectives and test questions if you have them.
- Listen, don't talk.
- Ask good follow-up questions.

- Don't interrupt to ask a new questions until the SME's thought is complete.

- When you move from general questions to specific questions, give the SME a chance to make the mental change.

- Don't use trainer terminology like *job aids* or *performance tools*. Ask it in their language, or they won't know what you are looking for.

- Use both verbal (ahh, uh-huh) and nonverbal (smiling, nodding, frowning, open body language, eye contact) behaviors to elicit more and better responses.

- Be careful not to ask multiple questions at the same time. Keep it simple to get solid answers.

- Keep your SMEs updated on the progress of the course, as they own part of it now. This will pay big dividends later when you need reviewers.

- When you have follow-up questions, instead of another meeting or even an e-mail, try posting them on the corporate intranet to get other SMEs interested.

Another rapid design hint is to plan to develop your SMEs into training professionals. Don't just tell them *what* to do but tell them *why* as well. Show them what happens with what they are giving you. Have them help you with some aspects of material development and even writing objectives. Over a period of time, they will be able to anticipate your needs and give you feedback that is effective and easy to use. This will drastically cut down the time you need to work with them and, more important, the time you sit there trying to decipher what they are talking about.

Prerequisite Learning

Whether you are the SME or you are using others as SMEs, one of the first things you need to do when gathering content is to develop a list of the prerequisite skills and knowledge that the trainees should come to your program having already mastered. This will give you a starting point and keep you from overdeveloping your content. This list could be in the form of a series of statements or an outline. Make it as detailed as you feel is necessary. Don't forget to list both knowledge and skills.

Here are some examples of prerequisite learning lists. An outline format such as this usually works just fine for this process:

Pilot Training

Main Task: Perform restart procedures in the event of an engine shutdown. Prerequisite skills:

    I. Identify location of engine feather switches

        A. Locate area of control panel

        B. Identify RPM gauges

   II. Recognize engine shutdown

        A. Recognize vibration decrease

        B. Recognize RPM decrease

Nuclear Maintenance Training

Main Task: Check electrical circuit for resistance. Prerequisite skills:

    I. Know how to read flow diagram for test points

        A. Recognize electrical symbols

        B. Calculate resistance levels

   II. Operate a multimeter

        A. Connect a multimeter to a circuit

        B. Read resistance values across points

Computer Technician Training

Main Task: Replace PCMCIA card. Prerequisite skills:

    I. Recognize card problem

        A. Know card location

   II. Remove underhousing of computer

        A. Recognize and utilize card removal tool

Setting prerequisite learning requirements is particularly important in self-instructional formats, in which there is no trainer to help the less experienced catch up, and in technology-based applications, for which it is a key guideline for scripting. It also helps in the development of test items and, of course, in prescreening, if that is part of your training.

Many designers list the prerequisite requirements in both the trainer's and trainee's guides. This helps set trainee expectations and gives the trainer information on what to expect of the trainees when they enter the class.

Other Sources of Content

Other places and methods for collecting content include the following:

- Technical manuals for equipment and processes. These might contain useful diagrams and other visuals as well. Be sure that you get the latest edition, and have an SME look over it for changes or "ways we do things" that are different.

- Existing training that may have material that is related to what your course is about. You might even find useful media such as videos or graphics.

- Quality control manuals that have information about how to do things right—and possibly about why the right way is not being utilized.

- Standardized tests for various professional certifications. Not only is there content here, but if your training leads to certification evaluations you will want to know whether you are preparing your trainees in all the certifiable aspects.

- Observation: you've done it before and you may want to do it now, particularly after you've worked with your SMEs. Watch how the tasks are done on the job. Look for areas of weakness in the content as you now have it described. Ask questions, particularly of new employees, about where they are having problems; then juice up the content in those areas. Find all the gaps in your content in as many ways as you can, then fill them.

 ### Enough Is Enough Is Too Much

You need to be careful, however, that you don't collect too much content. Give yourself a time limit and follow it. We've said that everything can be changed, but don't keep changing everything without ever going on. Choose a point somewhere at which you will stop collecting and begin structuring. Just as there is *analysis paralysis* (when designers never go beyond the analysis process), there is also *content paralysis* (when designers never feel they have all the content they need).

It's hard to say how you will know when enough is enough. It depends mostly on the course itself. However, if you wrote good objectives, based on a good analysis, and you have the information that will allow mastery of the objectives, you have enough content. Time to stop and move on.

ADDING STRUCTURE: THE INSTRUCTIONAL PLAN

Now that you have your content in hand, it is time to add some structure to it. Depending on the delivery method you have chosen, the final product of this structuring process may take the form of a script, storyboard, or lesson plan, or one of a variety of other documents. We'll discuss the creation of some of these later, particularly the lesson plan, as it is one of the most common structures and can be used as a preliminary step in the development of most other formats. However, before you get to this stage you must expand your topical outline and make some preliminary training decisions. As usual, there are a number of documents that may be used for this purpose. We'll focus on a simple one generally termed the *instructional plan*, which may consist of several elements.

Course Maps

Many designers like to create a course map as part of their instructional plan. A course map breaks a course into distinct units of finished training, with introductions, activities, reviews, tests, and so forth. These maps are useful tools for keeping on track as you develop materials and can even be used by the trainees as an overview. They are also important in rapid prototyping, a design shortcut discussed in Chapter Eight. Course maps normally have structure similar to each segment, with the simplest ones usually comprising the following parts:

- Pre-instructional activities
- Introduction
- Information to be presented
- Trainee activities
- Learning assessment
- Post-training evaluation
- Follow-up

Maps can be done in outline format, as a flow chart, or graphically. Maps are not really a necessary step in rapid instructional design, but if you like the concept, use it ("Using Mapping for Course Development," *Info-Line*, 104).

Expanded Outline

Whether you do a course map or not, the next step in developing your instructional plan is to create an expanded content outline if you do not already have one. Depending on how you collected your content and what you put into your design document or other items that you created earlier, you may have already done this.

If not, take the content you have collected and detail it in an outline format. Use the topical outline you already completed and fill in all the A's, B's, 1's, 2's, c's, d's, and so forth, until you have basically run out of content.

While doing an expanded outline, you can also be matching content to objectives. Throw out or least put aside for later any content that does not match up well. This will save you a lot of time later when you'll need to separate the "need to know" from the "nice to know."

Here is an example from a coaching program:

I. The purpose of coaching

   II. The four aspects of coaching

      A. Developmental coaching

         1. Human behavior and associated needs

         2. Wanting to help employees

         3. Skills for development coaching

         4. Corporate development system

         5. Developmental plans

         6. Developmental experiences

         7. Ensuring follow-through

      B. Performance coaching

         1. Performance standards

         2. Organizational obstacles

         3. Motivation

         4. Performance feedback

         5. Skills for performance coaching

         6. The performance improvement plan

      C. Coaching for innovation

         1. Creating a belief that innovation is important

         2. Recognizing innovators

         3. Providing problems for innovators to solve

         4. Teaming up to deal with corporate policy issues

         5. Rewarding innovators

         6. Maintaining innovation

    D. Outside coaching

        1. Team coaching

        2. Expertise coaching

        3. Independent coaching

III. The basic steps of coaching methodology

    A. Establishing a climate of trust

    B. Communicating a willingness to help

    C. Understanding issues from the employee's point of view

    D. Developing a behavioral plan

IV. Personal characteristics of good coaches

    A. Soft-spoken

    B. Articulate

    C. Respectful of employee's needs and concerns

    D. Dedicated to the project and the company

    E. Task and results oriented

V. Common coaching practices

    A. Clarity concerning purpose of activity

    B. Proceeding with tasks in an ethical manner

    C. Committed to the employee as well as the task

    D. Recognizing no limits to possible performance

    E. Being personally responsible for the success of the task and the employee

    F. Being both teacher and learner

    G. Saying what you'll do and doing what you say

VI. Effective coaching behaviors

    A. Skillful observation

    B. Productive analysis

    C. Effective interviewing

    D. Active listening

    E. Positive praise

    F. Constructive criticism

VII. Coaching documentation

In your expanded outline, the Roman numeral items should basically relate to your first-level objectives; the capital letter items should closely mirror your second-level objectives. Everything else is content information that relates to these aspects. This is not a hard-and-fast rule, but it works well most of the time and will particularly help the new designer to keep track of what's going on with the content.

 ## Sequencing

With your raw content more or less determined (but don't forget that everything can be changed), you can now sequence your training to make it as easy as possible for your trainees to use. This will require you to tear apart your outline and put it back together again, based on the type of sequencing you decide to use. One of the advantages of computers for instructional design is that they make this process relatively simple: just cut and paste the various blocks. In fact, it's so easy that you might want to try a couple of different sequencing methods to determine which one seems to work best. Here are a few ways to sequence:

- *General to Specific:* Start with an overview and present the whole, then break it up into its component parts. This is one of the more common sequencing methods.

- *Simple to Complex:* Start with the simplest tasks and work your way up to multitask complexity.

- *Known to Unknown:* Start with what you know the trainees know and use this as a base to move into what they do not know.

- *Problem-Solution:* Start with a problem and arrange your content to come to a solution.

There are a number of other ways to sequence, but most of them are simple offshoots of these five.

 Another sequencing possibility is what I term the *logical sequence.* Basically, you look at your outline and say this should be taught first, this second, and so on, based on your own content knowledge (or, if you are not an expert, based on your SME's experience). This is not necessarily the most scientific approach, but it usually works, and if you are uncomfortable with the outcome you can always fall back on one of the more standard sequencing methods.

One other comment on sequencing: you do not necessarily have to stay with one type of sequencing throughout your program. One unit of training may lend itself to a time sequence, while another is perfect for a problem-solution sequence. The important point is that you take a little time to ask yourself: "In what order can this material be best presented to make it easiest for the trainees to learn?"

Training Activities

Your sequenced expanded outline becomes the skeleton for your instructional plan. The next step is to note the training activities you want to add that make a training program out of a mass of content. Following are some things you may want to include, presented in the order in which they would appear in your instructional plan.

Pre-Instructional Activities

These are aspects—like pre-readings, instruments, meetings with supervisors, questions to answer, or other specialized activities—that the trainee can do before attending class. You might use these to gain the trainees' attention, motivate them, explain class prerequisites, present initial information, or discuss class objectives, and for many other purposes.

One thing pre-instructional activities do is to shorten the time needed in class. In fact, many designers develop entire self-instructional packages to be done before a class for this specific purpose. Knowledge-type information is provided in the self-instruction, then review, activities, and evaluation are done in class. This mixing of delivery methods, which we discussed earlier, allows you to create a shorter class or a less expensive and time-intensive self-instructional package, or both. One word of caution, though: you should decide on this approach during your delivery analysis. Waiting until now to say, "Hey, I could do it this way" will probably mean a lot of backtracking and fill work to get your design to where you need it to be to take advantage of mixed delivery systems.

With the advent of e-learning, there is a lot more mixing of delivery formats going on. Self-instructional e-learning (asynchronous e-learning) delivery of basic content, followed by live classroom sessions or even computer-mediated live classes (synchronous e-learning), is being used in many organizations. Throw in some chat room or bulletin board structures and it's getting to the point in some of these systems where it is hard to tell where the pre-work ends and the class begins.

Introductions

An introduction tells the trainee what is coming in the course. It is also a good tool for notifying the trainee that a change in what is being presented is about to occur. You might want to use an introduction at the start of your instructional plan or at any point in the unit of instruction at which an important change is imminent.

We'll discuss introductions in more detail in the next chapter.

Pre-Tests

A pre-test is a common training activity often found in an instructional plan. Pre-tests have a number of uses. Of the five common uses, the two most common are (1) to measure the amount of learning that takes place, by being paired with a post-test, and (2) to test out of a learning program or parts of a program; the other common uses are (3) to assess what the trainee already knows as a prerequisite to attending a class (that is, to prequalify them for a class), (4) to assess what the trainees already know to help the trainer in facilitating the class, and (5) to inform the trainee about what will be in the class.

Because each of these uses has a different purpose or end result, you'll want to consider carefully why you want to use a pre-test before developing one. You do not need to develop your pre-tests at this time. Actual test creation can be done during the material development phase, when you have completed the plan and are sure the pieces are right. However, you should determine why or whether you are going to use a pre-test and what type you will use, and place that information in your instructional plan now.

One possible disadvantage of pre-tests is that some trainees do not like to be tested; in fact, they may actually be afraid of tests. This can alter the results you get from your pre-test and send trainees off in an entirely wrong direction or reduce their motivation. This is particularly true if your content is highly performance based—such as teaching the use of a machine—or involves a major hands-on process. In these cases, a paper-and-pencil pre-test may do more harm than good, as it could say to the trainees: "This training is all talk and no action."

Be sure that you know why you are including a pre-test in your instructional plan, that it makes sense for this particular lesson, and that the test itself reflects your purpose. Like everything else in instructional design, don't do pre-testing simply because you like the idea or because "everyone else does it."

Trainee-Centered Activities

Any well-designed training should have plenty of trainee activities. These should be noted as well in your instructional plan. Once again, you will not want to develop the activities this early in the process, but you can start to make decisions on what they might be and where you want to place them. The two key issues for all activities are that they (1) must directly relate to the objectives and (2) must provide the trainees with feedback or information about their performance.

A list of many of the most common trainee-centered activities can be found in Chapter Five. Use it to help plan which activities you want to put where in your instructional plan.

Instructional Games

One specialized type of trainee activity that can be used to great effect in your training is the instructional game. These devices can be entertaining as well as informative, and they allow trainees to test their knowledge and skills in various types of environments. Some of the more popular ones can be found in Chapter Five. Design them into your instructional plan now and develop them later, once you are sure that everything fits—especially in light of the fact that activities in general, and particularly games, can use up large amounts of time.

Testing

An entire subset of training activities revolves around testing. In your instructional plan you will need to decide on the types and forms of tests that you will include. Like objectives, tests can measure knowledge or performance—and sometimes both. However, like objectives, it is usually better to keep them separate, as the testing format is often different for each of the processes. Remember that the tests themselves, and the test questions in particular, must relate directly to the objectives.

We have already discussed pre-tests. Other types of tests includes embedded tests, which can be placed anywhere in a instructional plan, and post-tests, which are usually found at the end of your instructional plan.

Embedded Tests. Embedded tests usually follow a small but complete piece of training and are normally used to assess what the trainees have learned from that particular area. Often they are used as summary activities. They can be oral or written and can be as short as one question or as long as needed.

In self-instructional programs, these tests are found at the end of an instructional unit and are usually self-administered. The outcome tells the trainees whether they have mastered the material in that unit or not. In more complex self-instructional programs, these embedded tests can lead to remedial branches that present the material in a different way, thus giving the trainees another method to achieve mastery.

Post-Tests. Most training includes some form of post-test. The purpose of these tests is to pinpoint what learning has and has not occurred for each trainee. Two key thoughts for post-testing are (1) the questions must be *criterion referenced* (more about this in the next section), and (2) they must provide some type of feedback. Your instructional plan should leave time for going over the post-test to discuss missed answers and concepts.

Information from post-tests can also be used to determine what areas of training have to be revised. This is done by looking at the questions that were frequently missed and determining whether the training was not as complete or in-depth as it should have been. This might also simply indicate that the test question was poor, in which case it will need to be rewritten. This process is termed *item analysis*.

As we noted in our discussion of pre-tests, the main disadvantage of other forms of testing is the fear that tests invoke in some people. Also, testing can be affected by the health of the trainee, which is a problem when a test is used to determine whether mastery has occurred for certification or for continuing in a job.

Summaries

Summaries allow you to restate the key concepts in a piece of training and reemphasize their importance. Many designers add summaries at the end of their instructional plans, but good designers put them throughout the training to aid in understanding and retention of key issues. Summaries can also help in the transition from one topic to another by saying: "We're going to move to something new, but let's make sure you understand the previous material before we do."

A well-thought-out series of summaries can actually provide a structure for your trainees to learn within, as each summary builds on the last.

Summaries can be straightforward talk or discussion, can be built around activities, or can be self-instructional, depending on what you as the designer feel will work best for any piece of content. They often restate objectives or learning goals and can even include thoughts on where to find more information on this particular aspect of the instruction. You might use an embedded test as a summary to help the trainees measure their knowledge gain or their change in performance and even to rank the trainees in relation to these changes to increase motivation.

There is no good rule for how many summaries to put in your instructional plan or where they should go. Just remember that they are important in your trainees' mastering of the topic, and put them where it feels right.

Post-Class Activities

The last aspect of an instructional plan is to add in activities for the trainees to do after the class. This is not always appropriate, but should at least be considered each time you create an instructional plan. There are two good reasons for including post-class activities: (1) to increase retention and (2) to help transfer the learning to the job. Well-designed post-class activities can actually become an evaluation of the effectiveness of your training.

Post-class activities can be as simple as an activity report sent back to you sixty or ninety days after the training that states how the trainees have used what they learned, or as complicated as an action plan with goals and objectives to be accomplished back on the job. These plans are often shared with and evaluated by the trainees' supervisors or by third parties.

Interviews, questionnaires, or long-term post-tests are other types of post-class activities that are used, although these are more evaluative than activity-based, unless they are very well designed.

Chunking

One final thought on instructional plans. All of these activities, summaries, structuring, sequencing, and so forth, mean that what you are doing is dividing your content into smaller and smaller parts. This process is called *chunking*. The idea of chunking is to break down the mass of content you have collected into pieces that are easy for your trainees to digest—that is, to learn.

There are many schools of thought on how big a chunk should be. Some designers contend that one objective equals one chunk; others say that a chunk should contain a maximum of three objectives, or four, or five. After our discussion on objectives, you may already realize that a lot of this depends on the level at which you are writing the objectives.

As is true for other ID processes, I don't think there is any hard-and-fast rule on chunking. Your responsibility as a good designer is to know that chunking is important—and then to simply ask yourself how much of this material should be covered before you design in an activity, or a summary, or a test, or one of the other processes that sets a boundary to a chunk. You may even want to factor in time, considering that ten or fifteen minutes is about the top attention span for your trainees before they stop listening and need to do something else. Once you have chunked, have at least one other person review your instructional plan and give you feedback on the size and complexity of your chunks.

TRAINEE EVALUATION (TEST QUESTIONS AND TESTS)

This may seem like a strange place to talk about test questions. After all, in our instructional plan we've already designed in things like embedded tests and pre-tests and post-tests; maybe even a second post-test as part of a follow-up activity. Actually, there is no one good (or for that matter bad) place to talk about tests in instructional design. The process is so integral a part of designing any training that it fits just about everywhere.

One place that creating trainee evaluations does not fit is just before you use them, which is often the exact point at which they are developed. Test questions, and the tests that they make up, are much too important to be done as afterthoughts. They should be developed as a part of your design process, not long after you've finalized your objectives. Any good test question must relate directly back to an objective of the training, so it is efficient to write test questions while the objectives are fresh in your mind. Let me repeat that any good test question must relate directly back to one of the objectives you have already developed for your training. This is not a "nice to do" or a "should do," but a must do. Anything less is not acceptable!

Relate Test Questions to Objectives

There are a lot of good reasons to relate test questions to objectives, but two of them are most important. First, it is not fair to your trainees if they don't relate to the objectives; second, you will never be able to show that your training is valid if they aren't related.

Be Fair to Your Trainees

Let's take the first reason first. I'm sure that any number of times in your schooling you sat down to take a test and had no idea what the teacher was asking for. Now, this could have been because you didn't study (my usual reason), but it might have been because you didn't study the right things; that is, you missed what the teacher felt was important. As we discussed, with good objectives written at the right levels and distributed to the trainees, this should not happen, unless the test questions do not reflect the objectives.

Get the picture? The test questions you develop must relate to the objectives you tell your trainees are important. Otherwise, you are being unfair to them. Remember the "trick" questions that your old history teacher used to use on her tests? As a good instructional designer, forget them. Remember those one or two "special" questions that separate the A's from the B's? Good instructional designers don't use them.

Good test questions are straightforward and based on the objectives. If the trainees mastered what was asked in the objectives, they should answer all the questions right. This is what we referred to earlier as mastery learning, and this process of matching questions to objectives is termed criterion-based testing.

Criterion-Based Testing

The second reason for basing your questions on the course objectives is that otherwise you cannot know whether the trainees learned what your analysis told you they needed to learn and what the objectives based on that analysis said they should learn (*Criterion-Referenced Test Development* by Shrock & Coscarelli, 1989). Unless your questions reflect your objectives, you won't know whether your training worked or was a good use of company resources.

Criterion-based testing brings up many other issues, not the least of which is the time and expertise needed to create good test questions. But I hope that you can see why it is so important and worth the time. I know you have heard this before, but in the end criterion-based testing will actually save you time. As you become experienced at developing these questions and having them ready for any type of evaluation that you need, your test development and course evaluation will become exponentially more efficient.

To give you a little help, here is a list of objectives and supposedly criterion-referenced questions based on them. See if you can figure out which ones are criterion referenced and which ones are not.

Objectives

1. SOLVE for total power in a given DC parallel circuit, given values for any two of the following:

   current

   voltage

   resistance

   The answer will be accurate to two places.

2. LIST the sequence of steps for setting up and connecting a multimeter to test a transistor's resistance.

3. Given the necessary tools and an operator's manual, SET UP a double-acting reciprocating pump in five minutes, according to the manual specification.

4. STATE the rule for finding total inductance in a series circuit.

5. Given any resistor with four-color bands, DETERMINE the ohmic value as indicated by the color bands.

6. LIST the steps of the procedure for message reception as listed in NTP-4.

7. STATE the four classifications of call signals.

8. USE the principle of electromagnetic induction to describe the operation of an AC generator. The description must contain the following points. . . .

9. RECOGNIZE the five functions of the reactor vessel.

10. Given a circuit diagram and decade box setting, CALCULATE the internal DC resistance of the electrical circuit with a wheatstone bridge.

Test Questions

1. In the circuit below, the current and voltage are given. Calculate for total power. Your answer should be two decimal places.

2. The sequence of steps for setting up and connecting a multimeter to test the resistance of a transistor can be reversed when using an Ames omnimeter.

3. Using your operator's manual, describe the necessary steps for setup of a double-acting reciprocating pump. You will pass this test if you complete this task within five minutes, in accordance with the manual specifications.

4. In the space below, write the correct rule for finding total inductance in a series circuit.

5. For each of the resistors pictured below, find the value in ohms and write the value in the space next to the resistor.

6. The steps of the procedure for message reception include which of the following?

picking up the phone

writing message

hanging up phone

all of the above

7. For each of the call signals listed below, write the type in the space provided.

8. For each of the following sets of parameters, describe whether an AC generator will function in terms of the principle of electromagnetic induction.

9. The five functions of the reactor vessel are

_____

_____

_____

_____

_____

10. In this circuit diagram, the resistance is calculated at 30 ohms, the decade box is set on 30 ohm, galvanometer reads zero, and Rx = 350 ohms. Could a wheatstone bridge be used as the resistor?

Answer Key

1. Criterion referenced

2. The objective asks to list, the question is more analysis—of the procedure, the instrument, and the outcome

3. The objective requires a performance, which cannot be evaluated by a test question

4. Criterion referenced

5. Criterion referenced

6. The objectives asks for a list, not to recognize a term as this multiple choice question requires

7. The objective asks for classifications, not types

8. The objective asks for a description, the test question for analysis

9. The objective asks to recognize, not to list

10. The objective asks for a calculation, but the question gives the calculation and asks for analysis

You may have picked up on another issue here. Because you have different types of objectives, you will have different types of test questions—and even different types of tests. If your objectives are knowledge-based, the good old paper-and-pencil type of tests will work well, but if the objectives are performance-based, your tests will need to be set in a performance scenario. You will have a difficult time writing a paper-and-pencil test question for an objective that says: "The trainee will be able to utilize a paper cutter to cut each of twelve pieces of paper into two equal pieces."

 Performance Checklists. The simple answer to this problem is a different type of test, called a *performance checklist* or *criterion checklist* ("Comprehensive Open Skill Test Design" by Desmedt, 1991). With this type of testing instrument, the trainee is asked to perform a task or series of tasks, usually after being instructed on how to do so and having practiced in a real or simulated environment. The checklist lists the task or tasks and gives the evaluator a place to check whether they were completed properly. More detailed checklists provide the evaluator with specific criteria concerning the tasks that they should be observing—and even ratios of how often each should be observed per component. The complexity of your checklist will be dependent on the complexity of the task and the expertise of the evaluator.

If your evaluators will always be SMEs, they won't need much guidance in proper task completion. Simply provide a checklist of what they will observe.

However, if the evaluator has only limited knowledge or if the person's expertise may be suspect, you'll need more detailed criteria on your performance checklist.

Each checklist should include directions for the evaluator, concerning how and where to evaluate the performance and a place for both the evaluator and the trainee to sign showing that mastery has been demonstrated. Here are some examples of simple performance checklists:

TRAINER CERTIFICATION CHECKLIST

Task Area: Instructional Design

Objective: To utilize effective techniques in assessing training needs and planning a course of instruction.

The candidate has submitted evidence that he or she is able to:

☐ Create a summary document for a training needs assessment

    ☐ Effectively determine the items that must be investigated for a training request

    ☐ Utilize proper data-collection methods to determine required and actual performance for items in a training needs assessment

    ☐ Determine possible causes of performance deficiencies

    ☐ Determine possible benefits of improved performance in training situations

    ☐ Recommend the type(s) of training that should be used

    ☐ Recommend management support processes for specific training situations

    ☐ Produce a training needs assessment narrative that can be used to further the training design and development process

☐ Perform accurate cost analysis for training programs

☐ Perform accurate benefits analysis for training programs

☐ Determine ROI for training programs and make accurate decisions concerning continuing their development

☐ Create an effective and complete list of constraints for specific training programs

☐ Develop a proper work plan checklist for the design of a course of instruction

_____   _____
(Master Trainer's Signature)   (Candidate's Signature)

OPERATIONS DEPARTMENT FINAL CHECKLIST

Directions: This checklist is to be used by the evaluator to check the trainee's ability to perform the tasks related to a particular objective. The trainer should observe the trainee performing each of the listed tasks, either in a real-life or simulated situation, and have the trainee discuss the items that are not observable tasks. Check the task as being completed only if the trainee has satisfactorily mastered it. If the trainee has not mastered a particular task, the trainee should be coached by the trainer, given time to practice, and then observed again. When all tasks on this checklist are completed, both the trainer and trainee should sign the document.

Objective 1: Utilize the computer system to perform the computer-mediated functions of the operations department

The trainee can:

☐ Discuss how the computer system affects the company in general

☐ Compare the purpose and uses of Novell and UNIX

☐ Describe how specific departments interface with the computer system

☐ Log on to the computer correctly

☐ Log off of the computer correctly

☐ Navigate through the computer system efficiently

☐ Compare the system specifics and interactions of ATRS and TRIMS

☐ Input data as needed for the operations department

☐ Extract data from the system as needed for the operations department

These tasks have been practiced, observed, and mastered.

_____   _____
(Manager's Signature)   (Trainee's Signature)

Another type of performance checklist is based directly on the objectives. Here is an example of a template that you can use for this type of checklist. Note that this is not an all-or-none (or what we called mastery) process but has gradations of successful completion.

OBJECTIVE CHECKLIST

Reviewer: _____   Trainee: _____

Course: _____   Date: _____

Objective	Performance	Comments
	☐ Exceeded expectations ☐ Met expectations ☐ Below required level	
	☐ Exceeded expectations ☐ Met expectations ☐ Below required level	
	☐ Exceeded expectations ☐ Met expectations ☐ Below required level	
	☐ Exceeded expectations ☐ Met expectations ☐ Below required level	
	☐ Exceeded expectations ☐ Met expectations ☐ Below required level	

Question Banks

In good instructional design, the trainee evaluation questions are always developed well ahead of the actual evaluation, with a minimum of one question—and preferably two or three—written for each objective. This allows you time to have each question carefully reviewed by both an SME for content reliability and another instructional designer to determine whether the question is properly written and directly relates to an objective.

Having your questions written and reviewed ahead of time allows you to simply pull questions from what will become your *question bank* for whatever testing procedure you need. Have you designed in an embedded test after objective five has been facilitated? Pull from your question bank one question for each of the first five objectives, and you have your embedded test. Did you decide on a pre-test for the purpose of testing trainees out of the first class? Take one question for each knowledge objective covered in the first class and put them together as a written pre-test. Now take the performances for the three objectives that are performance-based and make a checklist from them. Add these together and you have a comprehensive, valid test-out procedure.

The time savings I mentioned earlier comes in here. Instead of creating a new test for each class, you only have to go to your question bank and pick and choose. This is also great if you have large numbers of trainees in multiple classes and you don't want the answers to be shared. It works splendidly for self-instructional packages as well or for remedial testing.

Thoughts on Testing and Test Questions. Here are some thoughts on the importance of testing and on the development of various types of tests and test questions (*Test Construction for Training Evaluation* by Denova, 1979).

- Criterion testing provides a trail from job analysis to trainee evaluation that supports both certification and legal justification

- Writing test questions can serve as a check of the completeness and accuracy of both your objectives and your content before it is seen by the trainees

- Tests can save valuable employee time by preselecting only those who need the training

- Tests can help the designer or the trainer determine what content areas need further emphasis

- Tests can help course designers evaluate the effectiveness of the course and make revisions where necessary

- Create at least two test questions for each objective and develop a question bank that you can draw on when you need a test

There are actually two major aspects to developing test questions. First, are they fair? We make sure of this by criterion referencing all our test questions, and any other trainee evaluation as well for that matter.

The second aspect is, are they fairly written? This aspect engenders a lot of controversy, as there are about as many rules for writing test questions as there are people writing them. The following chart contains more information on specific rules for developing various types of test questions.

These rules are not set in stone; there are many others and often they disagree with the ones stated here. These are simply the rules that I use most often. The final decision, as always in instructional design, lies with you, the designer.

DESIGNING IN VARIOUS TESTING FORMATS

Multiple Choice Format

Characteristics   An item with two or more responses, one of which clearly provides the "best answer"

Stem identifies question or poses problem

Alternatives are responses

Trainee selects best answer

Advantages   Can measure all levels of cognitive ability

Effective to administer and score

Provides objective measurement of achievement (either right or wrong)

Allows wider sample of subject matter (covers a great deal in a short time)

Limitations   Difficult and time-consuming to construct

Leads exam writer to favor simple recall of facts (no real depth)

Hints for Stem Construction   Write as direct question rather than incomplete statement

Pose definite, explicit, and singular problem

Do not include unnecessary verbiage or irrelevant information

Include any words that might otherwise be repeated in each alternate

Emphasize negatives (if you use them at all)

Alternatives   Make plausible to less skilled trainee

Make stem and all alternatives grammatically consistent

When possible, presented in logical order

Present only one correct or best response to each item

Make of approximately equal length

Avoid clues that give away answer

- Grammatical clues, as "a" versus "an"
- Verbal association
- Connection between stem and answer

	Use at least four alternatives
	Randomly distribute correct response positions
	Avoid "none of the above" and "all of the above"
	Do not use item and alternatives to measure trainee opinion
Example	"Which of the following is the formula for Ohm's Law?"

a. I = 2RI   c. I = RE

c. R⁻= IE   d. E = IR

True/False Format

Characteristics	A two-choice item in which only one of the responses is absolutely correct
	Complete declarative sentence
Advantages	Allows widest sampling of subject matter per unit of time (big number in unit of time)
	Effectively administered and scored
	Objective measurement of achievement
Limitations	Extremely high guess factor (50 percent right versus 50 percent wrong)
	Leads exam writer to favor testing of trivial knowledge
	Exam writer often writes ambiguous statements when testing higher levels of cognitive skill, due to difficulty in writing unequivocally true/false statements
Hints for Construction	Base items on statements that are absolutely true or false, without qualifications or exceptions
	Write statement as simply and clearly as possible
	Express single idea in each item
	Avoid lifting statements from text, lecture, or other materials so that memory alone will not permit correct answer
	Avoid use of negatively stated items
	Avoid use of unfamiliar vocabulary
	Avoid use of specific words
	• Usually, sometimes, often (likely to be true)
Example	True or False: "Foam is the most effective agent for extinguishing a Class A fire adjacent to the containment building."

Matching Format

Characteristics

A list of conditions, a list of responses, and directions for matching the conditions to the responses

Trainee matches correct items between lists

Advantages

Efficient to administer and score

Objective measurement of achievement

Allows for fairly wide sample of subject matter

Limitations

Difficult to write items that measure more than simple recall

Difficult to select common set of conditions and responses

Hints for Construction

Include clear directions

Explain basis for matching items

State whether or not a response can be used more than once

Use same types of material, i.e., lists of like nature or kind

Make the list of responses longer (or shorter) than the list of conditions

Place the responses in the right column and in a logical order (alpha or numeric)

Avoid grammatical clues

Keep items and total number of items brief

Example

"Match the abnormal control rod drive flow conditions in the left column with the cause in the right column."

Conditions	Possible Cause
High flow	Air problem
Low flow	Directional
Zero flow	Solenoid problem

Completion Format

Characteristics

An item that requires the trainee to complete the sentence or write the answer to a question in a few words

Statement with usually one or more blanks to be completed

Advantages

Series of well-constructed completion/short answer items can measure knowledge similar to essay test items and with more consistency

Allows wide sampling

Minimizes guessing as compared to multiple choice or true/false

Efficiently measures lower levels of cognitive ability

Usually provides measure of achievement

Limitations	Difficult to construct so that desired response is indicated
	Typically limited to measurement of simple recall
	Possibility of containing more irrelevant clues as compared to other item types
	Takes longer to score than previously mentioned format types
	Improper preparation of item can lead to more than one correct answer
Hints for Construction	Omit only insignificant words
	Do not omit so many words that meaning is lost
	Avoid grammatical clues
	Make sure only one brief, correct response is possible
	Make blanks equal in length
	Multiple answer blanks should be avoided
	The main idea should precede the blank (blank at the end of the statement)
	Blanks should require key words
	Answer called for should be clear to the trainee
Example	"The function of total flow indicators is to provide _____ ."

Essay Format

Characteristics	Question to which trainee is expected to demonstrate ability to:
	• Recall facts
	• Organize facts
	• Present facts in logical, integrated answer
	May be either extended response or short answer
Advantages	Easier and less time-consuming to construct as compared to other types
	Provides means for testing trainees' ability to compose answer and present in logical manner
Limitations	Limits amount of subject matter that can be covered by exam
	Extensive amount of time required to score, delaying feedback to trainee

	Subjective measure of achievement due to possible bias on part of grader
Hints for Construction	Use questions that can be answered in a short time and space
	Question should be specific, phrased so trainee will be able to answer
	For questions requiring lengthy response, indicate in outline form information desired
	Prepare in advance scoring key that shows acceptable responses and relative weights
Example	"In the space below, describe in terms of the principle of electromagnetic induction how an AC generator works. Your answer should include the following points:"

Here's an exercise to help you determine whether questions are fairly written. Be sure to use the rules we just discussed or your answers won't match mine.

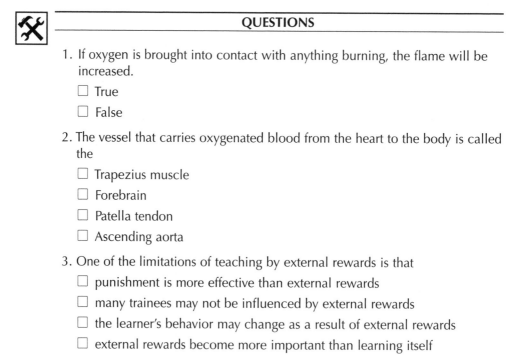

QUESTIONS

1. If oxygen is brought into contact with anything burning, the flame will be increased.
   ☐ True
   ☐ False

2. The vessel that carries oxygenated blood from the heart to the body is called the
   ☐ Trapezius muscle
   ☐ Forebrain
   ☐ Patella tendon
   ☐ Ascending aorta

3. One of the limitations of teaching by external rewards is that
   ☐ punishment is more effective than external rewards
   ☐ many trainees may not be influenced by external rewards
   ☐ the learner's behavior may change as a result of external rewards
   ☐ external rewards become more important than learning itself

4. Match the state with its capital city.

Alabama	Montgomery
California	Lansing
Indiana	Harrisburg
Michigan	Indianapolis
Minnesota	Los Angeles
North Carolina	Madison
Pennsylvania	Milwaukee
	Minneapolis
	Philadelphia
	Raleigh
	Sacramento
	St. Paul

5. Who discovered America? _____

6. _____ encourages the _____ of trainees' prior skill knowledge when developing and _____ learning objective.

7. After _____ second(s), the static type ABT will commence shifting from the normal source to the emergency source of power when a failure or reduction of voltage is sustained.

8. Resistance is measured by an:
   ☐ Voltmeter
   ☐ Wattmeter
   ☐ Oscilloscope
   ☐ Ohmmeter

9. Resistance cannot be measure by a (an):
   ☐ Oscilloscope
   ☐ Multimeter
   ☐ Ohmmeter
   ☐ Galvanometer

10. List the six trigonometric functions.

   _____   _____

   _____   _____

   _____   _____

Answer Key

1. Fairly written question.

2. Distracters are poor, as none are blood vessels.

3. OK, but get the repeated words out of the distracters and into the stem.

4. OK, but possibly too many choices in right-hand list.

5. So little information in the question that there could be a number of correct answers.

6. Too many blanks and too confusing for learner to really show knowledge.

7. OK, but try to position the blank near the end of the question.

8. The "an" makes some answers grammatically incorrect.

9. The negative word should be emphasized with boldface or italic.

10. Fairly written question.

Tests that are created from well-written questions will allow your trainees to prove their mastery of your objectives and allow you to prove the effectiveness of your program. But you must develop your questions properly, relating them directly to your objectives and what the objectives require. Create questions that fit the level of knowledge or performance of your objectives.

After you have designed your questions, a rapid design shortcut is to create a series of tests at various levels and to distribute them to the trainees along with the objectives they are based on. Explain to your trainees that they are responsible for mastering the tests, using their own initiative and finding their own resources. You might take this approach further by providing incentives for trainees for each level that they master. This shortcut will eliminate the need for you to develop instructional plans, lesson plans, and training materials.

Now that you have written your questions, you have finished the design component of instructional design. Your basic products are a decision on a delivery system, good objectives, an instructional plan of some type, and a bank of criterion-referenced test questions. All of these directly relate to the tasks to be trained on that you developed through your assessment and analysis activities. It's now time to take what you have done so far and create an actual training program, with content, activities, tests, and all the other things that are important aspects of good training. This is the instructional design component of development, and it's next.

HINTS FOR DESIGNING IN VARIOUS FORMATS
Classroom

- Plan your classroom design so all your trainees are at the same level of knowledge before the class begins. This requires a combination of good trainee analysis, pre-testing, and pre-work. Self-instructional technology-based training programs are a particularly good way to deliver this pre-work and bring everyone up to speed before class begins.

- For interpersonal skills, think classroom delivery first if your environment allows it.

On-the-Job Training (Job Aids)

- In OJT the costs increase in direct proportion to the number of trainees. This is not true in classroom training or self-instruction.
- Try to match your OJT trainers and trainees in regard to background, attitudes, language, and age, if possible.
- OJT is usually not a good approach in start-up situations.
- A simplified OJT design:

  Step 1: Prepare the trainer, the trainee, and the course material.

  Step 2: Tell the trainee what is to be done.

  Step 3: Show the trainee how it is done.

  Step 4: Allow the trainee to practice under supervision.

  Step 5: Evaluate the trainee under normal working conditions.

  Step 6: Provide transitional support as needed.

Thoughts on OJT or any type of one-on-one training:

Unlike in the classroom, there is no learning from peers

The trainer cannot be seen as the guru with all the answers

Tell, show, do, and let them make mistakes

Answer questions with "What do you think?" when possible, then say "OK, try it." And if it doesn't work, ask "What do you think went wrong?"

Trainer guides need to be minimal outline formats so the trainer remembers not to talk too much

Trainee guides need to be more complete, with plenty of job aids

Evaluations are often of the case study or problem-solving variety

You'll need deeper audience analysis when you have an audience of one

Build in more questions to check progress

When training one-on-one trainers, you can focus on basic communications skills as in a classroom, then give them lots of one-on-one practice

Here's a five-step approach to training with job aids:

1. Design it right
2. Explain to your learners what it is and isn't
3. Train them on how to use it (tell, show, do)
4. Let them practice using it
5. Evaluate them using it

Self-Instruction

- Self-instruction requires a higher level of motivation on the part of the trainees. Reconsider its use if your analysis indicates the trainees are not motivated.
- Use when concepts must be taught "just in time" to a large number of trainees.
- Use this checklist when planning a distance (distributed) self-instructional approach:
  - ☐ Facilitators have been determined
  - ☐ Control measures have been planned
  - ☐ Distribution hardware (if any) has been analyzed
  - ☐ Reproduction costs have been considered
  - ☐ Programs have job-specific activities as possible
  - ☐ Introduction, distribution, and revision costs have been considered
  - ☐ A plan for trainee preparation has been developed
- Use this checklist when planning a self-instructional learning center:
  - ☐ Designate a room or area that will be used only as your center
  - ☐ Hire and train a full-time facilitator
  - ☐ Be sure your center is in a central location
  - ☐ Be sure that a learning center will best meet the needs of the trainees and the training
  - ☐ Acquire the necessary funding to start and run the center
  - ☐ Look for shortcuts through the use of off-the-shelf programs
  - ☐ Create a good learning center selling plan
    - ☐ A critical need has been isolated
    - ☐ The center's main purpose has been defined

☐ The main users have been defined

☐ Center mechanics have been considered

☐ Cost has been estimated

☐ Integration with the current training system has been defined

☐ An effective presentation with concrete examples has been developed

Computer and CD-ROM-Based Training (TBT)

Use this type of training when

- There are a lot of repetitive actions in your training
- The performance conditions are hard to replicate
- Visualization and extended practice are important
- The program will be given often over a long period of time
- The audience is large or distributed widely
- Tracking of trainee evaluation is critical, such as in a regulated or certification environment
- Familiarization with equipment is important, but the equipment is not available

Course Treatment for Computer- and CD-ROM–Based Training
For this type of delivery system you might want to describe the look and feel of the course to your clients, material developers, and programmers. Items you may put in your treatment include the following:

- Course goal and major objectives
- Audience
- Theme (what the course will "feel" like)
- Tone (the course mood: formal, informal, down-to-earth, serious, fun)
- The environment or background for the course (where, when, what is going on)

Be sure to match the look and feel of the course's work environment to your audience's work space.

- Information about the main characters, such as
  - Personality
  - Speech habits

- Expressions
- Occupations

- Music style, if any

- Program colors (if you're not sure about colors, start with your corporate colors or ask an artist, but consistently use a single color scheme; watch the use of color cues, as some people are color-blind)

- The pace of the program (fast and furious, slow and deliberate, build slowly, or hit them between the eyes right away; use a faster pace when tasks are time-sensitive or involve risk; use a slow pace when "doing it right" and "being sure" are key issues)

- The point of view of key characters (first, second, or third person)

Design Hints for Computer/CD-ROM-Based Training

- Be politically correct or you will lose part of your audience
- Humor is good, but not if it offends
- Format your graphics so they follow the same pattern
- Don't change your user interface in midstream
- Use flow charts to detail interactions, branching, and other trainee-centered activities (flow charts also help when it's time to do a course revision.)

Course Overview for Computer/CD-ROM-Based Training

- This course overview functions in the same way as a course overview in a stand-up training class. You might include the following items in your course overview:
  - A description of the icons that will be found in the course
  - An example of how to navigate through the course
  - Testing and mastery requirements
  - The method for keeping course completion records
  - An introduction to the course tone, theme, and pace
  - A sampling of the music, graphics, and environment found in the program
  - An activity to capture the trainees' attention and make them comfortable with the program
  - If using a CD-ROM delivery, take advantage of its ability to administer high-level simulation-type test questions and branched testing

- Use the click-and-drag method to test for assembly processes and relationships

- Get double duty from your CD-ROM (or other technology-based) program by expanding the navigational possibilities and training your trainers on how to jump from place to place in the program when using it as instructional media in their stand-up or OJT training

- For multiple-language environments, CD-ROM–based programs provide easy translation if designed properly

- Branched CD-ROM is a good system for training in which the range of entry-level knowledge is great

Synchronous and Asynchronous E-Learning

The following points have been gleaned from many sources, including Margaret Driscoll's "Defining Internet-Based and Web-Based Training" (1997) and Brandon Hall's *Web-Based Training Cookbook* (1998). If you need to explore these formats further, see chapters Nine and Ten.

- Make sure you have a very good relationship with your IS department before attempting this type of delivery

- Trainees won't last long if your site is slow

- Trainees will also "bug out" if they don't see the relevance of the content

- Trainees won't even start if the navigation is hard to understand

- Test the user interface and its capabilities before developing your training

Here are ten things to consider when choosing an asynchronous delivery process:

- Do you have the expertise to maintain the content and structure of your website?

- Does your organization have a help desk to take calls dealing with technical issues?

- Do you need to install a training tracking system as part of the delivery? (The answer here should almost always be yes.)

- Can you install necessary plug-ins or other augmentations to the employees' computers?

- Are you prepared to help your trainees become efficient users of on-the-desktop training?

- Can you control your trainees' use of the technology (such as limiting web surfing)?

- Are the necessary media (video, animations, and so on) too complex for an e-learning delivery?

- Is there a concern about confidentiality of content?

- Does your organization have the basic technology in place?

- Do you have the technical skills to quickly update material if necessary?

You can do a simple form of synchronous e-learning by using your company's intranet and a conference telephone call. Develop activities that can be pulled off the server, discuss via the conference call facility, and share information by exchanging files. In this approach you can divide your class into teams and even small groups, directing them to call each other, then later bringing them all back on one conference call. This process will work asynchronously too.

You'll need the following software for your e-learning programs:

- Authoring, to create the content system

- Graphics, to convert graphics to net formats

- Server, to run the system

- Middleware, to translate databases to a net format

These are the levels of e-learning:

- Level 1: Communications. Done between trainer and trainee, possibly by e-mail or a chat room

- Level 2: Reference. Online libraries of technical documentation, articles, and course catalogs

- Level 3: Assessment. Online needs assessment, surveys, or trainee testing

- Level 4: Distribution. Training modules that are available from a central server for downloading to remote computers, then used as CBT

- Level 5: Delivery. Interactive real-time programming

Satellite-Based Training and Other Telephonic Formats

See Mantyla and Gividen's *Distance Learning* (1997) for an especially helpful discussion of this type of training.

- Be sure that you have a facilitator who knows, or is willing to be taught, on-camera training techniques.

- To add more interaction to your programs, plan to have SMEs available on the phone, but not as part of the broadcast, to answer trainee questions off camera. This works well for satellite-based programs, teleconferencing, and even synchronous computer-based classrooms. For satellite-based programs, it's also good to have a way for the off-camera expert to signal the on-camera talent if there is a particularly relevant question so that it can be put on the air.

- By mounting a document camera to a laptop in a video teleconference, you can broadcast what is on the trainer's screen to the various training sites. It's not pretty, but it works, and it's cheap.

- If you have a few more dollars, you can buy software—for example, one called Timbuktu (www.netopia.com/software)—that allows a trainer to access trainee computers remotely and even manipulate files on remote systems.

Chapter 5

Doing It Right: Development

This chapter will help you to:

- Discover the end products of development for various delivery systems
- Create effective lesson plans and participant manuals
- Consider various trainee activities that can be developed
- Determine and create the right media for your training

··········· With your training plan in hand, you should have chunks of content decided on and placeholders for introductions, activities, summaries, tests, and so forth. Your next task is to create the development end products that match your chosen delivery system. This is the process in training design known as *development*.

 END PRODUCTS OF DEVELOPMENT

The best way to think about the development aspect of training design is to look at it from the point of view of your end product. When you've completed the development, what should you have?

The specific answer to this question depends on what type of delivery system you have chosen, but in general you should end up with a sound piece of instruction. It's not finished yet—there is a lot of polish to be applied—but generally your end product should pretty much stand on its own as a training package: a package that helps your trainees to master the objectives you developed in the design aspect, which are in turn based on the needs and tasks determined in analysis and assessment. In other words, a package of effective training.

Classroom Training

If your delivery system is a classroom approach, you should have a viable lesson plan developed in detail that reflects who is doing the teaching (yourself or others) and the trainee materials that will help the trainer to teach effectively. Often the print portion of this is termed a participant's guide, training manual, trainee's manual, or something of this ilk. (We'll call it a participant's manual.) Any media—overheads, flip charts, PowerPoint presentations, videos, and so on—should be pretty much ready to use by the end of development.

On-the-Job Training

If your delivery is OJT, the products are much the same: a trainer's guide (same thing as a lesson plan, but developed for one-on-one teaching), a participant's manual (often called a trainee's package for OJT), and any other exhibits, job aids, or training items that the trainer and trainee will need to complete the training. Don't forget your performance checklists and other trainee evaluation instruments as well.

Self-Instruction

For a basic self-instructional delivery, you'll have the participant's package, which is generally the self-instructional program itself; a facilitator's guide; and, again, the media to be used with the package.

Technology-Based Training

For your technology-based training delivery systems, you'll have many of the products we've just mentioned. Which ones will depend on whether your delivery mode is a self-instructional or a classroom-based approach. The main difference will be the number of media that you've added.

For example, if you are using a multimedia delivery you'll have a script, storyboard, graphics, videos, animations, and the computer program, CD-ROM, or other technology in which you put all of these together. You may even have an old-fashioned paper-based participant's package to help get your trainees started or to perform other functions that you did not want to place on the technology.

On the other hand, if your technology delivery is asynchronous e-learning or a satellite-based classroom, you'll have a lesson plan, participant's package, and the media that will be used during the instruction, only this time developed for your particular technology delivery.

You can see that no matter what delivery system you are using, at the basic level the products of development are fairly similar. You have something for the facilitator and something for the trainee and some media and other stuff that will support them both as they take part in the training process.

THE LESSON PLAN AS AN END PRODUCT

Now that you have basically determined what you need to end up with, the next challenge is how you go about producing it. Like everything else in instructional design, there are about as many ways as there are instructional designers. A lot depends on what materials you already have picked up as part of your content gathering and also on your own knowledge of the subject matter. Some instructional designers like to pull resources and sources of resources together from as many places as they can find, and then they pick and choose the best. Others prefer, once they have a clear idea of what they need, to develop specific training segments one at a time, finding or creating the training material for each segment separately as they go.

For this book, we'll use the development of a lesson plan as a model for creating our development end products. Lesson plans are normally associated with classroom instruction, but they are just as important for OJT, particularly if you'll have a number of OJT trainers using your material. In this situation you will want to create an OJT trainer's guide, with plenty of trainer directions, objectives, key teaching points, activities to be performed, and possibly evaluations. To show you what we mean, here is an example of a page from this type of document.

	SAMPLE TRAINER'S GUIDE
Objective	1. Use the computer system to perform the computer-mediated functions of the operations department
Directions	To help the trainees master this objective, first review any references indicated below. Consider providing the trainees with copies of the references if applicable. Next, use the list of discussion points to guide your discussion with the trainees concerning the objective. Now demonstrate to the trainees how to perform the tasks related to this objective, following the list of demonstration points. Allow the trainees time to practice the practice points. When the trainees feel they are ready, use the OJT Checklist to evaluate their mastery of the objective.
References	• IBM systems documentation pp. 26–40 • Chi-text procedure manual Section 14–3

Discussion Points	• What the computer system is used for at Chi-text
	• What other departments use the system and how
	• How the system works
	Novell vs UNIX
	The importance of using the correct client number
	at all times
	• What ARS is and how it interacts with the system
	• What RIMS is and how it interacts with the system
Demonstration Points	• Logging on
	• Logging off
	• Navigating through the system
	• General input of data
	• General extraction of data
Practice Points	• Logging on
	• Logging off
	• System navigation
OJT Checklist	Can the trainee do the following?
	☐ Discuss how the computer system affects the company in general
	☐ Compare the purpose and uses of Novell and UNIX
	☐ Describe how specific departments interface with the computer system
	☐ Log on to the computer correctly
	☐ Log off of the computer correctly
	☐ Navigate through the computer system efficiently
	☐ Compare the system specifics and interactions of ARS and RIMS
	☐ Input data into the system as needed for operations
	☐ Extract data from the system as needed for operations

    Even if you are both the designer and the OJT trainer, using a document like this is not a bad idea. And who knows when someone else might need to use it?

A lesson plan is also important for any type of technology-based training in which a facilitator is involved. This would include synchronous e-learning programs, teleconference-based programs, and satellite-mediated programs.

Self-instructional programs do not actually require a formal lesson plan, but before you develop scripts and storyboards, you'll need more than just an instructional plan; the techniques of developing a lesson plan will help here too.

How detailed your lesson plan should be depends on what you are going to do with it. If it's for other facilitators, OJT trainers, or technology-based trainers, you'll want a lot of detail. On the other hand, if the delivery is going to be your responsibility and no one else's, or if you're simply fleshing out your instructional plan before writing a script, you might take your instructional plan, make notes on it where needed for activities and ideas, and stop there.

We'll take the middle ground here and discuss how to create a basic lesson plan that can be used by you or by other trainers and is complete enough to conform to most accrediting or certification processes, if necessary. As always, use what you need for your own situation, but make an informed decision about what you are leaving out.

Lesson Plan Formats

The first decision you need to make is which lesson plan format to use. One of the most popular is the two-column format, with one side showing content and the other containing trainer notes, media to use, activities, references, and anything else that the trainer might use to get the content across. Some designers put the content on the left and the notes on the right; others do the opposite. I've even seen lesson plans that are so complete that the notes side contains reduced-size examples of the handouts, other trainee materials, and the overheads as well. This is rather simple to do with a computer, and I find it very useful when developing lesson plans for other trainers, but it may be overkill for you. Following is an example of the two-column format.

As the trainee gains proficiency performing the task in an "ideal" environment, on-the-job noise or normal environmental factors are added.	Introduce noise *gradually.*
Aid the trainee in integrating new subject matter.	Display OH 12.
Use positive reinforcement, i.e., praise the person, criticize the action.	Display OH 14.

There are many other lesson plan formats. Two of the most popular are a three-column format with the columns labeled Time, Media/Activities, and Content, and a four-column format with the columns labeled Objective, Content, Methods and Media, and Testing.

EXAMPLE OF THREE-COLUMN FORMAT LESSON PLAN

Lesson Plan: 221   *Program Title:* Instructional Design   *Revision:* 1
Number of Pages: 12   *Module Title:* Objectives   *Time:* 4 hours

Time	Media/Activities	Content
45 min	OH 17	Review page 23 and discuss example 1
	PM pp. 23–25	Refer to task chart and audience analysis
	Flip chart	Ask: What do we want them to know?
		30-minute small-group interaction on pulling knowledge from analysis
30 min	OH 18	Discuss characteristics of good objectives
	Mager pp. 10–21	Complete and discuss activity page 27
	PM pp. 26–27	
45 min	LUNCH	LUNCH
60 min	OH 19–22	Discuss levels
	PM 28–32 and addendum 1	Read PM 28–30
	Pass out: Verbs	Discuss parts of objective
		Conditions
		Standards
		Verbs

TEMPLATE FOR A FOUR-COLUMN FORMAT

Objective (The trainee will be able to)	Content (Expanded Outline)	Methods and Media (Overheads, questions, activities)	Testing (The objective will be met when)

You can mix and match these formats, add new columns, or change the headings to suit your needs. The important point is to decide on a lesson plan format that works for you and use it.

 ### Pre-Activities

The first items you might want to put in your lesson plan are the pre-activities. If you have them noted in your instructional plan, then you've made a decision that some content should be learned or at least reviewed before the trainees come to class. Now you need to decide how this is going to be accomplished.

Depending on the content, you may develop a pre-reading assignment with some questions to answer or questions without any reading, in which case the trainees will need to find the information on their own if they don't already know it. You may give them some articles or references to look up, or you may put together the reading specifically for this class from your own or the SMEs' knowledge. There may be a survey or psychological instrument you want them to take. You may have them talk to their supervisor or other company employees to gather specific information on some problem or situation. You might even develop—or buy from an off-the-shelf vendor—an entire self-instructional package for them to complete before class, possibly on a CD-ROM, or an asynchronous e-learning package.

Trainee and Supervisor Pre-Activities

One of the most popular types of pre-activities links the trainees with their supervisors for some type of discussion or team-based task before coming to class. This can be as simple as an interview in which the trainee asks questions you have provided or as complex as an assessment tool that both of them take and discuss before class.

There are a lot of possibilities for how you can structure your pre-work. The important thing is to use a process that fits the content and that works best for your trainees. I've seen designers who have created a wonderful piece of pre-work, with the supervisor and the trainee both engaged in some heavy-duty team building, only to find out later that many of the trainees work entire states away from their supervisors and almost never see them. If the designers had done a good trainee analysis, they would have known this and developed the pre-work so it could be done over the phone, but. . . . Remember our saying in an earlier chapter that there are times you will need to redo or at least add to your analysis? One of those times is when you are doing your development and find you don't have enough information to be sure that a particular activity will work.

Product

When you've finished with the development tasks for your pre-work ideas, you should have a complete training segment with both trainee materials and a piece of your lesson plan that describes what the trainer is doing. Your lesson plan portion should also give your trainers any supplementary information, such as answers to questions or how to hold a discussion around the key issues of a survey that might help them debrief the pre-work. And don't forget our rule that everything can change. Simply because you planned for some pre-work as part of your lesson plan during your design process does not mean you must do it. Keep asking yourself if this is the right approach as you develop the pre-work (or any other part of your lesson plan). Does this work best for the content? Can my trainees do it easily enough that they won't just ignore it? Most important: Will it help them to master the objectives? As long as you keep saying "yes" or at least "I think so," you're doing fine.

Pre- and Post-Activities

If you are developing material for a multiple-day class, you might want to add activities to be done between classes. Some people call this *homework*, but let's not use such a loaded term. One possible approach is to divide up the pre-reading by having the trainees do some before each day's session rather than all before the first class.

I like to create activities that require the trainees to meet in small groups at the end of the day, possibly to discuss the day's activities or to plan items for the next day's work. Pre- and post-activities are great reinforcers of learning, both as an effective review and for adding depth to the learning through outside activities.

One of my favorite pre/post activities is to ask the trainees to come up with their own examples of on-the-job problems or situations, based on the day's discussions, that we can try to solve in the next class. This makes for not only a good summary, but also a good discussion the next time and some real job-related examples.

Another good pre/post activity when working with a topic that has electronic data applications is to have the trainees use the company intranet to find more information related to what was discussed in class that day or what will be discussed the next day. This only works if the trainees have personal computer access to the company net—that is, a laptop and modem—so be careful how you use this activity. Do not require your trainees to go back to the office or to a computer center, or even to share computers during the evening to complete the assignment. I know from experience that the chances are they will not do it, and it really is too much of an extra burden.

The only caveat I have concerning pre/post activities is to remember that after a long day in class the trainees may not have a lot of energy left, so don't overburden them with homework. I've often heard people say, "Well, we've paid all this money to bring them here, and they have nothing else to do at the hotel, so why not give them more training in the evening?" If these are your reasons for creating pre/post work, then don't create it. Your activities should help the trainees master the objectives, not just fill time. Never forget that trainees are human too. Just like you, they can only absorb so much in any given day.

One other thing I've learned about pre-work in general is that busy people tend to put things off until they have to be done. Sending the pre-work to participants three or four weeks in advance seldom gets them started early—

and often means that they forget about it completely. I usually plan on my pre-work assignments reaching the participants about a week before the class. For those do-it-now folks this is plenty early enough, and for those who wait until the last minute, it already is just about the last minute when they get it.

Introduction

Next in your lesson plan will probably be an introduction. Some of the purposes of an introduction are

- Gaining the trainee's attention
- Establishing the trainee's mind-set
- Helping the trainee recall prior knowledge
- Describing the goals of the program
- Setting expectations for the program
- Establishing the relevance of the program
- Making the trainee comfortable

Titles, objectives, and directions are usual parts of an introduction, along with a summary of what the next section will include. Mastery levels, testing procedures, and where this particular piece fits into the whole of the training are all good discussion points for a main introduction, but these are usually not used in the training unless something very unusual is about to happen.

Use the introduction to tie what has previously been learned with the new learning that is about to occur, thus making the new material more relevant to the trainee.

You can also use it to provide a general overview of the topic about to be discussed, and thus help the trainee prepare for the discussion.

In a self-instructional design, the introduction can tell the trainees why they should (or should not) complete a particular module, or it can interest them in a topic they might not otherwise have followed. It can also set the tone for a multimedia course by providing an example of what the screens will look like, who the players (voices) are, and what they can expect to see and do. If you have not done it earlier, the introduction could discuss navigation and record-keeping processes as well in a multimedia design.

The key to introductions is to make them short and sweet. Nothing will turn off trainees faster than a long introduction to a topic that they want to get to quickly. Produce a page for the participant's manual that states the objectives, and produce another for trainee directions if your content or course plan requires it. Note in the lesson plan how the trainer should use these pages.

If you've decided that you need a tie-in to previous material, you may want to draft a game or a series of review questions to be asked by the trainer. An approach for which the trainees break into groups and each group reports on a previous training aspect is another good possibility here. Don't forget to let the trainer know in the lesson plan what the key learning points are that need to be reviewed. Even if you are going to be the trainer, and you are developing a bare-bones lesson plan, a reminder here will help you when you're up in front of the class and dealing with a dozen unrelated issues at the same time.

Overview

Your introduction will probably include an overview. For your overview you might want to create some overheads or slides with flow charts and other graphics, depending on what your delivery system will support, to help preview the training that is to occur. You might decide to use a video of a high-level manager discussing the importance of your program or simply saying, "Good morning, we're glad you're here" to add credibility to your program. (This is another reason why you had to make many of the delivery decisions earlier. While you're developing material is no time to be asking yourself whether your delivery system can support what you want to develop. You should have made the decision much earlier and know going into development what is and is not possible. Again, a little up-front analysis can save you a lot of rework later.)

Whatever you need and do, be sure that your lesson plan tells the trainer how you think he or she should work with the material. For example, if it is that high-level manager video, list which points the trainer should reinforce.

Icebreakers

(www.susan-boyd.com/training.htm)

Most well-structured lesson plans include an icebreaker in the introduction as well. An icebreaker is an activity that helps warm the class up to the fact that they are going to be expected to participate in the training. Some icebreakers relate directly to the content being taught; others are more general in nature.

Icebreakers can be as simple as going around the room and asking everyone to introduce themselves (or each other), or as complicated as a full-scale role play in which each member of the class takes on certain characteristics that you are exploring in the content of your training. The type of icebreaker you develop depends in large part on your audience, your content, and your creativity (or someone else's creativity that you can borrow).

You'll usually want to develop an icebreaker of some type, unless there is a very good reason not to; for example, if you and the class have already been together in earlier sessions.

Breaking into teams is often a good icebreaker, particularly if you plan to use a lot of small-group instruction. Ask the teams to decide on a team name, color, song—anything to get them working together. Make it easy to assign a leader, scribe, or reporter by suggesting ideas, such as the oldest member is the reporter, or the newest corporate member is the leader.

To bring the actual course content into your icebreaker, you could use a brainstorming process in which each team tries to come up with the most new terms that will be discussed today. You might also ask for the most possible solutions to an issue that is going to be addressed in the training, such as how to make the plant safer or what will make computer software easier to learn.

Here's a list of other icebreakers that are commonly used:

- Brainstorm a list of topics or terms related to the course for further clarification and discussion
- Tell personal stories
- Show an unknown artifact or symbol to engender discussion
- Show videos (often humorous, thought-provoking, or both)
- Make introductions (of oneself or a partner)
- Learn something previously not known about everyone on your team
- Play *Jeopardy*
- Play "Who Am I?" using personal, professional, or other characteristics to guess who each of your classmates is

Here is a short list of things to consider when choosing an icebreaker:

- How much time will it take?
- What's the possibility that it will turn some trainees off?
- What's the possibility that it will become confrontational?
- Is it novel?
- Will it be fun or at least interesting?
- Will some information be produced from it that can be used later?
- Does it require active participation from trainees?
- Will it set the right tone for the program?
- Will it help energize the program and the trainees?
- Is there a possibility of failure for any trainee?
- Might it be embarrassing to some trainees?

Motivation

The final part of your lesson plan introduction should be a section on motivation. Here we take some time in the lesson plan to note to the trainees why they want to learn what is about to be taught and how it will help them personally.

That old radio station WII-FM or "What's in It for Me?" is always the key motivator. You might want to come up with a different way to describe this other than simply having the trainer list the WIIFMs, such as asking the trainees to discuss what they see as their personal WIIFMs or showing video testimonials from previous participants.

Pre-Tests

If you have decided in your instructional plan that you need to put a pre-test in your lesson plan, now is the time to develop it. Most often a pre-test is done in class, particularly if its purpose is to evaluate learning. However, there are times when you might give a pre-test as part of the pre-work activities. Be sure you have placed the pre-test where you want it, based on the purpose you have assigned to it.

If you followed our good instructional design practices from the previous chapter, you should already have a question bank developed. For your pre-test you need only to choose the questions you think cover the purpose(s) you assigned to the pre-test, create the test, and put answers and directions in your lesson plan for the trainer. Don't forget that a pre-test (or any test for that matter) is not worth the paper it is written on if feedback is not provided to the trainees. Leave room in your lesson plan for this, and let your trainer know how to do it.

In self-instructional programs, a pre-test can also be used as a formal or informal "test out" of one or more of the modules. If a trainee scores high enough on the pre-test, he or she can skip that particular unit of instruction. This test-out process can be used in classroom training as well, although it is more unusual for that delivery method.

In some self-instructional programs, particularly those using computers, the pre-test can be a couple of questions that lead the trainee down one learning path or another. This branching process is one of the major advantages of computer-assisted learning, and if you are using computers as a delivery system you will want to consider it strongly, as it is a technique that helps make the time and cost involved in developing computer-based training worth the effort by reducing the learning time.

Handouts versus Pass-Outs

Pre-tests bring up an interesting aspect of material development that I call the "pass-out versus handout" question. In classroom training particularly, but also in OJT, there are some pieces of trainee material that you do not want the trainees to see in advance. Pre-tests are a good example of this. So you probably do not want to put them in the participant's manual (or whatever you call it) that is normally distributed at the beginning of class or the start of an OJT program. Another example of a pass-out is the rules for a game that you don't want the learners to read until the game begins or that only some of the learners will receive. Items such as this become what I term *pass-outs* because they are passed out during the training (creative, huh?). I reserve the term *handouts* for the materials you include in the participant's manual or that you distribute at the start of a class. The two issues with pass-outs are (1) they need to be explained well in your lesson plan so the trainer knows what they are and when to use them, and (2) they are cumbersome. I've done classes where I've had an entire table full of pass-outs. Not only can this be confusing, but if you are taking your training on the road, instead of a nice simple participant's manual you have a bunch of loose papers to worry about.

A good instructional designer keeps pass-outs to a minimum. This does not mean not to use them, but use them only where it really matters, such as for a pre-test. Try to develop your material so as much of it as possible goes directly into the participant's manual as a handout. And when you use pass-outs, be sure your lesson plan has them marked with directions as to how they are to be handled and why. This "why" is important too. I've seen programs for which the trainer simply took the pass-outs and put them into the back of the participant's binder. He simply didn't want to be bothered with distributing them during class—and so another good instructional technique went down the drain.

Pass-outs are not as common in self-instructional programs or most of the high-technology delivery systems (with the exception of live satellite instruction), simply because there is usually no one available to pass things out. However, if you must have something such as a test passed out at a specific time, and not included as part of the participant's manual for your self-instructional or technology-based package, you need to figure out a way to do it. Usually this involves the trainee going somewhere and receiving the pass-out from someone. The someone needs to know what to do and how. This is one of the things that goes into a facilitator's package for self-instruction, or a site facilitator's directions for deliveries such as satellite or synchronous e-learning.

Lesson Plan Content: The Body

OK, so your introduction—including an overview, icebreaker, motivation, and pre-test (if you decided to use one)—has been developed. You've created some good trainee materials that you will place in the participant's manual, and you've added directions in the lesson plan for everything, especially those items that are pass-outs. You should be about ready to get into the main area of your content, what some people call the *body* of your lesson plan.

The main purpose of the body is to deliver the critical content that you identified through your content analysis. You might call this the facts-and-principles aspect. It includes how the processes work and how systems are structured and function together.

It is also used to create awareness of concepts and ideas, teach policies and procedures, guide trainees in their learning, and show good and bad examples of the learning in practice. It often is responsible for the development of problem-solving skills.

In your instructional plan, you made a first attempt at chunking the content and separating the chunks with ideas for activities or notes that you want an activity or something here and there. Development is the phase in which you complete the chunking and these activities become a reality.

Procedures

You might also have some notes and thoughts on pieces of content that you have gathered from other sources that you want the trainees to become familiar with. These pieces can be very significant to your training program, as they often describe how to perform procedures and can be real examples from the field. However, be careful that you don't rely on these content pieces too much and end up doing what might be called *procedure distribution* instead of training. I've seen a thousand so-called training programs for which training material consists of photocopies of procedures. They are put together in a trainee's package (I won't dignify it with the term *participant's package*) or, worse yet, passed out one by one in class. The lesson plan (if there is one) goes something like the following:

1. Tell trainees to read procedure

2. Go over procedure

3. Ask if there are any questions

4. Tell trainees to read next procedure

5. Wake up trainee as necessary

Obviously, the last entry is not usually listed, but it might as well be. Training plans that consist of handing out mounds of procedures do not constitute training. Even if the trainer spends class time going over the procedures, it is not good training.

This is not to say that you should not use company procedures in training. Much of technical training is procedure-based. But as the instructional designer, it is your job to turn these masses of procedures into real training. Leave the less-important procedures for supplementary reading, design some pre-work for other procedures, develop job aids and summary pages for complicated procedures, and above all create better activities than simply "read and ask questions."

 Having said this, I hasten to add that using policies, procedures, annual reports, memos—and all sorts of what would not normally be thought of as training materials—as training materials is actually another rapid design hint. Anything that you do not have to create makes your material development faster, so look for these things in your company and in the public domain. (In today's terms, check the Web.) You might find magazine articles, pamphlets, even pieces of television shows that you can incorporate rather than create. Just remember to choose well and to abide by copyright laws.

 ### Activities

Now I'll climb off my soapbox and move on to activities. The quality, and possibly the success, of your training program can be measured by the activities you develop for it. The thing to keep in mind with activities is that your job as an instructional designer is to create a course that doesn't just present information, but that helps the trainees to learn. Anything less is really nothing more than the procedural "nontraining" we discussed earlier.

The material you develop for your training should make it easy for trainees to interact with the content and with one another. Think about how you can help them practice what they are learning or help them learn it in different ways. Look for activities in which they can apply their new knowledge and skills. Build in ways for them to go beyond your training, to become involved, to expand on what they now know. Finally, build in structure that they can use to internalize their learning, that will help them to recall the important aspects when they encounter new situations.

Here is a list of possible activities you may want to include in your lesson plan.*

---

*Adapted from material contained in Langevin Learning Services' Langevin Instructional Designware software.

Anonymous Questioning. Trainees are asked to write their main question on a sheet of paper and pass it to the facilitator, who then reads the questions and may answer them or ask for responses from other trainees.

Behavior Modeling. A technique in which effective behaviors are shown to the trainees, with an outline of how to repeat the behaviors step by step. The trainees try out and practice the behavior with guidance and feedback. Used commonly in interpersonal skills and communication training.

Brainstorming. An idea-generation process in which a spontaneous non-judgmental flow of suggestions is facilitated. Later the ideas are explored in detail and their usefulness evaluated.

Case Study. A written, oral, or video account of a situation given to trainees. Either individually or in groups, the trainees are asked to analyze the case and present recommendations.

Colloquy. A modification of a panel in which half the group are trainees and the other half experts. The trainees ask questions, raise issues, and make comments for the experts to respond to.

Committee. The creation of a number of smaller groups from a large group of trainees, each of which is responsible for solving a particular aspect of a general problem. Through reports and feedback the general problem moves toward a solution.

Critical Incident. A variation of the case study, in which trainees are given incomplete data. By analyzing the case and asking the right questions, they are given additional data needed to solve the case.

Critique. Trainees are asked to analyze the strengths and weaknesses of a particular process and to make suggestions for improvements.

Debate. Two teams defend opposite sides of an issue. The purpose is to explore all aspects of an issue and not necessarily to win.

Demonstration. Trainees observe the performance of a task or procedure as conducted by an expert, either live or on tape.

Dialogue. Two individuals hold a conversation while the trainees observe. The conversation may present opposing views of a situation or simply be an exploration.

Discussion. An exchange of ideas between the facilitator and the trainees. It can be totally unstructured and spontaneous, but usually requires some structure to achieve a content-related purpose.

Drill. Repetitive practice designed to increase efficiency, improve the quality of performance, or aid retention.

Fishbowl. Division of a large group into two smaller groups, with one group discussing or role-playing an issue while the other observes and then offers feedback.

Forum. A trainee discussion and question-asking session about a presented topic. Trainees may ask questions of the speaker or discuss the topic among themselves.

Game. A structured exercise in which competition or cooperation (or both) are used to practice principles or learn new ones.

In-Baskets. Prepared items that are given to the trainees as if arriving in their in-baskets. Trainees must prioritize, make decisions, handle any difficulties, respond to time deadlines and pressure, and so forth, to complete the work.

Instruments. Questionnaires, checklists, or other forms filled out by trainees concerning themselves or others, usually to gain insight about themselves or a topic.

Interview. Questioning of a resource person by trainees to add to content knowledge or develop new approaches.

Job Aids. Items given trainees to assist them in doing their jobs. These might include worksheets, checklists, samples, flow charts, procedural guides, glossaries, diagrams, decision tables, and manuals. Training is often needed to help the workers use the job aids.

Laboratory. A training area set up to allow experimentation, testing, and hands-on experience by trainees. The processes occurring here may be extremely structured, totally unstructured, or anything in between, depending on the content.

Lecture. A prepared oral presentation by a qualified speaker.

Lecturette. A brief lecture, usually designed to cover a single aspect of a topic and lead into a discussion, games, or some other activity.

Listening Team. Group of trainees assigned to listen to a presentation, take notes, prepare questions, and then summarize a session. Each group is asked to focus on a different aspect of the presentation and report observations and conclusions.

Mental Imagery. An exercise that allows the trainee to relax and imagine doing the process that has been discussed. Also useful for quick stress breaks or as a transition when changing subjects.

Mini-Case. A case study in which the situation is described briefly to the trainees, who discuss how it might be handled. Often only one or two key facts are given, and usually the discussion is brief. Used to give examples of situations and procedures.

Missing Panel. A vacant chair that trainees can temporarily take to participate briefly in the panel discussion.

One-on-One Discussion. A method in which the trainees are asked to speak to the person beside them for a few minutes to discuss an issue, answer a question, or generate questions to ask.

Panel. A discussion among a group of experts that takes place while trainees observe.

Practice Exercises. An exercise in which trainees are asked to practice performing a task.

Question and Answer. Activity in which the facilitator covers content by asking a series of questions. Can be reversed, so the trainees generate the questions and quiz either the facilitator or each other.

Quiz. A practice activity of completing the answers to oral or written questions. Often used as a summary activity.

Reading. Materials assigned for trainees to read that cover course content or otherwise prepare them for further activities.

Reflection Activity in which trainees are given time for singular thought to consider what has been learned and its applicability in their work settings.

Role Play. Trainees' enactment of a situation, to try out new skills or apply what has been learned. Role plays might include the following:

- Confrontation, in which the trainee is confronted by another person and must handle problems or provide satisfaction.
- Court Techniques, in which a situation or person is "tried" as trainees work out the consequences of a mishandled task.
- Monologue, in which there is only one role and the player plays it while trainees observe.

- Triad, in which three trainees take on the roles of two individuals and an observer, often rotating roles.

- Role Reversal, in which the players assume the roles of others with whom they normally interact on the job.

Simulation. A training environment set up to allow the trainees to practice a task under conditions as close as possible to those on the job.

Skit. A short, dramatic presentation that is carefully prepared and rehearsed to illustrate principles or provide material for analysis and discussion.

Remember that activities need to be an integrated part of your training—something that assists in the training, not something that you design in because it is "neat," or you saw someone else use it and you liked it, or simply because you think you need an activity. Use some of the things you have already determined to help you choose activities, such as these factors:

- Who is the target audience? What are their expectations and preferences? What did your audience analysis say would interest and motivate them?

- What type of learning is required for your material? You determined this when you wrote your objectives by picking certain verbs. Use this knowledge to choose pertinent activities. Is the learning complex? Is it mostly knowledge? Does it require performances? Each of these suggests different activities.

- If you are using a technology delivery system, particularly in a self-instructional mode, you want to think interactivity. What activities can you design in that allow the trainee to respond to the material being presented—to become part of the process, not just an observer? How can these activities be designed to give the trainee feedback? This is a much more complicated process than using activities in an instructor-led approach; it's also more expensive, as good technology-based activities require a lot more development and often more programming time.

  However, interactivity is the key to good self-instruction. Ignore it at the peril of turning your trainees off, if not actually putting them to sleep as they use your training package. If you are buying self-instructional programs from vendors or having them custom made for you, interactivity—and plenty of it—is what to ask for.

 ### Games

Instructional games are a specialized activity that can motivate and spark trainee interest. They can also demotivate and make the entire class a somewhat substantial bore (*Games Trainers Play* by John Newstrom, 1980). And both of these can happen in the same classroom at the same time, depending on each person's perspective. Games can challenge the trainees to think beyond the box, but if the challenge is too great they can frustrate them as well. Too many rules, or games that are too complex can make the learning of the game not worth the result in content learning or application that you wanted to achieve.

There are actually two main categories of games: those that present new information and those that summarize.

Games can convey a variety of information, such as concepts, principles, system dynamics, problem solving, and even social skills. They can also have no connection whatsoever to the content or the objectives. The key, as always, is to make sure that the game is directly related to your objectives, that it instructs while entertaining, and that it gives those who grasp its purpose and content easily a chance for further learning.

A good example of a very simple instructional game is the old-fashioned spelling bee. Think of all the good points and bad points of any spelling bee that you participated in back in grade school, and you'll have a pretty good idea of the advantages and problems of most instructional games.

Choose your games so they maintain the interest of all your trainees while both presenting and developing the knowledge that your objectives indicate must be mastered.

You can use games as an activity almost anywhere in your lesson plan, although they are really great review and summary tools. But use them sparingly, particularly the complicated ones, as they can often detract from the message by their sheer complexity.

There is also a good argument going on in instructional design circles over whether games should be competitive or not. My recommendation is one I've given you before: know your audience. Highly competitive people, for example, actually do not do well with competitive games, as the competition becomes more important to them than the learning, and of course people who are not competitive won't like being forced into competitive situations. You can deal with these individual differences by having strong introductions and debriefings on either side of the game, but you need to be careful in your choices. The trainer also needs to monitor the game to keep things from getting out of hand. This is actually not part of this book's content, as it is a trainer skill, but the smart instructional designer will add to the lesson plan notes about what to watch for as the trainer closely monitors this particular activity.

Here are some things to consider when choosing games:

- What purpose do you hope to achieve?

- Does the game's focus relate to one (or more) of your objectives?
- Is the group the right size for the game?
- Do all trainees have the right experience and background to play the game effectively?
- Is the purpose of the game to introduce new material, demonstrate a concept, or reinforce learning?
- Is the game simple to play?
- Are the directions complete?
- Will the game be fun?
- Do you have the time to both play and debrief?
- Are there better ways to do what you think the game will do?

Here is a list of some of the more popular types of instructional games, adapted from the work of Sivasailam "Thiagi" Thiagarajan. Note that some of these game processes are actually game templates, and as such can be rapid design techniques. We've marked those with our rapid hints icon.

Action Learning. A combination of action and reflection by a team to solve complex, strategic problems in real-world organizations. Existing skills and knowledge are applied, and new skills, knowledge, and insight created through continuous reflection and questioning.

Board Games. Modeled after games such as Monopoly, Chutes and Ladders, and the like, board games use game cards and dice to encourage individuals and teams to demonstrate mastery of concepts, principles, skills, and problem-solving strategies.

Card Games. These games involve facts, concepts, technical terms, definitions, principles, examples, quotations, and questions printed on cards. Good for classifying and sequencing pieces of information.

Case Studies. Usually a written (sometimes a video) account of a real or fictional situation surrounding a problem. Participants work individually or in teams to analyze, discuss, and recommend appropriate solutions and to critique one another's work.

Cash Games. These games use cash transactions for the development of interpersonal skills.

Computer Game Shells. Games that permit the loading of new content (usually questions) by the facilitator during the game.

Experience-Based Learning. Physical activities and challenges such as rafting, rock climbing, walking on rope bridges, and so on, in regulated outdoor environments, used to build team reliance and self-reliance as well.

Framegames. Game templates that allow content to be replaced to create new games.

Interactive Storytelling. Fictional narratives in which participants listen to a story and make appropriate decisions at critical junctures.

Kinesthetic Learning Devices. Physical activities performed on electrical and mechanical equipment specially developed for a particular challenge or to make a specialized point. The best of these are often directly related to the workplace.

Magic Tricks. Tricks that can be used to provide metaphors or analogies for some important element of the content.

Metaphorical Simulation Games. Simulations that provide a simplistic, abstract view of real-world processes. They are good for teaching principles related to planning, generating ideas, testing alternatives, making decisions, using resources, and working under time pressure.

Puzzles. These can be used to preview, review, or test content for individuals or groups.

Read.me Games. Participants read a handout or pass-out and play a game that uses team support to encourage recall and transfer of what they read.

Role Plays. Participants act out characters, personalities, and attitudes other than their own. Often used to reverse roles in supervisory training.

Television Games. Structured like popular game shows, these are used to present content and to drill on concepts and terminology.

Thought Experiments. Participants mentally rehearse new patterns of behavior by placing themselves in unique mental situations, such as holding a discussion with George Washington to find out how he would solve a problem, or interviewing oneself. Through this process, new knowledge and insight are often gained.

Video Replay Games. Participants watch a videotape that presents content through a game situation, then replay the game live to apply the new concepts and skills.

Internal Summaries

In your instructional plan, you noted areas in which summaries of the presented material might be included. The most common summary activity is simply to have the trainer repeat the important points covered in the just-completed segment, perhaps with a slide to reinforce the points. This is also the most boring way to summarize a piece of content. That's not to say you should not use this approach from time to time; just don't make a habit of it.

To make your internal summaries more interesting and possibly more interactive, develop questions that the trainer can ask that will allow the trainees to review the main points, or put a series of questions in the participant's manual that the trainees will answer individually and then discuss as a group. You can have the trainees summarize the main points as they saw them, with the trainer adding comments where necessary. You can even make a game of it, with small groups vying to find all the main points of a particular piece of content and assigning points for the most complete summaries (although you'd better watch that competition thing).

You might have the learners do a one-minute paper on what they have learned so far, or a list of concepts they understand and those they find confusing.

One of my favorite summary activities in a multiday class is to have groups of learners come before the class and summarize what happened the day before. The groups are judged on thoroughness and creativity, and a prize is given at the end for the best morning summary.

Quizzes make good summaries at times, as do some of the simpler games. Videos can be used to summarize as well. Basically, any activity from the list we've already seen can be turned into a summary. The key is to find a variety of ways to achieve this important aspect—and don't forget that all summary items need to relate directly back to your objectives.

Imbedded Questions

The concept of summaries brings up another aspect of the lesson plan, which is questioning. There are a lot of rules and theory that relate to constructing good questions for use in a class or self-instructional program (*Test Construction for Training Evaluation* by Charles Denova, 1979). They deal with concepts such as open-ended and closed-ended questions, questioning techniques, and a number of other issues. Basically, imbedded questions—that is, questions that are found randomly throughout the program rather than in specific groupings—are a good idea. They are interactive, create new thinking processes, and can really drive home specific points.

Add imbedded questions where you can, remembering that as the instructional designer it is your job to add them, not the trainer's. Particularly if you have multiple trainers, your imbedded questions will be a key in maintaining consistency. You also do not want the trainers to be thinking up too many of their own questions, as this can easily get the class off track. Imbedded questions should be there in your lesson plan, with well-explained answers for the trainer to use during the discussion.

 ### Post-Class Activities

Post-class activities are done after the training has been completed, but they are yet another area of training that you need to develop now. Their purpose is to help the employees transfer their newly won knowledge and skills to the job, to reinforce those skills and knowledge, and, in the best-developed activities, to evaluate the success of the training by considering what the trainee is actually using on the job—that is, how his or her job performance has changed and, we hope, improved. This goes way back to our analysis of performance gaps and the fact that in many cases the purpose of training is to close them. We won't deal with the evaluative aspect of follow-up activities yet, as we will discuss it in the chapter on evaluation.

Good follow-up activities can also help your trainees to retain what they've learned through review and practice and even motivate them to learn more through enrichment activities.

Tried-and-true follow-up activities include contracts, diaries, letters to oneself, and action plans. The best follow-up activities involve the trainee's supervisor to one extent or another. This might include some of the ideas we discussed for pre-activities. Giving the supervisor a role in the activities mentioned earlier and those in the following list is good way to involve the person.

Here are some possible follow-up activities:

- Personal action plans
- Group action plans
- Phased action plans that occur between days of training
- Development of personal performance aids
- Training of others (colleagues, supervisor) on what the trainee has learned
- Contract with trainer, supervisor, or others
- Follow-up tests
- Follow-up questionnaires
- Returning reports to trainer on how information was implemented
- Follow-up phone calls or e-mail to trainer

- Postcards that are written and addressed in class, then sent back by the instructor

- Assignment of "parking lot" questions or concepts to be researched by learners, with the information sent back to all or posted on an electronic bulletin board

 ### Supplies List

One of the logistical items in your lesson plan is the supply list. This list identifies for the trainer everything needed to run the class. It should be very complete, with all media, special tools, or instruments, hardware and software, and any other items needed to facilitate the training, plus, if necessary, notations on where to obtain these things. Keep in mind that if the trainers do not have the proper materials and supplies at hand when they start the class, they won't use them, so all your wonderful activities that are dependent on them will be for naught.

Following is an example of a supply list:

Supply List for SS 100: Principles of Supervision

Training Materials

Leader's Guide (Rev. 2, 74 pp.)

Overhead transparencies (1–63)

Participant's package:
    Unit 1 (Rev 1, 18 pp.)
    Unit 2 (Rev 0, 23 pp.)
    Unit 3 (Rev 2, 40 pp.)
    Unit 4 (Rev 0, 19 pp.)

Pre-reading package (Rev 1, 22 pp.)

"I Prefer" survey

"Supervisory Styles" instrument and scoring sheets

Pass-outs:
    Performance management action plan (three per participant)
    Meetings checklist
    Interviewing guide
    Employee development case study

Videos:
    "Meetings, Bloody Meetings"

"Influencing Others"
"Man Hunt"

Equipment
Overhead projector
Overhead transparency markers
Flip charts (four) and markers
VCR and monitor
No. 2 pencils for scan form

Nice to Know Versus Need to Know

One problem with developing lesson plans, particularly activities, relates to content. It is very easy when using activities to move away from the "need to know" content and into the "nice to know." A little of this is not a bad thing, but often the entire class becomes sidetracked by some of the less important issues that the activities brings up. Help your trainer by including in your lesson plan some thoughts on how far to go with these aspects and what to watch out for.

The whole concept of nice to know versus need to know is actually a rapid design shortcut. If you're looking for a way to cut back on material development time, make sure that you have stripped the training down to what the trainees truly must know. To use an old adage, "When in doubt, throw it out." This will get you to the leanest possible content, which you will be able to develop and implement more rapidly.

Lesson Plan Reviews

That brings up one final thought on lesson plans. Just as we suggest for objectives (and for many other aspects we've yet to discuss), have someone do a review of your lesson plan if at all possible. Again, be sure to tell the person what you are looking for in the review. It might be chunks, activities, structure, sequencing, number of summaries, or all of the above. Give the person a list of what you need, and let a fresh set of eyes take a look before you proceed with material development. It will make your lesson plan better—and possibly save you a lot of time and revisions later.

Following is a lesson plan development job aid that will help you as you think through your lesson plan.

LESSON PLAN DEVELOPMENT JOB AID

1. What is the topic: _____

2. Who is the audience: _____

3. How many participants: _____

4. Location of program: _____

5. Who and what are my possible resources?

_____

_____

_____

6. What are the topics to be covered?

_____

_____

_____

7. Program objective: _____

8. Supporting objectives: At the end of this program the trainees will be able to . . . _____

_____

_____

_____

_____

_____

_____

9. Icebreaker: How am I going to capture the audience's attention?

_____

_____

_____

_____

10. Motivation: How am I going to create a desire in the trainees to listen and learn? _____

_____

_____

_____

11. Review/Overview: How will I review the previous lesson and give an overview of the next lesson? _____

_____

_____

_____

_____

12. Learning activities: What activities can I use to involve the trainees?

_____

_____

_____

_____

_____

_____

13. Media requirements: How can I visually enhance the presentation? What handouts and pictures will help me make my points? _____

_____

_____

_____

14. Summary: How will the main points of the presentation be restated?

_____

_____

_____

_____

15. Questions and answers: What types of question and answer processes will I use to make sure the trainees understand the material? _____

_____

_____

_____

_____

16. Trainee evaluation: How will measurement of trainee mastery be determined?

_____

_____

_____

17. Follow-up: What post-course activities can be useful in ensuring transfer to the job and/or retention?

_____

_____

_____

_____

Notes:

_____

_____

_____

_____

_____

SCRIPTS AND STORYBOARDS

As we've already mentioned, if you are going to use a self-directed delivery—such as a CD-ROM, DVD, or asynchronous e-learning—you'll need to develop a script and storyboard instead of a lesson plan. Actually, what you really need to do is take the lesson plan and add in all the articles, prepositions, and other grammatical constructions that make it read like a narrative. Here are some thoughts on developing scripts:

Script Hints

- Keep your sentences short
- Use repetition
- Remember to write for your audience, not yourself
- Write as you speak
- Scripts must be short, and script pieces even shorter
- Three items of information in each script piece is a good rule of thumb
- Stay on message
- Write when the time is best for you
- Do openings, closings, and even transitions last
- Plan for at least three drafts of anything you write
- Listen to your reviewers
- Use charts, graphs, bullet points, and the like as much as possible
- Define all technical terms (use hot links)

A storyboard is simply a script to which you add your ideas for the graphics to go with the words. These ideas may be anything from words themselves to stick figures to full-blown illustrations, if you have that kind of talent. Depending on your delivery system, here are some of the items you might find on a storyboard:

- Text or audio script
- Graphics
- Description of interactivity
- Sketches of visuals
- Branching instructions
- Programming notes

Here are some examples of the whole thing put together:

Text	Graphic File
Lesson 3: Objectives Objective: Create proper learner-centered objectives.	Stock
Reading Read pages 84-98 in your text on Objectives.	84-98
Exercise Answer the following questions based on your reading. We will discuss them in class. 1. What is the most important purpose of objectives? 2. What are the main parts of a well-written objective? 3. What are the two words that should never be used as behaviors for objectives, and why?	
Activity For each objective on the next screen, determine and record its behavior (B), standard (S), and condition (C). The correct answers will be discussed in class.	Bright Side "Mod 1 Job Analysis Form.doc"
Activity For each of the objectives on the next screen, state which part or parts of a well-written objective are missing. (Assume that "At the end of . . ." and "the employee will be able to . . ." are understood.) The correct answers will be discussed in class.	Dim Side "Mod 1 Job Analysis Form.doc"

Text	Graphic File

Activity
For each of the objectives on the next screen, determine if it is a well-written objective. If not, rewrite it. (Assume that "At the end of . . ." and "the employee will be able to . . ." are understood.) The correct answers will be discussed in class.

Sample Objectives
"Mod 1 Job Analysis Form.doc"

Activity
Using the content from a training program that you are responsible for, create three well-written objectives. We will critique your objectives in class.

Summary
In this module we have discussed the concepts of instructional design, analysis, and objective writing. For each of these broad concepts, list five learning points that you feel you have mastered.

Summary

FIVE WINDOW E-LEARNING STORYBOARD

PDF Storyboard Format
Project: __Fishing__   File Name: __Introduction__

Screen ID: _____   Last Date Saved: _____

Graphics	Text
Stock Fish	In order to catch a fish you must think like a fish

Action	Notes	Sound
Button to tutorial Fish to Main Menu	Tutorial should begin with file point A.1	Splashing water (.wav)

Screen	Content	Visuals
1	To complete this program we've included an activity and a "do it yourself" summary for you to work on	PDB Logo
2	Activity: Create a Process Map for Baking a Cake:	Stock graphic of cake
	List the major activities (at least five) involved in baking a cake on your "Notes" page.	
	Click here to check your list	
		At click, over cake graphic
	Select one of the major activites and break it down into steps that must be executed to complete the activity.	
		Major Activities for Baking a Cake
	Next, map them on your "Notes" page as a sub-process of baking a cake.	
	Include at least two decision diamonds for checking the quality of outputs from one activity as an input to the next activity.	Selecting a recipe Gathering ingredients Baking
	Be sure to include the proper symbols for beginning, ending, activities and decisions.	
	Check that your arrows flow in the correct direction.	
	When you've finished your process map find two places where there could be interrupts in the process and two kinds of errors that could cause sub-standard outputs (cakes).	
	After you've finished the previous activities click here for a cake-baking example process map.	
	Think about the remaining components of a Performance-Driven Business by considering the implications of measurements/metrics, roles/responsibilities, training, communication, and tools/technology to your cake baking process.	On click go to "Prepare Birthday Dinner for Eight" graphic from class-room participant guide. (3 graphics)

THREE-COLUMN STORYBOARD FOR TECHNOLOGY-BASED PROGRAM

The Six Components of a PDB Storyboard

Module 3

Activity and Summary

Objectives: Obtain hands-on experience with the activity of creating a process map using a familiar activity

Examine the six components of a performance-driven business

Review key points

 PARTICIPANTS' PACKAGES AND OTHER PRINT MATERIALS

By now you should have collected or created many different types of print materials that you can possibly use in your training. They may include fill-in-the-blank and other questions, directions for various activities and games, summary sheets, readings, graphics, diagrams to be referred to, and all kinds of other stuff. You'll have introductory directions, objectives, quizzes, and other activity-based material that you've developed concurrently with the lesson plan. These items will make up the bulk of your participant's manual, trainee's guide, or whatever you have decided to call your main handouts.

Basically, you'll need to gather all these pieces, relate them to your lesson plan or whatever you are using as your guide for material development, add whatever might be missing, subtract the superfluous, and then have it all nicely and consistently formatted.

One word of caution here: too many developers take the easy way out by simply putting copies of their overheads together and calling it a participant's manual. If you have lots of overheads, this can make for a nice fat package, but a pretty poor training experience. The trainees will pay attention not to what the trainer says, but to the prints of the overheads. They will also spend much of their time looking ahead or looking for overheads that may be missing, rather than listening and interacting.

If you want to use print copies of your overheads to great advantage, put them in your participant's manual with pieces missing so that the trainees will need to listen closely in order to complete them. Not too much missing; just blanks to fill in. This process also makes another great summary activity.

Here is a list of the most common items you might include in your participant's manual:

- Pre-work assignments (if the trainees will receive their manual before class)
- Objectives
- Introductions
- Reading materials
- Instruments
- Worksheets for skill practice or role plays
- Feedback forms
- Case studies
- Directions for activities
- Gaming materials
- Job aids
- Quizzes
- Reference materials
- Bibliography
- Glossary
- Evaluations
- Supplemental materials for enrichment, such as magazine articles, related corporate policies or marketing materials, and technical articles or information

When all the parts have been collected, you will need to decide on a format for your participant's manual. There are as many ways to format a manual as there are to format lesson plans—probably more. Some developers like a two-column format with room on one side or the other for notes; others put the objective each page is related to at the top of the page. Some use icons such as those you've seen in this book to note various aspects of the participant's manual; others like to place graphics, such as line drawings or cartoons, throughout the manual.

Participant's manual formatting is one of those aspects of ID in which the instructional designer is allowed to stretch his or her creativity a little. There are no hard-and-fast rules, and I've seen many wonderful formats that combine artistry and usability to perfection. I've also seen some in which the art gets in the way of ease of use, which is the main thing you need to guard against. The purpose of the participant's manual is to assist your trainees in their learning. Be sure to take this into account in whatever formatting decisions you make. Don't create a pretty package for the sake of being pretty. It's usually time-consuming, always costly, and—unless it supports the learning— time wasted. There are some good hints at the end of this chapter that can help you create a great participant's manual.

Whatever your format, be sure your participant's manual includes a title page, table of contents, and edition information.

Also, be sure to be consistent in your formatting, particularly in headings. The headings guide the learner, so decide on a template and stay with it; for example:

Heading 1 16pt Bold
Heading 2 14 pt Bold
Heading 3 Same as body text but bold
Heading 4 Same as body text but italic

Finally, get your participant's manual formatted and printed out by someone who knows good desktop publishing practice. Don't forget that this is your trainees' primary learning tool. Make it as easy to use as possible, with tables of contents, tabs, subtabs, page numbers, and anything else that will aid in their finding the things that are in it. Good desktop publishers know these tricks and more.

Also, remember that the participant's manual—more than anything else— will represent your training to others. Your trainees will show it to their colleagues and managers, and you will display it when someone asks you about your course. So make sure it looks good!

If you are using a self-instructional technology delivery, the chances are you will not be getting most of your participant's manual printed, but it is still there. It is made up of your screens, web pages, and whatever else you develop for your trainees to enhance their learning. Everything we've just discussed, up to the actual printing, is just as important for this type of delivery. Be sure you include all the "good stuff" you have found or created. Choose formatting that doesn't just impress, but facilitates. Don't forget the importance of seeing objectives, introductions, summaries, and all the other things that would appear in a printed participant's manual. You may actually want to make some of these downloadable documents that your learners can print for easier reference. Aspects such as the objectives, instructions for accessing the program, and self-quizzes are often printed out. Again, there are plenty of good ideas to help you in the hints section at the end of this chapter.

The following short checklist can help you develop good print materials.

CHECKLIST FOR DEVELOPING PRINT MATERIAL

- Leave plenty of white space (25 percent of the page is not too much)
- Leave space between blocks of content
- Leave space between headings and text
- Use only one or two fonts
- Use 10-point to 14-point type
- Justify the left margin
- Use running headers or footers with page number, unit, course, and revision numbers and course title
- Use simple sentences
- Be sure that the reference for each pronoun is easily understood
- Use illustrations instead of words
- Check readability
  - Have a table of contents
  - Use a new right-hand page for each major subtopic
  - Number the pages
  - Leave wide margins
  - Use "I" and "you"
  - Use the active voice
  - Explain *why* not to do something; don't just say "don't do it"
  - Use short sentences with ten to fifteen words
  - Make paragraphs short, with only three to four sentences
- Beware of
  - Stereotypes
  - Too much repetition
  - Technical jargon (without definition)
  - Acronyms (without explanation)
- Edit, edit, edit

OTHER MEDIA

Beyond print material, there are a number of other types of instructional aids—or what are often referred to as media—that you might develop for your course. Some of the more popular ones are flip charts, wall charts, overheads (or the newer PowerPoint presentations), slides (also being replaced by computer graphic presentation media such as PowerPoint), video, audio—the list goes on and on. Of course, if you are using a media-based delivery system, such as CD-ROM or e-learning, your media are an integral part of your content. The key thing to remember about using media is that it is a reductive, not a replacement process. This means that it can reduce learning time, but it should not be used as a replacement for hands-on or interaction-based activities.

Here is another job aid for helping you to think about the best media to use for various purposes:

JOB AID FOR SELECTING MEDIA

Media Type	Handouts and Pass-outs	Board	Flip Chart	Overhead	PowerPoint	Video
Uses						
Explain and clarify	1	2	2	1	1	1
Basis for discussion	2	3	2	2	2	1
Organize discussion	1	2	1	2	2	3
Summarize	1	3	3	2	2	2
Education	1	1	1	1	3	1
Size of Audience						
Small	1	2	2	1	3	2
Large	1	3	3	1	1	2

1 = Most desirable; 2 = Alternative; 3 = Least desirable.

There are entire books written on each media format, so we are not going to go into how to produce them or how to use them effectively here. We have included a number of thoughts on some of the more popular formats in the hints section at the end of this chapter. Use them and the references as needed.

 As you complete your material development, you will probably want to create a list of all the media, training materials, and so on that you've developed, for your facilitators to refer to. This is basically an enlargement of your supplies list, focusing specifically on the media aspects and giving much more detail on them. Here is an example of this type of reference. It should become a normal part of each lesson plan you create.

COURSE MATERIALS REFERENCE LIST		
Course: **Managing Change**		*Revision Number:* **1**
Material Number	Type	Description
1	Flip chart	3 steps of subtask 3.1.2
P1–2	Manual	Written role play
P3–5	Manual	Observer sheets
P6	Manual	3-step communication plan
1	OH	Course objectives
2	OH	Key steps to planning
3	OH	Change communication model
1	Video	Communicating change video role play 1

To summarize our discussion of material development, here is a checklist that you can use to review your (or other designers') lesson plans and make sure they are complete.

CHECKLIST FOR REVIEWING LESSON PLANS OR TRAINER MANUALS

☐ The learning objectives are stated.

☐ The learning objectives are followed.

☐ The introduction motivates and orients the trainees.

☐ The activities are based on the learning objectives.

☐ There are a variety of activities that will keep the trainees' interest.

☐ Time is adequate for activities and trainee participation.

☐ The activities have good debriefing questions attached where needed.

☐ There is a place and time for practice if required.

☐ Media are appropriate to learning and properly constructed.

☐ Summaries reinforce and pull together objectives.

☐ Questioning techniques are evident and appropriate.

☐ Evaluations are appropriate.

☐ A table of contents is included.

☐ A list of all necessary equipment and resources is included.

☐ Instructions for role plays or simulations contain enough detail.

☐ There is room for personalization.

When you have completed the development of your media aspects, you have completed your course. However, you're not done yet. Your training won't do your organization or your trainees much good until you actually deliver it to them. You determined a plan for this back in the design component; now it's time to put that plan into operation. The next chapter looks at how you do this, both generally and for specific delivery systems. In training design this component is termed *implementation*.

HINTS FOR DEVELOPING MATERIAL

Classroom

- Make sure the participants have read and understood any pre-readings by giving a quiz in class based on the pre-readings. Let the participants use pre-reading material to find the answers.

- When using videos in classroom situations, include a list of questions in the participant's manual that the trainees must find the answers to as they watch the video.

- A good introductory exercise, useful any time there is a lot of terminology involved, is to give the trainees a list of terms (twenty or so at most) and ask them to work, first individually and then in small groups, to define the terms. Allow about ten minutes for each aspect and follow with a group discussion, or turn it into a game by providing the "right" definitions and scoring the answers. This works best if your trainees have some previous knowledge or have been given pre-work to get them started, but it can be interesting and enlightening if they know little or nothing of the topic.

An Overhead Development Checklist

☐ No more than six lines per overhead

☐ No more than six words per line

☐ Sixteen-point font size or the equivalent is best (twelve-point is the absolute minimum)

☐ Use both upper and lower case letters—title case, not all caps

☐ Use either vertical or horizontal format, not both; horizontal (landscape) is usually best

☐ Use bullets, stars, dashes, and so on

☐ Each overhead should have a title

☐ Key words are best

☐ Keep your phrases and sentences short and simple

☐ Use overheads for emphasis, not instruction

☐ One main idea per overhead

☐ Check your spelling and grammar, then have someone else check it again

☐ Use the right kind of pen for your need (permanent, erasable, water-based)

☐ Use graphics when possible (charts, diagrams, line drawings, cartoons), but keep them simple and guard against clutter

☐ When developing overheads using a computer, all of the above guidelines apply, only more so (more capabilities = increased possibility of problems)

Keep your overheads large and legible. Test by placing your overhead on the floor and standing over it. If you cannot read it easily, it is too small.

More Ideas on Graphics

• Black-and-white transparencies just will not do any more, so use a color printer to make your statement

• Limit colors to no more than three

• Stick to the same color throughout to code similar elements

• Use red, orange, or yellow for items you wish to stress

• Pick red to call attention to main points, show priorities, or signal danger

• Use green to list things you want the audience to do or decisions you want them to approve

• Highlight goals and objectives with bright yellow: it signals optimism and confidence

• Use blue to calm; too much blue, however, can impair concentration

• Avoid large amounts of purple, which disturbs the eye's focus

Hints for Designing Computer Projections

• Keep each slide to one key thought; use builds to add new concepts

• Use charts and graphs rather than tables; they are easier to read at a distance

• Use the same format for all slides; don't switch from vertical to horizontal

• Never add sound or visual effects without good reason

• Keep the design clean and the effects simple

• Keep backgrounds consistent and subtle

- Use only quality clip art, and use it sparingly
- Check all graphics, especially gradient effects, on the projection system, to see how they will look
- Use the chart style that is appropriate for the data
- Use no more than four colors on one chart
- Use one thought per line, five to six words per line, five to six lines per slide
- Light colors on dark backgrounds attract the eye
- Use color cues to imply relationships
- Limit the number of colors on a single screen image
- Establish a color scheme at the beginning and stick with it
- Bright colors make small objects and thin lines stand out
- Don't use more than three fonts in a presentation
- Don't overuse boldface, italic, or all caps
- In general, don't use a font size smaller than 18 points
- Sans serif fonts such as Helvetica are easier to read when projected
- Use motion elements such as animation and transitions to attract attention—but don't overuse them

Activities
- As an activity or to get the trainees back on time, use "wuzzles" or other puzzle formats after a break.
- For big groups or multiple-day programs, give points when everyone at a table is back on time. Then award some type of prize at the end of the class.
- Remember, for both games and role plays, that the debriefing is the most important part. Be sure to give your facilitator debriefing points.
- Use five-minute physical action breaks in which trainees do something. Ask the trainees to recommend what these actions might be.
- Have trainees write down what they have learned at the end of the class and share.

Flip Charts
- Prepare complicated flip charts in advance
- Ten lines per page is a maximum

- Don't use the bottom third of the flip chart, as those in the back may not be able to see it

- Write key points only; no long, complicated sentences or paragraphs

- Title each page

- Leave blank pages between prepared sheets

- Use multiple colors, but use them systematically (red for emphasis, blue for key points, green for subpoints, and so on)

Print Materials (How to Write Training Materials by Linda Stoneall, 1991)

- Begin with the elements that you have or may be required to use. For example, your company or group may already have a logo you should incorporate, or you may be asked to use the same color scheme selected for the company brochures.

- Fonts matter, as do their sizes and colors. Fonts are used in

  - Content body (the main text on your page)

  - Header levels in the content

  - Page titles

  - Graphics and graphics captions

- Your best option is to use fonts commonly available on the computer—such as Times New Roman, Arial, and Helvetica—or to learn ways to specify specific fonts. For the font size, either use the default browser font and header sizes or select sizes that are easy to read (nothing smaller than 10 points).

  - No centered paragraphs

  - No decorative fonts in all caps

  - Lots of white space

- Emphasize with text attributes

  - Use highlighting or boldface to draw attention to the main points

  - Vary the size and rotation of text to attract attention

  - Avoid multiple fonts; pick a good font and work with its different styles

- Use boxes with restraint

  - Treat boxes with the same restraint as colors and fonts

  - Use boxes to emphasize important information, such as a sidebar or a pull quote

- Limit line length to forty to sixty characters.
- Tie headings visually to text they head; this means very little space between a headline and the following text, and a larger space between the end of the text and the next headline.
- Don't use all your fonts in one document.
- Don't center large amounts of text.
- Don't use all caps—especially if you're using a calligraphic font.

Developing Role Plays

- Know your purpose and follow it in the design.
- Keep the directions uncomplicated and as brief as possible.
- Make the role play challenging but nonthreatening.
- Provide enough time to do the role play and debrief.
- Use a template for the role play, such as this one:
  - The purpose of this role play:
  - Objective(s) that this role play deals with:
  - The time required for this role play:
  - The number of people needed and their roles:
  - Equipment or special seating required for this role play:
  - Step 1: Choose someone for each role
  - Step 2: Read one of the following role descriptions, depending on your role
  - Step 3:
  - Step 4:
  - Step X: Draw conclusions based on the role play and prepare to discuss them with the entire group
- If content matter is not all available or is very limited, use an open-ended role play in which the beginning is scripted but the trainer soon stops using the script and asks a participant, "Now what would you do?" then asks another participant, "And how would that make you feel?" and so on. This works as a class activity or in small groups as long as one member of each group takes on the trainer's role.

On-the-Job Training (Job Aids)

- Use overviews and "what's in it for me?" in your OJT, just as you would in a classroom delivery
- Why use job aids?
  - Cheap
  - Quick
  - Easy to design
  - Good retention
  - Consistent performance
  - Supports cross training or job transfer
- Types of job aids
  - Correctly filled-in forms
  - Checklists
  - Worksheets
  - Photo-diagrams
  - Task lists
  - Conversion tables
  - Graphs
  - Reference books
  - Step-by-step self-instruction sheets or books
  - Schematic drawings
  - Flow charts
- Have your trainees prepare their own personal job aids, based on the information provided in class and either a little or a lot of structure from you in the form of a template.
- A key to designing job aids is to organize the information according to how the user may see and use it, not according to the information itself.
- In OJT, instructor guides need to be a minimal outline so the trainer doesn't spend too much time talking from them.
- Participant manuals need to be more complete in OJT, as they provide a main reference for after the training is over.
- OJT learner evaluations are best when done as case studies or solve-the-problem types of evaluation, or the actual performance itself.

- Just because the audience is usually only one person doesn't mean the audience analysis isn't important.
- OJT requires more questions built into the design that check learner progress.

An OJT Development Template

    I. Materials

   II. Objective(s)

  III. Prepare trainee

      A. Purpose of session

      B. How session will be conducted

      C. Problems others have had

      D. Evaluation

      E. Any questions

  IV. Key learning points

   V. Expected results

  VI. Work standards

 VII. Sequence of activities

VIII. Demonstration

  IX. Observation of trainee performance

   X. Evaluation

If you are moving a piece of instruction for OJT to a technology-based self-instructional delivery in which you need a script, videotape the OJT instructor doing the training and use this as the basis of your script.

The 70 percent rule. If you're in a real design rush, 70 percent of the time you can do a good job by simply creating a job aid, training on it, and then evaluating its use. This is particularly true if your objectives are more performance-related than cognitive in nature. The other 30 percent is usually content that is fundamental to learning new concepts and so requires a more formalized training process.

Self-Instruction

- Your participant manual for any self-training package should include a piece on how users can learn on their own. This is true for any CD-ROM or asynchronous e-learning self-training package as well ("Preparing the Learner for Self-Directed Learning" by George Piskurich, 1992).

- Your participant manual should include the following:
  - Title Page
  - Course title
  - Course identifier
  - Department that course was developed for
  - Course date
  - Preface
  - Course purpose
  - Course objectives (high level)
  - Intended audience
  - Prerequisites
  - Course instructions
  - Self-directed learning instructions
  - The content, in whatever format you decide is most effective for the learners
  - Self-quizzes
  - Job aids
  - Summary
  - Glossary
  - Final exam instructions
  - List of other resources
  - Certificate of completion
- You can use a decision tree as an activity in your print-based manual. Each decision sends the reader to a different page in the manual, where new material is presented and another decision called for. A decision map at the end of the exercise shows the users where they could (or should) have gone with their decisions and why. This technique is even easier to develop and use in technology-based self-instruction.

Computer and CD-ROM-Based Training

- A rapid design shortcut for video production is to tape short video clips of SMEs doing what they do or talking about how they do it. These can be spliced in or spliced together to create video without going through the scripting and storyboarding process.

- A variation on this rapid design shortcut is to actually tape an SME doing the entire training process. Analyze what the SME did and add necessary aspects, such as objectives and evaluation. Pilot the new program and make necessary changes, then complete the self-instructional aspects and rerecord on a CD-ROM so you have a "brand-new" multimedia program.
- Use prototypes ("Rapid Prototyping" by S. D. Tripp, 1990).
- Create strong storyboards ("Storyboarding Tales" by Colleen Frye, 1998).
- Branch, branch, branch.
- Here are the basic roles for those involved in creating CD-ROM–based training.
  - Project manager
  - Training designer
  - Writer
  - Video producer/director
  - Graphic artist
  - Author/programmer
  - Reviewer
  - On-camera talent

Look for ways to combine two or more of these roles in one person.

- Use stock graphics where you can ("Playing the Stock Market" by John Hartnett, 1999).
- Develop a video shot list and a props list from your storyboard to make your production more efficient and share it with everyone involved. (An example can be found at the end of this chapter.)
- Use a video production checklist such as the one at the end of this chapter.

Scripts

- Take the time to write a good script ("Write Successful Video Scripts," *Info-Line*, 8707).

Storyboards

- Items you might want to include on your storyboard include the following:
  - Text or audio script
  - Graphics
  - Description of interactivity

- List of all previously prepared audio, video, or graphics files that will be used
- Thumbnail sketches of visuals
- Branching instructions
- Programming notes

CHECKLIST FOR CD-ROM (MULTIMEDIA) PROGRAM DEVELOPMENT

☐ Lesson or module test-outs used to decrease learning time

☐ Strong storyboards include the following:

     ☐ Text or audio script

     ☐ Graphics

     ☐ Description of interactivity

     ☐ List of all previously prepared audio, video, or graphics files

     ☐ Thumbnail sketches of visuals

     ☐ Branching instructions

     ☐ Programming notes

☐ Budget determined and approved

☐ Timeline determined, approved, and followed

☐ Objectives and their mastery used as basis of the program

☐ Alpha and beta testing planned

☐ Delivery hardware (and software) that adequately supports program

☐ Branching included where possible

☐ Installation instructions and hardware requirements included

☐ Troubleshooting tips included

☐ A good glossary that's easy to get to

☐ Online help for course navigation and content added where possible

☐ Frequently asked questions (FAQ) section included

☐ Course history screen that allows trainees to keep track of modules completed and those still to be done

☐ Tests with explicit directions on how to complete them

☐ Hot spots (hyperlinks) used wherever possible

☐ Simulations included to increase interactivity

☐ Examples of cause-and-effect relationships shown when possible

☐ Click-and-drag exercises included to help with sorting and sequencing behaviors

☐ Graphics just detailed enough to get the point across

☐ Color and shading used to attract the trainees' attention to particular areas of the screen

☐ Graphics with good, readable resolution, related to the content

☐ Lessons no more than fifteen to twenty minutes long

☐ Video production checklist used

☐ Scripts in active, not passive, voice and written for trainees

☐ Minimal screen text, as readable as possible

☐ All parts labeled with version numbers

HINTS FOR BETTER CD-ROM (MULTIMEDIA) PROGRAM DEVELOPMENT

- If possible, use professionals for everything; if not, use them for as much as possible.

- To save time and money, use a paper-based participant package with your CD-ROM.

- Use prototypes.

- Don't start media production before the storyboard is approved.

- Use good existing media when you can. Even if you have to pay for it, it will save you more in the end.

- In multiple-language situations or when literacy is a problem, keep text to a minimum and use audio—which is easily rerecorded in another language— to the maximum. Don't forget to watch the amount of text in your graphics as well.

- Use your course map or outline as an available screen to help guide the trainee.

- Use hot spots (hyperlinks) to turn the training into a discovery process by having the trainees decide what they want to learn about.

- Create simulations in which the trainee makes decisions and then sees what happens because of those decisions.

- Use both positive and negative behavioral models, with questions as to why they are right or wrong.

- Create dual examples in which the trainee must discriminate between the right one and the wrong one.

- Use story-based simulations as an evaluation process.

- When requiring a trainee response in a simulation, use a three-level feedback process for wrong responses:

  - First, the program asks the trainee to try again.

  - Second, the program branches back to show what should have been done.

  - Third, the program says: "Watch as I do it for you."

- The three-level feedback approach also works for self-quizzes, with the first wrong answer giving a "try again" response, the second branching back to the general area of instruction, and the third specifically showing the answer in a remedial branch.

- Use stock graphics where you can.

- Do your video pieces in small segments and use multiple narrators to make it easier to revise.

- If possible, have all the media ready before you start to program.

- Do videos on location if you can, and use real people for real situations.

- Don't forget that most videos will be displayed on a small screen, so keep them simple.

- Be sure your video budget has included audio recording and postproduction activities and money to pay both technicians and talent.

- When writing scripts for video:

  - Keep the sentences short

  - Use repetition

  - Remember to write for your audience, not yourself

  - Write in case studies and role plays

  - Remember that it's dialogue, not a magazine article

- If you have multiple programmers, be sure that screen layout and format remain constant.

- Use a professional narrator—nothing makes a program sound more professional and more interesting.

- Don't forget that your audio is as important as—and sometimes more important than—your video.
- Screen background should
  - Be chosen for emotional effect
  - Not be distracting
  - Use soft colors and simple patterns
- Screen text should
  - Flow the same way as the culture's written page
  - Be kept to a minimum
  - Not scroll automatically
  - Use the most readable font type for the software
  - Use a minimal number of font types (no more than two or three)
  - Usually use a blocked text design
- Keep your media sorted by lists (video, audio, graphic, animation, and so on)
- Be sure to label everything with version numbers, including scripts, media, and disks
- Use DVD when you need to expand the amount of stored data, particularly for serious games and large pieces of high-quality video. DVD is basically a CD-ROM that has been enlarged to accommodate demands for far greater storage capacity—and like CD-ROM, the more time and money it takes to develop, the harder it is to justify.

E-learning Design Hints

- Use the Web's ability to access references from other websites for both off-line and online activities.
- In instructor-mediated (synchronous) e-learning, case studies can be very effective, particularly if you have the case on a video that can be downloaded and viewed ahead of time so that online time can be used for discussion.
- Graphic illustrations work well in asynchronous e-learning, but don't forget to use good graphic design principles ("Applying Graphic Design Principles" by B. King, 1993).
- Your program should have a indexing scheme that the trainees can refer to at any time to show them where they are in a lesson, where they are going, and where they have been.

- Develop your material based on the characteristics of HTML.
- Use the power of a web browser to add links for enrichment information, literally from all over the world.
- The more hyperlinks you have, the more you'll have to watch them. Place them in a special reference section rather than throughout the training.
- Try your modules out in a print-based format.
- Use proper message design principles (*Handbook of HPT Message Design* by H. Stolovich, 1998).
- Build community in a synchronous classroom the same way you do in a face-to-face class: with introductions and icebreakers.
- Keep graphics, audio files, and video files as small as possible to avoid extended waits for downloading. Professionals in each of these areas and in web-based training can help you.
- Ideas for increasing personal interaction in synchronous e-learning:
  - Provide a chat room and schedule discussion times.
  - Have participants take turns presenting information and acting as the facilitator in online discussions.
  - Design and use online training games.
  - Structure online projects that must be completed outside of the synchronous aspect of the training.
  - Require online teams to make presentations on the topic.
  - Assign interactive exercises, with specific limits on the number of e-mail notes that may be exchanged between any two people.

Satellite-Based Training and Other Telephonic Formats

- Always prepare a study guide that is distributed beforehand and that includes questions that will be discussed and suggested readings.
- Stay away from talking heads.
- For tele-training with smaller groups, have people introduce themselves.
- Any singular activity should take under twenty minutes. This includes lectures, panels—anything.
- Don't forget to allow time for breaks—at least one for every two hours of broadcast.
- Start your program with a check on trainee expectations.

- Use other forms of technology for pre-work to shorten the length of your broadcast.

- Make sure your graphics fit the dimensions of the monitor or screen you'll be presenting on.

VIDEO SHOT LIST/LOG

Use this combined list to plan your video shots and record them as they are completed

Course Name: _____   Taping Date: _____

Location: _____   Master Tape Number: _____

Shot Description	Shot ID #	Time Code In	Time Code Out	Comments	Take (x)

VIDEO PRODUCTION CHECKLIST

Complete this checklist before you begin your video production.

Course Name:　_____

Location(s) of Shoots:　_____

Shoot Dates:　_____

☐ Storyboard approved by_____

☐ Budget approved by all parties

☐ Timeline, including production schedule, approved by all parties

☐ Locations checked out and scheduled

☐ Shot list ready and distributed

☐ On-screen talent approved and scheduled

☐ Video producer approved and scheduled

☐ Scripts ready and distributed to talent and technical people

☐ Rehearsal time scheduled

☐ TelePrompTer and/or cue cards prepared

☐ Props acquired

☐ Editing suite time scheduled

☐ Approval reviewers known and scheduled

Chapter 6

Getting It Where It Does the Most Good: Implementation

This chapter will help you to:

- Initiate effective beta tests and pilots
- Determine the types of reviews necessary for your training program
- Find out about common implementation problems
- Develop train-the-trainer training when appropriate
- Implement your training programs more effectively

$\textbf{N}$ow you've come to what should be the easy part. At least you would think or maybe hope so. You've planned so hard, designed and developed so well, that the actual delivery should be pretty simple. And it can be, if you follow a few good implementation practices.

BETA TESTS AND PILOTS

The first of these implementation practices, and perhaps the most important, are *beta tests* and *pilots*. The purpose of these two processes is to check the viability of your course before you actually implement it. Due to their nature, we're discussing them here.

Beta Tests

Beta tests used to be called *design tests.* The term *beta test* has more or less been borrowed from the computer world, and it is beginning to be the common term for this process. You run a beta test to see how the pieces of your course hold together and whether they work as a whole. Betas are also used to isolate (in a controlled environment) particular aspects of your course that you are not totally sure of, such as special activities, laboratories, complex simulations, and so forth. The importance of a beta test is that it is the first time you will receive feedback from a live audience concerning your course and its component parts.

For a beta test, your audience would include a few representative trainees and an SME or two to give you their viewpoint on the material. If you can, invite another instructional designer for an instructional design review as well. In an extensive beta you might also include the managers or supervisors of your target trainees, other training stakeholders, and anyone else you can round up to fill out the audience.

A beta test usually takes about twice as long as the actual training, due to the need for extensive feedback on all the various parts and pieces. You'll want to stop often during the test to receive that feedback, so be sure to schedule enough time, and let your subjects know why.

Designers approach beta tests in different ways. Some use a focus group; others like to do a managed "talk through." A beta test can be used as a first review or at the end of your first draft of the whole program. The following information describes how to handle a full walk-through type of beta test, usually done after other reviews have been accomplished and a fairly complete draft of the materials is available.

A Beta Test Simulation

Suppose you've just finished developing a two-day class on dealing with change. You have a lot of activities in it, and you want to be sure the activities work properly and that you've covered the material in the right depth and scope for your audience. You might hold a beta test to which you invite the department manager who requested this training, the three supervisors of your target audience, and two other trainers or instructional designers who will be responsible for critiquing all the little nuances of your instructional design. You also ask the supervisors to each bring along one of their best employees to give you feedback from the employee point of view.

Notice that using this approach also lets the invited managers know what is going to be in the training. As an extra added attraction, the process can sort of subtly train them on the change process you are about to institute. These are extra advantages of a beta test that you might want to consider when planning your audience.

Because this is a two-day class, you schedule the beta test to last at least three days. Four would be better, but that will probably not be possible with this group, so you take what you can get.

In your memo to the participants you explain the purpose of the training and of the beta test as well. You tell them what is expected from them in the way of feedback and why the beta test will take longer than the class (because of the feedback). You develop a series of questions for your beta participants, based on those aspects of the training that you want the most feedback on. You send the questions out ahead of time to help them prepare.

At the start of the beta test itself, you explain again why everyone is there and reiterate the importance of their feedback. Your plan for the test includes stopping points at which you will solicit feedback. You let participants know where these points will be and what particular aspects you would like them to focus on at each feedback opportunity.

A good technique is to have your questions or feedback needs prepared on a flip chart that your participants can refer to during each segment of the training. Let them know whether you want the feedback to be spontaneous or to be held back until a stopping point (usually the better approach, as it helps smooth out what is already a broken instructional flow).

Now you begin the training, just as you would if this were a regular class. At each stopping point, you solicit the feedback you have focused on and any other information that your group may provide. When you've finished with the entire program, you review the key issues you thought you heard for clarity and agreement, ask for general or overall comments concerning the training, and use this time to ask for the group's support in getting the employees interested in the program (another one of those little benefits of a beta test).

Other Beta Test Considerations

I've found that a beta test is often more effective if I, as the designer, am not also the facilitator. This gives me more time to watch reactions and make notes and allows me to focus all my attention on the audience and their reactions to the materials, rather than the instruction. However, many times this is not possible, as there is no one else to do the facilitation. In this case try to have one of your colleagues sit in as an observer and note taker, so you won't have to stop the flow to scribble something every time a good point is raised. Tape recorders can help too if they don't make your participants uncomfortable and if they do not require cumbersome activities like passing the microphone.

If you are creating a program that other trainers will facilitate, you will want to do a beta in which one of them does the facilitation to check on how well your trainer's guide can be used.

Beta tests are also a good place to do pre/post testing to check on knowledge acquisition. Even if you are not planning to use pre/post tests as part of the program's actual evaluation, using them as part of your beta will help you to see where your content is weak. If you have followed our good instructional design practices up to this point, you should have a question bank of valid, well-reviewed questions that you can choose from to develop a pre/post test in practically no time. If you did not follow this concept, it might be a good time to start.

Do not forget that this aspect is only valid for those beta participants who are representatives of your training audience. Knowing how managers or SMEs did on a pre/post is not of any value to you.

Many beta tests and pilots start the debrief with a question such as "What did you like and dislike about the program?" Often this leads to a lot of discussion about things that are not relevant to the design, such as policies and procedures the learners don't like, or even discussions of why the course is even being given, particularly if the pilot is also the actual training for the learners. I try to stay away from these types of open-ended questions; in fact, lately I've been eliminating the verbal debrief completely, relying on my written questions to give me what I need to know. One of the other problems with oral debriefs is that one or two individuals with an ax to grind tend to take over, and the others don't get a chance. If you feel you need to do oral debriefs, make your questions specific to what you need to find out about for your design.

 ### Beta Tests and On-the-Job Training

A beta test is just as important for your OJT program as it is for a classroom-based delivery. For your OJT beta you would most likely think of creating a one-on-one situation, but there is no reason why you couldn't have two, three, or even more participants involved to give you feedback. This includes those managers and other key players we mentioned when discussing the classroom beta.

The important thing about an OJT beta is that it be held in the actual training environment. If it is truly OJT, you will need to use the resources of that environment in the training, so you should be there. This can create a lot of scheduling difficulties, particularly when line machinery is involved, but it will be more than worth it in the end.

As with the classroom beta, use good focused feedback techniques and plenty of breaks in the training to get that feedback.

Beta Tests and Self-Instructional Programs

Beta tests are particularly important in self-instructional and technology-based implementations. This is the point at which you will find out whether the self-instruction actually is self-instruction (often it is not, and you'll need to revise some or many of your instructional pieces) and how the technology works with the content. Follow the same rules as we discussed for the classroom beta test as far as audience, breaking up the training with debriefs, and asking questions.

I've found it useful even for self-instructional or distributed deliveries to have all my beta test subjects in one room rather than spread out across a number of sites. In this way I can introduce them to the content and the concept of a beta test and observe as they go through the program. This gives me the ability to ask questions when and where they seem to have problems and to stop them at planned intervals for feedback, the same as for a classroom beta.

Some of you may be saying: "Yes, but that doesn't help you check on how the program runs in a real environment where trainees are on their own or connected from different work sites." Very acute of you, but that is more the venue of the *pilot* than of the beta test. We'll discuss that next. In the meantime, here is a list of ideas to help you plan and implement your beta test.

 ### RUNNING A BETA TEST

1. Explain what the participants will be doing and why they are here.

2. Describe how their feedback will be used.

3. Discuss the confidentiality of their feedback.

4. Audiotape if possible, but ask permission.

5. Keep track of time for first finished, last finished, and an average.

6. Don't forget breaks.

7. Ask the stakeholder to attend at least the debriefing.

8. Be sure to follow your evaluation criteria in the debriefing.

9. Give yourself enough time to gather all opinions and to write a good report.

Pilots

After you've done your beta testing and made revisions where necessary, you should run a pilot. The differences between the two are somewhat subtle, but the importance of those differences is monumental.

First, your pilot should run just a bit longer than your training normally will when you roll it out. The slight additional time is for a post-program debriefing and feedback session. Otherwise, if it's a two-day training session, the pilot should last two days.

Second, the audience for your pilot is different. Gone are the managers, instructional designers, and others who were part of the beta. Your audience for the pilot is the trainees intended for your program—and in the same numbers as your program will support when you roll it out.

So basically, if you plan for a class of twenty-five, your pilot should consist of a class of twenty-five. If your intended audience is all line workers, your pilot should be all line workers. If the class lasts two days, so does your pilot (plus a little extra for the debriefing). If your class is to be run off-site at a hotel, that's where to do the pilot.

Run your pilot within the exact parameters, and in the exact environment, as you will run the actual classes. The purpose of the pilot is to make sure the class will work just as you designed it to when you deliver it for real.

Pilots Versus Betas

A pilot allows you to evaluate things that a beta test does not. Timing is one of these items. You don't stop to garner feedback during a pilot, so you can check whether a two-day class can be run in two days and whether a one-hour activity takes one hour. Logistics should also be assessed during a pilot, which is why you always run a pilot in the actual training environment. A pilot might indicate that you need to have a bigger training room because of the amount of hardware you need, or that all materials must be sent to the training site at least a week in advance.

Obviously the pilot also allows you to check on the trainees' reaction to the training. Do they have the ability to do the activities? Do they need more pre-work to be ready for the class? Are they bored? Overwhelmed? You are probably thinking that we considered this as part of the analysis process, and you are right. However, the pilot is where you test all those assumptions you made back then, because they were just *assumptions* and remain so until real trainees validate them in a real training situation.

As was true for the beta test, you may want to develop questions to ask about particular aspects of the program, but in a pilot these are asked only at the end of the program, not during it. Distributing these questions before the pilot is not a good idea, as it tends to focus the audience on those issues when you need their reactions to the entire program.

Asking questions only at the end can be tough on the designer. As you instruct or observe a pilot, you'll want to jump in with "why's" and "how's" the same as you did during the beta. But control yourself! You'll lose many of the benefits of doing a pilot if you interrupt the flow of the instruction.

If you've done a good design job up to now, and particularly if you did a good beta test, what you learn from your pilot should neither surprise you nor cause you to do much in the way of revising the course. It is actually a final review, done to make sure that all those assumptions you made during analysis, design, and development are accurate.

Because this is (we hope) the case, your materials should be pretty much in final format for the pilot. Your handouts and other media should be finalized. Activities should be completely scripted, and technology should be complete. This is not true of your beta materials, by the way. Most often they will be in draft form for the beta test, and you will almost certainly need to make changes. If you consider the purpose of these two processes, and particularly the different audiences, you'll see why the materials should be at different stages of development for each.

Taken down to the lowest discriminator, you might say that you use betas to test the content and pilots to test the delivery and instructional flow.

Pilots for On-the-Job Training

 Your pilot for an OJT delivery should follow the rules already discussed. That means one trainee and one trainer in the OJT environment. Because of this restriction, you may want to run a number of OJT pilots to obtain enough feedback.

There is an interesting controversy as to whether the designer should be allowed to observe an OJT pilot. Some people feel this interferes with the reality of the pilot; others note that the designer needs to observe what is happening. I don't have an answer for this one. If you think it may be a problem, try to videotape or audiotape the pilot. Otherwise, be content with the debriefing at the end of the pilot and your debriefing of the OJT trainer. Of course, if you are the trainer the issue is moot.

Pilots for Self-Instructional Programs

The pilot is also of particular importance in distributed self-instructional training, whether technology-based or not. This is where you find out whether you can get the information to the trainees effectively and efficiently—and whether they can use it on their own. As with the classroom pilot, everything needs to be exactly as it will be for the final rollout. If you are sending CDs via the post office during rollout, this is what you do for your pilot. If facilitators at the training sites are going to do evaluations, they need to do them for the pilot. If you have a chat room running for one hour every other day as part of the rollout, you need to do it for the pilot. *"Everything exactly the same"* are your pilot watchwords, particularly when it comes to the distribution logistics and the training logistics of self-instructional and technology-based programs.

Once again, the pilot is where you check to make sure that what you expect to work for your program actually does work. Don't make the mistake one instructional designer made: for his pilot, he personally delivered the self-instructional materials to each test site because the self-instructional concept was new and he wanted to "get them off on the right foot." Unless he was going to do the same for every training site every time, this "personal touch" automatically reduced the validity of his pilot.

He failed to find out that the manager and facilitators he trained to do the introduction process for the rollout did not have the time to do it and had delegated the task to subordinates. Because these folks were not trained and thus had no idea how to introduce self-instruction to the target trainees, a major disconnect occurred. This resulted in the trainees being frustrated (as were the people who had this job delegated to them without training) and the program being viewed by many of the trainees and their supervisors as too difficult to bother with. A properly run pilot would have caught this problem and indicated that the delegates, and not the managers, should have received the facilitator training.

Other Thoughts on Pilots

A question I often hear is "Because I'm designing a class that will only be taught once, or to a very small group, do I have to go through all this beta test and pilot stuff?" The answer, as usual, is "It depends." A full-blown pilot is probably not necessary in many small-group or one-time environments. After all, if you only have one set of participants, and you use them for the pilot, what audience would be left for the training? However, some type of combination beta and pilot in which you delve into the areas you are less sure of wouldn't hurt. You can design a beta test, or for that matter a pilot, to do whatever you want. The procedures we have discussed so far are only a guideline, albeit a good one gleaned from hard experience. The important thing is that conducting betas and pilots is the only way you can really learn whether all your design decisions were accurate before they go to your trainees. So choose what works best for your situation, but don't send your training—or yourself—out there without giving it every chance to succeed.

One last comment on these processes that I've also gained from experience: if you are developing a class for delivery in different cultures, do at least a beta test, if not both a beta and a pilot, in each of these cultures. I learned this lesson when I designed a class with a whole range of great activities based on my own culture, only to find that in another culture one of the key activities was experienced and mastered by every grade school student, while in yet a third culture the follow-up activity was not acceptable, as it put too much stress on the trainee-supervisor relationship.

Even if you're designing within a multicultural team, you still need to test your program with real people from each of the cultures in which your program will be delivered, to determine whether cultural differences exist before the rollout.

Here is a checklist that you can use for both beta tests and pilots.

BETA TEST AND PILOT REVIEW CHECKLIST

(To be used by the instructional designer as a guide to completing a beta test, or for a reviewer to answer questions concerning a program.)

Design

- ☐ Amount of material is appropriate for time
- ☐ Task analysis is sufficient
- ☐ Objectives are clear and complete
- ☐ All terms are properly defined
- ☐ Important content is properly stressed
- ☐ Plan for transferring training to the job is adequate
- ☐ Evaluations are sufficient
- ☐ Objectives are met

Lesson

- ☐ Directions to trainees are clear and complete
- ☐ Pace is adequate
- ☐ Overview is adequate
- ☐ Sequence is logical
- ☐ Trainee benefits are explained in enough detail
- ☐ Links to previous training are established where necessary
- ☐ Content is relevant to trainee situation
- ☐ Practices are implemented where needed and for proper time
- ☐ Feedback to trainee is sufficient
- ☐ Activities are effective and timely
- ☐ Transitions are comfortable
- ☐ Reviews and summaries are adequate

Presentation

- ☐ Media are appropriate and effective
- ☐ Job aids are used where possible
- ☐ Reading level is appropriate for the audience
- ☐ Participation is adequate
- ☐ Atmosphere is conducive to learning
- ☐ Small-group involvement is sufficient

General comments:

Design comments:

Lesson comments:

Presentation comments:

 REVIEWS REVISITED

The pilot test basically ends what has been a lengthy review process for our instructional design. We've discussed a number of points at which reviews are important: after you write your objectives, after you develop your test questions, after the content has been written, for every piece of training material, and others. The problem with reviews is that they take time. If we are practicing rapid instructional design, this means by doing reviews we are not so rapid. However, reviews, betas, and pilots are important. In front of the trainees—whether in a classroom, on a computer, or on camera—is no place to realize that there are holes, gaps, or mistakes in the instruction, so *do all the reviewing that your time line permits.*

Here's one hint that I've found useful: give your reviewers a special pencil or pen to be used only for reviewing. Use this memory jogger to remind them of the importance of providing solutions as well as noting problems during their reviews.

Here is a summary of the various types of reviews that we've discussed. It might help you think of ways to combine them for your particular situation and thus make them more efficient in terms of time.

Type	Who	When	Comments
Content	SME	After content is written	1. Hold to scope of objectives 2. Obtain enough information ("this needs more" is not enough information; tell me *what* is needed)
Design	Experienced instructional designer	Starting with objectives, do after each step	1. Review objectives, usability, questions, and media 2. Review objectives when written, with the content, and with the questions
Editorial	Someone new, preferably with proofreading experience	Just before printing	1. Media too 2. Secretaries are great for this
Organizational	Anyone who should	Whenever you feel it's needed	Helps sell your training
Beta	Some subjects close to trainee level and experience	Before pilot	1. Prepare them 2. Observe and ask questions 3. Debrief extensively
Pilot	The real audience in the real environment	Before releasing any training	1. *Exactly* as the training will be used 2. Observe if possible, but do not interrupt 3. Debrief with planned questions and goals

If you are planning to use more than one review for the same purpose, a rapid design shortcut is to have your reviewers or validators meet as a group. This takes not only less of their time but also less of yours, as you do not have to collate their comments but can simply record what they all agree is right.

Here is a general review e-mail that you can use as a template when you send out any of your material for review. Notice that it gives accessing directions, asks specific questions of the reviewers so they don't go off on a tangent, sets a deadline, and provides contact information.

Training Review E-mail
Subject: SL Training Ready for Review

Joe:
The deliverables for Service Leader Training are now ready for review.
There are two deliverables to review for this segment:

- SL Training LG
- SL Training PG

To retrieve the soft copies, access:

1. Consumer on 'Nc-cic-vs14<\\>Hrtrain1<\\>Data'
The file names are
SL Training LG_5.5
SL Training PG_5.5
Please consider the following questions during your review:
Are the exercises and scenarios realistic?
Does the information represent reality in the workplace?
Does the information have language that is easy to understand?
Is the information presented in a logical order?
Is all essential information covered?
Is the information workable?

NOTE: If you answered No to any of the questions, please provide specific feedback on or in the documents.

If you have any questions, please call George Piskurich, the lead designer for this segment.

Please return all comments NO LATER THAN May 19 to

George Piskurich
409 Gentry Walk
Macon, GA 31210
478-405-8977

Only comments received by May 22 will be considered for review unless otherwise noted. The review meeting for this segment is scheduled for May 23 at 9:00 A.M.

Thank you.

COMMON IMPLEMENTATION ISSUES

Overall, if you have done your analysis well and remained true to it throughout design and development, your implementation should be relatively simple, particularly if you did beta testing, piloting, or both to make sure your training works as expected. The purpose of implementation is to get your program to where it does the most good—that is, to the audience that you determined needed it when you did your analysis.

 ### Classroom Implementation

For classroom delivery, implementation is pretty simple. You just have to arrange a meeting between the trainees, the trainer, and the materials, preferably all at the same time. Of course, anyone who has ever taught a class, particularly away from his or her home base, will tell you that it is much more difficult than you think. There are a lot of issues—enrollment, room size, facility support, travel plans, material reproduction, or even the weather—that can interfere with the smooth delivery of your class.

The art of administering and facilitating a classroom training delivery goes well beyond the scope of this book. (See "Basic Training: Getting Ready to Present" by Bill Withers, 1999.) You'll find a few helpful hints at the end of this chapter and a checklist or two. Generally, the most cogent advice I ever received for a classroom implementation was: "Sweat the details." Check everything twice, then check it again. Have a backup plan, and a backup plan for your backup plan. Get there early and be ready before your trainees come in. And, most important, *be flexible.* Anything can happen, from materials that never get there to an earthquake to lost or impounded luggage. Expect anything to happen; don't get flustered when it does; and do what you can with what you've got. Remember that the oldest, and possibly most effective, classroom instruction ever done consisted of a master, a few apprentices, and a stick for writing in the dirt.

To keep your field trainers from wearing out during large implementations, design your programs for a maximum of three days. That way they can travel on Monday, teach Tuesday through Thursday, and still have Friday to travel home or be back in the office catching up.

One problem with classroom implementation is no-shows. Solve this by charging the employee's cost center a noncompletion charge if they don't show up.

A second problem is that the learners do not finish the post class work. Charge them for the course for this if it's not done in a specified time.

A third problem is the learners who come to the class without having done the pre-work. Send them home! Word will get around quickly enough that you mean business.

 ## Implementation of Self-Instruction

Implementation is a bit more difficult when you use a self-instructional delivery. You have reproduction needs to consider and possibly a facilitation aspect as well. You'll need to train your facilitators well—well in advance of the actual implementation. Be sure they have the time, ability, and motivation to do what your program requires of them.

You may also want to do a little training of your trainees to make them comfortable with self-instruction if this is the first time they've attempted this learning method. This might require an orientation to self-instruction, or even a small practice program that they can easily succeed at before they tackle the real training.

A key to good self-instructional implementation is simply to make sure that the programs are available when the trainees need them. If you do a good job at this and at facilitator and trainee preparation, most everything else you do will simply be polish to make the implementation shine a bit brighter.

Learning Center Deliveries

A self-instructional learning center delivery is usually simpler than a distributed self-instructional delivery, as you have only one (or possibly a few) sites to worry about. These sites most often come with a full-time facilitator who can handle program distribution, trainee angst, and a number of other issues. However, you pay for this resource on the front end by having to set up the center and hire and train the facilitators. If you are using a preexisting center for your program delivery, this will not (or at least should not) be a problem, but if you are creating a center for your programs to reside in, you'll have a lot to do to make the center ready before the first trainee sits down (*Self-Directed Learning* by George Piskurich, 1993).

In a learning center delivery, it is critically important to make sure your training is available when the trainees want and need it, and that it is not subject to hardware availability. This is one of the main advantages of self-instruction, and if it is not part of your delivery process you have missed the boat somewhere. For example, I once saw a self-instructional system in which the learning center computer could be used only from 4:00 P.M. to 6:00 P.M. when it was not busy doing other things. What do you think the compliance level was for the "mandatory" training that was available on this delivery system?

This goes for the facilitator too. If the trainees have to hunt for a facilitator to provide them with materials or to monitor their test, and then have to wait until the right planets are aligned for the facilitator to have the time, your program will most likely fail to achieve its stated goals—particularly those requiring heavy facilitation, such as evaluation.

Distributed Deliveries

If you are using a distributed delivery for self-instructional implementation, distribution problems and breakdowns can be added to the above list of delivery difficulties. These include everything from late post office deliveries to a balky intranet. Package couriers don't always deliver on time, papers are lost on the job site, CD-ROMS go bad, and LANs go down. Higher technologies such as satellite delivery or web-based classrooms can make things much simpler—or much more complicated—for distributed delivery systems.

As with classroom delivery, expect Mr. Murphy to be a big part of your technology-based delivery; plan for anything to go wrong, because sooner or later it will. Have backup machines, backup materials, and backup plans for those times when the machines just refuse to work.

Since one of your biggest problems in a distributed delivery such as asynchronous e-learning is to prepare your learners, you might consider setting up temporary mini-learning centers that they can go to for their first couple of experiences. This will help them get off to a good start and will reduce their anxiety and frustration when things don't go quite as planned.

 ### Train the Trainer

Another aspect of delivery is what is normally referred to as T-3 or *train the trainer*. If you are both the instructional designer and the only trainer, you do not need to worry about T-3, so just skip this area until your situation changes. However, if others are going to train using your material, this is a big issue. A well-trained instructor can make your training sing; a poorly trained one can hamstring it.

The main issue here is to spend some time with the trainer. This does not have to be formal (although formal is better), but it should be systematized. Discuss your analysis and the reasons for the class. Go over objectives and exercises, particularly any that might be tricky. Elicit input and listen to suggestions. Some of my best design ideas were not mine at all, but concepts or simply random thoughts that came out of a T-3 session.

If you can create a more formal approach, all the better. This might consist of having the trainers observe you or someone else teaching the material, then observing them while they teach. The beta test is a good place to do the first observation, and the pilot is not half bad as a place for the second or the first. I've often had anyone who might possibly teach my course as a guest or participant at one or both of these processes. You'll have to use another person as an observer if you are doing the instruction of a beta or pilot, but this is simply one more of those tradeoffs that you'll need to make. Is it more important for you to observe the pilot or to give your trainers a full model of how the instruction works? The choice is yours.

Be sure you supply the trainers with your well-constructed lesson plan, and make it known that these are their copies to write on as they wish. For some reason new trainers are often hesitant about marking up "your" lesson plan, so make a point of letting them know how much of the course is open to interpretation and which parts must be done as written.

T-3 as we've discussed it is so far is for experienced trainers only—those you are helping to learn the way your course is structured. For people with no training experience, T-3 takes on an entirely different meaning, as you need to teach presentation and facilitation skills as well as content and lesson plan flow. Again, there are many good sources of information on this type of trainer preparation if you need it, but find out what your trainers' needs are first, then meet them. Here is a general outline for a T-3 program for inexperienced trainers:

Basic Classroom Facilitation Outline

    I. Introduction

        A. What makes a good facilitator

        B. What doesn't

        C. The basic presentation styles

   II. Adult Learning Principles

        A. Which principles are most important for facilitation

 III. Preparing for Facilitation: Long Before the Class

        A. Knowing your audience

        B. Knowing your design

        C. What resources you need; what resources you have

        D. Practice, PRACTICE, **PRACTICE!**

  IV. Preparing for Facilitation: Right Before the Class

        A. Getting there early

        B. Setting up the room

        C. Name tags and name tents

        D. Setting up equipment

        E. Setting up your area

   V. Delivery

        A. Building rapport

        B. The keys to excellent facilitation

           1. Vocabulary

           2. Voice

           3. Eye contact

           4. Appearance

  VI. First videotaped presentation

VII.   Using the Lesson Plan

    A. Objectives

    B. Ice breakers

    C. Motivation

    D. Overviews

    E. Activities

    F. Summaries

VIII.   Leading lectures, discussions, and demonstrations

  IX.   Question-and-answer sessions

   X.   Facilitating small group instructions

  XI.   Classroom control

    A. Time

    B. Dealing with characters

 XII.   Using Media

    A. Handouts and pass-outs

    B. Flip charts

    C. Overheads

    D. Computer projection of PowerPoint files

    E. Other media

XIII.   Evaluation

    A. Feedback to the learner

    B. Feedback from the learner

XIV.   Final Videotaped Presentation

 Your T-3 can be a rapid design technique as well. The better your trainers are at training, the less explicit your lesson plans will have to be and thus the less time you'll have to spend developing them. If you have the luxury of doing a T-3 for a specific program, you can really reduce your lesson plan size by providing information there instead of in the document.

Train the Trainer for Self-Instruction?

No T-3 exists for self-instructional training, which is obvious. However, in many self-instructional deliveries, particularly distributed ones, you will need to do facilitator training. Self-instructional facilitators are not trainers. This is both good and bad. It is good because they won't need the depth of content knowledge training or classroom skills that a trainer needs; it is bad because in most cases they have no facilitation skills at all and know little to nothing of what is expected of them as facilitators.

There are any number of ways to do facilitator training for your self-instructional program, all based for the most part on what you need the facilitators to do. Remember when we did facilitator analysis to try to determine whether the right facilitators were available? Use this information and your design work to put together a training program that gives the facilitators the skills and knowledge they need to do the things you thought might be necessary back in the analysis stage.

If you do a beta test, have a few (or more) of your possible facilitators as beta subjects and ask them about your facilitator requirements. Your pilot will tell you where other facilitation problems may lie. Use all of this information in formulating your facilitator training.

The problem, particularly in a distributed self-instruction delivery, is to get that training to the facilitators. You may be able to develop a facilitator's manual, or you may need actual face-to-face time with them. The key is to know what is needed and then to create a system that works best for the facilitators in your company's environment.

An approach I like to use is a self-instructional package on how to facilitate each program. Using this method, the facilitators learn what is expected of them and at the same time they experience self-instruction. This approach can be expensive and time-consuming with some of the higher-level technologies, but there is no reason why you cannot mix your media and make the facilitator self-instruction a print-based package with references to the main technology program blended into the process. Also, use some type of monitoring check to make sure your facilitators complete their package and understand it. The usual post-quiz is a good tool for this purpose, although I've used everything from phone calls to videotapes, depending on the program.

And remember, a facilitator of self-directed learning:

- Doesn't know everything

- Doesn't have all the answers

- In fact, doesn't even know all the questions, as most often the learner provides these

Here is an example of a facilitator checklist for a self-instructional delivery that might be helpful for you.

SELF-INSTRUCTION FACILITATOR CHECKLIST

Each time a trainee takes a self-instructional package, use this checklist as your guide to help them start properly.

☐ Allow sufficient time for the trainee to complete the package.

☐ Provide quiet space.

☐ Explain that the trainee is responsible for his or her own learning.

☐ Give the trainee an answer sheet from a provided supply.

☐ Explain that all answers are to be recorded on the answer sheet.

☐ Check on the trainee every twenty minutes.

☐ Be available to answer questions.

☐ Record the trainee's name, program title, and completion date on the program completion record.

☐ Have the manager sign the program completion record.

☐ Provide at least one opportunity for guided practice.

On-the-Job (One-on-One) Trainer Training

Training for OJT trainers has its advantages and difficulties as well. Because OJT trainers are usually SMEs, you won't need to deal much with content. However, they are not usually trainers, so you will have to train them on training techniques, particularly one-on-one training techniques. You will want to show them how to use the materials you designed, and you'll want to go over any instructional or logistical aspects that might cause them headaches. I normally make it a priority to remind the OJT trainers how important it is to keep to both the time schedule and the required content. In fact, I remind them of these two factors continually, as they seem to have the most difficulty with these concepts.

I like to teach my OJT trainers the seven-step approach to successful OJT:

1. Tell Me

2. Show Me

3. Do It for Me

then

4. Let Me Tell You

5. Let Me Show You

6. Let Me Practice

and of course,

7. Evaluate Me Doing It

I also remind them that they must not be seen by the trainees as the guru with all the answers, so they should use the four-step question-answering technique:

1. The learner asks a question.
2. Answer, "What do you think?"
3. If it's not a safety problem, then say, "OK, try it."
4. If things did not go right, follow up with "What do you think went wrong?"

If job aids are being used, I discuss this five-step process with them:

1. Review the job aid to make sure it is right.
2. Tell your learners what it is and what it is used for.
3. Train them on how to use it through demonstration.
4. Allow them to practice using it.
5. Evaluate them using it.

You can do OJT trainer training one-on-one or in a classroom, depending on numbers. The most important skills they need to review during this aspect are the basic communications skills (listening, verbal, non-verbal, empathy, and so on) that you would teach any facilitator. However, whatever your approach, make sure you give them plenty of *observed* practice time to bring their skills up to speed before they meet their first trainees.

 Administration Guide

Another good implementation practice is the creation of a *program adminis-tration guide*. This is useful if your program is going to be instructed by a number of people in various environments. The administration guide details overall information about the course—such as goals, objectives, audience, and so forth—and provides helpful information on what is needed to run the course, such as supplies, hardware, materials, registration, prerequisite con-cerns, room size, and all the other logistics processes.

These aspects are often part of the design document and lesson plan or, in the case of a self-instructional program, the facilitator's package. But in some cases there is an administrative person involved in doing the planning and organizing who does not receive the lesson plan or who doesn't know how to use it. The administrative guide helps these folks to do their job effectively, which will make your training more effective. You can pull the majority of information directly from these documents and add to it as needed. In your implementation planning, don't forget to at least consider whether you'll need an administration guide.

 ## Management Guide

Closely related to the administration guide—in fact, for many programs it is the same thing—is the *management guide.* A management guide is used to tell the manager(s) about the course, what it will do, what their responsibilities are, and how they can help make it a success. If you invite managers to your beta test, this is a good takeaway for them. I like to add a sheet in my management guide that gives them hints on how they can talk to their employees about the importance of the course and lay the groundwork for their accepting and being motivated for it.

I have a rule concerning management guides. If I don't seem to need one, I go back and find out why. Managers and supervisors are an important element in almost every training program's success. They perform important functions, from allowing their people to attend to following up on the training through post-class activities that help transfer the training to the job. Every program should have a tie-in to management, and the management guide explains to the manager what that tie-in is.

With your implementation under way, you are pretty much done, right? Wrong! Remember back in Chapter Two when we discussed the fact that the only real reason for doing training was to meet an organizational need? Well, how do you know whether you've done that, or even whether your trainees have learned anything? The answer is the instructional design component of *evaluation,* and that's Chapter Seven.

HINTS FOR IMPLEMENTATION

Classroom

- Give trainers in training a chance to observe the training before they do it.
- Give the designer or developer and trainer a chance to talk together.
- A good trainer will have these competencies:
  - Can use course material effectively
  - Can use trainee information effectively
  - Prepares well
  - Establishes and maintains credibility with trainees
  - Demonstrates good classroom management techniques

- Is an effective communicator
- Is an effective questioner
- Relates well to trainees with questions and problems
- Provides positive reinforcement
- Uses instructional media properly
- Is a keen evaluator of trainee performance

Flip Charts

- If you have prepared flip charts, keep them on one easel and write on another.
- Talk to the class, not to the flip chart.
- Post key sheets on the wall to make them easier to refer to and for better retention.

Logistical Items to Discuss in a Classroom Introduction

- Emergency exits
- Rest rooms
- Location of phones
- Contact phone number at training site (on flip chart)
- Vending machines
- Ground rules

Presentation Pointers

- When using a PowerPoint presentation, print out the slides six to a page for your trainer's manual so your trainer has a better idea of what's coming up next.
- Things your trainers should never have to say:
  - "I know that I'm not supposed to read these overheads to you, but since those in the back can't see them. . . ."
  - "I don't have a handout, as I did not want anything to interfere with your learning from my presentation."
  - "I'll answer questions at the end of my presentation."
  - "I'll lecture for about an hour and then we'll do an activity."
  - "I know we only have twenty minutes left, so let me spend some time talking about the objectives on your list."

Hints for Facilitators

- Overprepare.
- Build a presentation kit with all the things you need for your media, from markers and a stapler to extension cords for computer projectors.
- Observe others as they facilitate and note what they do that works.
- Stay up to date on content.
- Memorize your introduction and have it down pat.
- Resist the temptation to make any significant last-minute changes to your lesson plan.
- Eat light before you facilitate and at lunch.
- Get there early.
- Use both name tags and name tents, depending on the classroom environment.
- Start and STOP on time.
- Don't be a slide narrator.
- Reinforce each learning point.
- Know where you're going and what you're going to do when you get there.
- Don't be afraid to be seen using your lesson plan.
- Use quotations, metaphors, analogies, and stories to illuminate the content.
- Silence can be golden.
- Use nonbreak breaks, like throwing a ball, stretching, or mind relaxers.
- Take a walk during the breaks to clear your mind.
- Use games to get them back—team games work best.
- Everyone likes prizes.
- Candy breaks, particularly in the afternoon, are real energizers.
- He who laughs last was probably offended by your joke.
- Summarize.
- Have fun.

Guide to Room Size

For approximately twenty trainees:

> Minimum = 20 × 24
> Maximum = 24 × 30
> Best = 22 × 26

On-the-Job (One-on-One) Training

- Train (certify) your OJT trainers in how to do one-on-one training, as well as in how to use your materials.

- When demonstrating the job, sit or stand in the exact position that the trainee will be in when doing the job.

- When the trainees are practicing for the first few times, as they do each step have them explain what they are doing and why.

- Provide feedback on each step as needed.

- Correct errors immediately.

- Give praise for a successful performance.

- Be sure the trainees know where to obtain help before being left on their own.

- Be sure your trainers realize that learning must take precedence over production during the training.

- Remind the trainers that unlike in classroom training, there is no learning from peers in OJT, so the trainer is the source.

- If you use OJT because your content changes often and rapidly, be sure to use a printer who can provide you with just-in-time printing for your materials. You lose a lot of cost effectiveness if you have to keep throwing away outdated material.

- Recognition for completion of OJT is often not considered. As you do for your other programs, use certificates, plaques, and mailed copies of completed training records. For multiclass programs, issue stickers at the end of each portion to be placed on a certificate. This also works well as recognition for completed projects on the way to long-term certification.

Self-Instruction

If you plan to develop a learning center, sell the supervisors on its advantages and capabilities first.

Training Centers

- Plan enough space for trainees to work and keep documents open.

- Post a sheet of instructions on how to adjust "adjustable" chairs.

- Have enough room for the trainer to spread out his or her material.

- If you use a lending library format as part of your center, use a fax request form to allow trainees to sign up for programs or put them on reserve for borrowing.

- In distributed self-instruction systems, charge a noncompletion penalty against the trainees' department's budget if evaluations or monitoring reports are not returned.

Computer Training Centers

- Use red and green cups that trainees place on their computers to notify the facilitator that they have a question: red for immediate help, green to signify a question that can wait.

- Styrofoam hamburger boxes stuck on the wall in the proper order and labeled with a magic marker make a great instructional aid for teaching keyboard skills in software training.

- Use the following checklist to help you implement a distance (distributed) self-instructional program of any type.

 CONDUCTING A DISTRIBUTED SELF-INSTRUCTIONAL IMPLEMENTATION

☐ An effective, efficient delivery system for the programs is being utilized.
- The human touch is being used, if possible.
- Contingency plans for lost packages are in place.
- A procedure is in place for packages that arrive without explicit instructions.

☐ Effective control measures are being used.
- Packages are in a good physical location and available when needed.
- Record-keeping techniques are in place to maintain control.
- Formal and informal management observations will be made at the training sites.
- Personal observations, facilitator reports, training-completed reports, and other control measures are being implemented.
- Top management is being kept involved to keep their support high.

☐ Specialized evaluation measures of trainees and the packages are being implemented.

- Trainee performance evaluations are being done correctly.
- Package effectiveness (training transfer) evaluations are being done.
- Program compliance is being checked.

☐ Procedures to ensure continued compliance and support are in effect.

- The programs are being updated on a timely basis.
- Revision and updating procedures are in place.
- Revision data from the sites is being collected.
- Edition control procedures are in place.

Use the next checklist to help you implement a learning center for self-instructional programs.

OPERATING A LEARNING CENTER

☐ Adequate furniture has been purchased.

- Special consideration has been given to chairs.

☐ Storage space is sufficient.

☐ Lighting, heating, ventilation, air conditioning, and interior decoration have been considered.

☐ Electrical needs have been satisfied.

☐ Hardware requirements have been satisfied.

☐ Prepackaged materials have been obtained when possible.

☐ Facilitators have been selected.

- Staffing will be continuous.

☐ Hours of operation have been set.

- Contingencies for shift workers have been developed.

☐ Scheduling policy and procedures have been set.

- A decision about sign-in sheets has been made.

☐ A card catalog system or its equivalent has been developed.

☐ The mechanism by which trainees obtain packages has been tested and determined to work.

☐ Center directions have been posted.

☐ Program directions accompany programs when needed.

☐ Directions for using machines have been posted.

☐ A center orientation for new users has been developed.

☐ Center initiation publicity has been done.

- Group initial orientations have been done.
- The corporate newsletter has been used.
- A center program booklet has been developed.

☐ Center evaluation mechanisms have been developed.

- Package effectiveness as a function of job transfer has been considered.
- Evaluation of trainee learning has been systematized.
- Center efficiency evaluation through use of sign-in sheets and opinion-naires have been considered.
- Enough data for a center cost-benefit analysis is available.

COMPUTER AND CD-ROM-BASED TRAINING

- Items to check for a CD-ROM beta or pilot:
  - Course runs on appropriate hardware.
  - Screen colors are appropriate.
  - All navigation points work as specified.
  - All branching works as specified.
  - Course can be entered or exited where necessary.
  - Menus are available as needed to make the course efficient to use.
  - "Tone" of course is appropriate for the audience.
  - Narration is appropriate for the audience.
  - Graphics are constructed well and appropriate for the course.
  - Test questions are criterion-referenced.
  - Feedback is available where needed and facilitates learning.
  - Quality of audio and video is up to the standard set for the course.
  - Objectives can be met through the content.
  - Activities are plentiful and timed to keep trainee interest high.
- Have your storyboard validated by SMEs and other necessary reviewers, as it's much easier to change things here than later.

E-LEARNING

- General items you might need to determine during an e-learning pilot ("Synchronous Distance Learning: The Interactive Internet Classroom" by J. Stewart, 1999):
  - Is the training appropriate to the audience?
  - Does the audience have the proper computer skills?
  - Does the audience have the right prerequisite knowledge?
  - Will the hardware support the program effectively?
  - Do all trainees have necessary add-ons and peripherals?
  - Do all trainees have correct software versions?
  - Can all participants connect to the network?
  - Is the connection speed what is required?
  - Is the connection reliable for all sites?
- Ideas for increasing personal interaction in e-learning:
  - Seat more than one participant at each computer.
  - Have online team members interact among themselves before responding.
  - Pose challenges that require online teamwork to answer.
  - Provide prizes and incentives (such as downloadable games) for participation.
  - Post ideas on your bulletin board that require comment from each trainee and reactions to their colleagues' comments.
  - Introduce facilitators and trainees through e-mail or precourse questionnaires that all see.
  - Share common likes and dislikes through your bulletin board or chat room.
- If you are using a web-based delivery, or even if you are not but have an intranet, you can do your trainee tests in a computer format instead of paper and pencil. There are a number of programs available to help you do this, and it will save you a great deal of logistics time in distance environments.
- Use the computer screen as you would a flip chart, allowing each participant to type in a response, then showing all the responses to everyone for discussion.
- Train your synchronous e-learning trainers on how to use this delivery system effectively.
- Use a nongraded preclass session to allow the trainees to become accustomed to synchronous technology and to test your system. Make it something fun, like a discussion of current events.

SATELLITE-BASED TRAINING (TELECOMMUNICATIONS)

- Determine your downlink sites based on where your employees currently travel to and from for training.
- Keep track of the people who do not participate and try to involve them in future discussions.
- Flip charts and whiteboards don't work well with satellites or cameras.
- Use a graphics camera to show prepared visuals.
- Be specific on ground rules and communications do's and don'ts during the training.
- Check out all equipment and links before the trainees arrive, starting two to three hours in advance of the broadcast.
- Rehearse, rehearse, rehearse.
- Keep a name map to show you who is where.

Chapter 7

Did It Do Any Good?
Evaluation

This chapter will help you to:

- Discover why evaluation is important
- Find the key to appropriate evaluation
- Consider the applicability of the types of evaluation to your training situation
- Master the evaluation of self-instructional programs
- Create a revision plan for your training

..........*U*p to this point you've analyzed, designed, developed, and implemented, but there is still one more step. Sooner or later (more likely sooner), someone is bound to ask, "Did it work?" Did your training do what it set out to do? Was it any good? These questions and others are what evaluation tries to answer. To finish our house metaphor, this would be the inspection before you move in.

WHY EVALUATION?

Evaluation is sort of like the weather—as the old saw goes, everyone talks about it, but few seem to be able to do much about it. You can probably see the main reason why. By now you've already spent a lot of time and energy on this training, and you may not want to invest more. You may also have been given new priorities or new training to do, or simply gone through any of a number of other business changes that have you telling yourself: "You don't have time to mess with evaluation."

However, you must evaluate. If you do not evaluate, you might just as well not have analyzed, or developed consistent materials, or implemented properly,

267

because the end product is the same: training that is suspect, that may be good or may not be—you just don't know.

You evaluate for one of two reasons: (1) because someone else wants to know whether the training you designed was effective or (2) because you want to know. These might seem to be the same thing, but they are not, and the difference between them is the difference between good evaluation and an exercise in futility.

Let's look at an example. Suppose you have done a little reading and you've found that there are at least four different kinds of evaluation (*Evaluating Training Programs: The Four Levels* by Donald Kirkpatrick, 1994). Being a good instructional designer, you decide to do all four kinds for your program. So you have the trainees evaluate the program with a reaction sheet, you evaluate the trainees' learning with a good criterion-based test, you monitor their use of the new skills back on the job through observation and supervisory interviews, and you develop a return on investment (ROI) evaluation that compares program costs with achievement of corporate goals.

You write a report that details the ROI, but no one in upper management ever really reads it. You compile data that shows that 87.6 percent of the trainees felt the course was outstanding, but since it is not being given again, no one really cares.

You get the point. What you've done was right from a pure instructional design viewpoint, but wrong (or at least worthless) for your organization. "But wait," you say. "What if *I* wanted to know these things?" That's great, but do you have the time to satisfy your own curiosity when there is so much else to do? "But wait," you say again. "Didn't you just hammer into me the fact that evaluation *must* be done or the training is suspect? And aren't you saying now that evaluation doesn't need to be done at all?"

The answer to that last question is both a resounding NO and a possible YES. No, I'm not saying you don't have to evaluate, but yes, evaluation can easily be a waste of time and not worth the effort. This is another one of those "clear-cut" instructional design issues that we keep running across.

 THE KEY TO GOOD EVALUATION

The solution to this conundrum is to *know what to evaluate*, and this in turn is based on what you are going to do with the evaluation.

First, if doing evaluation means you get to keep your job, then by all means do evaluation. This may be a bit of an overstatement, but basically, if your manager or some other manager needs to see that the trainees liked the course, then evaluate for that. If this or that person needs to know that the trainees learned something, then evaluate for that. If the big boss wants to know whether your training was cost-effective, then evaluate for that. But know *why* you are evaluating, *who* your evaluation audience is, and *what* they want to know before you start. Sound familiar? If not, go back to Chapter Two and begin the whole design process again.

Evaluation is a lot like analysis. In fact, in really well-designed training systems it is difficult to see where evaluation ends and the next round of analysis begins. But for now, let's just deal with the concepts mentioned above. Know why you are evaluating, who you are evaluating for, and what they want to know, and then design your evaluation for that purpose.

For the most part, when others ask whether your training did the job, what they really want to know is whether it is helping the organization to meet its goals. If you have followed our instructional design approach, you should be able to link the training back through test questions, content, objectives, and tasks, all the way to corporate needs. So if your trainees learned, the training was effective, although to convince others you may need to do a little more than just say so.

This Evaluation's for You

But what if you are evaluating for yourself as the instructional designer? What do you evaluate then, and how? The answer to this is even simpler. If you are only evaluating your training for its own sake, let what you evaluate be dictated by the training—and by the amount of time you can spare to do evaluation instead of the other things expected of you .

For example, one tried-and-true method of evaluation is the *class reaction sheet*, often known as the opinionnaire, and even more disparagingly known as the "smile sheet." We've all filled out dozens of these. Ever wonder what happens to them? Well, sometimes they are looked at; sometimes statistical analysis is done on them and they are summarized; and some are filed away in drawers and never see the light of day again. You might think it's a waste, but not necessarily. Remember our key to good evaluation. If the reason for this reaction sheet evaluation was to do it so that there was proof it was done, because someone might ask to see these evaluations some day, then it served its purpose.

But what if you planned to give this course again next year, and you were interested in which topics the trainees thought were covered well and which were not? Now your course has told you what to evaluate. Or perhaps in the next iteration you will only need three trainers, not the current six. Do you hear what your course is asking you to evaluate?

Obviously, asking questions such as "Were there enough breaks?" "Was the room too hot or too cold?" and "Did you like the donuts?" won't get you information about content, but the right questions will. And if you want to know whether the same facility or the same bakery would be a good choice for next time, then these other questions might be valid as well.

Or, if your course tells you that for it to be successful your trainees must take what they've learned and apply it to the job (remember the objectives from back in the design phase), then you need to evaluate its success by determining whether the trainees did transfer the skills to the job. This may require observation instead of a smile sheet; in fact, you may not use an opinionnaire at all for this training if it doesn't tell you what you need to know. Observation is the type of evaluation that your course demands, so that's what you want to do.

Thinking this way about evaluation even answers the age-old question "To test or not to test?" Put philosophy and sociology and all the rest aside. If your training, through its objectives, says that success is measured by knowledge retention or skills mastery, then the right kind of test, as we discussed in Chapter Four, is the right kind of evaluation. If these things, or the other things that tests measure, are not important, then neither is a test.

There is an old saying: "Don't ask a question you really don't want to know the answer to." This works very well in marriages and to some extent in instructional design evaluation as well. Let's change it to read: "Don't ask evaluation questions that nobody (including yourself) needs or cares to know the answers to." Know *who will review* your evaluation data and *what data* he or she wants. This will tell you what you need to capture and how and when to capture it.

To make this whole evaluation thing simple, try asking yourself these five questions:

- Why do I want to evaluate?
- What am I going to evaluate?
- Who should I involve as part of the evaluation?
- How am I going to do the evaluation?
- When should I do the evaluation?

If you cannot come up with reasonable answers for these five questions that support each other when taken as a whole, you might want to rethink the whole idea.

 What we have just discussed is in itself a rapid design shortcut. Don't play "follow the leader" by evaluating everything you can. Only evaluate what you need to evaluate—what there is a good "why?" for. Otherwise, forget it. You'll save tons of design time and record-keeping time and a lot of headaches.

TYPES OF EVALUATION

From the preceding discussion, you may have discerned that there are four major types of evaluation. We've already mentioned them all and discussed a couple in some of the other chapters, but here they are, in order of popularity:

- Trainee reaction to the course
- Skills and knowledge mastery and retention (*same concepts, just different timing*)
- Transfer to the job, which can also be defined as improvements in job performance
- Return on investment or corporate goal fulfillment

This system of evaluation was created by Donald Kirkpatrick, and he assigned levels to each type of evaluation. By levels, it looks something like this:

Level 1: Reaction

Level 2: Learning

Level 3: Behavior

Level 4: Results

Some authors have split some of these, added to this system, and rearranged it, the most common change being a fifth level added in which the results level is broken out into corporate goal fulfillment and ROI, so it looks something like this:

Level 1: Reaction

Level 2: Learning

Level 3: Application

Level 4: Business Impact

Level 5: Return on Investment (ROI)

Let's look more closely at each level in turn.

Level 1: Trainee Reaction to the Course

As we've discussed, this is the most used and probably most abused type of evaluation. Many designers do it for no better reason than that they think it *should* be done, and then they have no idea what to do with the data. Here are some good reasons for doing this type of evaluation:

- You are giving this particular course again and want to know what was received well and what was not
- You are thinking of using the trainer again and want information on the trainees' opinion of him or her
- You are the trainer and want to know what you can do better
- You are going to revise the course and want information on what you should revise
- You want to know what the trainees thought about certain aspects of the course (activities, exercises, and so on)
- Someone or something is forcing you to do this type of evaluation (boss, accrediting agency)

Ways to Do It

For all the above reasons except the last one, you should design an evaluation instrument that asks the trainees exactly what you want to know. If it's about the trainer, ask about the trainer. If it's about donut freshness, ask about donuts. The worst thing you can do is have a general trainee reaction instrument that asks a little about a lot of things and so tells you very little about anything (but does keep you busy collating and summarizing data).

The exception to this rule is that last bullet. For this category, develop and have approved a reaction instrument that you use every time. If you think you can actually get some use out of it, frontload it with the questions you really need to ask, but otherwise just collect the data and have it ready and statistically manipulated when asked.

These written surveys come in all sorts of styles, with three-choice answers (good, bad, indifferent), four-choice answers (all the time, some of the time, occasionally, never), five-choice answers, and so on. They are all pretty much the same and none is really any better than any other, although there are those who believe an odd number is best and others who fight for the even.

Pick a type of answer that you are comfortable with, and make sure your questions all match the answers—that is, read your questions and the possible answers to ensure that the answers make sense for the type of question you wrote.

You might use an answer format in which the trainees write a paragraph or two (or ten!) on what they thought of particular course aspects, but these are hard to summarize and often not worth the effort. Leaving a place for comments at the end of a multiple-choice type evaluation works just as well.

You don't even have to use an instrument at all. You might pick random trainees and conduct an interview, or simply request a show of hands for a series of questions that you ask at the end of the class.

One of the best general reaction instruments I've ever seen was three questions asked verbally at the end of the class, with the answers written on any old piece of paper the trainees happened to have. Here it is:

1. Rate this class on a scale of 1 to 5.
2. State the one thing you liked best about the class.
3. State the one thing you would most like to change about the class.

I sometimes add a fourth:

4. What do you think was the most important thing you learned from the class?

If you like a bit more formality, here is another four-question Level 1 instrument, to which the learners can answer simply yes or no, that I think works well:

1. The instructor was well prepared and organized, and did an effective job of facilitating the material.
2. The course contained the appropriate amount and level of information.
3. I gained new knowledge that I did not previously have.
4. I will be able to apply what I learned here on the job.

You can take these questions, add a 1 through 4 scale and a place for further comments, and have a pretty good paper Level 1 instrument as well. Short, to the point, and about as much information as you are likely to need, or receive, from a reaction evaluation.

The key issue in trainee reaction evaluation is to make sure you ask questions (1) that the trainees have the expertise to answer, (2) that are important parts of the training design, and (3) that you control. If you have no control over an aspect, it's not worth asking a question about.

Here are some other examples of reaction evaluation instruments. Note that the questions in each of them may not all be valid all the time, so customize them according to the comments we just made concerning the key issues.

REACTION INSTRUMENT 1

For each statement below, circle the response that best indicates your opinion.

1. Quality of the material	Poor	Fair	Good	Very Good	Excellent
2. Ability of the facilitator	Poor	Fair	Good	Very Good	Excellent
3. Usefulness of the content	Poor	Fair	Good	Very Good	Excellent
4. Quality of the training facility	Poor	Fair	Good	Very Good	Excellent
5. Relation to your job	Poor	Fair	Good	Very Good	Excellent
6. Quality of the media (slides, video, etc.)	Poor	Fair	Good	Very Good	Excellent
7. Practice sessions	Poor	Fair	Good	Very Good	Excellent
8. Fulfillment of objectives	Poor	Fair	Good	Very Good	Excellent
9. Meeting of your training needs	Poor	Fair	Good	Very Good	Excellent
10. Overall impression	Poor	Fair	Good	Very Good	Excellent

Comments:

REACTION INSTRUMENT 2

Use the scale below to indicate your opinion on each of the following statements.

3 = agree   2 = neutral   1 = disagree

1. This course was relevant to what I do on the job. ____
2. I was able to master the course objectives. ____
3. The course was interesting. ____
4. The course gave me practical information. ____
5. The course materials helped me in my learning. ____
6. The role plays were useful activities. ____
7. The trainer helped make the learning easier. ____
8. We had the time to complete all the course material properly. ____
9. The course was well organized. ____
10. Overall, the course was worth the time I spent in it. ____

Comments:

REACTION INSTRUMENT 3

This session:

1. Was taught well	6 5 4 3 2 1	Was poorly taught
2. Had value for me	6 5 4 3 2 1	Was worthless
3. Was well organized	6 5 4 3 2 1	Seemed disorganized
4. Was too easy	6 5 4 3 2 1	Was too difficult
5. Had enough skills practice	6 5 4 3 2 1	Needed more skills practice
6. Went too quickly	6 5 4 3 2 1	Went too slowly
7. Was related to my job	6 5 4 3 2 1	Was not related to my job
8. Was active	6 5 4 3 2 1	Was passive
9. Met its objectives	6 5 4 3 2 1	Missed its objectives
10. Met my needs	6 5 4 3 2 1	Did not meet my needs

Comments:

You can make your Level 2 evaluations more effective by adding technology to them. Even if your delivery system is not a form of e-learning, you can have your tests put online for the learners to complete. There are software packages that will allow you to do this and that will also gather statistics on your questions for item analysis. They allow you to give immediate feedback to learners on what they missed, and you can even use them as a diagnostic tool.

Self-Instructional Reaction Evaluations

In self-instructional courses, one aspect that is usually included in the survey is the amount of time spent by the trainee in doing the course. This is different for each trainee, but there should be an average time that you were aiming for when you started your design. This is the place to find out whether your estimate was accurate or whether the course is too difficult (or too easy) for that particular time frame.

You can also ask the trainees if they thought the course was too short or too long, but be sure to give them a place to explain why, as this will help you redesign the training if necessary. Note that this question is often asked for classroom-based courses as well. I never have figured out why, and I don't ask it myself, but if you think it gives you some important information, make it part of your classroom survey. I prefer to ask whether there was time enough to complete the activities and master the material.

Level 2: Skills and Knowledge Mastery and Retention (Learning)

We've already spent some time discussing this type of evaluation. Basically, it is the learner evaluation process that we started with criterion-based question writing back in Chapter Four.

In developing your lesson plan you decided where and when you wanted these tests. Your objectives told you what kind of questions you needed to create and what type of tests you needed to construct. As an evaluation process, the information on who mastered what and who did not and how many they had right and wrong tells you much about the effectiveness of your material and your instruction.

Your aggregate test scores indicate whether the content has been successfully transmitted to the trainees, both individually and as a group, and if they can perform as required based on your analysis. If this is not important to you, you may need to go back and ask why you are doing the training in the first place. There is an old adage: "If it's worth teaching, it's worth testing." We've already noted that this may not be true in all cases, but it is in the vast majority.

These tests, or at least the test questions, can also be used to evaluate retention. Simply administer another test later. When you do this depends on the length of time you want to check—thirty days, ninety days, six months, whatever. But don't forget our prime directive: if no one needs to know, don't ask.

Evaluating Your Skills Evaluation

You may also want to evaluate your tests themselves, or at least the questions that make them up. The simplest way to do this is to keep track of the questions missed. If you see the same question missed a lot, you should look back at the objective and the content related to the question. You may find that a question was written poorly, that the content did not cover this point in enough detail, or that the objective simply does not make sense. If any of these is true, you'll need to change whatever is wrong or out of synch. This is another one of those places in instructional design where evaluation leads you back into analysis again, and the circle is complete.

Some evaluations in this category also look at the time various levels of trainees spend taking a test. Usually more experienced individuals take less time for the test. If this is not true for your test, it may indicate that the questions are too difficult or are off the mark in relation to the job.

Everything we just said, although aimed toward paper-and-pencil tests, is also true of your performance tests, so use them and evaluate them in the same way when needed. However, remember that the best performance tests are those that are conducted in an environment as close as possible to actual job conditions.

 Level 3: Transfer to the Job and Improvements in Job Performance (Application)

The third type of evaluation, often termed application, is evaluating how—or if—the training was transferred to the actual job, and whether the job is being performed at a higher level now because of the training. This is a popular aspect of evaluation to talk about, and you can see why if you remember that way back in the beginning we were tying our training to job performance. However, it is not done quite as often as it is talked about, mostly because it is quite time-consuming. Also, because it is done after the training, it is seldom monitored too closely because of time and resource constraints.

Basically, transfer to the job tries to answer the question: "Are the trainees using the knowledge and skills taught in the class in their everyday work?" You can also evaluate whether their work has improved (productivity increased) due to this transfer, although this is also considered part of the next evaluation category.

Methods

It is often possible to intertwine this type of evaluation into activities that begin in class. For example, a contract or action plan that incorporates the important learnings is developed in class, then shared with the supervisor, and reviewed (read "evaluated") at a later date.

The supervisor can also play a role in another evaluation method for this category, the *post-training interview.* This is a simple process of interviewing the trainees and their supervisors some time after the training has occurred and asking whether they have seen the transfer to the workplace of the skills that were taught in the training. You may ask this a number of different ways, but the basic idea is still the same.

You can also perform this type of evaluation through a written instrument that you send to trainees, supervisors, managers, customers, and other individuals who might know. You will need to be very specific with your questions or the data you collect will not be worth much. Restating the objectives as pure behaviors and asking whether these have been observed is usually a good approach.

The simplest approach usually works best. A five-question "transfer to the job" evaluation might go something like this:

1. Did the training address the requirements of the job?

2. Were the trainees performing the job requirements competently before the training?

3. Are the trainees now performing the job requirements competently?

4. What are the trainees still not doing correctly?

5. Were there any unintended consequences of the training?

Another quick method for doing a Level 3 evaluation is to develop a five-question yes-or-no instrument that asks the learners and their supervisors if various concepts that were taught are being used on the job. Send these questions every six weeks or so for six months to a year to obtain some trending data and also for reinforcement.

Here are some examples of transfer-to-job instruments using the objectives listed in Chapter Four. Note that all of these forms can be given to the employee, colleague, or supervisor.

TRANSFER TO JOB INSTRUMENT 3

On a scale of from 1 percent to 100 percent, estimate the employee's ability to complete each task before and after training:

	Before Training	After Training
Choose the correct tread size	_____	_____
Reverse the interior matrix	_____	_____
Lay on the steel belt	_____	_____
Sequence the assembly machine	_____	_____
Trim excess rubber	_____	_____
Inspect for proper seal	_____	_____

Other comments concerning trainee performance after training:

As a shortcut you might also use your performance checklists as a transfer evaluation. Simply rename them, then go to the job site some interval of time after the training (how long an interval is up to you), and either observe or ask if the performances are being exhibited on the job.

You can create more general Level 3 instruments and use e-mail to distribute them. For these, simply restate the objectives as necessary, and for each ask the following questions and ask the respondents to check the proper response:

Before the class my level of knowledge on this performance was	High	Average	Low
After class my level of knowledge on this performance was	High	Average	Low
Before class my level of ability to use this performance was	High	Average	Low
After class my level of ability to use this performance was	High	Average	Low

You might even add a really general question to the e-mail, such as "I feel I am using _____ percent of the knowledge and skills I gained in this class."

Here are some other general questions you might add to a Level 3 e-mail evaluation:

What can you do on the job now that you couldn't before the class?

How have you used the knowledge and skills you acquired in class back on the job?

What was the most useful thing you learned to do in the course?

What has stopped you from using something you learned in the class back on the job?

A new and very interesting approach to Level 3 evaluation is to use the questions just suggested, or something like them, as postings on a corporate training evaluation electronic bulletin board. This method works particularly well for younger learners who are used to the bulletin-board process.

Of course the replies are always anonymous, but if you allow others to react to the evaluative postings, you could end up with a lot of electronic gripe sessions if you don't design your questions well. However, the evaluation data you can gain from this methodology—and the increased retention that is a natural outcome of the process—can make it more than worthwhile.

 Level 4: Results (Business Impact)

This level of evaluation is concerned with your training's effect on the goals and objectives of the business. This is not as statistical a measure as ROI; in fact, it has little to do with numbers at all, except maybe profit numbers. If you did a good job back in Chapter Two of linking corporate needs with your training, then this evaluation is a simple process of taking some of the credit for meeting those needs (or goals) through your training. If you did not spend the time in the beginning of your design work doing this, you will have to try to retrofit the training to the corporate goals to do this type of evaluation. Retrofitting works sometimes, but at others it becomes a real stretch. If you plan on doing this aspect of this type of evaluation, start at the beginning as described in Chapter Two.

One hopes that you've just had another one of those blinding flashes of the obvious and said: "Hey, I have to start planning for evaluation back when I start planning my training!" No doubt about it! You've probably also seen, once again, the connective nature of instructional design. Everything is related somewhere along the line, from analysis through material development to evaluation. You really need to think of your training design as one piece of cloth made up of a number of interwoven threads.

When doing Level 4 evaluation, some of the data points that might be assessed depending on the corporate goals are as follows:

Customer satisfaction	Stakeholder satisfaction
Employee satisfaction	Investor satisfaction
Regulatory compliance	Time to market
Percent of market share	Turnover
Diversity	Health and safety
Bench strength	Profit per employee
Business metrics	Human capital metrics
Financial reviews	Growth and capability measures

Of course this isn't a complete list by any means; there are as many possibilities as there are corporate goals and objectives. However, this should give you an idea of what Levl 4 is trying to evaluate.

 Level 5: Return on Investment

In its simplest form, ROI is how much you've spent on the training and how much you will save or the company will make because of it, converted into a ratio.

Although the amount you've spent on the training is usually pretty easy to determine, what you have saved or made because of it is often much less clear. Beyond simple profit gains or increased productivity, there are aspects such as increased efficiency, quality improvements, better personnel performance (less absenteeism, reduced grievances) and decreased accidents or down time to consider, and some less tangible processes as well, such as increases in capability or capacity, customer and employee satisfaction, increased teamwork, reduced conflict, and possible or realized growth potential.

There are some intangibles in the "how much you spent" category too. For example, many designers forget to factor in time off the job for the employee while attending training, particularly as it relates to benefits costs or lost productivity in their cost estimate. You might even want to factor in the cost of wasted training investments for training the wrong person at the wrong time, or the cost of lost opportunities for sales, or satisfying current customers because the trainees were not trained properly, were trained too late, or were never trained at all.

This gets pretty esoteric after awhile and sometimes degenerates into a best-guess process, so make sure that if you are going to do ROI you can find hard valid data to use in your analysis.

We discussed some of this ROI process in Chapter Two as part of your pre-analysis work when doing a cost-benefit analysis to decide whether the training should even be attempted. If you did a cost-benefit analysis then, evaluating ROI will be pretty easy now. If you did not, but are now interested in the process as part of evaluation, go back to Chapter 2 and use the methods described there. Just remember that your new goal is to evaluate your program's success in relation to ROI, not to analyze the logic of doing the program to begin with.

Your cost-benefit analysis will allow you to produce a basic ROI as a ratio of the benefits to the cost expressed as a single number. The formula looks something like this:

$$ROI = \frac{Net\ Program\ Benefits}{Program\ Cost} \times 100$$

Where the net program benefits is calculated by subtracting program cost from the dollar amount assigned to the benefits of the program.

Remember that positive ROIs are good, and the more positive the better. How positive a number you want depends on your ROI goal. This is often set by upper management. If it is not, any positive number is good. Even a break-even goal is good in some circumstances. A negative ROI means that *as far as can be calculated* the company is not getting enough of a benefit to justify the expenditure for your training program.

Don't forget that "as far as can be calculated" phrase. There may be a number of reasons for doing training (employee satisfaction, long-term development, accreditation) that cannot be expressed in dollar values and so do not produce a valid ROI. Employee orientation, software training, new employee technical skills training are all required in any company, but their ROI is difficult to determine, even if you assume that the company will go out of business without them. This makes ROI a less than ultimate measure of a training program's success.

In an ROI evaluation it is most imperative that you isolate the effects of your training solution and attempt to express them in terms of numbers, and that you look at as many possible data points as you can in relation to these effects. Often, however, these effects are not numerical; you then need to use conversion factors for your ROI evaluation. These factors can be obtained from books, by examining historical or industry-wide costs, by forecasting trends, through customer input, by expert estimation, or by using contributor and supervisor estimates. They may not always be the same across companies, or even within a company if one department functions differently from another, and it is better if you use more than one source for the conversion factors, possibly averaging them if they are significantly far apart.

Effects can also be gleaned from business metrics (revenue, profit, cash flow, margins, and the like), HR statistics, internal performance measures, and industry comparisons, but again you will need to isolate the effects of your program on these statistics and, more often than not, use conversion factors.

If you know that you will want to evaluate for ROI, it is helpful to gather baseline information on the aspects that you will use to measure your gains from training. For example, your company may keep records of the scrap rates from various machines. By comparing the scrap rate before training to the scrap rate after the training, you will have one measure of ROI. If dollar amounts can be assigned to the scrap, annual savings can be computed, further augmenting your ROI process.

For another type of training, you may want to capture any records that document the number of times employees in an area are "written up." After your supervisory training, you can see whether this has changed. If you have information about how much lost time is incurred during the process of writing up an employee (by management and employees) and multiply the time by the cost per hour, you can use the figure as another measure for your ROI.

 EVALUATION OF SELF-INSTRUCTION PROGRAMS

Self-instruction, particularly in technology deliveries such as CD-ROM or e-learning, is becoming an increasingly important part of training design. If you have designed your training as self-instruction, no matter what the delivery system, you may want to do a special form of evaluation that looks a little deeper into the self-instructional aspects of your program. This type of evaluation is usually divided into five parts: sufficiency, usability, currency, compliance, and effectiveness.

Sufficiency

The first aspect to evaluate is the *sufficiency* of your training, by asking the basic question: "Is all the information that is necessary to the training in the program?" You can ask this of the trainees who have completed the program (after they have been using the training on the job for a period of time), their supervisors, and other subject-matter experts. If you did an SME review before implementing your self-instructional training, you will already have some SME feedback, but look for new ways to do this post-review.

You can do your asking by personal visit (this way you can see what's going on as well as listen), phone, e-mail, or through a formal (or informal) opinionnaire. Be sure, if you use the opinionnaire approach, that you keep your questions focused on the sufficiency issue. This is probably the wrong audience to answer other types of evaluation questions, and an evaluation that asks the wrong audience the wrong questions is worthless.

Following is an example of a simple self-instructional sufficiency instrument:

STORE MANAGER QUESTIONNAIRE

Below is a list of all the self-instructional CD-ROM packages in use by your employees. Place an X in the box next to the ones that you have reviewed or completed. Then tell us whether there is any information missing from any package that you feel would be helpful to a new employee.

☐ Orientation

☐ Inter-store Transfers

☐ Merchandising

☐ 1:1 Ordering

☐ Order Receiving

☐ Outside Vendors

☐ Photofinishing

☐ Recalls

Other comments on content of programs:

Usability

The second aspect of a self-instructional package to evaluate is *usability*; that is, "Was the training package as easy to use as possible?" The audience for this aspect is, obviously, the users: your trainees. There is no one question for this aspect, and the questions you do ask will be dependent on your particular delivery process. They may include such queries as these:

- Was the text hard to read?

- Were there problems obtaining the necessary supplies?

- Was the layout of the screens effective for reading and navigation?

- Did you have trouble getting onto the network?

- Could you find a facilitator when needed?

You might use a personal visit, a phone call, or a questionnaire to collect this information. An example of a usability instrument follows.

SURVEY ON SELF-INSTRUCTIONAL PACKAGES

This survey is designed to give the Training Department an idea of how the self-instructional learning packages are working. There are no right or wrong answers to these questions; just tell us how they work in your store. Circle "yes" or "no" in each case.

1. Is the print portion of the packages easy to read?	Yes	No
2. Are the instructions in introductory screens clear and easy to follow?	Yes	No
3. Were the activities and practice exercises "doable" in your store?	Yes	No
4. Did the activities and practice exercises help you perform the actual task?	Yes	No
5. Did the objectives give you a clear picture of what you were to know and be able to do at the end of the program?	Yes	No
6. On the average, how long does it take you to complete a package? _____		
7. Are you usually able to complete a package from start to finish without interruptions?	Yes	No
8. How often does the store manager check on your progress when you're completing a package? _____		

9. Where do you usually go to complete a package? _____

10. When you finish a package, does the store manager   Yes   No
    watch you perform the procedure before you're
    expected to do it on your own?

Currency

One major problem with all self-instructional programs is that they can rapidly become dated. This is not as true of classroom or on-the-job training, as the trainer can make changes on the fly. However, your CD-ROM or CBT package must be called back in and redone if changes are necessary. That is why it's important in self-instruction to evaluate its currency. The main question here is: "Are the materials in your package up to date?" The people you ask may include your SMEs or the managers, but a better source is to find the people responsible for policy and procedure or job task changes and ask them.

The best method is to keep track of whoever might be making changes to your program content and to give them a call periodically. Ask them to put you on their distribution list for all changes. It is particularly important to make these contacts when it is time to make a revision, but it's also a good idea to make a "just checking" call from time to time.

Compliance

The next aspect is *compliance,* which evaluates whether your package is being implemented according to your plan. If you are only responsible for a single self-instructional package, compliance is not a major issue, but if you have a number of packages—what you might call a self-instructional system—you will want to find out who is and is not doing the training, how those who are are doing it, and if they are not doing it, why. You can find out this information from users, from their supervisors, and from your facilitators. You can also look at training records to see an overall picture of compliance, but you'll have to go to the source to learn the why's and why nots. Another good way to check compliance is simply to observe and ask questions.

Effectiveness

The last evaluation aspect for a self-instructional program is *effectiveness.* The questions here are concerned with mastery of objectives by the trainees. Remember that in a good instructional design, if the objectives are mastered then the training was effective—at least as far as getting the right content across to the right people.

For this aspect, you need only to go back to your trainee evaluations for the data. You might also want to do a little spot checking by asking some of the trainees how they mastered the objectives. These two pieces should give you what you need to know.

Of course, in most cases effectiveness also relates to using what has been learned back on the job. The methods for doing this are pretty much the same for self-instructional or instructor-led training, as discussed earlier.

 ## REVISIONS: WHAT TO DO WITH WHAT YOU'VE LEARNED

A new task that often comes from evaluation is revision. In most organizations things change rapidly, and you will need to revise your training to keep up with those changes. We mentioned earlier the importance of considering revision possibilities when choosing your delivery system, so you already have a fair idea of its significance.

Any of the evaluation data you collect might be useful for the revision process, as there are really two types of revisions that might happen: *as-needed* and *planned.*

As-Needed Revisions

As-needed is what most people think of first when you mention revision. You usually do an as-needed revision because you find your content is out of date. This could be because a policy changed, a procedure was revised, or a whole new system was introduced. Whatever the reason, an as-needed revision may mean a change in your lesson plan, participant materials, or the whole darned CD-ROM.

You can't stop as-needed revisions; in most situations you won't even be able to control them. You simply need to keep in close contact with those people who may create a change that will necessitate an as-needed revision. By doing so you may at least know that one is coming.

Planned Revisions

It becomes a much more serious issue if your training needs revising and you aren't aware of it. To guard against this you need to have a systematic plan for periodically revising your training. If you're doing periodic evaluations such as those discussed earlier, then these should be the impetus for your planned revisions. The revisions will be based on the data obtained through the evaluation.

Timing of Planned Revisions

There is no simple formula for doing revision planning. It is dependent on your program's content and your company environment. The amount of change that occurs to policy and procedures in some companies requires that planned revisions occur at least every six months. I worked in the nuclear power field for a time, in which each course was revised every year. For other courses with more stable content such as management training, two or three years is a good time period between revisions. Technical subjects need planned revisions more often, basic topics less. Companies that are fast growing or in crisis will demand shorter revision cycles. Stable companies can use longer ones.

Decide what is best for each of your programs, then set a schedule, and—most important—keep to your schedule. It's easy to put off a revision if you're in the middle of a big project and it comes up on your schedule. You might just give it a quick look and say, "Well, I don't think anything has changed, so we'll wait till the next round." *This is the last thing you want to do.*

The purpose of planned revisions is to find out whether anything has happened *that you don't know about.* If nothing did, that's fine, and your revision becomes simply a review with no changes made. But if something did change, and your program doesn't, you will have lessened its effectiveness and its usefulness for your trainees.

Information for Revisions

There are many sources of revision information. These include your own evaluation process, policy and procedure changes that come via interoffice snail mail or e-mail, memos, and meetings.

Your best source for good revision information is the initiator of your training; that is, the individual or department that requested the training in the first place. It is critical that you ask the right people. As we discussed in the evaluation process, look for the people who know what is going on in their area. Open lines of communication with them. If you can, work out a relationship in which they feel a responsibility for the information in your training program. One good idea I've seen used is to distribute a phone sticker with your number and e-mail address so you can be easily notified if a change in content occurs.

Other sources of information might include trainers, facilitators or site implementers for self-instructional programs, and field trainers. If you talk to these individuals as part of your evaluation process, be sure to keep in touch with them concerning revisions. As these people continuously work with the subject matter, they'll have first-hand knowledge of areas that are out of date or now contain erroneous information.

 ### Who Should Perform a Revision?

If you are a team of one, responsible for design, development, and instruction, then you will be the one who does the revising. However, if there are other resources available, you may want to have another person work on the revision. He or she can often come at the topic with some fresh ideas. This is usually not as efficient as having the original designer revise the material, but can be more effective in the long run.

As usual, I think the answer lies somewhere in between. Who does a revision is dependent on why the revision is being done. If it's simply a matter of looking at how up-to-date the material is, the original designer will be most efficient at adding, subtracting, or changing material. However, if usability or effectiveness is an issue, you might want to try a somewhat different approach from a new person.

A lot also depends on who is available to help, the time the person has, and the time you can afford in general to do revisions. The key is to consider the alternatives and needs before assigning revision work. Too often the original designer is the choice by default—and sometimes not the best choice at all.

 ### Controlling Revisions

When the content has been revised, the next step is to make sure that everyone is using the latest revision of the course. This is particularly important in self-instructional courses, in which the stories of two, three, or even four revisions of the same program all floating around the same company are legend. I've had it happen more than once myself.

To guard against this, use a revision tracking mechanism. For example, each of your programs should have a very visible revision number on it, preferably on the front or back cover of all print pieces and on the first screen of any technology-based material. You don't need codes or cryptic numbers: something as simple as "Rev. 1" or "Revision 2" and a date will be more than adequate. Some designers like to put a header or footer on each page with the revision number. This probably is not a bad idea, and with computers it is easy enough to do.

You will also need a way to inform your users of which revision is most current. If you have more than one trainer using your material, the best approach is to call in the old material and send out the new. In a learning center delivery process, your facilitator should find it easy to keep up with revisions. If you are using a distributed self-instructional delivery, where you have programs at sites in various locations, you will need a revision list that you keep current and send out often. In fact, this type of list is a good idea for any training system. You should have someone at each training site who is responsible for checking revisions. To formalize the process you can have this person sign off on your revision list and return it to you. If you want to be even more formal, you can have out-of-date material returned to you.

In the nuclear industry, correct revisions are so critical to the training process that some facilities have a department whose only job is to keep revisions up-to-date in the files and to check to make sure there are no invalid copies in the plant. I'm not suggesting that you go quite that far. However, if you are going to put the time and energy into doing revisions properly, be sure you work out a mechanism to ensure that the correct revisions are being used.

Of course, all of this means a lot less if you are a one-person operation, but it is still a good idea to keep track of your revisions in case this changes somewhere along the line, or someone else asks to use your program.

Other Revision Considerations

We discussed the relationship between revisions and delivery systems earlier, and if you did not consider it before now, you may be in deep trouble when a revision is needed. Costs of reshooting video, redoing computer animation, and so on may make revisions almost impossible from a budgetary viewpoint. If so, you may need to go back to the drawing board and redo your entire training program now that a revision is necessary.

Another revision argument concerns whether to revise pieces or to revise the whole training program. This is particularly important with self-instructional materials. The answer is dependent on you and the particular needs of your program(s). However, this decision affects everything else that goes into your training, from binding of print pieces to media choices and development, so be sure that you consider all the ramifications before you decide.

In anticipation of revisions, keep intact masters of all current materials stored where no one can use them or take them accidentally. I've found that you should also have a handy official revision copy of everything available and easily accessible. That way, when anyone thinks of something or finds out about something that needs to go into the next revision, it can be recorded where the reviser can find it.

This is true not only for printed materials, but for video scripts and storyboards, slide and tape programs, and computer materials as well. If your training program is large enough, I'd suggest a file drawer that has revision copies of everything that you have in current use and another locked one for your master copies. I used such a system when I had a staff of four designers working on thirty different self-instructional packages, and it functioned quite well. Even when one of my designers left, we had all her thoughts on how to revise her materials where we could find them for the next revision.

This pretty much ends our formal discussion of instructional design. However, the title of this book is *Rapid Instructional Design*. We've given you a few ideas of how to speed up the process throughout the chapters, but we'll take one more chapter to look at some more complex techniques for making instructional design less time-consuming. If you are an occasional designer or new to the field, many of these may be a little more than you can handle until you get some more design experience, but you might want to read on anyway to see what else is out there. For more experienced designers, we hope that Chapter 8 will provide a useful overview of the more common rapid instructional design techniques and will whet your appetite for more information on those you find useful.

HINTS FOR EVALUATING
Classroom

- An evaluation plan should be based totally on company profits: dollars spent = new skills learned = behavior changed = performance changed = increased productivity = increased profits

- For a really well-considered evaluation, and to guard against the last-minute evaluation rush, give out your opinionnaire type evaluations at the start of the class so the trainees know what to look for; give them time every so often during the class to pull it out and make notes.

- If you have multiple trainers for a program, make sure each receives his or her own evaluation from the trainees.

- Never underestimate the power of a good lunch.

On-the-Job Training

- Here's one of my favorite evaluation scales for trainee opinionnaires of training and trainers:
  - Excellent
  - Exceeded my expectations
  - Met my expectations
  - Below my expectations
- Does the OJT program
  - Identify the work tasks to be taught?
  - Have organized learning objectives?
  - Produce technical competence?
  - Develop social competencies as necessary?
  - Convey clear expectations of results to trainees?
  - Assess progress toward competency properly?

- Provide feedback to all interested parties as required?
- Provide clear teaching roles and responsibilities?
- Provide trained trainers to handle the teaching role?
- Support the trainers as necessary?

Self-Instruction

Here's an example of a form that can be part of your self-directed learning (SDL) package, completed by the site facilitator and sent back to you to monitor compliance. You could use this form with some modification for a technology-based self-instructional package or even use it electronically.

SELF-INSTRUCTIONAL LEARNING FACILITATOR SURVEY

We need your help in determining how well the [self-directed learning system title] is working now that the first packages have been in the field for almost a year. Please take five minutes to complete the questions below. Return this survey to [name of person and department]. Thank you for your time!

Region: _____ District: _____ Store: _____

Store Manager's Name (optional): _____

1. Have you used any of the SDL packages?   Yes   No

2. How many employees have completed one or more of the SDLs?

3. What is the average length of time it takes an employee to complete an SDL package?

4. Are there any SDL packages that are particularly difficult for associates to complete or understand? Be specific please:

5. Do you think the activities and practice sessions are   Yes   No
   realistic and helpful?

6. Are the instructions in the SDL packages clear and easy   Yes   No
   to follow?

   If not, why not?

7. When your employees are working through an SDL package, how often do they need help from you or other employees?

   Never   Sometimes   Frequently

8. Do you have any other comments about this self-directed learning system?

Here is an example of a form that can be used to gather evaluation data from site facilitators on how well a distance self-instructional program or system is operating:

Computer and CD-ROM-Based Training

Here is a short trainee opinion survey for a CD-ROM course:

1. What is your overall opinion of the course?   ☐ Favorable
                                                 ☐ Not favorable

2. Did the course prepare you for your job tasks?   ☐ Yes
                                                    ☐ No

3. The course presentation was   ☐ Interesting
                                 ☐ Boring

4. The instructional segments were   ☐ The right size
                                     ☐ Too large
                                     ☐ Too small

5. Was it easy or difficult to exit and return
   to the course?   ☐ Easy
                    ☐ Difficult

6. The directions for how to use the course were   ☐ Clear
                                                   ☐ Confusing

7. Compared to other multimedia programs
   I have used, this course was   ☐ Better than others
                                  ☐ Not as good as others

8. I found the material presented in this course   ☐ Useful
                                                   ☐ A waste of time

9. I would recommend that others take this
   course   ☐ Yes
            ☐ No

10. To make this course better, I would . . .

Multimedia program evaluation questions you may want to ask:

- Is the computer interface appropriate for the target audience?
- Does the content properly and completely match the objectives?

- Do the trainee evaluation processes match the objectives?
- Does the interactivity support and reinforce the learning?
- Do the multimedia pieces support and reinforce the learning?
- Was there transfer to the job?
- Were there any unanticipated outcomes?
- Were the trainees satisfied with the program and this form of training?
- Did the program meet the proposed cost-benefit goal?

Asynchronous E-Learning

- Possible evaluation criteria for asynchronous e-learning:
  - Reduction in training time
  - Reduction in travel cost
  - Reduction in errors committed
  - Reduction in facilitator time
  - Reduction in customer complaints
  - Increased consistency
  - Delivery of training just in time
- Have as much of your evaluation and record keeping on the system as possible

Here is a list of questions you might consider when evaluating a technology-based training program. Some are restatements of what we've already discussed, while others speak specifically to the use of technology. These should work for almost any technology delivery, with a few modifications.

- What is the course intended to do? (Is it simply for practice or does it present new information, or both?)
- Who will be looking at the evaluation?
- What will be done with the evaluation data? (What decisions might be made using it?)
- Must the records be kept private?
- What system requirements (disk space, memory, and so on) are needed for running data-gathering processes and storing the gathered data?
- Will there be technology problems involved in getting the gathered data to the right place (other software programs, other networks, and so on)?

- Will the record keeping cause new problems (need for special disks, finding people to collect, requiring evaluation administration)?
- What is the real purpose in gathering the data?
- How long must the evaluation data be kept and where?
- Are there any legal or organizational requirements regarding the data that must be met or considered (use for performance appraisal or promotion, and so on)?

Satellite-Based Training

- When doing multiple-broadcast programs, do not solicit or take too heavily into account random feedback from individuals or even downlink sites, as it is not systematic and can lead to knee-jerk reactions that you don't want and that may play havoc with your program design.
- Call participants prior to the session to establish rapport.

Chapter 8

Doing It Faster: More Rapid Design Shortcuts

This chapter will help you to:

- Consider the usefulness of various types of instructional design software
- Find out about the technique of rapid prototyping
- Discover what learning objects are and what they can do
- Determine the appropriateness of performance support based training for your training needs
- Consider other techniques of rapid instructional design

---

*T*hroughout this book we've tried to supply you with a variety of hints, shortcuts, and other ideas to make your instructional design process more efficient as well as more effective. Most of these have been tied to the various aspects of instructional design and were mentioned as we discussed the area they were related to. However, there are a number of shortcuts that don't really fit one particular part of instructional design but can be great time savers and are certainly worth mentioning, if not exploring in detail. Many of these are pretty cutting-edge in nature, as they are based in the newer technologies or related to new advances in instructional design theory, but that doesn't make them any less useable, even for a new or occasional designer.

If you are an SME trying to keep your head above water as you create your training program, these shortcuts may not be your cup of tea. I hope you'll have a little time someday to explore them, but for now they may not be particularly relevant to your needs. For everyone else, they are worth at least a look to see what they have to offer. Under the right circumstances, one or more of these shortcuts may save a great deal of time and effort.

We've divided the chapter into shortcut sections, with no consideration of where they fit into the instructional design process, as many overlap a number of areas. Some of them are full-blown processes, others just a little more than a hint. Add customization as you wish to make them your own.

SOFTWARE FOR INSTRUCTIONAL DESIGN

A number of vendors sell various types of software designed to help you through an instructional design process. We've mentioned this type of software earlier, particularly authoring systems and conversion software, and noted that some of the packages claim you don't need to know about instructional design to use them. Stay away from anything that makes such a claim. If you've been through the rest of this book, you know that no software can fully take the place of understanding what instructional design is and how to make it work.

That said, there are some really great packages out there that can help you mightily, if you already know what you are doing. They will correlate data into reports for you, give you hints on how to do things when you forget, provide advice from experts on the how's and why's of instructional design, and basically speed up most of the administrative parts of the instructional design process. Some have templates to help you create attractive, consistent, and understandable reports; others give you models of what your outputs should look like. Many include online coaching. All the market claims aside, they still will not do your thinking for you.

I'm not comfortable with recommending any particular product, but I can tell you to look for software that matches your intended training plan, especially your delivery system. There are some packages that work best for classroom instruction, others that are multimedia-based, and still others that are meant for use with an e-learning delivery. Each type leads you toward outputs that fit into the end product it has been developed to produce, so make sure you pick the right one. For example, the software that you would use for a CD-ROM program will (or should) lead you to a script and storyboard as outputs, one for classroom training helps you create lesson plans and participant packages, and an e-learning software program should provide you with end products that are formatted to be delivered on a network.

The software should also match the way you like to do instructional design. If you prefer a limited design document and plenty of multilevel objectives, your software should support your required outputs. If you like to write test questions as soon as you finish your objectives, the software should allow you do just that (some do, some do not).

There are a number of these programs that also come with a public workshop to help you learn to use them. These are often designed for a beginner audience, and by now you may be beyond that point as an instructional designer (I hope so, or this book was not very successful at meeting your needs), so look the curriculum over carefully before you spend your valuable time going to a seminar that tells you what you already know. My rule of thumb is that if it takes more than two days to learn to use a piece of software, then either the software is not worth it or they are talking about more than just the software itself.

You can find a list of vendors for instructional design software (and just about anything else in training) on the ASTD Website (www.astd.org). Call or e-mail your vendor(s) of choice and ask for a demonstration or evaluation copy. Play with the demos until you find the one that works best for you.

ANALYSIS SOFTWARE

We mentioned in Chapter Three that there is software on the market to help you perform the various types of analysis. These packages may also come equipped with a facility that allows you to do both paper-based and net-based questionnaires. Like the instructional design software already discussed, the marketing gimmick for many of these programs is that you don't need to know analysis to use them. This is akin to going out onto a football field without your helmet. It may work fine. But then again.. . . .

The best of this type of software includes a training cost analysis function, the ability to create graphs and flow charts from your data, and file conversion facilities so you can move the analysis data to other types of software such as a design package or authoring system.

If you know what analysis is about and the types of analysis you need to do, a number of these packages can be helpful and time-effective. Check them out, and if you find one that's right for you, use it.

TEST DEVELOPMENT SOFTWARE

Another software-based instructional design shortcut is the use of test development software. The warnings concerning the use of these packages are the same as for the analysis and instructional design software. Know what you're doing first and they will make you more efficient in certain situations, when and if a package fits your style.

One thing that all this type of software does is to make computerized testing and computer-generated tests possible. If you are doing a lot of knowledge testing in a distance environment, the ability to generate tests and administer them totally on the computer can save you large amounts of implementation time. If you are going to use information from these tests as part of your evaluation process, you'll save even more data-gathering time.

With this type of software you can deliver tests via CD-ROM, disk, e-mail, or a network. Most come equipped with random question generators, so no two tests are ever the same. Using this type of shortcut is another good reason for developing a question bank, as we discussed in Chapter Four.

Some of these programs allow you to add pictures, video, and audio to your test questions, thus making it easier to do performance-based testing—another cost and time savings, particularly for your examiners.

When considering using this type of software, look for

- Ease of use
- Whether the system grows as your needs grow
- Whether it has the capabilities you need now (random generator, video support, and the like)
- How easily tests can be printed
- Whether there is an integrated spell checker

MISCELLANEOUS SOFTWARE

There are many other types of software that can increase your instructional design speed, particularly in the material development aspect. These include flow-charting systems, outlining software, word processing software (of course), grammar checkers, graphics design packages to help you create professional-looking graphs and charts, and even presentation software that can be used to produce entire stand-up presentations.

Again the question becomes one of investing time. If you don't know how to use the software and you are not going to use it often, is it worth the time investment to learn how to use it? Often it is more efficient to find someone who already knows how and have that expert do it for you. Of course, if you don't have the budget this is not an alternative.

The issue here is to know what is out there and what it does and then to use it as efficiently as possible to cut down on your design time.

RAPID PROTOTYPING

A relatively new shortcut, but one that is growing in popularity, is the concept of *rapid prototyping*. This idea was developed by technology-based designers, but is useful in almost any design process. Basically, it stresses the development of only a portion of the training, but with all of the bells and whistles that the entire program will have. It is literally a process of taking only one aspect of your training program all the way from analysis through evaluation before you do any other piece of the design. Much more than an outline, it is an actual piece of finished training that will allow the client (external or internal) to have the real "feel" of the finished product.

At times more than one prototype is developed and evaluated to analyze the strengths and weaknesses of various approaches and to choose one, or a combination, that will work best.

There are other conceptualizations for prototyping as well. Some go beyond the above description; others are much simpler. One of these simpler approaches suggests that the user interface, navigation, and other technology aspects be developed quickly (and maybe not too prettily) and then tested with content that is not yet complete but filled in enough for testing purposes.

The key to these and most other systems is that the rapid prototype is a continuing process, with new aspects being added and evaluated in this mode each week until you finally have the complete program.

You can see the importance of this type of approach to technology-based designs. Client questions or trainee problems can be caught early and fixed before too much of the heavy-duty media work (video, graphics, or even programming) is done. Interfaces can be changed, screen design altered, colors reprocessed, or the whole tone of the program redeveloped for much less than what it would cost when changes became necessary due to data gathered at a beta or even an alpha test. Some proponents say that rapid prototyping, when done properly, can even do away with storyboards, although I'm a bit skeptical.

As an instructional designer, you'll want to do rapid prototyping where it fits to save you time and money on edits; as a purchaser of instructional design expertise, you'll want your designers to use it for the same reasons.

LEARNING OBJECTS AND GRANULAR TRAINING

These two concepts mean roughly the same thing, although the term *learning objects* (often referred to as *object-oriented learning*) is quickly becoming the more widely accepted one. What both entail is the creation of very small, discrete pieces of training that are reusable in a number of different circumstances. How big "small" is and how the learning objects are reused differ in different systems. Some proponents feel that each object should encompass no more than one objective; other feel that two, three, or even five objectives can make up an object. Their reuse is dependent on the training system of which the objects are a part. For example, if you developed a learning object that dealt with the skill of paraphrasing, you might use that piece of learning in a course on listening skills, interviewing, questioning skills, or dealing with the media, or even in doing a training needs analysis.

In some systems the objects are stored as a database and can be called out when their learning objective matches a proposed objective for a program.

The key here is to develop the piece of training once, but make it both basic and general enough to be used in a number of programs. Systems have already been created to keep track of learning objects and to guide designers in how to choose them. Perhaps in the near future there will be a system agreed to for designing and standardizing them, which will in turn make it possible to share them.

At the moment, learning objects are most useful for designers working within a large training system in which there are many opportunities for the creation of reusable training. Standardizing them might make it possible some day to buy learning objects off the shelf the same way one can now buy a video, a graphic, or a training program.

PUBLIC COURSES

You can cut your development and implementation time way down by using public courses where appropriate. Make the courses your own by creating a special participant's manual for your trainees, based on your job analysis of what they need to know. Add objectives (sadly missing from most public courses, or when present, inadequate), guidance on the key concepts that the trainees need to consider in detail, precourse and postcourse activities, and even self-quizzes that are completed at breaks or at the end of the day for a self-assessment of mastery.

OFF-THE-SHELF PROGRAMS

You can use off-the-shelf programs (video, CD-ROM, or web-based) in much the same way as we just discussed with public courses. Focus your trainees on the content areas that are important to your company and their jobs through objectives, directions, special activities, and testing found in a companion participant's manual that you create specifically for the needs of your company. Modify the content of these programs as needed to make them even more effective shortcuts. Just be sure you obtain permission first from the vendor.

Here are questions to ask vendors about their off-the-shelf programs:

- How do your courses use sound instructional design methodology?
- What is your testing philosophy?
- How do you design in interactivity?
- How do you handle skill objectives?
- What media do you prefer and why?
- What are my training requirements as you see them?
- How do your courses integrate with my need?

TECHNOLOGY VENDORS

Technology vendors can help you reduce your design and development time in a number of ways. We've discussed the possibility of using professional programmers for your multimedia productions in lieu of your learning an authoring system, or simply handing a storyboard and script over to a multimedia production house and letting them take it from there. As a less drastic approach, you can hire graphic artists to do your graphics for any type of program or a custom video house to do your videos.

If you are designing e-learning, there is a type of vendor who can take your previously existing media and convert it to net-compatible formats ("Outside Services for Converting Audio and Video to the Web" by Maria Palazzolo, 1997) for you to use in both your instructor-led and self-instructional e-learning programs.

Some general questions to ask technology vendors:

- How long have you been in business?
- Can I talk to your long-time customers?
- Who is your primary competitor?
- What are your pricing models?
- How many new courses are you currently developing?
- How will you pilot your course for us?

Some things to consider when choosing a technology vendor:

- Is there an established track record?
- Is this their main business?
- Are their definitions of terms like yours?
- Are there trained IDs on staff?
- Is their technology current?
- Are their programs interactive?
- Does the program meet your objectives and your audience needs?

PERFORMANCE SUPPORT-BASED "TRAINING"

We've talked a bit about this shortcut before. It is based on a strong analysis, particularly a performance analysis, and its precursor is our old friend the job aid. Performance support based training is not really training, but rather the process of looking for places where the performance need can be met by the creation of something other than training. Depending on what this other "something" is, it is possible to save a great deal of design time and money, not to mention the costs associated with training delivery, by creating on-the-job support materials rather than actual training.

These materials can be as simple as the aforementioned job aids or as complex as an electronic performance support system (EPSS) (*Electronic Performance Support Systems* by Gloria Gery, 1991). However, when you get into these more complex processes, performance support based training becomes a questionable instructional design shortcut, as you may spend more time designing the EPSS than you would have to create training.

An example of performance support-based training would be the "flip file" that you often see on registers in retail stores, or behind airline ticket counters. These performance support tools give the user explicit directions on how to do various tasks. If the system is designed well, these are tasks that are done infrequently or are very complex and are therefore difficult to memorize.

During training, the tasks that are done more frequently are covered in detail and tested on, whereas infrequent tasks are covered with a quick reference to the support tool and are not tested on except as part of the process of using the support tool. This means that a lot of training material development related to these infrequent tasks is done away with, creating a true design shortcut.

Other performance support-based training tools include decision matrices, wizards, interactive guides, pop-ups, and hypermedia glossaries.

When considering performance support–based training, ask yourself the following questions:

- What tasks will the performance system support?
- How will the system relate to the training?
- What training will be needed for the system?
- What are the features and benefits you need from the system?

Performance support-based training has few disadvantages and should be considered each time you develop a training program. Of course, this means strong analysis—particularly what we referred to as *criticality analysis* in Chapter Three—but you've been convinced that analysis is important anyway, right?

You can use the following quick design method for software training within a performance support methodology:

1. Perform a criticality analysis of software tasks

2. Train on only those tasks that are most critical, using a performance support tool

3. Distribute performance support tools for the noncritical tasks

4. Evaluate learning with a series of simulated cases for which the learners choose the correct performance support tool(s)

5. For changes to software, don't design training at all. Simply create a three-column performance support tool that lists the function, the old method, and the new. Then distribute self-directed and -evaluated simulations with the tool for practice using the new change.

PROBLEM-BASED LEARNING (PBL)

Cut down material development time and increase trainee interaction through problem-based learning. Here is the six-step approach to this training method:

1. Trainee teams meet in class and are given problem(s) to solve.

2. Each team works together, with facilitator available if needed, to discern needs and steps to solve problem.

3. The team distributes pieces of problem-solving process to each individual member.

4. Each member goes out and individually gathers what's needed to complete his or her aspect of the problem-solving process.

5. Teams reconvene either in class or on their own and information is shared.

6. Teams meet in classroom environment to use gathered information to develop and share a solution(s).

TRAINING MANAGEMENT SYSTEMS

Training management systems are so new that there is no real consensus yet on what they truly are. They combine a number of the shortcuts we have discussed already—such as computer-based record keeping, often computer-based testing, sometimes computer-based analysis, and even separate programs—to create and deliver e-learning and other technology-based training programs. I say "often" and "sometimes" because different systems have different capabilities. Some systems actually maintain files of learning objects and can use them to deliver training, have a place for you to store your task and objective lists, and include templates for design, analysis, and evaluation.

The obvious shortcut here is that many of your design processes are contained in one piece of software that has a common interface, so it is easier to learn. There is also a common output structure that makes the products of the system easier to use and understand. Naturally these systems also have all the efficiencies of their component parts.

Depending on the product, a training management system can also prescribe training modules to an individual based on an individualized assessment, link with your human resources information system to download training and other relevant data, notify individuals of new critical training necessary for their job due to procedural or other changes, become the beginning of a knowledge database for object-oriented learning, and link your training directly to an organizational competency process for hiring, advancement, or even performance appraisal.

MISCELLANEOUS

Here are some one-liners I've gathered from here and there to help you "think rapid":

- The only course description you must have is a statement of the objectives.

- If you're stuck for an explanatory analogy, remember that movies are the single most commonly shared experience in modern culture. And there are probably as many analogies as you'll ever need at the Internet Movie Database (http://us.imdb.com).

- Don't forget telephone conferences for distance learning needs. If they will fit the bill, they are easy to design and cheap to implement. Send a participant's manual out ahead of the call to add structure.

- E-mail is another way to save design time and implementation dollars for *some* distance learning needs.

- Busy people put off things that are not due immediately. Send them your pre-work a week in advance, and don't schedule multiple classes more than two weeks apart.

- Use MP3 player technology for corporate newsletters, training tips, and even for your EPSS.

Here is one additional hint for rapid instructional design. Don't forget to use *situational design*. Now that you know what the instructional design process is all about, you should be able to see places where you can create your own shortcuts. For example, decrease the complexity of your lesson plan because you know that your trainers are all top-notch and will need only limited guidance. *Consider your own situation carefully and design accordingly*; that's probably the best shortcut we can think of.

Chapter 9

Asynchronous E-Learning Design

This chapter will help you to:

- Differentiate between asynchronous and synchronous e-learning
- Determine what planning must be done by the organization in advance of designing an asynchronous e-learning program
- Formulate basic criteria for choosing a learning management system
- Analyze the offerings of e-learning vendors
- Develop effective, activity based asynchronous e-learning programs
- Prepare your learners for the self-direction necessary in asynchronous e-learning
- Properly implement and evaluate asynchronous e-learning programs

---

Asynchronous e-learning is just the latest in a long line of technology-based training deliveries that have been touted as the wave of the future, flaring up for a time, only to be eclipsed as their often overhyped promise is tempered by their inherent disadvantages.

We have mentioned the concept of e-learning at various places throughout this book, as well as its two basic components, synchronous and asynchronous. However, let's do some redefining of the concepts now, just to make sure we are all on the same page.

DEFINITIONS

E-learning is the delivery of training using the Internet or a company's intranet. It differs from older technologies, such as computer-based and CD-ROM–based training, and newer technologies, such as DVD-based training, in that the computer being used by the learner is not a stand-alone machine but rather part of a computer network. The learning programs are delivered through the network to the learner's computer, either ahead of the actual learning experience or just as the learner is engaging in the learning. This leads to a number of instructional design advantages,and, of course, disadvantages, just like any delivery system, which is what e-learning is in the final analysis.

Asynchronous e-learning is e-learning done in a self-instructional mode. This means, among other things, that there is no instructor available to answer learner questions or clarify issues, and that the learners can avail themselves of the learning at any time that works best for their needs; hence the term *asynchronous*. When most people talk about e-learning in general terms they are referring to this aspect of the process, with its self-instructional advantages and disadvantages. However, it's not uncommon for them to confuse the two components, ascribing advantages and disadvantages of both to the general concept, to the point where no one is really sure what they are talking about.

Synchronous e-learning is a slightly newer and vastly different concept. The only thing the two processes actually have in common is the use of networked computers. In a synchronous e-learning delivery, all the learners are on line at the same time, and a facilitator is present via the computer to lead the learning. The term *synchronous* indicates that all the learners are engaged in the learning, with an instructor, simultaneously. Of course, this negates the self-instructional advantages of the learners learning at their own pace and at a convenient time, but it does provide the advantage of a human component that enhances interactions and allows for the immediate exploration of questions.

Blended E-Learning

As we've come to better understand the intricacies of the Internet and its usefulness for learning, we've begun to realize that you can blend aspects of synchronous and asynchronous e-learning to create a hybrid delivery system that uses both components for maximum effectiveness. So you might have an asynchronous program that includes an electronic bulletin board function so that independent learners can still pose questions for an SME, or even a chat room function so that questions can be discussed in a synchronous environment. Or you may design a synchronous delivery that requires asynchronous pre-work to be done in the form of a self-instructional e-learning package. Even e-mail can be blended into an asynchronous e-learning system to provide a place for answering questions and holding discussions.

These e-learning blends can be very effective, but they can add to the confusion that occurs when discussing or determining the effectiveness of e-learning. If the designer is not careful, these blends can also bring an entire new set of design problems into play, such as record keeping and the efficient use of trainer time.

Chapter Ten will deal with synchronous e-learning design and, to some extent, with the blending of e-learning components through another form of e-learning that I term *online learning*. For the rest of this chapter, let's talk asynchronous. (*Blending E-Learning* by Karen Mantyla, 2001.)

CREATING AND IMPLEMENTING AN E-LEARNING SYSTEM

The design process for asynchronous e-learning is basically the same as that of a classroom design until you get to material development. The only major difference is that all of your design steps must be more rigorous, due to the simple fact that there is no instructor in an asynchronous delivery to make up for your design errors. We've already discussed this important design consideration when considering any form of self-instructional program, so it shouldn't be a big surprise to you when I say that your synchronous e-learning program succeeds or fails based on what you put into it, not on how a facilitator delivers it.

But before you can even think about designing an asynchronous program, you need to have a general e-learning system functioning in your organization. The creation of such a system should not be the job of the instructional designer, but knowing how the system works so you can design your courses properly *is* your job. Having a well-thought-out and properly implemented e-learning system is critical to the success of your programs, so let's talk a little about e-learning systems first.

Some Sad Statistics

Sixty-eight percent of eligible learners never register for voluntary e-learning courses, 31 percent don't register for required e-learning courses, and a 60 to 80 percent dropout rate for an e-learning course is not uncommon. When you hear averages such as these, you may begin to wonder if designing is such a good idea. Add to this other reports—62 percent of a poll of top executives said e-learning failed to meet their expectations, and less than 25 percent felt their e-learning system improved corporate performance—and you may feel sure that asynchronous e-learning isn't a good idea. However, you may be wrong in this assumption. As usual, statistics don't necessarily tell the whole story.

In many cases, the surveys and polls did not take into account whether the programs and the system itself were properly created. Good asynchronous e-learning programs in a well-implemented e-learning system can produce remarkable learning results. The problem is developing that good system.

When asynchronous e-learning first came on the scene, the planning basically consisted of "If we build it, they will come." Well, we built it (though in truth we often didn't do a very good job of it), but they didn't come, or at least they didn't stay for long.

The first attempts at major e-learning systems were learning portals that allowed learners access to hundreds, sometimes thousands of programs. But few companies prepared their learners to take advantage of these amazing resources, even fewer prepared them for the difficulties that transitioning from being taught to being a self-directed learner created, and fewer yet took the time to consider the quality of the programs being offered on their portal. I even had one very large and well-respected company tell me, when I asked how they evaluated their e-learning, that as far as their e-learning system was concerned, "Any training is good training."

So as they say, experience is the best (sometimes the only) teacher, and we realized that a more systematic approach was necessary. It would be easy to write an entire book on just the processes involved in creating an effective e-learning system, but as this is a book on instructional design we'll try and keep it to some basic thoughts for you on how to determine if your company has what you and your learners need to make asynchronous e-learning work (*E-Learning: Strategies for Delivering Knowledge in the Digital Age* by Marc Rosenberg, 2001).

The key to a successful e-learning system is outstanding planning—not proper planning, or even good planning, but outstanding planning. This includes the following:

- Determining a comprehensive e-learning strategy
- Designing and developing good programs
- Preparing the organization globally for e-learning
- Planning for a smooth, successful implementation
- Creating an effective monitoring and evaluation plan

DETERMINING A COMPREHENSIVE E-LEARNING STRATEGY

This planning step has three substeps:

- Analyzing your motives for using e-learning
- Determining your organization's readiness for e-learning
- Creating an e-learning vision

Analyzing Your Motives

When analyzing your motives for using e-learning, ask questions such as these:

- Why do we want to do this?

- Can we link this process to our business goals and strategy?

- What baseline technology do we have available?

- Can we build a business case for instituting e-learning?

If your motives for planning to use asynchronous e-learning are mostly concerned with saving time and saving money, then you'd better think twice or even three times, and do a comprehensive cost-benefit analysis before going on. Under the right circumstances, asynchronous e-learning can accomplish both of these goals, but it seldom does. It more often simply replaces one form of cost and time expenditures with another. For example, you may save learner and instructor time that would have been spent traveling to a class, but you end up spending much more design time and dollars on programming and graphics. Your CBA can help you determine if you really will be saving resources with a asynchronous e-learning delivery.

We discussed cost-benefit analysis earlier, so I won't go into it again, but the key indicator for comparing e-learning to other delivery systems is cost per learner for the delivery. Add up all the design, development, and implementation costs of e-learning, including the hardware, software, and other ancillary factors, then divide by the number of learners who will take the course or use the system. This will give you a per-learner cost. If you find out that this number is less than the per-learner cost of a classroom or other delivery method that you are using, you may actually have a cost savings. The problem is making sure you calculate in all those ancillary costs, on both sides of the equation.

Other "not so good" motives for deciding to try e-learning include the following:

- We'll put our classrooms on the Web and the trainers won't need to teach anymore

- We might as well use it because all our employees know how to work computers

- We need to do it because everyone else is and it works for them

- It's self-directed so it will be easy for the employees to use

- It's a better way to learn

If any of your motives sound like these, do some more thinking on it!

Determining Your Organization's Readiness for E-Learning

Organizational readiness for e-learning is somewhat subjective, but here is a short instrument you can use to help you think about some of the factors involved in this process ("Analyzing the Organization's Need for E-Learning" by Tom Floyd, in *The AMA Handbook of E-Learning*, 2003).

 Questions to Consider When Analyzing Your Organization's Readiness for E-Learning

- Do the strengths of e-learning match the content we must deliver?
- Do the delivery advantages of e-learning match our learning environment?
- Will e-learning save us design, development, and implementation time?
- Will e-learning be more efficient for our learners?
- Overall, will e-learning provide us with any real cost savings?
- Will our culture support the nonclassroom environment of e-learning?
- Are our trainers or instructors ready to make the shift to asynchronous e-learning?
- Do we have the technology infrastructure in place to support e-learning?
- Do we have the funding to augment the technology as necessary?
- Will we be able to support and maintain the e-learning initiative under current or future conditions?
- Will our learners be ready to become e-learners?
- Is there visible high-level support for the process?
- Do we have the right design resources for e-learning?
- Are our learners comfortable with computer operating and e-mail systems?

This certainly isn't everything you'll need to consider, and you may want to add your own items or subtract those that are not applicable, but it's a good place to start.

Creating an E-Learning Vision

If you are comfortable with your organization's motives and readiness, you are now ready to create an e-learning vision. Start by determining what your e-learning is and isn't.

- Is it just another delivery system or are you looking at a complete shift in your approach to learning?
- Will it be driven by the training function, or is it something much larger in scope?
- Who will it serve, and who won't be included?

- Who will it serve first, or most?
- What will it look like to the executive level, the business units, the line supervisors, the learners?
- What are the goals and objectives of the process?
- Are they linked to business goals and strategy?
- What change management issues will need to be addressed?

By answering these questions you should be able to create a succinct paragraph or two that states your e-learning vision. Don't skip or pay short shift to this part of the planning, as it will guide everything else you do in your e-learning process.

DESIGNING AND DEVELOPING GOOD PROGRAMS

We'll be discussing the instructional design component of this step in detail a little later. Actually, we've already been discussing it throughout this book whenever we talked about self-instruction, so our discussion may be shorter than you expect. However, a key planning question to ask yourself here is: do we have or can we obtain the resources required to create effective asynchronous e-learning programs? This includes instructional designers who understand how to create self-instructional packages; programmers who have the experience and, especially, the time to do it right (no overworked IS personnel need apply); graphic artists to make it sing; software for design and implementation; the list just goes on. If such resources are not available, your programs and your learners will suffer.

Policies and Procedures

The second component in this planning step is to create the policies and procedures (P&P) that will facilitate the success of your programs. This includes all the who, what, where, when, and how that make up the infrastructure of the system, what special roles will be played by various people in the organization, what committees will be needed, and what their responsibilities are. Special consideration should be given to who owns the process and who will be allowed to publish on it and under what circumstances.

You'll need to write P&P on who has access to the learning and how, what aspects require management approval, how learners can request learning, how scheduling of classes is to be done, who can author courses, who can change or edit courses, penalties for not completing required courses, rewards for achieving learning goals, record-keeping processes, and anything else you can think of specific to your own culture and learning environment.

Preparing the Work Environment

The third component is planning the preparation of the work environment for e-learning. This means making sure you have the right computer hardware where it is needed for the learner, working with your IS department to get necessary software loaded properly, determining if the e-learning will be delivered to the desktop or in learning centers, or both, and generally ensuring that the delivery environment is amenable to learning. One organization I visited was having such a difficult time with the privacy problem that they created "knowledge closets" where a learner could go and literally shut the door. Everyone was made aware that people in the knowledge closets were not to be disturbed unless it was an emergency. Some of these facilities actually were closets; the stored materials and, in one case, even the brooms and mops were replaced with a chair, desk, and computer.

You also need to determine if the time for asynchronous e-learning actually exists in the work environment. The tales of learners who couldn't learn because the work place gave them neither the privacy nor the time to do it are already legend, and those of entire e-learning systems failing because no one realized that the IS department bought computers without sound cards or some other necessary item are so common that they're not worth repeating. Basically, this happens because of incomplete planning.

LEARNING MANAGEMENT SYSTEMS AND LEARNING CONTENT MANAGEMENT SYSTEMS

One special and particularly important aspect of the work environment is the existence of a learning management system (LMS) or learning content management system (LCMS). You can use asynchronous e-learning without one, but having one available sure does help.

These software systems assist in both the design and the administration of e-learning—and any other type of learning for that matter. They track registrations, course access, time spent on courses, learner progress, and grades, and they can be used to design courses, provide a learner interface, create knowledge libraries, implement threaded discussions and chat rooms, assign learners to courses, and create and administer evaluations.

You'll see both acronyms still in use, but the difference between an LMS and an LCMS is becoming harder and harder to distinguish. Early on, an LMS was an administrative tool that handled everything but the actual course content, whereas an LCMS managed course content to the point where you could actually reuse screens and even whole sections of asynchronous content that you developed for one program in another.

The following list compares some of the aspects of an LMS to a LCMS:

ASPECT	LMS	LCMS
Who uses it	Trainers, administrators	Designers, trainers, administrators
Ability to provide collaborative learning	Usually no	Usually
Ability to plug in development tools	No	Usually
Integration with HR software	Usually yes	Usually no
Event scheduling	Yes	Normally no
Learner progress reporting	Yes	Usually no
Learner profile information	Usually yes	Usually no
Results tracking	Yes	Yes
Content creation	No	Yes
Learning object manipulation	No	Yes
Test question development	Yes	Yes
Test administration	Yes	Yes
Pre-testing	No	Yes
Navigational controls	Normally no	Yes
Complete learner interface	Normally no	Yes
Compliance with Shareable Content Object Reference Model (SCORM)	Yes	Yes

Today all of these functions are usually included in a single package, or at least enough of them that the difference between the two systems is not critical—that is, if you are buying a new one. If your organization already has one and has had it for some time, you'll need to look very closely at what it can and cannot do.

A number of questions must be answered when considering an LMS. For example, will it be used for administrative purposes only or to create and deploy e-learning as well? Will it be integrated with other corporate HR and customer service systems? How expensive it will be to customize it? Here are some questions of more interest to the instructional designer concerning the usefulness of an LMS:

- Can HR data be imported from other databases?
- Is there automatic synchronization with these databases?

- Can the naming conventions be customized if needed?
- How are learner guides, facilitator guides, equipment, and software tracked?
- What learner transactions (registration, attendance, cancellation, testing) are tracked?
- Are learner transactions tracked automatically?
- How difficult is it to generate transaction reports?
- Can custom courses be created, tracked, and maintained?
- How does the system handle pre/post activities?
- Can the system tag, store, and retrieve various kinds and pieces of content?
- Does the system work with our e-mail system?
- What are the graphics standards that it supports?
- Does it allow the sharing of normal business documentation?
- Are the search functions and organizational tools easy to use?
- How is stored content outputted, and can it be translated when necessary (HTML to XML to PPT and so on)?
- Can the system combine vendor and custom courses and even course content?
- How flexible are the content creation templates?
- How simple is it to make small content changes?
- Can more than one designer work on a course simultaneously?
- Does it have bulletin board and chat room functionality?

In the end, a major problem with many of the big LMS programs is that they try to be all things to all people, including designers, administrators, HR, programmers, graphics designers, and so on, so they end up being entirely too complicated for anybody to use effectively. The key to an effective LMS is to determine what you absolutely need and then apply the tried and true KISS principle when choosing one. The best LMS programs reside entirely on a single server, not on individual machines, and can be used by anyone with minimal training.

Beyond an LMS, here are some questions that sum up what you need to know about the general availability of technology in your organization for asynchronous e-learning:

- Do all targeted learners have access to the Internet or our intranet in their work environment?

- Do the learners use corporate websites that are already on line?
- Do we have an effective LMS?
- Is there easy access to the corporate servers for obtaining learning programs?
- Is there space on the corporate servers for the learning programs?
- Is the necessary hardware (computers with minimum system requirements, sound cards, access lines and modems, graphics cards, CD-ROM or DVD drives, monitors of sufficient resolution) available to all targeted learners?
- Is the proper software (current browsers, plug-ins, presentation software) on the learners machines or can it be easily downloaded?
- Will IS supply needed support as necessary?

Of course, you will want to talk to your IS department about these questions and make sure they are on board with the whole idea of using "their" computers for training and all that entails. ("Learning Management Systems" by Bray Brockbank, in *The AMA Handbook of E-Learning*, 2003.)

PREPARING THE ORGANIZATION GLOBALLY FOR E-LEARNING

This is the planning step that has been forgotten so often in the past, and unfortunately still is. It includes marketing the concept of e-learning to the organization through the use of benefits, WIIFMs, and even branding; preparing management by discussing their role and their benefits, doing the same with supervisors, and then preparing the learners themselves, both for becoming self-directed learners and for the use of your particular system—especially the use of the learner interface and the procedures for signing up for a course.

You'll need to help management understand that this is a three-to-five-year commitment of time and resources if you really plan to reap the benefits that e-learning offers. You'll also need to help the supervisors understand their role as e-learning gatekeeper, coach, and support person, and the advantages self-directed employees can have for them in terms of higher levels of performance, higher employee satisfaction, and better-trained workers. (*Selling E-Learning* by Darin Hartley, 2001.)

Here is a partial list of e-learning selling points that you might use in this planning step:

Selling Points for E-Learning

- Cost savings (be careful)
- More effective
- Greater learner choice

- Greater manager control
- Reduced training time
- Geographic implications
- Allows learning 24 × 7
- Easily updateable
- Provides a consistent message
- Trains large numbers in a short time

There are various methods for preparing the learners and their supervisors for e-learning, one of them (strangely enough) being the holding of classroom sessions for this purpose. We don't have the space to deal with these methods in detail (*Preparing Learners for E-Learning* edited by George Piskurich, 2003), but to help you get an idea of what might be included in this aspect of preparation, here is a list of objectives from a section of one of those learner preparation classes.

At the end of this session you will be able to:

- Define the concept of e-learning
- Discuss why self-directed learning is an important aspect of e-learning
- Discuss why SDL is important to you personally and to the organization
- Develop an appreciation of how much SDL you already do
- Determine your SDL readiness level
- Recall various corporate resources that can be used in learning activities
- Determine SDL strategies that will be effective in your personal work environment
- Isolate environmental obstacles and barriers to e-learning success
- Create an e-learning plan for a personal on-the-job learning need

Here's another objective list from a supervisor preparation class:

- Discuss the importance of e-learning to the organization from a managerial perspective
- Describe methods by which managers can help or hinder the development of self-direction in their workers
- Determine how you will create an environment that is conducive to e-learning for your work group
- Use the e-learning contract to manage self-direction in your individual contributors

Learner preparation and motivation is such a critical aspect in the success of asynchronous e-learning that you just can't talk about it too much. So, here are a few more resources for you to use as you create your learner preparation process. The first is a list of things you might do to prepare and motivate your e-learners; the second, a job aid to distribute to your learners to help them succeed at asynchronous e-learning; and the third, a self-assessment you might have them do as part of your preparation plan.

Other Thoughts on Preparing and Motivating E-Learners

- Know your learners and their goals
- Know the work environment they will be learning in
- Match their values and motives to your program
- Create a personal stake in the learning for the learners
- Make giving time for the learning an organizational priority
- Allow them to evaluate their learning
- Inform them that you will be monitoring their learning
- Focus on learning results
- Make the learning process important in the company
- Make the programs hands-on where possible
- Celebrate successes
- Provide support before, during, and after
- Make sure your program content is valuable to the learners
- Try to keep the technology as unobtrusive as possible
- Design the learning in small chunks to make it easier for them to learn and leave
- Don't sacrifice learnability for glitz

We've already covered some of these, some are related more to program design, and others are just good common sense. Use them as you can.

 How to Prepare to Be an Asynchronous E-Learner Job Aid

- Develop the drive to be a lifelong learner
- Practice self-motivation
- Learn to be an excellent time manager of your own learning time:
  - Make learning checklists
  - Turn off the phone when working on a program
  - Post a "Do Not Disturb" sign
  - Add time for learning to your weekly schedule

- Learn any time you have spare time
- Negotiate for learning time with your supervisor
- Become comfortable with computer and web technology
- Know your e-learning system:
  - Where are assignments, due dates, and other notifications located?
  - What tools are available to set my personal learning profile and calendar?
- Know your e-learning program:
  - How do I navigate?
  - What help structure is available?
  - What interface facilities (toolbars, icons, bookmarks) are available?
  - What learning facilities exist?
    Objectives
    Outlines
    Summaries
    Testing
    Activities
    Hyperlinks
    Remediation
    Enrichment
- Build your personal learning network with other asynchronous learners
- Know your purpose before you begin your learning
- Scan the content to develop a learning map before getting into the details
- Find ways to apply your learning to the job as soon as possible

E-LEARNING SELF-ASSESSMENT			
Statement	*Yes*	*No*	*Comment*
I am comfortable using a computer			
I have little difficulty learning to use new software			
I can use a web browser effectively			
I have used electronic bulletin boards in the past			
I have engaged in threaded discussions using a computer			
I participate in chat rooms			

Statement	Yes	No	Comment
I'm comfortable interacting on line with people			
I'm comfortable using my computer as a learning tool			
I am self-motivated to learn			
I feel I can manage my own learning time effectively			
I feel learning can happen in other places than the classroom			
I believe I can manage my own learning			
I have good access to a computer in my work area			
I have access to a computer and the Internet at home			

PLANNING FOR A SMOOTH, SUCCESSFUL IMPLEMENTATION

("Implementing E-Learning" by Loretta Donovan, in *The AMA Handbook of E-Learning*, 2003)

To achieve this planning step requires a good rollout and continuation plan. There are literally hundreds of aspects that may be included in your rollout, but here is a sampling:

- Use quick start guides to help the learners hit the ground running
- Run focus groups ahead of time to determine learner needs and build excitement
- Have a pop-up support function available inside your programs
- Make sure your start-up phone-in support is 24 × 7 for the first few weeks
- Create help screens in your program introduction
- Have a help desk number available as a menu pop-up
- Create a major launch event that goes throughout the organization
- Use giveaways to remind the learners about e-learning
- Use personal contact where possible
- Step up your marketing to all levels
- Use e-mail to announce new programs
- Communicate learner and departmental successes

- Write reports and send them to all interested parties
- Develop rewards and incentives for learners and supervisors:
  - Produce printable completion certificates that can be exchanged for prizes
  - For management development and other multiprogram processes, create a wall display plaque with spaces for stickers as programs are completed
  - When a program is completed, have a copy of the completion certificate sent to the learner's boss's printer or computer
- Create a culture that prizes learning
- Find incentives for sharing learner learnings with others
- Develop peer recognition processes:
  - Learner of the month
  - Special events
  - Group e-mails
  - Learner chat rooms or electronic bulletin boards
  - E-news letters

Your responsibility here is to create a plan that initiates the system successfully, then allows for both sustainability and adaptability as needs of the organization change. It should also include a variety of methods for continuing communications, which brings up the final planning step.

Help your learners learn more by advising them to take time off between modules of a program. A day or two will allow them to internalize the information better and possibly have a chance to practice it on the job

CREATING AN EFFECTIVE MONITORING AND EVALUATION PLAN

A major part of ensuring that your e-learning system is sustainable and adaptable is the way you monitor and evaluate it. You'll need to create a monitoring plan that includes conversations with and surveys of everyone, particularly the learners and their supervisors. They will give you on-the-firing-line information about whether your e-learning is succeeding and what needs to be done to make it better.

Monitoring is usually an informal process, but for your formal evaluation you should consider the five levels as we discussed earlier and create an evaluation plan that encompasses all of them. Since this is self-instruction you'll also need to consider the five aspects of self-instructional evaluation that were discussed in the evaluation chapter:

- Sufficiency of information in the program
- Usability of the program itself by the learners
- Currency of the material in the program
- Compliance of the learners with the program process
- Actual effectiveness of the program at both Level 2 and Level 3

As noted, we've already discussed this process so we'll not go into detail again, but be sure you cover everything in your evaluation plan.

One other important aspect of evaluation planning, particularly if you need to do a Level 5 (ROI) evaluation, is to define your success metrics. These are the numbers that will indicate to you and, more important, to management that your system is succeeding.

Here is a list of criteria that you might use for success metrics:

- Number of courses taken
- Number of courses completed
- Number of courses created
- Revenue
- Help desk calls
- Customer service ratings

You might also use some more esoteric but just as important results-based criteria:

- Reduced training or other costs
- Improved individual and work group performance
- Maintenance of core competencies
- Increased flexibility and reactivity of organization

By now you may once again be thinking that if you need to do all this just to get to the point where you can create an asynchronous e-learning program, it may not be worth the effort—and you may be right. Asynchronous e-learning is not an easy delivery system to use, no matter who says that you can go from PowerPoint to e-learning in fifteen minutes. Without proper preparation, most people in your organization, particularly your learners, won't understand what it is you are trying to do or how to do it.

The best asynchronous e-learning processes are integrated into the corporation's culture and business strategy, and that takes time. You can't just drop an LMS and a bunch of content on the employees and figure that sooner or later it will take. A few learners will learn, simply because their need is great enough to overcome all obstacles—including your lack of planning—but the majority will simply turn away. Even the design process itself, which we will discuss next, is much more rigorous and more loaded with pitfalls than some would want you to believe. However, there is an old Chinese proverb that states:

> *When the learner is ready, the teacher will appear.*

Through outstanding planning and good instructional design, you can change that concept to a new asynchronous e-learning proverb:

> *When the learner is ready, the learning resources will be there.*

ASYNCHRONOUS E-LEARNING DESIGN AND DEVELOPMENT

As we've already noted, much of asynchronous program design is the same as what we've already discussed for a classroom delivery, at least until you get to material development. So let's look at the process using the same format that we used for the rest of this book: analysis, design, development, implementation, and evaluation.

ANALYSIS

The early stages of analysis remain pretty much the same for asynchronous design. The first important change occurs in your job and task analysis (JTA). This process must be much more exacting for an asynchronous delivery. It can't be repeated too often that there will be no instructor to augment your analysis of the tasks that need to be taught or to fix places where it wasn't quite what it should have been, so completeness and clarity are critical. Also, once your program is finished it is usually very expensive and time consuming to make changes in it, so your JTA needs to find everything out the first time through.

Delivery Analysis for Asynchronous E-Learning

Your delivery analysis also has a new twist to it in asynchronous designs. In its basic mode this analysis tells you if asynchronous is the right delivery system, but beyond this decision you also need to consider whether your program will be created in a linear or nonlinear format. We're all somewhat familiar with the linear format, in which the learner begins at the beginning, follows each learning step to its conclusion, and ends at the end. This is the way most asynchronous e-learning is developed.

However, there are asynchronous programs in which the learners are given no more than a problem via the computer and asked to solve it using what can be gleaned from a list of computer-based learning resources. Or they might be given a task through a computer-based scenario and asked to decide how to do it, using another list of learning resources to determine key decision-making points, and then submitting their task completion plan for critiquing. (*Designing World-Class E-Learning* by Roger Schank, 2002.) There is even a nonlinear methodology in which the learners are required to develop their own learning objectives based on a personal learning needs analysis, come to a conclusion on what computer-based learning resources they'll need to meet their objectives, and then use those resources to complete a self-evaluation process that tells them and the learning facilitator whether the objectives have been achieved. This is often done through the use of individual learning contracts.

The main thing that all of these nonlinear designs have in common—and have in common with linear designs as well—is the need for precise performance-based objectives, present in enough depth and number to guide the learning and the learning evaluation. Even though the learner is much more self-directed in the nonlinear formats, the objectives are just as critical, perhaps more so. As you may have already realized from our previous discussions, intensive preparation of your learners for the high degree of self-directedness required in these nonlinear formats is of critical importance.

Following is an example of a self-directed learning plan or contract that can be used in a nonlinear asynchronous learning format, followed by lists of advantages and disadvantages of asynchronous e-learning that can help you make that basic delivery decision of whether to use asynchronous e-learning at all.

SELF-DIRECTED LEARNING PLAN

Learning Objectives	Learning Process	Possible Resources	Target Obstacles	Dates	Evaluation
What do I need to know or be able to do?	What steps will I need to take?	What resources will I need?	And how to overcome them	When will I complete each step?	I will have succeeded in my learning when . . .

Advantages of Asynchronous E-Learning

Once a program is completed it can be used by thousands of learners simultaneously

It enhances self-direction

It can be used to create very effective blends

It can be very effective for knowledge-based content

It can save large amounts of learner personal time

It can save large amounts of instructor face time

It can save large amounts of travel time and expense for learners and instructors

Asynchronous programs can meet the needs of small groups of your learning population for specialized classes, advanced classes, or simple enrichment

It works well for learners who just don't like to sit in a classroom

It is just-in-time training

Learners can move at their own pace

Learners can use it to learn just what they need or their situation demands

It's available 24 × 7

Disadvantages of Asynchronous E-Learning

Creating and implementing the system can often cost more than the courses

The design costs can wipe out any travel cost savings you were expecting

It is seldom effective as a training system; it's even questionable as to its effectiveness for an entire subsystem of training such as management skills or software training

It requires a higher level of self-direction

It is difficult to use for performance-based content

It requires the learner to have some degree of computer comfort and ability

It requires specific hardware and software

It requires you to work closely with the IT department

It requires detailed implementation planning

It does not work well for collaborative learning

It is not simply putting classroom courses on line

Audience Analysis for Asynchronous E-Learning

As you might already expect, your audience analysis needs to be more thorough, as the instructor isn't there to gather more information at the start of the class and make on-the-fly changes. Your analysis also needs to ask more specific questions concerning the learners' computer skills and level of self-direction. We've already given you some tools for audience analysis during the discussion of learner preparation. You may want to modify them by adding questions from the earlier material on audience analysis, as well as other questions that reflect your own environment, to create an audience analysis instrument specific to your situation.

MATERIAL DEVELOPMENT

I'll spare you another diatribe about the importance of objectives for asynchronous e-learning design, as I hope that was made more than clear in our earlier objectives discussion. Suffice it to say that the quantity, quality, and use of objectives will be the primary make-or-break factor in your program as far as your learners are concerned. Their creation is exactly the same as it is for the classroom, so let's move on to where the real differences are: material development.

The workhorse of asynchronous e-learning material development is the storyboard with its accompanying script. We discussed scripts and storyboards in Chapter Five and gave you some examples as well as a lot of hints for their development, but here are a few more examples of storyboards created specifically for the asynchronous e-learning delivery process (see figure, "Web-Based Training Layout").

WEB-BASED TRAINING LAYOUT
(form edited to fit this participant guide)

Project Name: <u>Learning@Acme</u>   File Name: <u>c:\20Acme Learning Presentation\WBT Scrip Rev 2.doc</u>

Screen ID <u>1</u>   Last Save Date: <u>7/31/05 1:41PM</u>

Programmer Notes	Text
Acme Brand and Sam Smith picture	You are part of one of the most successful financial institutions in the world. Our annual revenue is close to 20 billion dollars, and our net profit is nearly 4 billion dollars per year.
Audio voiceover with fading replacement of brand with generating station graphic, automobile assembly line graphic, then large crop.	How do we do it? What do we have that createsthat kind of revenue and profit? In other words, what are Acme's assets? It's easy to see the assets of, say, an automaker or the power company, or even a farm . . .
Replace Sam's picture with dissolved-in Flash "video" of customer service rep on headset, "Welcome to Acme. How may I help you today?"	. . . but what are our assets? "Welcome to Acme. How may I help you today?"

Action/Buttons	Related File Names
Related File Names "Next" upon end of audio on all screens	Graphics, audio, script, and graphic list are located at gfx01.jpg: Acme Signature gfx02.jpg: Picture of Sam gfx03.jpg: Assembly Line gfx04.jpg: Generating Station gfx05.jpg: Agribusiness aud01.wav: Sam's Intro aud02:wav: Welcome

As you can see in the first example, in this template there are windows for the script (text), notes for the programmer, audio pieces or functionality of specialized buttons, and the names of the files that contain the information to be added to this screen. This tells the programmers just about all they need to know to make your screen concept come to life.

You should also be able to see why the designing of asynchronous e-learning can be so lengthy. This is the necessary information for just one screen of one module. Multiply this by fifty or so screens, and maybe three or more modules for just one program, and you have an idea of why designing asynchronous e-learning (when done right) is so time consuming.

The "Introduction Module" figure is an example of a column-type asynchronous e-learning storyboard, in case you prefer this template format:

Take learner literacy out of the problem mix through the use of narration.

Learner Guides

Your learner guide for an asynchronous e-learning program may be little more than a couple of pages of directions sent down to the learners electronically, or it may be an entire document, including objectives, notes pages, activity pages, and anything else you feel your learners should have in hard copy. However, during your materials design don't forget to consider it.

If nothing else, your learner guide should always include a piece at the start on how to learn on your own. It doesn't need to be a big deal, just a reminder that this is self-directed learning, what that means, and that good self-directed learners are resourceful, have initiative, and are persistent in their learning. It should also have information on how to access the course, and where to go for help if the learner has problems.

Beyond this you might include course objectives, a content outline, prerequisites, a materials list, and possibly information on the interface (such as what the buttons and colors mean) What you include is part of your design decision, but use this resource to help your learners get started properly and learn effectively.

 If your learners have PDAs, make your learner guides are downloadable for them as well so they can use them to take notes.

Asynchronous E-Learning Program Activities and Interactions

(*Michael Allen's Guide to E-Learning* by Michael Allen, 2003)
We've said it before, but we'll say it again, and probably again: one of the most vital aspect in making asynchronous e-learning work is the creation of learner

		INTRODUCTION MODULE		
Screen #	*Topic*	*Content*		*Animation*
1_0_00	Course Introduction	Animated Flash Screen		
1_0_01	Welcome Screen	Course objective		
1_0_02	Course Overview	Modules - interactive menu format		
1_0_03	Navigation	Instructions - optional link from 1_0_02		
1_0_04	Instructions	(Scoring, contacts, and so on)		
		Module 1: Introductory Period		
1_1_00	Module Introduction	Animated Flash Screen - similar to 1_0_00		
1_1_01	Module Objectives	**What You Will Learn** *Module 1 prepares you to complete your supervisory responsibilities during the introductory period for new employees. Specifically, it addresses:* • Identifying the four possible outcomes of the introductory period • Helping employees during the introductory period • Making decisions after the introductory period • Extending the introductory period if necessary • Transferring within BHCS • Fulfilling your supervisor responsibilities • Handing a separation from employment *Click Next to continue.*		
1_1_02	Introducing Our Trial Basis Approach	Employees are hired on a trial basis for the first ninety calendar days of employment. During this introductory period, you will evaluate their • Performance • Behaviors • Work habits • Interactions with coworkers It's also a time for them to evaluate their satisfaction with the position and work unit. *Click Next to continue.*		Picture: Group of employees Interaction: Family Feud style board with four bullet points as answers— hit the buzzer button to display the answers.

interactions and activities. This doesn't mean a pop-up that appears during a mouseover, or having the learner click a button to move to the next screen. Those are navigational processes, not interactions. It does mean any creative methods you can come up with to involve the learner.

Activities may be as simple as using a storytelling methodology to deliver the content, perhaps with the learner's name inserted in the story, and a group of questions to be answered at the end—or as complicated as a branched decision-making scenario in which each decision the learner make moves the learner along a different path and often to a different conclusion. By the way, you can insert the learners' names and even other facts about them into these interactions too, which can be really cool, not to mention motivating.

Of course the problem is that creating these interactions takes time, so just as in a classroom delivery, they are usually the first thing we skip and the last thing we should have skipped.

When considering interactions, you need to keep in mind the amount of time you have to design them, the amount of time the learner will devote to doing them, and what your software capabilities are. I like to outline possible activities and interactions on my storyboard, and then when I present it to the programmer we talk about what is possible and what isn't. The programmers usually have some great ideas too, particularly if they have been doing this type of programming for awhile and have seen what other designers have used.

In a more or less random order, here are some thoughts on possible asynchronous e-learning activities and interactions:

- Present the learner with a piece of completed work and ask them to evaluate it according to the criteria they've just learned
- Have the learner label a graphic or complete a flow chart
- Exhibit a series of simulated scenarios and ask the learner to label which ones were right, wrong, require _____, and so on
- Get rid of any video talking heads; these are neither activities nor good learning methodology
- Get rid of any book pages scanned onto a screen
- Tell stories that illuminate content using animations and narration
- Use video demonstrations
- Use games (but not too often)
  - Jigsaw puzzles
  - Crosswords
  - Game shows

- Web treasure hunts
- Interactive calculators
- Beat-the-clock games (these really add excitement to your program)
- If you have the capability, get them on the Web to do web research or just to search provided websites
- Create computer-based role plays in which they play a role by answering questions concerning what they'd say or do next
- Start each program with an activity, the same way you would a class
- Use integrated timers to create timed activities that build suspense
- Create competitions by developing activities that are scored, then posted like a video game
- Create on-screen avatars to take learners through the learning by talking to them or just being there throughout
- Send learners on "field trips" to websites to come back with information
- Use instruments such as questionnaires, surveys, checklists, or other types of forms
- Create printable job aids that the employee can practice using in simulations
- Be careful not to use the same type of interaction too many times in a program; three is probably too many
- Click interactions—in which a learner is given a series of choices and clicks on the right one—are OK, but note the preceding comment
- Cross-link material so learners need to go to other screens to get the whole story. This also keeps your screens from getting too complicated
- Keep your sessions (including activities) to no longer than 45 minutes
- Drag-and-drop interactions work very well for sequencing processes
- Text-entry interactions provide little in the way of feedback
- Don't overuse mouseovers and pop-ups
- Use voting or polling activities in which the learners compare their own reactions to those of a predetermined group
- Use click and drag to present a series of problems and solutions and ask learners to choose which works best for which; make it more difficult by having solutions that don't work, multiple solutions, or even the need to take parts of different solutions to solve a single problem

You can make e-learning activities out of electronic policy and procedure manuals by having learners answer questions about what they find there, doing word searches, creating a series of scenarios that require use of the content, or requesting a search for the newest additions.

Graphics

(Web-Based Training: Using Technology to Design Adult Learning Experiences by Margaret Driscoll, 1998)
We already talked a lot about graphics design in Chapter Five, and the basics of design are the same for screens as they were for print. I've found that you can't beat the art of a true graphic designer, so for my programs I try to save the money to hire one. It has always been well worth it.

However, in case you don't have the money, or you think you are close to switching careers and becoming the next Picasso, here are some thoughts on graphic design for asynchronous e-learning screens:

- Keep your format consistent

- Know if your company has a format and if so, use it

- Incorporate your company logo where possible

- Graphical elements to consider:

  - Colors

  - Fonts

  - Navigation bars

  - Buttons

  - Backgrounds

  - Animations

- Use a web-safe color palette

- Times New Roman, Helvetica, and Arial make the best screen fonts

- Font size should always be 10-point or greater

- Do not use bold, italic, caps, or small caps

- Try to place graphics with text, not on a separate screen

- Use compressed file formats for pictures (GIF, JPEG)

- Watch for contrast between your chosen background and text

- Graphics help learning—but

- Too many graphics, particularly combined with other sensory inputs, can hinder learning

- Use colored backgrounds on your charts and graphs to add color to your programs at no additional bandwidth

- Use different color fonts for the main path, enrichment paths, or remedial paths

- Too many screens is better than too few

- Use general examples (farming, fishing, sports) rather than corporate-specific where possible

    In limited-bandwidth situations in which you want to use video, have the video set to download to the learner's machine ahead of time, then played from the hard drive when a hot link is clicked.

LEARNER EVALUATION

In asynchronous e-learning, learner evaluation takes on a number of forms. However, the one common aspect is that it must be criterion referenced. Since the learners are guided by the objectives, they must be evaluated by them as well if the evaluation is to be both valid and fair.

A good designer places evaluations throughout the program, at the end of sections, after modules or units, and of course at the end of the entire program. Many of these evaluations, particularly those found internally at the end of sections, can be self-evaluations: the learner is provided with the correct answers after the evaluation is completed and, if possible, with the area of the program where the answer came from. This enhances not only the evaluation process but the learning as well. However, be sure that your software allows you to branch back immediately to the correct answer in self-evaluation processes for maximum reinforcement. Waiting until the end of the test to provide the right answer and context is usually too long.

Of course, this multiple evaluation methodology means you'll need a lot of test questions, preferably written as a question bank (described in Chapter Four). Most good asynchronous e-learning software comes with a question bank facility, or it may be included in your LMS if you have one. If you don't have this capability I suggest that you try and purchase one of the evaluation software packages that have it in a form that can be integrated into your system. It will make your design life a whole lot easier. One of the other advantages of creating a question bank for asynchronous designs is that it can be used outside the actual program for retests, make-up exams, practice, or a number of other purposes.

A big problem with asynchronous design is that it is difficult to evaluate performances. This should be a major consideration when you are doing your delivery analysis. Performance evaluation is not a strength of asynchronous designs, and content that requires it might be best delivered in another way or possibly blended with OJT to create the right setting for the evaluation.

If you do need to evaluate performances in an asynchronous environment, and you must do it through the computer, you can create a performance simulation type of process in which the learner evaluates the simulation to determine if the performance has occurred. For self-tests you can use a "three strikes" technique, with the computer asking the learner to "try again" after the first mistake is made, explaining what should have been accomplished after the second mistake is made, and if a third try comes up empty, actually taking the learner through the performance process again step by step. This system also works well as a practice process when the learner is first learning a performance, and it isn't a bad way for a human to teach performance tasks either.

LEARNER INTERFACES

For being so important an item in the design of asynchronous e-learning, there are probably as many opinions concerning learner interfaces as there are designers out there worrying about them, and just as many controversies. Some of the controversy revolves around screen size, background color, even color and size of buttons on the screen, but one of my favorites is the discussion concerning whether you should add a pacing function to each screen; that is, telling the learner how many screens have been completed and how many are left.

I usually try to stay away from including these on my screens, as it is just another item to take up space or confuse learners, and it really doesn't tell them much of anything. The fact that they have completed ten screens in twelve minutes has no bearing on the length of time it might take to complete the next two screens, or ten. Good design tells us that screens that are basically text are completed quickly, whereas activity screens may take much longer. It's your program, so you make the choice as to whether to include screen completion information or not.

Actually, most often this decision and most other interface decisions are made for you in advance by the software you are using or your IS department. However, here are some thoughts you might consider if you have a say in the process, or if you think you may need to make a change to your current learner interface:

- Create screens that do not require the learner to use the scroll bar, if at all possible

- Learning objectives should appear often, certainly on the first screen of each chunk (section, module, and so on)

- Titles, captions, and headlines on screens should be well thought out and not just continual repeats

- Have a main path and options off the main path
- Test your interface before you develop your learning modules
- Be sure each program begins with a title screen; a preface that describes the purpose, background, and scope of the program; and a menu
- Create an interactive glossary for each program and a glossary button
- Make sure the purpose of all buttons is absolutely clear to all learners
- Decide where your navigation bars are going to be and leave them there
- Every screen should have next, back, and end buttons, as well as a way to get to any other part of the program without clicking through every screen between here and there
- A course map that can be accessed on every screen is usually a good idea
- Don't over-tech your presentation with so many bells and whistles on the screen that it gets confusing
- When you want the learner to take a break, program in a blank page with a note that reads "This page intentionally left quiet"

BETA TESTS AND PILOTS

We discussed beta tests and pilots at length earlier; they are much the same for asynchronous e-learning as they were for a classroom delivery. A particularly important aspect to remember, though, is that you use beta tests for content and pilots to determine flow. The flow of an asynchronous program is critical, as is the timing, and these should be the two aspects that you are most concerned with in your pilot. Final decisions on content, activities, and particularly the learner interface should have been made before the pilot.

At the beginning of a beta test, have the learners do only two or three screens before stopping them for feedback. This will help to get them comfortable with the feedback you are looking for. As their comfort level increases and their comments become more specific, you can make the chunks larger.

Another thing I've found useful is to condense all feedback from the beta test before working with it. Look it all over generally as a first step, discarding anything that is repetitious. Consider thoughts that are mutually exclusive (the course was too long, the course was too short) and make a decision on which one you will accept. Whittle it down to the basic comments that appear to be common and then make changes based on them. This will spare you a lot of headaches and having to make changes to your changes later.

Finally, be sure you have regularly scheduled review and revision meetings for your programs once they are out there. Nothing is more damaging to a program's credibility than having out-of-date content, and there is no instructor in asynchronous e-learning to bring the content up to date.

SOFTWARE

The basic software for asynchronous e-learning is the authoring system. There have been many different brands of authoring systems and all of them have had advantages and disadvantages. For the most part, although the good ones are easy to learn as far as the basics go, even the best of them take a lot of time and practice to become really expert at.

Currently the most popular authoring systems are Lectora, ToolBook, and Authorware, but if you are reading this book a year or two from the time of this writing, it's a good bet that there will be another one or two to add to this list, and maybe one of the three I just mentioned will no longer exist. I've learned to use four or five of these systems in my career, and I think only two of those are still around.

The problem with these systems is that they take you through a very specific approach to asynchronous design, which may or may not meet your needs. It's a pretty safe bet that if you are planning to use one of the nonlinear methods we discussed earlier an authoring system won't be of much help at all.

Things to look for in a good authoring system include

- Adherence to a systematic instructional design process such as the one we've discussed in this book

- Ease of use, ability to get quick and varied help

- Ability to go outside the system's design box if needed and a good integrated graphics program

- A good integrated test construction and question bank facility

- Video editing capability (not a must, but a plus)

Actually you don't really need an authoring system at all if you use vendors to do your graphics and programming. You simply do your design work as usual up to and including the creation of a storyboard, then turn it over to the experts. They will do it faster, better, and—if you consider the time it will take you just to learn the authoring system—cheaper than you can. Of course it won't seem cheaper when you get the bill, but in the long run it really is, and your program and learners will benefit from their expertise. If vendors are not a possibility for you, there are plenty of good authoring tools available out there. Look at them all, try them out, and choose the one that fits your needs.

There's one class of tools you'll want to be careful of, however: the ones that tell you they can help you create e-learning in thirty minutes, or make a PowerPoint presentation into e-learning as fast as you can type—what some refer to as conversion software. Let's just say that these software applications tend to stretch the truth a bit. Sure, by using them you can create a program that runs on a computer, but beyond that it will seldom have the activities and evaluations necessary to be truly effective e-learning. There is no magic bullet here. Designing synchronous e-learning that really works takes time, expertise, and imagination—and all three of these in good measure.

One good piece of software to consider, if you don't already have it, is a message board facility that allows learners to communicate asynchronously with the instructor and each other by posting questions, thoughts, and ideas, and even engaging in threaded discussions. These discussions, which can be spread over time, create some of the best learnings because, unlike in the classroom, the learners have time to assimilate and analyze their new knowledge. Your boards can be populated by learners, instructors, and SMEs for basic and extended content development. You can use message boards as help facilities as well.

REPURPOSING

("Repurposing Materials for E-Learning" by Carole Richardson, in *The AMA Handbook of E-Learning*, 2003)

 One way to cut down on the amount of design time needed for asynchronous e-learning is to repurpose your current programs. This has been the holy grail of vendors for about as long as there has been computer-based training. As we've already noted, there are a number of software programs that guarantee you e-learning from your classroom training in three easy steps, or that promise to change your PowerPoint to e-learning in fifteen minutes, and the interesting part is that they all work—just not very well.

Repurposing software usually starts with a rather large assumption: that the programs you begin with have been well designed. Notice I didn't say that they were good, but that they were well designed. This means, as you now know, that they began life with a strong analysis and have proper objectives, criterion-referenced learner evaluation, learner-centered activities, and all the other good design stuff we've discussed throughout this book. If they don't, your repurposing software will only translate a poor classroom program into a poor e-learning program. Remember the old computer saying: "Garbage in . . . , garbage out."

Even if your existing program is well designed, you've still got work to do—work that the repurposing software seldom considers. You've got to make sure that the activities your facilitators use in their classes translate well to an asynchronous environment. Some do, some don't; some repurposing software forgets that activities are important and has no way to translate them at all.

Your objectives will need to be looked at and probably supplemented, as classroom objectives are seldom in the number or depth needed to take the place of the instructor as they do in asynchronous deliveries.

Next, you need to move your tests to an e-learning environment. You may need to buy another piece of software for this, as we've mentioned before, for both test distribution and record keeping as well as question banking. You'll probably need to augment your question bank too, as asynchronous learning uses a lot more questions. You'll need to change the introductions, as the ones that work in classes seldom fit e-learning, and you'll need to boost the WIIFMs to create the learning need in your e-learners.

You should sort of be getting the picture by now: it ain't as easy as it seems. Even if you have well-designed courses, you'll still need to do much more than hit that one button to repurpose them for an asynchronous e-learning environment. That's not to say repurposing isn't a good idea. It is. It can save you time, money, and a lot of work. Just go into it with your eyes wide open, and don't expect much in the way of magic. Most important, don't sell your asynchronous e-learning concept to your organization with the idea that you can quickly and easily repurpose all the courses you now have into e-learning courses. This will doom your intervention to failure about as quickly as anything you can think of.

If you are considering repurposing, here are some thoughts to consider:

- Start by redoing your curriculum plan. You may find out that the order of courses changes when you go asynchronous, and that there is a lot of overlapping content that you can delete.

- You'll need to rechunk your content; when you do, think about possible resequencing here as well. Asynchronous learning often flows differently from classroom learning, both on a macro and a micro scale.

- Look for missing content when you're chunking and get it in there.

- Look for places to add more and different asynchronous-based interactions; you almost always need more of these than were designed into a classroom lesson plan.

- Add those real-life examples that the facilitators talk about but that aren't in the lesson plan.

- Try to find places to set up scenarios and problem-solving activities. These are the things that keep a learner interested and learning in an asynchronous environment.

EVALUATING ASYNCHRONOUS E-LEARNING PROGRAMS

(Evaluating E-Learning by Bill Horton, 2001)

We discussed the evaluation of your e-learning system back when we were looking at the planning process, but as part of your evaluation methodology, or to decide if an off-the-shelf program is worth the price, you also need to consider how to evaluate singular programs. Here are some things to look for when evaluating an asynchronous e-learning program, whether a vendor's or your own:

- Indication that a JTA, delivery analysis, and audience analysis were done
- Well-written objectives at various levels
- No need for an instructor
- Directions evident at the start of the program and the start of each chunk as needed
- Proper chunking of content
- Self-tests sprinkled throughout
- Good use, but not abuse, of media
- Plenty of activities and interactions
- Criterion-referenced learner evaluation where needed
- Inclusion of continuing postcourse activities
- Whether the amount and quality of the content is adequate
- Whether the content meets the objectives
- Whether the tone and examples match the needs of the intended audience

SUMMARY

To end our discussion of asynchronous e-learning design, I thought you might like to see what we've talked about from a number of different perspectives through the use of a few checklists and job aids.

This first one is a summary of the general characteristics your programs and system should exhibit.

Your programs and your system must

- Be easy to access
- Be relevant to the learners' needs
- Have excellent help functions for both technical and content help
- Be easy to navigate and allow learners to determine their own course
- Give learners control of the learning (no lockstep)
- Provide immediate practice
- Have a solid program evaluation process
- Have simple, uncluttered screens
- Allow for learner evaluation and record keeping

The next one is a job aid that summarizes most of the things we've discussed concerning program development, and maybe a few we missed:

E-Learning Design Hints

- List all the materials, tools, equipment, and training aids your learner will need for the program.
- Include a final summary activity.
- Use test outs where they make sense to decrease learning time.
- Use branching processes for individualization.
- Include a glossary and balloon definitions.
- Include a frequently asked questions screen where possible.
- Design in plenty of examples.
- Use click-and-drag activities to teach sequencing and sorting.
- Label all materials with version numbers.
- Modules should be twelve to fifteen minutes long, maximum.
- All self-tests and other evaluations should have specific directions.
- Make note of your sources of authority for the content.
- Provide sources of further information on topics for clarification or enrichment.
- Chunk, and then chunk again.
- Provide a content help number.
- Use chat and threaded discussion functions to increase interactivity.
- Be sure your scripts are politically correct.
- Be careful that your use of humor is not offensive.
- Reduce scrolling as much as possible; minimize graphics if necessary.
- Provide information with the fewest possible clicks.
- For lots of information use hot links; for small bits use pop-ups and mouseovers.
- Create pop-up and hotlink windows that do not require enlargement or scrolling.

To augment this program design job aid, here is a summary of thoughts on creating the overall e-learning system:

Questions for E-Learning System Development

- Have you performed an analysis of the content you plan to deliver?
  - Does it meet one or more organizational needs?
  - Does it meet individual employee development needs?
  - Is asynchronous e-learning the right delivery for the content?
- Have you created a proper design?
  - Are there enough objectives, are they learner based, are they useable?
  - Is there plenty of interactivity in your programs?
  - Are there both self and formal assessments of the learning?
- Do you have the right user interface or learning site?
  - Has it been tested by your users for ease of use and intuitiveness?
  - Will it meet all your e-learning needs?
  - Are you using it consistently?
- Have you scheduled beta tests and pilots for all your courses?
- Do you know what you need to evaluate and how you plan to do it?
- Do you have the right policies and procedures for your corporate environment?
- Do learners, instructors, designers, and administrators know what their roles are and how they will fulfill them?
- Are there job descriptions for individuals with special roles in your intervention?
- Have the necessary committees been created and populated?
- Is your technology adequate for your implementation?
- Have you chosen the place for the e-learning to occur, and will it be adequate?
- Have all time constraints been considered?
- Has the right help desk function for your intervention been created and staffed?

Next is a series of questions in the form of a checklist that you can use to determine how ready your organization is for asynchronous e-learning.

Your Twenty Questions for E-Learning Checklist

Place a check in the first column if you and your organization have an answer for the question; place a check in the second column if you are going to need help finding the right answer.

We know	*We need help*	
☐	☐	How do I motivate my employees to be responsive to my e-learning?
☐	☐	Is e-learning effective for all my levels and types of learners, particularly those with low literacy levels?
☐	☐	How do I create time for e-learning?
☐	☐	What are the minimum technology requirements for effective e-learning?
☐	☐	How do I re-tool my stand-up trainers to become e-proficient? What is available to help me?
☐	☐	How do I work with corporate IT to communicate my e-learning needs?
☐	☐	Why does e-learning sometimes fail?
☐	☐	What criteria do I use to pick the best e-learning programs?
☐	☐	Is it more efficient to deal with e-learning internally or to use outside agents? Do I build it or buy it?
☐	☐	What strategies do I use to get executives involved in not only supporting e-learning but in helping to implement it and make time for it?
☐	☐	What technical or other problems can be anticipated and avoided when getting started with e-learning?
☐	☐	How do I determine the ROI of e-learning?
☐	☐	What is the right blend of e-learning and classroom instruction?
☐	☐	Is e-learning effective for soft skills?
☐	☐	How do we measure e-learning success rates?
☐	☐	Are there ways to reduce e-learning development time?
☐	☐	How do I pick the best e-learning tools, software, platforms, and so on?
☐	☐	What do I need to do to support and maintain my e-learning process?
☐	☐	How do we make e-learning interesting?
☐	☐	How do I transition my learners to e-learning?

And last, but certainly not least, some comments on program design and implementation from those who are closest to the process: the learners.

Twenty-Five Significant Comments on E-Learning Made by E-Learners

On Course Design

"Don't give me a failing mark simply because I never finished the course. Maybe I learned what I needed without finishing."

"More links to outside information please."

"Don't organize the course according to your plan. Let me organize it the way I need to."

"Don't overwhelm me with too much content. Give me activities to learn a little at a time."

"I hated writing on the bulletin board, but liked to read what others said. I think I learned a lot that way."

"I don't want to be forced to contribute to threaded discussions to 'learn' from my peers. I don't think they know any more than I do."

"The best part was talking to other employees in the chat sessions."

On Preparation

"It's hard at first, but stay with it."

"If you are used to having a teacher tell you everything, you need to break that mold first."

"Initially, finding the right resources is the hard part. Once you start e-learning you develop a curiosity to find new resources."

"I can't learn what nobody teaches me."

"When I first started I needed someone to show me how, and then leave me alone."

"The only way to get good at it is to practice using it."

"Being comfortable with learning on your own makes it easier to succeed at e-learning."

On Technology

"My computer wouldn't show the videos, so I missed a lot."

"Once you master the software, learning the content material comes easy."

"I get confused in the technical terminology from the start. Can't they use words to describe what the stuff is that isn't 'computerese'?"

"It takes too much time to get on line and get started, especially when you just wanted to look something up."

"Having experience with computers, any computers for any reason, is a major advantage."

On Support

"No one ever told me how to use the buttons."

"I learned by trail and error and word of mouth, which isn't the best way. Look for a coach or mentor who can help you become a more efficient e-learner."

"They never give me time to sit down and do it."

"I found no place where I wouldn't be interrupted."

"My boss doesn't believe I'm working."

"I don't know what to do when it freezes up."

In the next chapter we'll look at synchronous e-learning, its advantages and disadvantages as a delivery system, and how to create an effective design for it.

Chapter 10

Synchronous E-Learning Design

This chapter will help you to:

- Discuss various advantages, disadvantages, and myths concerning synchronous e-learning, and their basis in reality
- Determine when synchronous e-learning is the best delivery system to use
- Design, redesign, and repurpose materials for synchronous e-learning
- Repurpose leader guides and learner guides for the synchronous environment
- Create effective media for synchronous classes
- Effectively implement a synchronous e-learning class
- Differentiate between synchronous e-learning and online learning

---

Synchronous e-learning, sometimes referred to as *online learning*, has been rapidly evolving into a delivery system of choice for many companies. This is partially due to its real advantages and partially due to some perceived advantages that are not necessarily so, and that can cause a great deal of difficulty for you as an instructional designer.

ADVANTAGES

("Getting Ready for Synchronous E-Learning" by Jennifer Hoffman, in *The AMA Handbook of E-Learning*, 2003.)

The obvious major advantage of synchronous e-learning is that neither the learners nor the instructor need to travel to a certain location to work together. Instead they interact through the mediation of a computer and computer network, most often using a specially designed software package. With synchronous designs you still have the ability to create learner-facilitator and learner-learner interactions, very much as in a classroom, but without the physical classroom itself and all that that entails.

Another significant advantage, at least over asynchronous e-learning, is that synchronous e-learning is faster to design. Unlike asynchronous designs, there is an instructor or facilitator present. Therefore the need to design the learning program as perfectly as possible is no longer quite as critical. As in a face-to-face classroom, the instructor provides a way for the learners to have their questions answered (it is hoped), and if your material is not quite as sharp as it might be, there is someone there to fill in the gaps and cover for the design flaws. This also means the program will be easier to revise as, in a pinch, all you need to do is talk to the instructor.

Here is a short list of advantages of synchronous e-learning:

- Efficient for a geographically dispersed audience
- Easily revised if content is unstable
- Efficient when delivery of content is limited to once or a few times
- Allows real-time access to an expert
- Effective when learner collaboration is important
- Useful when content requires classroom delivery
- Can be developed quickly when design time is short

An exciting use of synchronous e-learning is to use it for communications; that is, simply to stay in touch. If you have a highly dispersed workforce, do ten-minute mini-learnings every week or two, with a discussion board added in for later feedback.

DISADVANTAGES AND MISCONCEPTIONS

Unfortunately, synchronous designs also suffer from the same disadvantages as classroom designs, the main one being, of course, the instructor who we said was such an advantage in the last paragraph. Even more than in classrooms, many synchronous implementations seem to consist of a data dump from an SME. This may be because it's so efficient and simple for an SME to teach a synchronous class, they only need to find a computer, not go to a classroom. Or it may be because the instructor can't see the learners becoming bored and tuning out his or her droning PowerPoint presentation, or because the SMEs—and, in many cases, even the professional trainers—have not been taught to use this delivery methodology properly. This brings up the first of those perceived advantages we mentioned that are not necessarily so.

It Ain't That Easy

Synchronous e-learning has been and continues to be sold to organizations as a process that requires their facilitators to do nothing more than put their presentations on a computer, then talk through a microphone to the learners who are at their own computers. This is true, if your goal in implementing a learning program is to have practically no learners paying attention to the presentation about fifteen minutes after the class begins. Since no one is "watching" them, if learners get bored they don't zone out as in a classroom—they multitask out: working on other assignments, surfing the Web, answering e-mails, even talking with people who happen to drop by their cube during the class.

An effective synchronous class often requires not just repurposing of classroom material (which some define as switching media formats and adding an activity or two) but redesign of the program, including changes in activities, the inclusion of large numbers of small interactions, the design of polls and interactive media-based activities (often called *annotating*), and quite possibly resequencing of content and objectives. And we're talking here about beginning with a good design in the first place. If the classroom design and materials are slipshod, with poor objectives, less than adequate learner evaluation, and content that has not been validated, you literally need to start from scratch.

Beyond design considerations, you must also address concerns about the facilitators. Saying a classroom facilitator can step right into a synchronous environment is akin to saying a good single-engine pilot can step right into the cockpit of a 767. Sure, the basic concept is the same, but the differences can be rather daunting. These include simply using the software effectively, knowing when to answer questions and when not to, gathering feedback when no one is there, deciding when to relinquish control of the network and when to take it back, figuring out when and how to turn various software functions off and on, and facilitating small group interactions when you can't see the small groups—just to mention a few. We'll discuss these tasks in more detail later, but for now let's just say that no matter how good they are at classroom facilitation, if your facilitators have not taught in a synchronous environment before, they are in for an eye-opening experience.

Another of those perceived advantages is that you can teach hundreds of learners simultaneously using synchronous e-learning. Actually, that is true as well, or at least as true as the misconception that you can teach hundreds of students in a college lecture hall simultaneously. As the saying goes, you can teach 'em, but that doesn't mean they'll learn anything. The maximum effective learner number for synchronous classes is about the same as for a stand-up classroom, and maybe just a bit smaller. To get good interactive learning, fifteen or so learners is optimum in a synchronous environment.

Another disadvantage of this type of delivery is that it is a *synchronous* distance learning process. You may say "Duh," but consider what that really means. All of the learners, and the facilitator as well, must be on line at the same time. So if you have learners in Europe, Asia, and Australia, your class may start at four o'clock central time, but it's nine in France, tomorrow morning in Tokyo, and the middle of the night in Australia. Often synchronous e-learning is perceived, at least subconsciously, as e-learning, which to many means *asynchronous*, with its wonderful ability to be around the world at any time the learner chooses. Synchronous has many advantages, but this isn't one of them.

Designers try to overcome these time zone problems by saying, "Well, we'll record the class for those who are asleep when we give it." This has about the same amount of charm (and success) as recording a live stand-up classroom and making it available on a DVD. If you've been following along so far, you know that any relation between this and an effective self-instructional learning package is purely coincidental.

Let's look at a list of some of synchronous e-learning's other disadvantages and misconceptions:

Disadvantages

General

- Requires proper software or technology
- May be ineffective due to lack of trained facilitators
- Requires learners to be prepared for e-learning delivery
- Not effective when content requires face-to-face delivery
- Not efficient when the class needs to be run many times

For the Facilitator

- No eye contact
- No idea of what the learners are doing
- Learners can't use facilitator's visual cues
  - Body lean
  - Movement
  - Smiles
- Facilitator can't use learners' visual cues to speed up, slow down, go over again

- Voice is everything
- Positive reinforcement is difficult
  - Not used to sending or receiving reinforcement via phone line
  - Emotions sound different on the phone

For the Learner
- No eye contact
- Multitasking allure
- No justification for participating
- No nonverbal instructor feedback
- Less verbal or nonverbal feedback from colleagues

Misconceptions Concerning Synchronous E-Learning

- Learners aren't comfortable with it

Sometimes they are more comfortable than in a classroom.

- There is less demand for instructor's time

Depending on the design, it may take more instructor preparation and follow-up time, though they do not need to travel.

- Interactions are limited

Only by the instructional designer or facilitator's knowledge and creativity.

- There is less social interaction

Only if the instructional designer or facilitator allows this to happen through poor planning.

- Hundreds of learners can learn at once

They can be taught, but that has nothing to do with learning.

So, now that we've gotten all those misconceptions out of the way, we can consider what synchronous e-learning really is: simply another delivery system. As we've already said about all delivery systems, it works where it works and doesn't where it doesn't. It is your job as an instructional designer to decide if it will work in your situation, and then to properly design it.

DESIGN CONSIDERATIONS FOR SYNCHRONOUS E-LEARNING

(*Lessons from the Cyberspace Classroom* by Rena Palloff & Keith Pratt, 2001)
The key to designing effective synchronous e-learning is to remember that
almost anything you can do in a face-to-face class you can do in a synchronous
class; it's just done a little differently. As with asynchronous e-learning, the
design process for synchronous is pretty much the same as a face-to-face class
until you reach the point of material development. Here it continues to reflect
classroom design, but with a few critical differences.

MINI-INTERACTIONS

The first of these differences is the need to develop more of what I term mini-
interactions. These are simply small one-minute activities that the learners can
participate in to keep their interest high. They include singular questions that
require a response and tabulation, polls in which the learners express their feelings about issues or even content, statements to which the learners respond
with a yes or no and a why, and chances to annotate documents, graphics, even
websites on line, using the synchronous software's drawing tools.

A great example of the use of mini-interactions is for icebreakers. A good
synchronous designer might create a quick icebreaker that simply shows a map
and asks everyone to note where they live on it. This is particularly good for a
national or international groups of learners. Another is for the instructor to ask
each participant to input on the screen what they had for dinner last night. This
not only personalizes what is a somewhat impersonal delivery, but also gives
the learners practice at using the annotation tools if you plan on doing more
extensive activities with them later.

A somewhat longer icebreaker involves the learners answering four or five
agree-or-disagree questions about the content, and having the facilitator (actually the software) tabulate the responses as a percentage of the class. This can
lead to a lot of discussion. You can use this type of mini-interaction to help
introduce class concepts as well as create interest. It works particularly well if
some of the content might engender more than one answer or opinion.

Polls are also great mini-interactions. They are good for icebreakers and
summaries, as well as a process for taking the class's temperature on things, both
before and after discussion. You can use polls as pre- and post-debate or argument interactions to engender further discussion or choose a debate winner.

If you're really creative, you might create graphics that present question-
type mini-interactions. One of my favorite examples is to call up a previously
created document or graphic and have learners annotate by checks or circles
what is new or unknown to them. This works well with objective lists, too. You
might also create lists, then ask learners to vote for their top five on the list via
number annotation, or check ones that they are unsure of.

The number of these mini-interactions you should create is somewhat open to debate. Some say they should happen at least every twelve minutes or so, as that is the average attention span of adult learners. Others say that because synchronous classes feel so impersonal, and there are so many possibilities for multitasking, you could lose your audience quickly. Therefore, a mini-interaction every ninety seconds or so is important.

My experience, as usual, falls somewhere in the middle of these extremes. I think that you need to change styles more often than the twelve minutes that we use as a rule of thumb for stand-up classrooms, but every ninety seconds is a bit extreme, particularly when some of the mini-interactions can take that long to do.

I try to design in a mini-interaction every five minutes or so, assuming that the learners are not engaged in some other activity. This takes the spotlight away from the facilitator and puts it on the learners, and it can also help to bring back those who might have strayed into e-mails, office conversations, or simple daydreaming.

I'm also in favor of asking directed questions as mini-interactions, and I design them in as well, letting the facilitator know to watch out for learners who are slow or not complying with the other interactions, and then pointing a question right at them.

For even shorter mini-interactions, design in stop points where the facilitator simply asks the learners for an emoticon, or to respond with the fast and slow buttons that are part of most software packages.

REPURPOSING AND REDESIGNING OF SYNCHRONOUS E-LEARNING PROGRAMS

Before we go any further, it's probably a good idea to define a few terms that we've already used, and that we'll be using again in this discussion. In the synchronous e-learning environment we often speak of designing a program, redesigning a program, or repurposing one.

Design, of course, means starting from scratch and going through the entire ISD process as we've discussed it in previous chapters of this book, though in this case our delivery is synchronous e-learning, so our materials will be developed for this approach. We'll focus most of our attention on this process, because if you can design effective synchronous e-learning you will be able to redesign or repurpose it as well.

A redesign of materials for a synchronous delivery usually means that you have a learning program already, but it isn't very good, or at least it's not good enough for synchronous learning. In a redesign you often have to rewrite objectives and learner evaluations, and possibly even do more analysis. You may need to redetermine the criticality of the current content, and you must almost always add more activities.

Repurposing means taking a current course that's already well designed and simply making it ready to be delivered in a synchronous environment. You may need to polish an objective or a test question here or there, maybe even design in a new activity or two, but the major task in repurposing is to add plenty of those mini-interactions that we discussed earlier.

For both redesign and repurposing you should remember the following:

- Objectives are more critical in a synchronous delivery, so review them and tighten them up as needed.

- Planning is more vital, particularly precourse communications.

- Questioning techniques will be different.

- Activities may need to be translated.

- The facilitator guide needs to be more technology specific.

- Watch for areas of the course that contain "talking heads" or "talking PowerPoints."

- Know the hardware and software needs of both the learners and the facilitator and make sure they are met.

- Know the level of computer proficiency of each as well.

- Know what the "need to know" content is.

- Know the time expectations, both for design and in-class time.

- Know the number of learners and where they are located (twelve to fifteen is optimal, twenty is the maximum).

Everyone talks about repurposing for e-learning (both synchronous and asynchronous), but most designers end up redesigning. This increases the project time significantly—as you can imagine, now that you know about writing objectives, learner evaluations, activities, and so on. Cast a wary eye on anyone who comes to you and says, "Oh, this will only need to be repurposed to be a good e-learning program." It's that term "good" that's usually the sticking point.

One final thought: not all classroom programs can be repurposed into the synchronous environment, so don't stress yourself out trying if it just won't work.

OTHER SYNCHRONOUS ACTIVITIES

(*Live and Online!* by Jennifer Hofmann, 2004)

Beyond the mini-interactions, there are a number of other activities that are unique to synchronous delivery, or that require you to do some special design work if the facilitator is to use them properly. One of the most obvious ones is the chat function, which allows learners to talk to learners or to the facilitator without disturbing the rest of the class. There are some great activities you can create using private chat, particularly for paired collaborative learning.

Here are some of the various types of chats you might consider designing into your program:

- Learner to instructor
- Learner to learner
- All learners to all learners
- Learner to panel
- Learner group to panel
- Panel to learner
- Panel to learner group

You can expand on the "star your top five" or "checkmark the ones you don't know" mini-interactions we mentioned earlier by using a private chat room function to allow learners who feel they have mastered various listed concepts to talk with those who have said they are not confident with the same concepts. If a large percentage of your learners checkmark a concept, then bring a panel member or SME into the chat mix to work with them while others work in different content areas in pairs or small groups. When your time is limited, rather than discussing concepts, simply ask the learners to share possible resources that they are aware of and that can help their colleagues obtain further information on "don't know" concepts that they've checked.

 Chat rooms and threaded discussion facilities are also useful for post-class activities; they usually part of any good synchronous software package. As always, you need to carefully design the topics or questions that will be discussed, and keep in mind the amount of facilitator time that will be spent monitoring these processes. In other words, use them, but use them sparingly so you don't abuse your facilitator.

When doing asynchronous discussions, create two for each topic: one that is more the threaded or focused type, and the other a coffee-shop variety in which any thoughts concerning the topic can be posted. This works for chat rooms too, but is more difficult to do as it requires double the amount of facilitator time

Synchronous e-learning also allows you to design in activities in which the facilitator and learners can share documents, applications, websites, even entire desktops. Using annotation tools, the learners can work on these processes as a group, noting places in applications where they are having difficulties or changing documents on the fly. Again, these activities require a very strong design with plenty of directions for the facilitator on how to get the most out of them.

In shared-type applications, usually only one learner can annotate at a time. If you want multiple learners to annotate, create your document for the whiteboard, then have the learners do activities such as circling or checking what is new to them or what they want to learn more about. Using the whiteboard function, you can involve them all at the same time.

Another technique is to do a brainstorming session using a shared document, but with a general chat window open to allow the learners to really "storm" their ideas as they read or think.

Synchronous activities can include many of your tried-and-true classroom interactions, such as role plays, simulations, games, and small group or break-out processes. The basics for these types of activities are about the same as what we've already discussed for stand-up classrooms. However, because you have technology mediating the facilitator-learner interface, the instructional designer must have a good grasp of how this interface changes the implementation of the activity and must provide complete directions on these changes to the facilitator. Here are some of our usual classroom activities that translate well into a synchronous e-learning environment, and a few that are synchronous specific:

- Pre-tests
- Knowledge sharing
- Collaborative problem solving
- Team teaching
- Roundtable discussions (via open chat)
- Learner manipulation of facilitator software
- Collaborative writing and editing
- Individual coaching
- Private or group discussions during breaks
- Debates
- Critiquing of information
- Brainstorming
- Individual problem solving with written solutions
- Observation of demonstration
- Games
- Annotative activities: make a list, create a time line, draw a map, draw flow charts, create spreadsheets

- Questioning
- Discussions
- Creating class glossaries
- Application sharing
- Guest experts or panels
- Learners' resource from Web
- Learners taking over and teaching
- Team competitions
- Using breakout rooms and offline messaging
- Short quizzes to check comprehension and for retention

These quizzes and any Level 2 evaluation questions can be enhanced through the use of graphics and even videos in a synchronous environment.

- Single and multi-user whiteboard activities
- Timed games that increase the excitement and competition, such as Beat the Clock or Ten Thousand Dollar Pyramid

MORE DETAILED FACILITATOR GUIDES

Which brings up the next difference between a synchronous classroom design and a face-to-face one: the depth of the facilitator guide. We've already talked about facilitator guides or lesson plans—or whatever you've chosen to call them—so you know their basic purpose, but in synchronous designs they become more critical and more detailed, even if you're designing the package for yourself to facilitate.

One of the reasons for this is the need for those mini-interactions. Your facilitator guide should have each of them spelled out in detail, with the purpose, directions, a general time frame for how long they should take, and approximately when each should start during the lesson.

Another specialized aspect of a synchronous facilitator guide is to note places for icon-based feedback stops. One of the major disadvantages of synchronous classes, particularly for experienced instructors, is that there is simply no nonverbal feedback from the learners—and very little verbal feedback. Therefore you need to note in your guide where the facilitator should stop and ask for feedback, even if that feedback's as simple as learners sending a smiley icon or clicking the "too fast" or "too slow" button.

One of the biggest differences, however, is the amount of technical direction you'll need to add to your facilitator guide. You simply can't go overboard on this aspect, particularly if you suspect that the facilitators will not be well trained in the use of the software.

Information on how to use the various functions of the software for polls, questions, annotation, breakouts, and the like are all important if the facilitator is going to do the job properly. Hearing this, you might say, "Then I'll need to be an expert on the software as well," and you'd be right. Actually, you don't need to be an expert if you have one available who can tell you how these things are done. However, my question for you is this: how will you know what is even possible in the synchronous instruction world if you don't know the software? This aspect is so important that if you'll look at the following leader guide template, you'll notice that an entire column is devoted only to technical instructions.

		FACILITATOR GUIDE TEMPLATE	
Time	*Content and Notes*	*Technology*	*Learner Activity*
	Add content outline and any notes to the facilitator here	Place names and numbers of slides of handouts; instructions for other forms of media, such as still camera, sound or video; special technology comments; and instructor notes on demonstrations or other technology aspects here	Describe learners' roles and each activity they will be involved in here

Other Facilitator Guide Enhancements

Another aspect of the facilitator guide that you need to enhance is the information you give the facilitator on setting up and starting the class. In a face-to-face classroom delivery, the facilitator usually has a pretty good idea of what to do, but if they try to translate this to a synchronous class they are going to miss a few rather important things, such as how to access the software, where to go if there are technical problems, and most important, how to get the learners started.

 Here are a few items you might want to include in your facilitator package to help the facilitator with class setup:

- Hardware and software requirements
- Network access information
- Setting up of delivery area and computer(s)
  - Check for background noise
  - Ensure freedom for distractions
  - Privacy: use "Do Not Disturb" signs
  - Space for all hardware and note taking
  - Power outlets and extension cords if needed
  - Internet connection
  - Comfort: seating, heat, and so on
  - Lighting
- Reminder to create class rosters
- Perform final program review

And here are some reminders for your guide of items the facilitator might want to send the learners before class:

- Study guides
- Objectives
- Class start time:
  - Get on line fifteen minutes early if possible
  - Be sure to label A.M. and P.M., particularly in global programs
- Level 1 evaluation
- Access procedures

- Contact information: instructor and other participants
- Bios and pictures via bulletin board posting
- Technical problems job aid if available

And one more list, of items you might remind the facilitator to do when he or she actually starts the class:

- Be on line fifteen to thirty minutes early to hang out with learners (virtually) until start time
- Start promptly
- Welcome participants; ask for personal introductions
- Ask for confirmation that everyone is on line and can hear
- Provide assistance phone number for emergencies
- State objectives and ask for feedback on them
- Tour synchronous classroom highlights, particularly feedback mechanisms
- Explain how class will be conducted, particularly aspects such as random, nonvolunteer questions, interactions with peers, amount of informality, and special types of activities
- Have a good introductory activity ready

LEARNER GUIDE

Along with the facilitator guide, you also need to think about the learner guide when designing for synchronous e-learning. You might say, "What learner guide? This isn't a classroom." But it is, and all the good reasons for having a learner guide in the face-to-face classroom are equally important in a synchronous classroom. Just to review, some of those reasons include:

- Providing the learner with extra information on processes and procedures
- Increasing the learner comfort level by providing something they are used to and comfortable with
- Setting up activities
- Providing enriched information

What you put into your learner guide is up to you and your program's needs, but some common items you might consider are the preclass communications that we discussed earlier, directions for accessing the course and using the software effectively, directions for activities, objectives, reading material, bibliography, a glossary, and troubleshooting checklists.

One of the ways you *don't* want to use your learner guide is to simply send your learners a copy of the slides you plan on showing during the class. That doesn't mean you shouldn't send copies of your slides to the learners if you feel they might enhance their learning, or as a backup in case the technology fails, but your learner guide needs to be much more than just that. Of course, when we say send it we don't mean snail mail. Since you're in an e-environment, use its capabilities to send downloadable learner guides and even slides.

Other People Involved in the Process

Yet another design consideration for synchronous e-learning is that there may be other individuals involved in the learning process, such as

- Panelists
- SMEs, not only for content development but also as online or offline experts
- Technical experts who could be available to the learners and to the facilitator before and during the class
- A cofacilitator who takes on some of the actual teaching aspects
- An assistant, who doesn't share the teaching but handles any necessary support roles, such as technical help, offline questions, and media staging
- A producer, usually used in a more complex program design to call up media, give cues, and stage panels, experts, or demonstrations

For any and all of these positions that need to be included in the design, the designer must create a document that clarifies roles and explains to the facilitator how to use and not use these added resources. This document should contain directions for both the facilitator and the people filling the roles. The designer should also note to the facilitator the importance of planning and practicing with cofacilitators and support personnel.

GENERAL TECHNOLOGY CONSIDERATIONS

Although most of the technology considerations for synchronous e-learning are directly related to the software being used, there are a few general aspects that are common to any synchronous environment. First and most important, the facilitator must be comfortable with the technology and tools being employed. The only method for achieving this is practicing with them, both generally and for each specific program. Your design should include information on training the trainers. We'll discuss this aspect in full a bit later.

Also, the facilitator needs to be properly equipped. This means the best, fastest, and most up-to-date PC you can buy, a high-quality microphone and speakers, a high-quality headset (preferably wireless), and a second PC that emulates the learner's equipment, so the facilitator can see what the learner is seeing.

Next, the learners need to be provided with as much technical support as possible. The facilitator or a technical expert should be on line at least half an hour before the class starts, to help learners with technical problems. The learners themselves, particularly those new to synchronous learning, should be required to log in at least fifteen minutes before the scheduled start time in case they have technical problems. Ideally there should be a technical expert available on line during the program to deal with issues that come up, but this is seldom the case. As an instructional designer you have very limited to no control over technical support, but you need to make its importance clear in your documentation.

It's critical as well to remind the facilitator that the rest of the class shouldn't be held up waiting for one or two technical issues to be resolved. Help desk phone numbers and e-mail addresses should be given to the learners in their learner package, and their problems should be routed there.

The facilitator needs to have a contingency plan for technology breakdowns, either individual or groupwide. Your facilitator guide should note this fact and provide some ideas. One approach is to send out any graphics that will be used in the program as part of the learner guide. In that way, a learner can at least listen over a phone line and look at the graphics during the presentation. If a general technology crash includes the phones too, well, as one experienced online facilitator noted, "There's always tomorrow."

Another use for the learner guide in handling technical problems is to include in it a job aid on common technical problems and how to deal with them. Often this entails simply logging off and then on again, but such directions, when written as a job aid, can keep distracting technical help calls to the facilitator to a minimum. The use of the telephone as a contingency plan can also be spelled out in the learner materials so the learners know what to do in case this becomes their only option.

Your documentation should make the facilitator aware of the need for a backup plan for times when files (either graphic or document) are lost. The best approach here is to have all the files that will be used in a presentation backed up on a mass storage device such as a flash card or USB drive. Then it's only a matter of a few keystrokes to call up the missing files or send them out to the learners. The instructional designer can make sure this is normal procedure and note to the facilitator where and how to access the files.

Finally, the facilitator needs to be reminded that there may be some learners who can't do even the simplest of technological tasks. These learners need to be identified through audience analysis (a simple questionnaire sent out before the class will do it if you don't have the time for a full-scale analysis) and introduced to the technology well before the day of the class. You might also remind the facilitator to try and team novice learners with experienced ones, both before and during class, to give the novice someone other than the facilitator to ask questions of.

MEDIA

Media is a major issue in synchronous design. In many cases it is the media that carries the message to the learners, unlike in a face-to-face class in which the media basically augments and emphasizes. Therefore the instructional designer needs to consider the types of media in the design with even more than the usual care and provide plenty of direction for the facilitator on how to use it.

Most of the media considerations for synchronous e-learning are related to the capabilities of the software and the network being used, so once again the instructional designer needs to know the technical capabilities of the system the program will be delivered on. This also means that the media you used when designing a face-to-face classroom may not translate as well as you hoped (or as some people suggest) to the synchronous environment. Often it needs to be reworked, if not completely redesigned.

Here is a list of the most common types of media found in synchronous e-learning, in descending order of use:

- PowerPoint
- Whiteboards
- Graphics
- Web pages
- Hard copy or photographs
- Sound
- Video

One of the advantages of using media in a synchronous environment is that the media can become interactive through the use of annotation tools. The whiteboard is an obvious candidate for this, but so are your PowerPoint presentations, other graphics, and even web pages. You might design an activity in which learners take a graphic of gauges on a control panel and draw in their probable readings based on a scenario, or move an icon across a world globe as you have them follow a weather satellite in orbit. The possibilities are unlimited.

Your learners can redraw your graphics, add or subtract from your Power-Point presentations, even redesign web pages that you capture, and of course do almost anything that they can normally do with a whiteboard. Again, the key is to make sure you know what the software will support, design it so that it will be easy for the facilitator and the learners to use, and provide the facilitator with good information on how to do it and, just as important, how to debrief it.

You can use different media formats for different purposes, but some are better for some things than others. The following chart gives you a quick look at what works best in a few general categories.

Media Type	Hand-outs	White-board	Hard Copy and Pictures	Power-Point	Sound	Video
Uses						
Explain and clarify	1	1	2	1	3	1
Basis for discussion	2	2	2	2	2	1
Organize discussion	1	1	1	2	3	3
Summarize	1	1	3	1	2	2

Here are some thoughts on both the design and use of each of these common synchronous media formats.

PowerPoint

- Keep each slide to one key thought; use builds to add new concepts.
- Use charts and graphs rather than tables, as they are easier to read at a distance.
- Use the same format for all slides; don't switch from vertical to horizontal.
- Never add sound or visual effects without good reason.
- Keep backgrounds consistent and subtle.
- Use only quality clip art, and use it sparingly.

- Use no more than four colors on one chart.
- Use one thought per line, five to six words per line, five to six lines per slide.
- Don't overuse boldface, italic, or all caps.
- Use motion elements such as animation and transitions to attract attention, but don't overuse them.
- Give learners enough quiet time to comprehend each visual.
- Be sure you have backup media just in case, both electronic and hard copy.
- PRACTICE.

 If your system is slow or your graphics very memory intensive, you can save time by downloading your PowerPoint slides to the learners ahead of time. This can also act as a backup if your system goes down.

Whiteboards

- Use a whiteboard in activities the same way as you might use a flip chart in a stand-up class.
- Capture new or interesting points brought up by both participants and facilitator.
- Capture discussion points or reports from small groups.
- Prelabel whiteboards to help guide discussions.
- Archive whiteboards and send copies to participants.
- Use prepared whiteboards as an organizer, highlighting aspects as they are presented.
- Have participants be responsible for whiteboards.
- Use whiteboards for games such as tic-tac-toe or hangman.
- Use whiteboards for polling by having participants check which of a group of thoughts they are most in favor of.
- Use whiteboards for brainstorming by opening them up to all participants.
- Know the tools and limitations of your whiteboard software and practice with it.
- Save whiteboards if possible.
- Paste graphics or screen shots into whiteboards if possible.
- Provide instructions to learners and facilitators on how to use the whiteboard properly.

Using Hard Copy or Pictures

- Remind the facilitator to practice using the still camera.
- Follow the same rules as for any other graphic piece.
- Be sure pictures have enough resolution to be seen properly by learners.
- Leave a note on both the graphic and the camera stage that says "This Side Up."
- Remember, digital pictures usually look better than projected ones.
- Use still cameras only when absolutely necessary, as they add another level of complexity to the facilitation.
- DON'T design in the projection of pages of books.

Graphics

- Light colors on dark backgrounds attract the eye.
- Use color cues to imply relationships.
- Limit the number of colors on a single screen image.
- Establish a color scheme at the beginning and stick with it.
- Bright colors make small objects and thin lines stand out.
- Pick a font that fits the message.
- Don't use more than three fonts in a presentation.
- Don't overuse bold face, italic or all caps.
- In general, don't use a font size smaller than 18 points.
- Sans serif fonts such as Helvetica are easier to read when projected.
- Use the chart style that is appropriate for the data.

Sound

Audio is perhaps the most underrated and least understood aspect of synchronous media, due in part to the fact that voice audio is almost always in use, and little attention is paid to any other aspect. It is extremely easy to import, record, and edit sound elements in the digital age. Today there is no excuse not to take advantage of the persuasion power of music, sound effects, and pre-recorded narration. Sound has the power to heighten attention levels, improve retention rate, enhance emotional responses, add emphasis to the message, and provide, when necessary, some comic relief.

Follow these guidelines for effective sound presentation and design:

- Keep sound and music clips brief.
- Keep volume levels consistent.
- Suit the mood of the music to the mood of the message.

- Invest in quality music clips.
- Do not use copyrighted music without the proper license.

Video

The human eye loves movement. We can scarcely stop ourselves from following action within our view. Careful use of motion can add depth, clarity, and dynamism to a message.

Motion elements, including video, animation, and transitions, can

- Attract attention
- Engage the audience on a deeper level
- Present testimonials
- Depict remote locations and activities
- Overcome barriers of language and culture
- Lend credibility to the presenter
- Tell a story without words
- Create subconscious associations

The element of motion puts extra demands on the presentation design and the presentation system.

- Be certain your software can play back the digital video.
- Start with a high-quality video source, if possible.
- Frame the subject tightly to compensate for small on-screen images.
- Experiment with different frame sizes and frame rates (the number of frames per second) to get the best image playback.
- Set objects in motion that you wish to dominate the screen.
- Combine scene cutting and on-screen action to create the desired pacing and rhythm.

Web Pages

- Use web sources instead of recreating content.
- Have participants find web sources to share.
- Use web searches as an activity, such as a web scavenger hunt.
- Go to competitor websites for comparisons.
- Know the functionality of the web browser in your software system.
- Use hyperlinks to allow independent searching.
- Use bookmarks if possible to make browsing faster.

DESIGNING CONTINUING INTERACTIONS

("Synchronous Collaboration" by Harvey Singh, in *The AMA Handbook of E-Learning*, 2003)

A design advantage of synchronous e-learning is the ability to add post-class interactions, often called *continuing interactions,* to the program. Almost all synchronous software has the capability to support both asynchronous message boards and synchronous chat rooms. These facilities allow you to design in learning that occurs well after the actual class ends, give and received feedback from the learners, enhance learning transfer, and perform Level 3 evaluation.

Message Boards

Message boards, sometime referred to as *electronic bulletin boards* or *e-boards,* provide for asynchronous post-class activities. These might include almost any of the post-class assignments you use in a face-to-face class. The postings can be one-way—that is, strictly from the instructor—and therefore be basically informational in nature; or they can be two-way, in which case you ask the learners to respond with their own postings and possibly even comment on each other's postings. You can use message board postings for FAQs, parking lot issues that the facilitator didn't get to during the synchronous class, enrichment commentary from SMEs, and for preclass assignments as well.

In some designs the post-class activity is to write a short paper concerning oneaspect or another of the course and then post it for commentary by the other learners. If your synchronous class runs for more than one session, you might use this function for between-class assignments and communications.

The key to effective use of message boards is to design your interactions with solid goals, good objectives, and obvious intent, and then make sure the learners know what they are. If you are following good instructional design methodology, this should not be a problem.

You also need to be aware of the amount of time your bulletin board activities will require of your learners and your instructor. Keep them short and easy for both their sakes.

Use your message board facility to keep learners up to date on content changes as they occur. Send an e-mail to tell them that there is a new posting. If you need to do recertification training, you can use this method to show that the learners are up to date on the issues, possibly even forgoing a class.

Chat Rooms

Chat rooms are simply live meetings held by computer. Everything just said for message boards goes for chat rooms too, particularly the part about considering the amount of time they require for both learners and instructors. Chat rooms also have the added problem of being synchronous, so everyone will need to attend at the same time. On the other hand, they can produce wonderful interactions if designed and handled properly.

Chat rooms are excellent for post-class brainstorming on unresolved or even new issues. You might want to design them in for preclass brainstorming as well, where applicable and possible. They provide a good way to reduce the class time spent on introductory activities by having the learners introduce themselves and even form learning teams before class begins.

To make your chat rooms more effective, use prewritten questions or exercises to define the limits of the chat and help keep the learners on track. Give these to the learners ahead of time. You also need to remind the facilitator that the chat room should be monitored closely, otherwise it often becomes an electronic gripe session or, worse, leads to negative interactions called *flaming* by those in the e-know.

For both chat rooms and bulletin boards, you'll need to create solid instructions for the facilitator as part of the lesson plan and even a one-pager for the learners in their material that discusses how they should best take advantages of these learning opportunities.

AUDIENCE ANALYSIS

("Discussion Groups and Chats" by Saundra Wall Williams, in *The AMA Handbook of E-Learning*, 2003)

Whether designing or redesigning for synchronous e-learning, you should take another look at your audience analysis data. The successful synchronous learner isn't a lot different from the successful classroom learner, but there are a few learner characteristics that are unique to the synchronous environment and some others that they need in greater measure. Following is a list of the more important of these.

Synchronous learners need

- More self-direction, even though the process is instructor led
- Better listening skills
- The ability to read between the lines
- To be proactive with their learning experience
- To find ways to deal with the isolation
- To be comfortable learning with partners or teams
- To overcome the fear of new technology
- Adequate technology support
- A basic level of technology skills
- A predetermined literacy level
- Physical work space in which to do the learning
- Time to do the assignments
- A common language
- To overcome time zone barriers
- More structure:
  - Comprehensive schedules
  - Deadlines
  - E-mail progress checks
- The ability to ask questions off line
- More reinforcement, particularly if they are high achievers, as they will not get it from the group
- Individualized contact with the facilitator from time to time in long classes

You may have noticed that not all of these items are strictly internal to the learner. Some require the presence of external tools or functions as well. However, they are all necessary for the learner to succeed at synchronous e-learning.

The chances are pretty good that your current audience analysis won't provide you with enough information on these issues. You will need to do a supplementary one before completing your design, and particularly before writing your instructions for the facilitators, as they will need to know in detail what to expect from their learners.

The best way to do this is to send a survey to the learners, asking them questions based on these characteristics. You might want to break the survey up into two parts, one for technical issues such as their familiarity with both the hardware and software, and the other for nontechnical issues such as their time zone, language skills, and the like.

As with all surveys, keep your questions short and to the point, with as little jargon, particularly technical jargon, as possible. Don't forget to include the results of the survey and your entire analysis in the facilitator package.

Just as in a regular classroom, and possibly even more so in the synchronous environment, you need to know early on in the design who your learners are and what they can and can't do—particularly in relation to the technology.

IMPLEMENTATION

(*Sustaining Distance Training* by Zane Berge, 2001)

Implementation of a synchronous delivery, like most training implementations, is not the purview of the designer, but rather belongs to the facilitator. However, you still have some responsibilities, the most critical of which are facilitator training and helping ensure that the program gets off to a good start.

Facilitator Training

There's an enormous amount of misinformation concerning a competent classroom instructor's ability to easily step into a synchronous e-learning environment, as we have already noted. Basically, if your facilitators attempt to teach a synchronous class without adequate training, they will fail; your design, no matter how well done, will fail; and worst of all, your learners will fail to learn.

The synchronous environment is different from the face-to-face environment: nonverbal cues are almost nonexistent, feedback is more difficult, and even the lesson plan is more complicated due to the presence of both computer hardware and software. Your facilitators will need to understand these differences and work with them every time they go on line.

To help them accomplish this, you should create a solid facilitator training program that illuminates the differences they will experience, helps them see what facilitation skills are more critical in a synchronous environment, teaches them the software, and then gives them a systematic way to practice until they become comfortable with the process. Here is a four-part approach that I've found works well in most situations.

1. Basic Facilitation Skill

This discussion concerns what is it like to be a synchronous facilitator: what is the same as in a face-to-face classroom and what is different. You may want to discuss the advantages and disadvantages lists that we looked at earlier, particularly the ones specific to the facilitator and the learner.

Once you have convinced your facilitators that this isn't going to be quite as simple a task as they might have heard, you don't want to spend a lot more time on this aspect. Summarizing with a couple of job aids such as the ones that follow can give competent facilitators what they need and allow your training to move on to other issues.

JOB AID: GENERAL SYNCHRONOUS FACILITATION SKILLS

- Be a good motivator.
- Use all possible communications methods well.
- Lead learner-centered discussions.
- Listen well.
- Use your voice with a full range of inflections to express emotion.
- Direct less, suggest more.
- Use your facilitator guide.
- Practice prompt starts and ends.
- Create a safe environment.
- Use humor wisely.
- Learn to multitask well, as you'll be managing multiple activities at the same time.
- Don't lecture.
- Maintain a nonauthoritarian style.
- Read between the lines.
- Stand up and roam as you facilitate, just as you do in any class.
- Know your software well and plan out how to use it effectively.
- Practice 20 to 30 percent more than usual.
- Record your sessions for later use and critiquing.
- Use more directed questions.
- Plan to take more time for everything in the lesson.
- Summarize or have learners summarize often.
- Use "fun" activities to build community.
- Reserve comments until after all learners have a chance to reply.
- Model proper online behavior.
- Be positive.
- Encourage lurkers to interact by asking them random nonvolunteer questions.
- Don't read off the screen; say it in your own words.
- Change your inflections; allow your voice to express.

- Call on people using their names.
- Use multiple voices where possible.
- Minimize any references to the technology (such as "Please wait while I launch this application").

JOB AID: FACILITATING SYNCHRONOUS INTERACTIONS

- Ask provocative questions.
- Work to pull a variety of ideas, answers, and stories from the learners.
- Use open-ended questions to elicit more thoughtful responses.
- Listen to or read the learner comments carefully (don't think ahead).
- Be concise and clear in what you write on the screen or say.
- Validate all replies with positive feedback.
- Debrief.
- Allow the group to exhaust all possibilities before going on.
- Mini-interactions, like a simple hello, are important.
- Take breaks.
- Look for unifying threads during discussions (use them for summaries).
- Encourage learners to assess each other's work.
- Allow learners to help form behavior standards and program goals.
- Encourage; never judge or allow others to judge.
- Be provocative but not argumentative.
- Take time to allow the participants to form answers (dead time is OK).
- Bring in lurkers with nonvolunteer Yes or No questions or by assigning a presentation or question to them in advance.
- Clear response screens periodically.
- Observe breakout rooms and review chat logs.
- Erase whiteboards when needed.
- Talk off line to overly aggressive participants.
- Create special interest groups to work on extraneous issues off line.

2. How to Use the Technology

The second aspect of the facilitator training deals with the specific ins and outs of the software program that will be used, including how to use text chat, web boards, breakout sessions, hardware, and graphic projection, and how to create accounts, enroll learners, download, start the program, and handle technical problems.

For this last item, here is a small job aid that works well to minimize class disruptions and get learners back up as quickly as possible.

When you encounter a technical problem with the system, follow these steps:

1. Have the learner call back in first.
2. Ask the learner to try to reconnect.
3. Send the learner to your technical expert or the help desk.
4. Try reloading the presentation (if it is a group problem).
5. Try restarting the presentation (if it is a group problem).
6. E-mail the media if that is the problem, or reschedule the class if the problem is more serious.

3. Observation

In this aspect of the training the facilitators attend a couple of synchronous programs as learners (if they haven't done so already) to get a feel for what it will be like for their learners. Then they observe a seasoned facilitator or two facilitating a program from the facilitator station to see how they do it right. Finally, the facilitators team-teach with a seasoned facilitator to try their wings in a safe environment.

4. Practice

Now, as with any other facilitation, the facilitators need to practice. Have them practice first off line, just to get comfortable with the technology and the feel. Then have them practice on line with some friends or colleagues acting as participants. The participants should make it easy for them at first, then give them some problems, so they can determine how to deal with them. Finally, have them do their program live, and record it for self-critiquing and to look for areas that need improvement.

Learner Training

(*Getting the Most from Online Learning* edited by George Piskurich, 2004) You will need to do a bit of training for your learners as well if they are to become effective synchronous e-learners. This is not really the designer's responsibility, but a good designer will prepare material for this purpose anyway and will counsel managers on how to use it.

In this training, remind the learners that they need to set up an environment conducive to synchronous learning. This includes finding or creating a quiet, private space. They can accomplish this through the use of posting signs, giving verbal reminders, forwarding calls, turning off cell phones or pagers, and notifying people that they will be in training during certain hours.

Provide them with a list of things with which they need to concern themselves, such as the one that follows.

PREPARING TO BE A SYNCHRONOUS E-LEARNER

Prepare yourself
- Think about how you feel about the virtual classroom.
- Consider your responsibility to participate and your need to feel connected.
- Be ready to answer questions and participate in discussions.
- Create a list of questions to ask the facilitator.
- Practice how to speak into the microphone.
- Practice sending questions to the instructor.
- Identify and complete preassignments.
- Review the content outline and session objectives.
- Create your personal objectives.

Prepare the technology
- Check for proper hardware
  - Sound card
  - Microphone
  - Headset
- Install all software ahead of time
- Test everything
  - Audio and microphone tuning
  - Software functionality
  - Connection

Prepare your environment
- Locate a space
  - Where there is room for your computer, documentation, and notes
  - Where you can talk online
  - That has power for the computer and an internet connection
  - That has good lighting for working with a computer
- Reduce as much background noise as possible
- Eliminate all distractions (phones, colleagues, other work)

(Just before class time (a half hour early)
- Gather all course materials and paper to write on.
- Check for last-minute class communications.
- Review your list of questions.
- Close all other applications running on your computer.
- Place "Do Not Disturb" signs.
- Log on to the course to check connectivity.

You could also give them a quick overview of proper online behavior, such as this:

TIPS FOR INTERACTING SUCCESSFULLY ON LINE

1. Remember, you are dealing with a person	E-mail, chat rooms, and speaker phones can hide this important fact.
2. Behave in the virtual world as you would in the real world	In a class strictly for personal development, you may develop informal friendships, complete with gossip and note passing. If you are in the course for your job, or others are, expect to develop more professional, businesslike relationships.
3. Share	Give back to the class. Give your experiences, your learning, and your opinions (when relevant). You do have value to add.
4. Forgive	Assume others in your class mean the best and that slip-ups and misinterpretations of your brilliance are accidental.
5. Communicate	Write and speak clearly and concisely. Say what you mean and then stop. Those who are not primary speakers of the language in which the class is held will appreciate it.
6. Pause before clicking the Send button	Make sure you review your posting once, maybe twice before sending.
7. Don't be too casual	Stay away from slang, and check your spelling.

8. Keep your comments short and on topic

If it has to be long, note "long" in the subject line.

9. Be sure to add your name to a thread message

Always sign your name at the bottom of a message.

10. Reset the subject line when you change topics

This keeps everyone from becoming confused about what you're talking about.

Note: Adapted from Chapter Ten, "Building Successful Online Relationships," of *Getting the Most From E-Learning,* by Doug Liberati.

You might even provide them with an assessment like the following one to get them thinking about becoming synchronous e-learners.

A SELF-ASSESSMENT OF PERSONAL SYNCHRONOUS E-LEARNING CHARACTERISTICS

- Can you accept the responsibility for your own learning?
- Are you comfortable using a computer?
- Are you self-motivated when learning new skills?
- Are you self-disciplined?
- Do you have the desire to learn?
- Are you good at setting goals for yourself and then meeting them?
- Are you able to complete assignments or study for tests without undue procrastination?
- Do you work well in groups?
- Are you comfortable interacting in a chat room or posting to a threaded discussion?
- Do you use e-mail effectively?
- Do you tend to participate in class discussions?
- Are you comfortable working with others when you never see them?
- Can you learn from your fellow students' sharing of their experiences?
- Are you comfortable sharing your experiences and expertise with others to enhance their learning?

All of these tools, and any others your own creativity can aid you in developing, will help your learners and therefore your instructional design to succeed.

Getting Started

The instructional designer's other critical responsibility in the implementation of a synchronous e-learning program is to make sure it gets off to a good start. Of course you can't do this yourself unless you are also the facilitator, but what a designer can do is provide the facilitators with a good program initiation checklist. These checklists are somewhat dependent on the software you are using and your own organization's procedures, but here is an example of one you might use to help you design your own:

SYNCHRONOUS CLASS INITIATION CHECKLIST

Before the first day of class:

- Send preclass communications:
  - Learner guide and slides (download)
  - Objectives
  - Time and date of class; label time A.M. or P.M. if program is global
  - Evaluation procedures
  - Procedures for logging on: password, dial-in number
  - Contact information for both instructor and participant
  - Posting of bios and pictures
  - Technical problems job aid if available
- Complete software requirements:
  - Schedule session.
  - Create password.
  - Invite attendees.
  - Invite yourself as an attendee.
  - Set up conference call (if needed).
  - Plan for necessary reports.
- Locate proper facilitation environment.
  - No background noise
  - Distraction free
  - Private: use "Do Not Disturb" signs
  - Space for all hardware and note taking
  - Power connection
  - Comfort: seating, heat, and so on
  - Lighting

- Other
  - Create session folder for storing materials.
  - Prepare class roster.
  - Perform final review of program.
  - Coordinate with other resources if they are part of the program.

On class day:
- Set up delivery area.
  - Post "Do Not Disturb" sign.
  - Turn off phone ring and forward calls.
  - Notify colleagues and other key people that you'll be facilitating.
  - Get water.
  - Put clock in view.
  - Set up notes and guides for easy reading.
  - Check in with other resources.
- Set up computer(s).
  - Set up participant machine so you can see what participants are seeing.
  - Close all nonessential applications.
  - Clear browser cache and reboot machine.
  - Set monitor for proper resolution.
  - Check network connections.
  - Check audio and phone.

When class starts:
- Start the session fifteen to thirty minutes early to deal with problems and chat with learners.
- Check for screen resolution problems.
- Begin the program promptly.
- Welcome participants.
- Ask for personal introductions.
- State objectives and ask for feedback.
- Ask for confirmation that everyone is on line and can hear.
- Provide assistance phone number again for emergencies.
- Tour virtual classroom highlights, particularly feedback mechanisms.
- Explain how class will be conducted, particularly aspects such as random nonvolunteer questions, interactions with peers, amount of informality, and special types of activities.
- Be ready with your introductory activity (ice breaker)

(A similar class checklist appears in the "Other Facilitator Guide Enhancements" section of this chapter.)

ONLINE LEARNING: A SPECIAL TYPE OF E-LEARNING

(147 Practical Tips for Teaching Online Groups by Don Hanna, 2003)

There is a variation of e-learning used mostly in academic settings and often referred to as *online learning*. In organizational learning we tend to use this term interchangeably with synchronous e-learning, but there are some major differences between these two delivery methodologies, and those differences may help you to create a more time- and cost-effective design whereby the process's advantages can work for you.

Basically, online learning is both synchronous and asynchronous because its major delivery processes are chat rooms and threaded discussions via electronic bulletin boards. In the academic model the delivery usually begins with a face-to-face class, after which there are no more class meetings except through computer mediation. This first class is an effective but not critical aspect of the process, and it can be replaced by a synchronous e-learning class, a web meeting, a chat room, or even a simple conference call.

After the first meeting the class is facilitated through a series of assignments that are completed by the learners individually, in pairs, in groups, or in learning teams. Learning resource lists for each assignment are provided and learners are encouraged to post other resources they come across. The products of these assignments are posted to the bulletin board for commentary and discussion, or presented in a synchronous chat room that has been scheduled for that purpose.

As a competent instructional designer you may have already realized that this delivery system is most effective for programs that stretch over a number of weeks, such as a college class, but it can also be effective in lieu of a multiday class such as what we often do for leadership or management training. In fact, because you can stretch the learning out over a longer period of time using an online delivery, reinforcement is enhanced, and the complaints of learners that they can't afford to be out of the office for two, three, or more full days are negated.

With this major advantage in mind, here is a list of possible effective uses for an online delivery:

- Long-term development activities
- Blending with OJT for skills building, cross training, or remedial training
- Recertification
- Orientation

- Multiday classes of any kind
- Management development
- Most any soft skills
- Team building
- Learning new computer software

Advantages of Online Learning

The cost and time savings inherent in an online delivery are sometimes obvious and sometimes not so obvious. One of the most obvious is the savings in both travel time and costs. This is true of synchronous e-learning deliveries as well, but an online delivery has the further advantage of being an easier process for both facilitators and learners to use. The facilitators do not need extensive training in how to use the software, and most learners these days are quite comfortable with posting to bulletin boards or interacting in a chat room.

There is a tremendous advantage over traditional asynchronous e-learning as well. Even though much of the work done by the learners is asynchronous, in online delivery there is still a facilitator available for learners to interact with, making the self-directed aspects of the learning less daunting to learners who have lower levels of self-directedness. Other advantages of an online delivery include the following:

- Efficient for geographically dispersed audiences
- Suitable for unstable content
- Efficient when the content is being delivered once or just a few times
- Allows real-time access to SMEs with minimal loss of their productivity
- Effective when content requires classroom delivery
- Provides continuous learning
- Multiple reinforcements mean greater retention
- Design time is less than for asynchronous, but program can be mostly asynchronous
- Time to learner comfort level less than with asynchronous
- Facilitator learning curve less than with synchronous
- Learner learning curve minimal
- Cheaper software
- Provides interactive and collaborative learning

- Allows for as much or as little self-direction as you feel the learners can handle
- Allows for many learners learning at the same time, though in different groups
- Research indicates team building is enhanced by collaborative learning projects online

Disadvantages of Online Learning

Of course there are disadvantages to an online delivery as well, not the least of which is that it often takes more time to design than a synchronous program. This is due to the nature of the assignments. They need to be well thought out, leaving plenty of room for individual exploration, yet focusing on a result that can be posted or discussed in the chat room. Your objectives also need to be sharper than ever. They guide the learners to the focus of the assignments and, as always, to the required learnings.

On the other hand, the design time is much less than for asynchronous e-learning. The nature of the delivery and the fact that a facilitator is available make a perfect design less critical. Yet the majority of the learning that takes place is asynchronous, with all the advantages that are implied.

One disadvantage of an online delivery is that it can actually take up more facilitator time in the monitoring of bulletin boards, threaded discussions, and chat rooms. However, instead of being in large blocks of time such as a day or a week, online time is measured in hours here and there, often over many weeks. As a designer you need to consider carefully how much facilitator time your activities will demand, then design appropriately.

Now let's look at some of the other disadvantages of an online delivery.

Weaknesses of Online Deliveries

- The same as for any delivery process, it is not good for everything.
- The learners may not come back for session two.
- Instructor "face time" is often greater.
- Design time is usually greater than for face-to-face classroom, but less than for asynchronous e-learning.
- Learners can easily lose interest or begin to multitask during chat discussions.
- It requires learner personal discipline and corporate learning discipline.

Designing Online Learning for Organizations

By merging our good instructional design principles with this methodology, we can create a delivery process that takes advantages of the aforementioned strengths while reducing or eliminating the weaknesses. Such a delivery has these characteristics:

- It is analysis based, relying on good needs and job and task analysis to isolate the right content to base the activities on.

- It is objective centered, with plenty of good, well-written objectives that help the learners determine the proper end products of the learning.

- It is learner centered. The learners know the objectives, the goals, where they are going, and why they want to get there. Much of online learning is often self-directed and contract-based—two learner-centered methodologies.

- It is activity based. The entire program revolves around the activities and assignments you design into it.

- It is criterion evaluation based.

 Here are some hints for designing a good online delivery, followed by a job aid to help you determine if an online delivery will work for your training need.

- Be sure to create a strong learner guide, with activities, preclass communications, objectives, reading material, learning resources, and a glossary.

- Always begin assignments or activities by stating the objectives they will cover.

- Use readings and websites in lieu of creating new content as you normally do in an asynchronous design.

- Build in progress checks that are completed and sent to the facilitator during long individual activities.

- Build in plenty of reviews and summaries, especially at the start of each segment.

- Place objectives everywhere, even allowing learners to create their own objectives.

- Use learning contracts as much as possible.

- Use collaborative or group learning contracts, particularly in team environments or for team-building processes.

- Create a help board for posts to group or instructor, for both technical and content problems.

- Make sure your learning resource lists are as complete and rich as possible.

- Structure large resource lists by objective.

- Allow for learners' evaluation of their own learning. In group learning scenarios, provide group evaluation activities of the group's learning.

- Use negotiated, mastery evaluation-based contracts where possible.

- Add more structure in the form of

  - Comprehensive schedules

  - Deadlines

  - E-mail progress checks

- Create open-ended questions as part of your activities to elicit more thoughtful responses.

- Be sure your audience analysis is accurate and complete.

- Create a strong facilitator guide, even if you are the facilitator, with room for completion dates, notes, and other records.

- Create an FAQ posting.

- Develop evaluation instruments for both course and learners.

Following is a handy job aid for you to use to generally determine whether an online delivery might be right for your training need.

ONLINE DECISION JOB AID

Yes	No	Is the content is mostly knowledge based?
Yes	No	Can any skill-based content be handled in the online environment or by blending?
Yes	No	Can effective activities and exercises be developed?
Yes	No	Are applicable paper based graphics available, or can they be developed?
Yes	No	Is the need for human interaction during the learning important to its success?
Yes	No	Is there a need for collaborative learning?
Yes	No	Are team-based problem-solving and decision-making activities and practice important?

Yes	No	Is the background knowledge of the learners known?
Yes	No	Is corporate learning discipline strong enough to expect the learners to attend scheduled chat rooms and make posting deadlines?
Yes	No	Are critical content SMEs available often enough to share their expertise during chat room functions or on the discussion boards?
Yes	No	Are the employees who need the content in different locations?
Yes	No	Are competent designers available to create the online program?
Yes	No	Must the content be taught on a periodic basis no matter what the size of the audience?
Yes	No	Is the technology available for online learning?
Yes	No	Are trained online facilitators available?
Yes	No	Can the content be taught in an environment that is not face to face?
Yes	No	Is there a relatively short design window?
Yes	No	Is the content unstable?

WHAT THE LEARNERS SAY

Let's wrap up this look at synchronous e-learning with some thoughts from the people who matter most in the process, the learners. When asked "What are the most important characteristics of e-learning facilitators?" the learners said they were

- How well they used humor
- Their interpersonal skills
- How fast their response time was
- Having a positive attitude
- Their ability to create a stimulating learning environment
- How well they adapted to their learners' needs
- Their ability to establish clear guidelines
- Their ability to motivate and engage
- Their content knowledge
- Their ability to make the learners feel that they are part of a team
- Their listening skills

- How well they can manage online discussions
- Their ability to provide feedback
- How well they used e-mail
- Their questioning ability

When asked what they felt their e-learning facilitators could have done but did not do on line, the learners said they could have

- Directed my learning
- Relinquished control
- Provided a clear overview
- Made me feel more a part of a team
- Provided a telephone contact
- Established clear guidelines
- Shown empathy
- Had a positive attitude
- Provided better feedback
- Allowed for group collaboration activities
- Communicated more often

When asked what were their top three barriers to being successful e-learners, the learners said these were

- Technological problems
- Minimal and tardy feedback from the facilitator
- Ambiguous instructions on the website as well as via e-mail

Well, that about does it. If you stayed with us for the whole book, you should now have a pretty good idea about how to do good instructional design; that is, how to create training that effectively and efficiently meets the needs of your organization and your trainees. If you've only dipped in here and there to read about the concepts that were most relevant to you, that's OK too. We hope it helped you to become a better designer.

We have one more list for you that summarizes everything we've discussed. We call it *seven rules for good instructional design.*

Thanks for reading and for caring enough to want to be a better (and faster) instructional designer.

SEVEN RULES FOR GOOD INSTRUCTIONAL DESIGN

1. Know that what you are going to do is important for your organization.

2. Know that the content you are going to provide is what your trainees need to learn.

3. Know that the way you plan to present the content is the most time-, cost-, and learning-effective way for your trainees and your organization.

4. Know that the training materials and methods you are going to use in presenting the content to your trainees are the best ones for your training situation.

5. Do it all right!

6. Know that what you did was what your organization needed, and that it did some good.

7. Use whatever works for you to make instructional design easier, faster, and cheaper.

Glossary

Action Verb: A word that conveys actions and behaviors and reflects the type of performance that is to occur. Action verbs reflect behaviors that are measurable and observable.

Active Performance Support System: An electronic performance support system that actually monitors the employees' work and stops them to lend advice and support when necessary. There are few of these in existence.

Advance Organizer: A brief introduction to a training aspect that outlines its structure and defines how the content builds on existing knowledge.

Alpha Test: The first evaluation of a technology-based program, used to test the user interface and to determine overall usability.

Analog Audio and Video: Audio or video information normally stored in a tape format; it is differentiated from digital audio and video, which usually use some type of computer format as the storage medium. Digital video and audio are needed for e-learning and CD-ROM training deliveries.

Animation: A sequence of graphics presented in succession, animation is widely used to simulate motion in computer-based or e-learning deliveries.

Aspect Ratio: The relationship of height to width of an image size (for example, 4:3 is a standard aspect ratio for NTSC television).

ASTD: An organization of training professionals encompassing all aspects of the profession.

Asynchronous: Usually in reference to e-learning, asynchronous refers to non-instructor-led training using a computer-network-based delivery system in which the trainees are not online at the same time nor in direct, immediate contact. The technique sometimes includes the use of electronic bulletin boards and chat rooms. It is often a mixed-media format combining a self-instructional aspect with one or more instructor-facilitated processes.

Audience Analysis: An evaluation of a training audience to determine the background, needs, interests, preferences, and demographics of the group.

Authoring System: A software application used to create courseware by combining text, graphics, video, audio, and animations.

Bandwidth: Technically a concept that has to do with the size of the wire that connects computers in a network and how much information can flow over it. Usually the more bandwidth the better, as more information can be sent faster. Bandwidth limitations can make e-learning using high-level video, graphics, and even audio is very difficult to do smoothly. It's the same reason surfing the net can be so slow at times.

Barriers: Organizational factors that get in the way of performance.

Beta Test: An evaluation for a course or product, done by actual users and others, not necessarily in a real-life environment, to determine instructional flow and answer questions that surfaced during development of materials. It is also referred to as a formative evaluation, although this term is being used less frequently.

Brainstorming: A technique for idea generation in which each person suggests as many ideas as possible, with no discussion of viability until after the session is complete. A recorder usually writes the ideas on some medium for this later discussion.

Branch Back: A technique whereby a wrong answer causes the program to replay the area of instruction where the correct answer resides.

Branching: An instructional technique in which the learner's next step is determined by his or her response to a previous step. Branching makes a course more interactive by allowing students to take different paths through a course, based on their needs and interests.

Browser: A software program that allows trainees to navigate through a web-based training program.

Bug: A programming error that causes a course to run improperly or stop running unexpectedly. Alpha tests are used to find bugs. Bugs are also known by the euphemism "undocumented features," although usually only by programmers.

Bulletin Board: Software that allows trainees to post class information, activities, or questions electronically for reading by other participants, the instructor, or both.

Button: An object on the computer screen that initiates an action when clicked.

CAI (see Computer-Assisted Instruction).

CBT (see Computer-Based Training).

CD-I (see Compact Disc–Interactive).

CD-ROM: A delivery technology for multimedia-based programs. It is used mostly for self-instructional training designs. It has some compatibility and storage size problems, and is being slowly replaced by DVD.

Chat Room: An electronic "place" where individuals can connect by sending typed text to one another in real time.

Checklist: A tool used to ensure that the important actions or steps in the performance of a task have been taken.

Chunking: The process of dividing a portion of training material into smaller pieces that are easier to deal with.

CMI (see Computer-Managed Instruction).

CMI (see Computer-Mediated Instruction).

Color Scheme: A group of complementary colors used in computer-based training to give a course a consistent look.

Compact Disc–Read-Only Memory (see CD-ROM).

Competency: The specific knowledge and skills and the application of that knowledge and those skills to the standard of performance required for a particular job.

Competency Analysis: An analysis process in which the competencies necessary to superior performance of a job are determined. In a second stage of the analysis, competencies of individual performers are determined, based on the new competency model, to develop individual or group training needs.

Completion Item: A test item requiring the completion of a statement, phrase, or concept.

Compressed File: Files that are reduced in size to allow for quicker transfer and more efficient storage. Particularly used by audio and video files across computer nets.

Computer-Assisted Instruction (CAI): Another term for computer-based training or computer-managed instruction.

Computer-Based Training (CBT): Can be a general term for any training done through the use of computers rather than through instructor facilitation, but is also often used to signify only text-based computer-facilitated instruction. This is usually referred to derogatorily as an "electronic page turner" and is not considered good instruction.

Computer-Mediated Instruction: Can be the same as computer-based technology, but often signifies an approach in which the computer is used in conjunction with an instructor, either in a classroom or in a distance-learning format. Similar to if not the same as synchronous web-based training.

Condition: The part of an objective that describes the situation, environment, or limitations under which the learner must exhibit the behavior.

Content: The concepts, ideas, policies, and information that a training program comprises.

Content Outline: An outline that organizes course content into topics and subtopics.

Cost-Benefit Analysis: A method of assigning dollar values to the cost of training development and implementation and to the benefits derived from the training, to determine whether it is worth the effort.

Course: A complete, usually integrated series of lessons identified by a common title. Courses usually make up a training curriculum, and in turn are made up of modules, units, sections, and so forth.

Course Map: The major concepts from a course depicted in a visual arrangement, usually with lines drawn between associated concepts and relationships shown between the connected concepts. Maps usually break the course into units, lessons, frames, or segments, and they detail objectives, treatment, teaching strategies, and a skeleton storyboard if needed.

Courseware: The media (text, computer program, CD-ROM, and so on) that contain the content of the course.

Criterion: The standard by which learning is measured.

Criterion-Referenced Testing: Testing of the objectives as a learner progresses through the course of instruction. Success depends on the trainees' attainment of the objectives and not on how well they do in relation to others.

Critical Incident Method: A method of analysis through which experts identify the critical job incidents and their products. Incidents are classified as positive or negative, summarized, and then validated by the experts for completeness.

Criticality Analysis: A model for selecting tasks for training in which tasks are identified as critical based on their difficulty, importance, and frequency of performance.

Cross-Training: Providing training in several different areas or functions. This provides backup workers when the primary worker is unavailable.

Data Analysis: Analysis of records and files collected by an organization, reflecting actual employee performance and results, such as sales figures, attendance figures, call-backs for repair, employee evaluations, and so on.

Delphi Study: A data-collection technique in which groups of SMEs respond to repeated cycles of prepared questions, each cycle of questions becoming more and more specific, based on answers to the previous cycle's questions.

Design Document: A conceptual report that gives all those involved in the development of a training program a picture of the overall course design. Items might include a mission statement, an audience profile, course objectives, content outline, a course map, an evaluation plan, and a visual motif.

Designer: An individual who attempts to make it easier for learners to learn by systematically discovering what a learner needs to know and then determining the best way to make that information available.

Desktop Training: Any training delivered by computer to a trainee's desk.

Dial-Up Connection: Using a modem and telephone line to connect to a computer net.

Digital Audio: Audio information stored as discrete numeric values. Computer disks, digital audiotape (DAT), and CD-ROMs are typical storage media for both digital audio and video.

Digital Versatile Disc (DVD): DVD is another advancement in delivery technology. It allows full-motion video and all the other goodies of multimedia on a small-sized disc with plenty of storage capacity.

Digital Video: Video that is digitized on a computer instead of residing on a magnetic tape. Digital video is easier to store, edit, and play on a computer. This also makes it more expensive, and it takes up large amounts of storage capacity.

Digitize: To store media (graphic, audio, or video) in digital form. Often used to note the conversion from an analog to a digital format.

Distance Learning: Probably one of the most overused and much-abused terms in technology-based training. At the basic level it simply means that the instructor and the learner are either not in the same physical location or not there at the same time, or both. However, it is often used to refer to satellite-mediated learning, even though computers, video players, and even telephones can be used as distance-learning delivery systems.

Distributed Implementation: A self-instructional delivery process in which there is no designated learning center. The packages are sent to the trainees' job locations and usually facilitated by a supervisor or other line individual.

Distributed Learning: A newer and also older term that means roughly the same thing as distance learning, but is coming into use due to distance learning's perceived relationship with satellites.

Downlink Site: The earth station in a satellite-based system that receives programming beamed from the satellite.

Download: To receive and store information from another computer or system.

Drill-and-Practice Exercises: Instructional activities designed to allow a learner to review previously learned information through repetition and rehearsal. Often a major activity set for computer-based training.

DVD (see Digital Versatile Disc).

E-Learning: Technology-based training using the Internet as the delivery system. Advantages of this delivery system include reduced hardware compatibility issues, easier and quicker revisions, and the possible maximum size of the distribution network. The disadvantages include security problems, speed, and bandwidth limitations, which reduce multimedia capability. E-learning can be instructor-led or self-directed.

Electronic Performance Support System (EPSS): Computerized applications that provide support for the user in accomplishing specific tasks, particularly those that are difficult to memorize or are done infrequently. An electronic performance support system may provide needed information, present job aids, and deliver just-in-time training on demand. Electronic performance support systems will often take the place of some training, although the employees need to be trained on how to use the system effectively.

Entry Skills (Entry Behavior): Skills or knowledge that the trainee must master before he or she can begin a training program.

EPSS (see Electronic Performance Support System).

Ergonomics: An approach to job design that focuses on the interactions between the person and his or her environmental elements.

Evaluation: Reviewing a course to determine its impact and improve its effectiveness.

Expert System: A type of electronic performance support system, normally a decision-making tool, that has been developed in conjunction with an expert on a job or process. It is designed to help the employee make correct decisions concerning particular tasks related to the job. It is the precursor to an active performance support system.

Facilitator: An individual who is responsible for helping trainees to learn, not by presenting information, but by listening, asking questions, providing ideas, suggesting alternatives, and identifying possible resources. Facilitators are found in the classroom and for self-instructional delivery as well, although their responsibilities are usually very different for these delivery systems.

FAQ (see Frequently Asked Questions).

Feedback: Providing learners with information about an action and its result in relation to some criterion of acceptability. Feedback can be positive, negative, or neutral.

Field Production: A media production shot on location rather than in the studio.

Focus Group: A method of data collection using facilitated group discussions with SMEs. The facilitator leads the process, tries to make sure everyone is involved, and collects data for analysis.

Frequently Asked Questions (FAQ): A file with commonly asked questions and their answers, created to help trainees in self-instructional or asynchronous deliveries.

Graphical User Interface (GUI): A process for allowing the user to communicate with computer software through the use of graphic icons instead of words. Graphical user interface has become the preferred method for communication with computers, but can be tricky if the user does not understand what the icons represent. This is a particular problem in a multicultural environment. (Think Apple versus Windows.)

GUI (see Graphical User Interface).

Guided Simulation: A simulation in which learners receive coaching or feedback during the activity.

Handout: Supporting information used by the learner as reference or activity material in a training program. Handouts are often contained in the participant's package.

Hands-On: An activity in which the trainees practice on actual equipment, simulators, or special training aids.

HTML (see Hypertext Markup Language).

Human Performance Technologist: An individual responsible for using various technologies designed to enhance human performance and capabilities in the workplace. These technologies include methods and procedures from many fields, such as instructional technology, organizational development, career development, motivation and feedback, human factors, and employee selection.

Hyperlinks: A feature in computer-based training that allows you to program places on a screen that, if selected, will "jump" the trainee to a further explanation of a concept, an example of it, or some other information concerning it or a related topic. This allows for the important process of learner control and for enrichment or remedial activities.

Hypermedia: Interactive computer-based instruction technique in which video, slides, graphics, or other media can have or even be hyperlinks that, when selected, send trainees down a new learning path.

Hypertext: More or less the same as hyperlink, except it is an older term that was used when only words were hyperlinks.

Hypertext Markup Language (HTML): A code used to create web pages.

ID (see Instructional Design).

ID Software (see Instructional Design Software).

IDL (see Interactive Distance Learning).

Immediate Feedback: Feedback given to learners at the moment they complete an action or provide some form of input, such as answering a question.

Individualized Instruction: A learning design in which each trainee works on materials without regard to what other trainees in the same class or facility are doing. Sometimes the learning is prescriptive, and it is often self-paced.

Instructional Activity: An activity designed to promote learning and transfer of knowledge. A course is typically a series of lessons made up of instructional activities.

Instructional Design (ID): A systematic approach to creating training that meets the needs of the trainees and the organization while being as effective and efficient as possible.

Instructional Design Software (ID Software): Similar to authoring systems but used before them to guide trainers in making important instructional design decisions for any type of training, but particularly for technology-based training. Instructional design software is usually easier to use than authoring systems, but it is a rare individual who can employ one without some instructional design knowledge. It is sometimes referred to as pre-authoring software.

Instructional Game: A game designed to teach concepts, behaviors, attitudes, or procedures. Can be part of an instructional activity.

Instructional Plan: An intermediate step in program design in which the topic outline is expanded to include sequenced content notations and possible activities.

Instructional Setting: The location and physical characteristics of the place in which a form of instruction takes place. The setting can be in a classroom, laboratory, workplace location, learning center, or any other place in which people receive training.

Instructional Systems Design (ISD): A systematic process of designing learning activities. By following ISD, designers increase the likelihood that their course designs will be appropriate and effective. The most basic form of the ISD model is a five-step process of analysis, design, development, implementation, and evaluation. ISD is often referred to as the ADDIE process as well, using the first letter of each phase in the acronym.

Instructional Technologist: One who is an expert with instructional technologies. This is a dying breed, as no one person can be expert in all the varying technologies available today. Most practitioners consider themselves expert in one or two aspects of technology and work with teams of other experts to create great technology-based training. If you run into someone who claims to be a truly general instructional technologist, watch out for the snake oil.

Instructional Technology: The use of technology (video, computers, CD-ROM, modems, satellites, and so on) to deliver or support training.

Instructor: An individual who provides knowledge or information to learners by directly presenting content and directing structured learning experiences.

Instructor-Led Training: Training that relies on the instructor to present content and create an effective environment for learning.

Interactive Distance Learning (IDL): An interesting term that should simply be redundant, but often is not. It is used mainly to differentiate the old "talking head" tele-courses from more modern techniques in which trainee involvement in the distance-learning process is designed in. It is also used less frequently for the same purpose when differentiating the old "electronic page turners" from newer, more interactive computer-based training approaches. Good instructional design for technology-based training (or any instruction, for that matter) demands plenty of student interaction, so methods in which there is none should not be considered valid training techniques, which is why the term is redundant.

Internet: A global network of networks connecting millions of computer users worldwide.

Internet Service Provider (ISP): A company or group that connects users to the Internet.

Interviews: A data-collection technique in which the collector meets with individuals, such as SMEs or managers, usually to ask them a series of prepared questions.

Intranet: A private network based on the internet standards, but servicing a known organization from behind a secure access point.

Introduction: A major section of a lesson plan designed to establish common ground, capture and hold trainee attention, outline the lesson, point out benefits of the learning, and lead the trainee into the body of the lesson.

ISD (see Instructional Systems Design).

ISP (see Internet Service Provider).

Item Analysis: The process of evaluating test items by determining how well an individual item is answered by examinees, its relative difficulty value, and its correlation with objectives.

IVD (see Interactive Video Disc).

JIT (see Just-in-Time).

Job Aid: An easy-to-carry summary of a procedure that the learner can use on the job to aid transfer of learning. It provides guidance on the performance of a specific task or skill. Job aids are used in situations in which it is not feasible or worthwhile to commit the procedure to memory before on-the-job activity.

Job Analysis: A technique for breaking a job into component parts such as duties and tasks.

Job Duty: A combination of related tasks equals a duty, and duties combine to form a job.

JTA (Job/Task Analysis): Job analysis and task analysis are often spoken of together (mostly for convenience sake as they are two different processes) as a JTA or Job/Task Analysis.

Just-in-Time (JIT): A method of providing training when it is needed by the trainee rather than when a class is held or a trainer is available.

Learner Characteristics: The traits, such as reading level, education, position, interests, and so on, possessed by learners that could affect their ability to learn.

Learning Center: A designated facility, usually staffed by one or more facilitators, where trainees go to view self-instructional programs.

Learning Content Management System (LCMS): A software application (or set of applications) that manages the creation, storage, use, and reuse of learning content. An LCMS combines the record keeping functionality of a learning management system with the ability to manage the actual content as well. An LCMS may actually include an authoring system for this purpose.

Learning Management System (LMS): Software that automates the administration of training. The LMS registers users, tracks courses in a catalog, records data from learners; and provides reports to management. An LMS is typically designed to handle courses by multiple publishers and providers.

Learning Technology: See Instructional Technology and substitute "learning" for "instruction."

Lesson: A portion of a course. Courses may be organized by topics, modules, lessons, or units.

Lesson Plan: A written guide for trainers that provides specific definitions and directions on learning objectives, equipment, instructional media, material requirements, and conduct of the training.

Linear: A programming method characterized by short steps of ordered instruction followed by constructed responses. Also known as lock step.

List-Serve: Subscription mailing list on a computer network that automatically sends the user information on a particular topic.

Location: The place a video or still shoot will take place.

Mastery: Meeting all of the specified minimum requirements for a specific performance.

Mastery Learning: A design characteristic in which the trainee is expected to achieve a preset level of mastery for the material to be learned. This mastery level is usually measured through a criterion-referenced evaluation.

Media List: A master list of all media elements included in a program (overheads, print, video, audio, graphics, and animations).

Model: A representation of a process or system that shows the most important aspects of the system in such a way that analysis of the model leads to insights into the system.

Module: A unit of instruction. This term is often used to delineate a self-contained instructional unit that includes one or more learning objectives, appropriate learning materials and methods, and associated criterion-reference measures.

Multimedia: Most commonly refers to the use of text, graphics, sound, video, and computer-generated animation, or any combination of the above, usually in a self-directed, computer-based format, often employing a CD-ROM or other large-capacity storage devices as part of the delivery system. Multimedia is usually designed and developed by a team of experts.

Multimedia Training: A delivery system that incorporates various technology-based instructional methods, such as graphics, text, animation, audio, and video. It is most often delivered on CD-ROM.

Narration: The spoken portion of a video or audio production, especially anything spoken directly to the audience instead of dialogue between the actors.

Navigation: How a user moves through a technology-based training program. Navigation controls are typically a series of buttons or icons.

Need: The difference between the way things are and the way they ought to be.

Needs Assessment: A process used to determine the difference between current and desired states, often related to the development of a training program. A needs assessment may use many data-gathering techniques to discover needs expressed by management, the target audience, or subject-matter experts.

Nominal Group Technique: A data-collection technique related to brainstorming but more structured, with participants recording their own ideas, then bringing them before the group and discussing them one by one. In the end, the group ranks the ideas.

Object-Oriented Design: Creating training as single concepts or small "packets" of information that can be used and reused for many different training needs or programs.

Object-Oriented Learning: A training design in which reusable pieces of content learning, termed objects, are created for both a specific training need and for use in other programs.

Objective: A specific statement of what learners will be able to do when they complete a training program or a piece of a program.

Observation: A data-collection technique in which the collector physically observes the subjects' job performance.

Off-the-Shelf: Training produced by an outside agency for use by other organizations. Normally used by organizations when in-house produced training programs would be more costly or take too much time to develop.

OJT (see On-the-Job Training).

On-the-Job Training (OJT): Training in the skills and knowledge needed to perform a job, taking place in the actual work environment.

Online Learning: Often used to mean synchronous e-learning, it is also a delivery method in which the learners communicate with the instructor through discussion boards and chat rooms as they complete preplanned activities and exercises on their own. It can be an excellent methodology for the practice of collaborative learning.

Open-Ended Test Item: A question that can be answered in a variety of ways, such as an essay question.

Organizational Need: The reason for doing training. A difference between where the organization is and where it should be, determined through various analysis methods.

Organizational Needs Analysis: A needs-analysis technique that identifies a gap between what the organization expects and its current performance.

Parking Lot: A classroom facilitation term used to signify a place (usually a flip chart) where questions or ideas that will be dealt with at a later time are recorded or "parked." Usually discussion of these items occurs at the end of class, during breaks, or when an expert who knows something about the topic appears. Parking lots can also be used in e-learning programs; in that case, an expert reads the "parked" questions and answers them via e-mail.

Participant's Package: A set of materials that presents information for use in a learning experience, usually in a classroom setting. This might include general information, procedural and technical use data, or design information, activities, and references.

Passive Performance Support System: Making up the majority of electronic performance support systems, these require the user to recognize the need to stop a task and refer to the system when information is required or a problem that cannot be solved with current knowledge is encountered.

Pass-out: Trainee material, usually in a classroom setting, that is passed out at a specific time in the learning process rather than at the beginning of the program as part of the participant's package.

Performance Analysis (Performance Assessment): Process through which opportunities and problems of an organization are determined by using systematic analysis methods that look at the performance of the individual and the organization as a whole.

Performance Checklist: A list of elements that must be correctly performed to determine whether each learner satisfactorily meets the performance standards described in the learning objective.

Performance Criteria (Performance Standard): Part of a learning objective that describes the observable learner behavior that is acceptable as proof that learning has occurred.

Performance Evaluation: Evaluations related to the mastery of specific skills rather than knowledge.

Performance Gap: The difference between optimal and actual performance of a person, group, or organization.

Performance Intervention: Any one of a number of interactions that are developed and implemented to close a performance gap or help an organization realize a performance opportunity .

Performance Objective: A measurable statement of the behavior that students will be able to demonstrate at the end of the course, the conditions under which they will be demonstrated, and the criteria for acceptable performance.

Post-Production: The processing of video or audio after it has been recorded into a completed piece of instructional media. This might include video editing, sound editing, synchronization, mixing, and special effects.

Post-Test: A test administered after a program or part of a program to assess the level of a learner's knowledge or skill.

Pre-Instructional Activity: Introductory course activities that are done before the actual program is received. Often called pre-work.

Preproduction: Everything done to prepare for a video shoot, including location scouting, casting, planning, testing, and so forth.

Prescriptive Learning: A learning design in which each learner is measured against a set group of skills or competencies and then assigned work based on this measurement. The learning may be individualized, self-paced, or both.

Pre-Test: A test administered prior to a program to assess the level of a learner's knowledge or skill. The results may be used to determine prior learning and readiness or as a baseline to compare with the results of a post-test to determine learning or behavioral change.

Problem-Based Learning (PBL): An instructional methodology in which the participants (usually in teams) are given a specific complex problem and asked to solve it as part of the learning experience. The teams work on their own to finalize a solution, then meet as a group to discuss not only the solutions but also the methods by which they were achieved. In the health-care profession this is often called case-based learning, as the learners are provide with actual cases to diagnose.

Programmed Instruction: A learning design in which trainees are provided information in small steps, with immediate feedback concerning whether or not the material was learned properly. This allows the trainee to choose the pace at which he or she goes through the material. This concept is often termed self-instruction, self-directed learning, and self-paced learning, although each of these concepts has other definitions as well.

Props: Items used in a production by the actors (such as hats, canes, books).

Prototype: An early version of a course developed to test and gain approval of the look and feel and the functionality of the course.

Questionnaire: A data-collection technique, usually a form comprising a list of questions. Questionnaires are often used during analysis when the potential audience is widely distributed.

Quick-Time: A digital video process in which the speed of the image is slowed to fifteen frames per second from the normal thirty frames per second. This allows for more video to be stored in a smaller amount of space on the computer, but also creates the slightly jerky motion that is often found on multimedia programs (and MTV). Quick-time is usually not full-screen video, which bothers many trainees.

Quiz: A short test to measure achievement on material recently taught or on any small, newly completed unit of work.

Reading Level: A number representing a person's ability to read and comprehend what he or she is reading based on academic grade levels.

Refresher Training: Training that reinforces previous training or helps trainees regain previously acquired skills and knowledge.

Remedial Branch: A technique whereby a wrong answer causes the program to present a new piece of instruction designed to help the trainee master the material, usually from a different point of view.

Satellite-Mediated Distance Learning (SMDL): A general term applied to the use of satellites as a training delivery system. This can include two-way audio or two-way video communications. If well-designed, satellite-mediated distance learning can be an effective distributed training method. If designed badly, it becomes a technology-based and very expensive talking head or group of talking heads, often termed an expert panel.

SCORM (see Shareable Content Object Reference Model).

Script: A list of all spoken lines in a self-instructional course or media production.

SDL (see Self-Directed Learning).

Self-Directed Learning (SDL): Often referred to as individualized instruction or self-managed instruction, in its basic form it is simply training for which there is no instructor present to guide the trainees, who therefore learn on their own. This concept is open to a number of interpretations and more than a little controversy.

Self-Paced: A design characteristic whereby the learner works at his or her own speed to complete the learning assignment.

Self-Quiz: A short assessment, usually self-scored, that allows learners to determine their own understanding or abilities.

Self-Study Guide: A trainee document containing a series of lessons arranged in discrete steps, each of which ends with a self-quiz. It usually includes objectives, subject-matter content, references, review exercises with feedback, and directions to interact with training media, if any.

Sequencing: Arranging the content, objectives, or both into the most appropriate order for effective learning.

Server: A computer that acts as a link to other computers in a network.

Setting: The physical surroundings in which a scene takes place, including the time, period, and ambiance.

Shareable Content Object Reference Model (SCORM): A web-based e-learning standard.

Shot List: A list of still, film, or video images to be captured, organized by location.

Simulation: An instructional technique in which the trainee is presented situations resembling real life that usually involve choices and risks. The players are reinforced for making the right decisions.

Skill: The ability to perform a specific task.

Small-Group Instruction: A training method that places the responsibility for learning on the student through participation in small groups divided out of a larger class.

SMDL (see Satellite-Mediated Distance Learning).

SME (see Subject-Matter Expert).

SME Review: A review of instruction material done by a subject-matter expert to correct technical errors.

SME-Based Training: Training that is facilitated by an SME who may have, but often does not have, any training experience or formal instruction. The SME is chosen as the facilitator based mainly on his or her being an "expert" on the subject.

Soft Skills: Skills needed to perform on jobs for which outcomes may vary depending on interactions with individuals, such as counseling, supervising, and managing.

Stakeholder: The individual in an organization who requests training or who is responsible for the individuals whom the training will affect.

Stem: The part of a test item that is common to all possible answers, as in multiple-choice or fill-in-the-blank questions.

Storyboard: A document containing sketches of interactions specifying the placement of screen elements (text, graphics, buttons, video windows, and so on) and branching information for CBT, or the scene layout, actions performed, camera angles, and accompanying audio elements for video training.

Streaming: A method for moving digital audio and video over networks such as the Internet. It solves a problem with waiting for large audio and video files to download (but creates security issues) by allowing an audio/video (A/V) file to start playing before it has finished downloading. This is accomplished by buffering (temporarily storing) a small portion of the video during the first few seconds after the (A/V) file is launched and then play begins. While the file is playing the buffered segment, more (A/V) content from the file is loaded into the buffer for the file to continue playing.

Subject-Matter Expert (SME): A content expert who works with the instructional designer to ensure the accuracy of information in a course.

Subtask: Component performances, behaviors, or procedures that make up a task.

Supporting Objective: Objectives that describe something trainees must be able to do prior to accomplishing the terminal or program objective. Also termed enabling objectives.

Survey (see Questionnaire).

Synchronous: Most often combined with e-learning, synchronous refers to instruction using a net-based delivery system in which the instructor and trainees are online at the same time. It is often called online learning as well.

Talent: The actors or narrators used in a media production.

Target Audience: The specific audience for whom the program is designed.

Task: A performance, procedure, or behavior. The smallest essential part of a job.

Task Analysis: The process of analyzing a task and breaking it down into its subtasks, skills, and necessary knowledge.

TBI (see Technology-Based Instruction).

TBL (see Technology-Based Learning).

TBT (see Technology-Based Training).

Technology-Based Instruction (TBI; see Technology-Based Training).

Technology-Based Learning (TBL:): See Technology-Based Training and substitute "learning" for "training."

Technology-Based Training (TBT): An overall term for training done with the help of what can be defined as technology. This might include anything from a pencil to a Cray computer, but usually means a device that plugs in, often but not always a computer. Although technology-based training is sometimes used synonymously with computer-based training, this is often not accurate. Technology-based training is also often considered to be a self-instructional process, but this is not always true either.

Teleconferencing: Meetings held through the use of telephones or satellites. Often considered a form of training, teleconferencing normally lacks any objectives or learning focus. Basically the term is invalid for technology-based training.

Tele-Learning: Simply using the telephone as a training delivery system. It can be an effective and very inexpensive form of distributed training if used for the right reasons and well designed.

Template: A prebuilt element that can be used and reused in different programs to speed up the design and development process.

Test: A device or technique used to measure the performance, skill level, or knowledge of a learner on a specific subject matter.

Test Items: Specific items that test trainees' mastery of objectives.

Topical Outline: An outline of the topics to be included in a training program. It may provide course learning objectives; a listing of part, section, and topic titles; and statements of rationale to explain or justify the training.

Trainee Guide: Often used interchangeably with participant's package or workbook, this term is used at times to indicate a more complex document that guides the trainee through a self-instructional activity.

Training Curriculum: A number of programs or classes that make up all of the training requirements for a job position, department, or entire organization.

Training Needs Analysis: Process of determining which needs may require training to be met. Usually done by reviewing work tasks, identifying performance factors and objectives, and defining a training plan.

Transfer of Training: The ability of trainees to apply to the job the knowledge and skills they gain in training.

Treatment: A written description of a technology-based project, including the story line, the look and feel, how it will work (course flow), and how the course goals will be achieved.

VHS: A standard consumer video format that uses half-inch tape. VHS is the lowest-quality video format in common use.

Video Conferencing: Conferencing in which participants both hear and see one another. Usually done over telephone lines.

Video Editing: The process of selecting sections of raw footage and placing them in proper order to create a completed video piece.

Video Still: A single video frame digitized and used as a still image.

Virtual Reality (VR): Not necessarily the goggles and gloves of science fiction (though this is already a possibility), virtual reality is an entire series of photo-realistic and three-dimensional modeling technologies that lend a new level of realism to technology-based training. Virtual reality machines allow trainees to practice complex tasks before they ever see the factory floor, and virtual reality environments permit employees to learn critical skills without going in harm's way.

Virtual Reality Markup Language (VRML): The computer language used to develop virtual reality training. (See also Hypertext Markup Language.)

Voice-Over: A type of narration in which the speaker's voice is heard without his or her image being displayed on the screen.

VR (see Virtual Reality).

VRML (see Virtual Reality Markup Language).

WBT (see Web-Based Training).

Web-Based Training (WBT): Instruction delivered over public or private computer networks and displayed by a web browser. Web-based training is usually not downloaded computer-based training, but rather on-demand training stored in a server and accessed across a network. Web-based training can be updated very rapidly. Usually uses a Web browser as the basis for navigation.

White Space: The amount of blank space between areas of print on a piece of printed material.

Workbook (see Self-Study Guide).

Wuzzles: Puzzles consisting of combinations of words, letters, figures, or symbols positioned to create disguised words, phrases, names, places, sayings, and so on. Used to energize classrooms and even e-learning experiences.

Suggested Readings

Instructional Design

Basics of instructional design. *Info-Line*, 803. Alexandria, VA: ASTD.

Building for adult learning. Cincinnati, OH: LDA Publishing. J. Leed. (1987).

Easy-to-use instructional systems design methodology. *Performance & Instruction*, pp. 10–16. K. Overfield. (1996, April).

How does instructional systems design differ from traditional instruction? *Educational Technology*, pp. 9–14. W. Hannum. (1982, January).

Mastering the instructional design process: A systematic approach. San Francisco: Jossey-Bass. W. J. Rothwell & H. C. Kazanas. (1992).

Producing workshops, seminars, and short courses. New York: Follett. J. Loughary. (1979).

Survey of instructional development models. Syracuse, NY: Information Resources Publications. K. Gustafson. (1993).

The ASTD handbook of training design and delivery. New York: McGraw-Hill. G. M. Piskurich (Ed.). (1999).

The ASTD training and development handbook. New York: McGraw-Hill. R. Craig (Ed.). (1996).

The systematic design of instruction (6th ed.). Boston: Allyn & Bacon. W. Dick & L. Carey. (2004).

Trainer basics. Alexandria, VA: ASTD. G. M. Piskurich. (2003).

Assessment

An analysis of front-end analysis. J. Harless, in *The Best of Performance & Instruction*, 26(2), 7–9. (1987).

Be a better needs analyst. *Info-Line*, 8502. Alexandria, VA: ASTD.

Benefit-cost analysis for program evaluation. Thousand Oaks, CA: Sage. M. Thompson. (1980).

Building a management competency system that yields results, not scorn. *Training Director's Forum Newsletter*, 11(12), pp. 1–2.

Needs assessment by focus group. *Info-Line,* 9401. Alexandria, VA: ASTD.

Return on investment for technology-based training: Building the business case. J. J. Phillips, in G. M. Piskurich (Ed.), *The ASTD handbook of training design and delivery.* Alexandria, VA: ASTD. (1999).

Strategic needs analysis. *Info-Line,* 9408. Alexandria, VA: ASTD.

The three R's of ROI. *Technical Training.* K. Ruyle. (1998, May/June).

Training needs assessment. Englewood Cliffs, NJ: Educational Technology Publications. A. Rossett. (1988).

Where have all the dollars gone? *Technical Training,* pp. 22–25. R. Schriver. (1998, July/August).

Performance Assessment

HPI essentials. Alexandria, VA: ASTD. G. M. Piskurich (Ed.). (2002).

Performance basics. Alexandria, VA: ASTD. J. Willmore. (2004).

Performance intervention maps. Alexandria, VA: ASTD. Sanders and Thiagarajan (Eds.). (2001).

An ounce of analysis is worth a pound of objectives. Harless Performance Guild. J. Harless. (1996).

Analysis for improving performance. San Francisco: Berrett-Koehler. R. Swanson. (1994).

ASTD models for human performance improvement. Alexandria, VA: ASTD. W. Rothwell. (1997).

First things fast: A handbook for performance analysis. San Francisco: Jossey-Bass. A. Rossett. (1997).

Handbook of human performance technology. San Francisco: Jossey-Bass. H. Stolovitch (Ed.). (1992).

Human competence. Amherst, MA: HRD Press. T. Gilbert. (1996).

Improving performance. San Francisco: Jossey-Bass. G. Rummler. (1990).

Introduction to performance technology. Washington, DC: ISPI. M. Smith (Ed.). (1986).

Leading organizational change. Alexandria, VA: ASTD. E. Holton III. (1997).

Performance Improvement, 36(10), pp. 27–33. [Special issue]. (1997, November/December).

Rapid analysis: Matching solutions to changing situations. *Performance Improvement,* 36(10), pp. 16–21. D. Brethower. (1997, November/December).

Transforming organizations through human performance technology. G. Rummler, in H. Stolovitch (Ed.), *Handbook of human performance technology.* San Francisco: Jossey-Bass. (1992).

What is your problem? Seven steps to analyze and define performance problems. *Performance & Instruction,* pp. 15–18. A. Marrelli. (1993, August).

Analysis

An introduction to competency analysis and modeling. *Performance Improvement,* pp. 8–17. A. Marrelli. (1998, May/June).

Analyzing jobs and tasks. Englewood Cliffs, NJ: Educational Technology Publications. K. Carlisle. (1986).

Be a better job analyst. *Info-Line,* 903. Alexandria, VA: ASTD.

Be a better task analyst. *Info-Line,* 503. Alexandria, VA: ASTD.

Brainstorming updated. *Training & Development, 38*(2), pp. 84–87. S. Grossman. (1984).

Costs, benefits, and productivity in training systems. Reading, MA: Addison-Wesley. G. Kearsley. (1981).

Figuring things out. Reading, MA: Addison-Wesley. R. Zemke. (1982).

Job analysis. San Francisco: Jossey-Bass. S. Gael. (1977).

Managing the job analysis process. *Training & Development,* pp. 64–66. J. Markowitz. (1987, August).

Surveys from start to finish. *Info-Line,* 612. Alexandria, VA: ASTD.

Training Settings

Designing laboratory and simulation instruction. B. Lierman, in *The ASTD handbook of instructional technology.* New York: McGraw-Hill. (1993).

Effective training delivery. [Best of Series, Number 4]. Minneapolis: Lakewood. (1989).

Individualizing instruction. San Francisco: Jossey-Bass. R. Hiemstra. (1990).

Instructing for results. Minneapolis: Lakewood. F. Margolis & C. Bell. (1986).

Self-directed learning. San Francisco: Jossey-Bass. G. M. Piskurich. (1993).

Which technology to use? How to select the right media to deliver training. B. Bailey, in G. M. Piskurich (Ed.), *The ASTD handbook of training design and delivery.* Alexandria, VA: ASTD. (1999).

On-the-Job Training

Designing on-the-job training. L. Tyson, in *The ASTD handbook of instructional technology.* Alexandria, VA: ASTD. (1993).

On-the-job training. D. A. Gallup, in G. M. Piskurich (Ed.), *The ASTD handbook of training design and delivery.* Alexandria, VA: ASTD. (1999).

On-the-job training prescriptions and practice. *Performance Improvement Quarterly, 8,* pp. 19–37. G. Semb. (1995).

Structured on-the-job training. San Francisco: Berrett-Koehler. R. Jacobs. (1990).

The instructor coach. *Performance Improvement,* pp. 26–31. E. Mager. (1999, February).

Job Aids and Performance Support Systems

A handbook of job aids. San Francisco: Pfeiffer. A. Rossett. (1994).

Basics of electronic performance support systems. *Info-Line,* 9412. Alexandria, VA: ASTD.

Creating motivating job aids. *Performance & Instruction,* pp. 13–20. A. Tilaro. (1998, October).

Designing electronic performance support tools. Englewood Cliffs, NJ: Educational Technology Publications. E. Stevens. (1995).

Developing intelligent job aids intelligently. *Technical and Skills Training,* pp. 25–28. K. Ruyle. (1991, February/March).

Electronic performance support systems. New York: Ziff Instate Publishers. G. Gery. (1991).

Expert systems in education and training. Englewood Cliffs, NJ: Educational Technology Publications. R. McFarland. (1990).

Making EPSS work for your organization. *Info-Line,* 9501. Alexandria, VA: ASTD.

On using job aids in lieu of or as an adjunct to training. *Performance & Instruction,* pp. 32–33. D. Mitchell. (1993, May/June).

On-line help supports performance. *Performance Improvement,* pp. 32–35. B. Miller. (1999, April).

Performance support systems and job aids. S. W. Williams, in G. M. Piskurich (Ed.), *The ASTD handbook of training design and delivery.* Alexandria, VA: ASTD. (1999).

Quick and dirty job aids. *Performance & Instruction, 28,* pp. 35–36. J. Nelson. (1989).

Objectives

Guide learning with objectives that take a student perspective. *Performance & Instruction,* pp. 46–48. R. Dodge. (1987, November/December).

Organizing a lesson plan by objectives. *Technical Training,* pp. 8–10. S. Parry. (1998, July/August).

Preparing instructional objectives. Belmont, CA: Pitman Learning. R. F. Mager. (1975).

Write better behavioral objectives. *Info-Line,* 505. Alexandria, VA: ASTD.

Writing objectives with style. *Training.* J. Heines. (1990, July).

Design Documents, Instructional Plans, and Lesson Plans

Analyzing and selecting instructional strategies and tactics. *Performance Improvement Quarterly, 3*(2), 29–47. D. Jonassen. (1990).

Breaking the ice. *Training & Development,* pp. 26–27. R. Herman. (1989, January).

Course design and development. *Info-Line,* 905. Alexandria, VA: ASTD.

Getting inside an expert's brain. *Training & Development,* pp. 55–62. D. Gayeski. (1992, August).

Icebreakers: Warm up your audience. *Info-Line,* 8911. Alexandria, VA: ASTD.

Instructional design strategies and tactics. Englewood Cliffs, NJ: Educational Technology Publishers. C. Leshin. (1992).

Lesson plans: Strategies for learning. *Training & Development,* pp. 15–18. M. Toney. (1991, June).

Organizing a lesson plan by objectives. *Technical Training,* pp. 8–9. S. Parry. (1998, July/August).

Planning effective instruction. Englewood Cliffs, NJ: Prentice Hall. W. Dick.

Thirty-five lesson formats. Englewood Cliffs, NJ: Educational Technology Publications. P. Lyons. (1992).

Using mapping for course development. *Info-Line,* 104. Alexandria, VA: ASTD.

Activities

Ten great games and how to use them. *Info-Line,* 411. Alexandria, VA: ASTD.

Active training: A handbook of techniques, designs, case examples, and tips. San Francisco: Pfeiffer. M. Silberman. (1996).

All together now. San Francisco: Pfeiffer. Lorraine Ukens. (2003).

Games that teach. San Francisco: Pfeiffer. S. Sugar. (1999).

Games trainers play. New York: McGraw-Hill. J. Newstrom. (1980).

Great session openers, closers, and ice breakers. New York: McGraw-Hill. M. Caroselli. (1998).

How to use (not abuse) role plays. *Performance & Instruction,* pp. 16–22. V. O. Wright. (1989, May/June).

Making training active. K. Lawson, in G. M. Piskurich (Ed.), *The ASTD handbook of training design and delivery.* Alexandria, VA: ASTD. (1999).

More games trainers play. New York: McGraw-Hill. J. Newstrom. (1989).

The wuzzle book. Minneapolis: Resources for Organizations. T. Underwood. (1996).

Classroom Instruction

Basic training: Getting ready to present. B. Withers, in G. M. Piskurich (Ed.), *The ASTD handbook of training design and delivery.* Alexandria, VA: ASTD. (1999).

Classroom facilitation: The art and the science. Bellevue, KY: MicroPress. G. M. Piskurich. (2005).

Creative training techniques handbook (2nd ed.). Minneapolis: Lakewood. B. Pike. (1994).

Effective training delivery. [Best of Series.] Minneapolis: Lakewood. (1990).

Instructing for results. Minneapolis: Lakewood. F. Margolis & C. Bell. (1986).

Point°click°wow: A guide to laptop presentations. San Francisco: Pfeiffer. C. Wilder. (1996).

Technology in the classroom: Velcro for the mind. W. W. Turmel, in G. M. Piskurich (Ed.), *The ASTD handbook of training design and delivery.* Alexandria, VA: ASTD. (1999).

Print Materials and Graphics

Applying graphic design principles. B. King, in *The ASTD handbook of instructional technology.* Alexandria, VA: ASTD. (1993).

Designing instructional text. London: Kogan Page. J. Hartley.

Designing multimedia: A visual guide to multimedia and online graphic design. Berkeley, CA: Peachpit Press. L. Lopuck. (1993).

Handbook of HPT message design. H. Stolovich. (1998).

How to write training materials. San Francisco: Pfeiffer. L. S. Stoneall. (1991).

Making instructional design readable. *Performance & Instruction,* pp. 26–27. E. Parker. (1999, April).

Non-designer's design book. Berkeley, CA: Peachtree. R. Williams. (1996).

Playing the stock market. *Inside Technology Training,* p. 34. J. Hartnett. (1999, April).

Preparing the learner for self-directed learning. G. M. Piskurich, in H. Long (Ed.), *Self-directed learning application and research.* Tulsa: University of Oklahoma Press. (1992).

The technology of text. Englewood Cliffs, NJ: Educational Technology Publications. D. Jonassen. (1992).

Write, design, and produce effective training materials. *Info-Line,* 508. Alexandria, VA: ASTD.

Media (Nontechnical)

Audio, film, and video. *Info-Line,* 8509. Alexandria, VA: ASTD.

Corporate instructional video design and production. Englewood Cliffs, NJ: Prentice Hall. D. Gayeski. (1983).

Create quality videos. *Info-Line,* 8607. Alexandria, VA: ASTD.

Designing audio for effective listening. *Training & Development,* pp. 71–76. J. Bunch. (1982, December).

Don't sing the first time video blues. *Training & Development,* pp. 59–61. P. Schleger. (1983, December).

Flip charts: How to draw them and use them. San Francisco: Pfeiffer. R. Brandt. (1986).

How to write training materials. San Francisco: Pfeiffer. L. Stoneall. (1991).

Instructional video. New York: Focal Press. S. Deluca. (1985).

Planning and producing audio-visual materials. New York: HarperCollins. J. Kemp. (1989).

Selecting and developing media for instruction (3rd ed.). New York: Van Nostrand Reinhold. R. Anderson & A. Reynolds. (1992).

Storyboarding tales. *Inside Technology Training,* pp. 26–28. C. Frye. (1998, September).

The ASTD media selection tool for workplace learning. Alexandria, VA: ASTD. R. Marx. (1995).

The corporate scriptwriting book. Poatch, IN: Communicom. D. Matrazzo. (1985).

What instructional media producers should know about using music. *Performance & Instruction,* pp. 21–23. S. Deidman. (1981, March).

What's the story? Creating and using story boards. *CBT Solutions,* pp. 36–40. D. Adams. (1997, May/June).

Write successful video scripts. *Info-Line,* 8707. Alexandria, VA: ASTD.

CBT and Multimedia

About face: The essentials of user interface designs. Boston: IDG Books. A. Cooper. (2001).

Design standards for visual elements and interactivity for courseware. *T.H.E. Journal,* p. 84–85. P. Thibodeau. (1997, February).

Engaged! The nature of computer interactivity. *Training,* pp. 53–58. B. Filipczak. (1996, November).

Getting friendly with authoring tools. *Training & Development, 50*(5), pp. 36–46. T. Barron. (1997).

How to build an interface. *Info-Line*, 9303. Alexandria, VA: ASTD.

Mapping hypertext. Lexington, MA: The Lexington Institute. R. Horn. (1989).

Selecting off-the-shelf courseware and suppliers (CD-ROM, LAN and Web). D. Woodall, in G. M. Piskurich (Ed.), *The ASTD handbook of training design and delivery.* Alexandria, VA: ASTD. (1999).

Text, context, and hypertext: Writing with and for the computer. Cambridge, MA: MIT Press. E. Barrett. (1988).

Asynchronous E-Learning

A trainer's guide to web-based development. Alexandria, VA: ASTD. J. Alden. (1998).

A tough audience: Getting employees revved up about e-learning can be difficult. *Online Learning.* D. Raths. (2001, June).

Analyzing the organization's need for e-learning. Tom Floyd, in G. M. Piskurich (Ed.), *The AMA handbook of e-learning.* (2003).

Blending e-learning, Washington, DC: ASTD. Karen Mantyla. (2001).

Defining internet-based and web-based training. *Performance Improvement,* pp. 5–7. M. Driscoll. (1997, April).

Designing and managing computer mediated learning. OmniCom Associates. D. Gayeski. (1998).

Designing internet-based and intranet-based training. *Multimedia Training Newsletter.* G. Tansy. (1996, December).

Designing world-class e-learning. New York: McGraw-Hill. Roger Schank. (2002).

E-learning: Strategies for delivering knowledge in the digital age. New York: McGraw-Hill. M. Rosenberg. (2001).

E-learning: If we build it will they come? E-Learning Motivators and Acceptance Levels, ASTD/Masie Center. (2001, June).

Enhancing your readiness for self-directed learning: A workbook for the Learning Preference Assessment. King of Prussia, PA: HRDQ. L.M. Guglielmino & P. J. Guglielmino. (1991).

Evaluating e-learning. Alexandria, VA: ASTD. B. Horton. (2001).

Guidelines for designing web-based courses. *Solutions,* pp. 25–28. A. Barron. (2002, March/April).

Interacting with interactions. *Inside Technology Training,* pp. 40–41. J. Hartnett. (1999, July).

Michael Allen's guide to e-learning. Hoboken, NJ: Wiley. M. Allen. (2003).

Outside services for converting audio and video to the web. *Multimedia and Internet Training Newsletter,* p. 6. M. Palazzolo. (1997, February).

Preparing learners for e-learning. San Francisco: Pfeiffer. G. M. Piskurich (Ed.). (2003).

Selling e-learning. Washington, DC: ASTD. D. Hartley. (2001).

The AMA handbook of e-learning. New York: AMACOM. G. M. Piskurich (Ed.). (2003).

The e-learning question and answer book. New York: AMACOM. A. Henderson. (2003)

Using audio and video over the web. D. S. Metcalf, in G. M. Piskurich (Ed.), *The ASTD handbook of training design and delivery.* Alexandria, VA: ASTD. (1999).

Web-based training cookbook. New York: Wiley. B. Hall. (1998).

Web-based training: Using technology to design adult learning experiences. San Francisco: Pfeiffer. M. Driscoll. (1998).

Synchronous E-Learning

147 practical tips for teaching online groups. New York: Atwood. D. Hanna. (2003).

Distance learning. Alexandria, VA: ASTD. K. Mantyla & J. Gividen. (1997).

Getting the most from online learning: A learner's guide. San Francisco: Pfeiffer. G. M. Piskurich. (2004).

How to be a successful online student. New York: McGraw-Hill. S. Gilbert. (2000).

How to build an e-learning community. *E-learning, 2,* pp. 18–23. R. Blount. (2002).

Interactive distance learning activities that really work. Alexandria, VA: ASTD. K. Mantyla. (1998).

Lessons from the cyberspace classroom. San Francisco: Jossey-Bass. R. Palloff & K. Pratt. (2001).

Live and online! Tips, techniques, and ready-to-use activities for the virtual classroom. San Francisco: Pfeiffer. J. Hofmann. (2004).

Preparing students for the task of online learning. *Syllabus,* 38–42. J. E. Reid Jr. (1997, March).

Sustaining distance training. San Francisco CA: Jossey-Bass. Z. Berge. (2001).

Synchronous distance learning: The interactive internet classroom. *CBT Solutions,* pp. 25–28. J. Stewart. (1999, May).

The synchronous trainer's survival guide. InSync Training Synergy, LLC. J. Hofmann. (2001).

Getting the most from online learning. San Francisco: Pfeiffer. G. M. Piskurich (Ed.). (2004).

Other TBT

A new dimension in CBT. *Inside Technology Training, 2*(9), pp. 14–16. J. Bell. (1998, October).

ASTD models for learning technologies. Alexandria, VA: ASTD. G. M. Piskurich & E. Sanders. (1998).

Lessons from the virtual world. *Training, 32*(6), 45–48. N. Adams. (1999).

Training via videoconferencing. *Training & Development,* pp. 15–17. T. Poppell. (1998, July).

Video conferencing: "You ought to be in pictures." *Inside Technology Training.* G. Keizer. (1999, July/August).

Virtual reality: Is it for you? C. G. Mohr, in G. M. Piskurich (Ed.), *The ASTD handbook of training design and delivery.* Alexandria, VA: ASTD. (1999).

Betas and Pilots

How to pilot web-based training. *Training & Development*, pp. 44–49. M. Driscoll. (1998, November).

Keeping your pilots on course. *Training & Development*, pp. 69–73. J. Chernick. (1992, April).

Reviewing to ensure quality and build skills. *Performance Improvement*, pp. 17–20. K. Lutchner. (1997, October).

Usability testing. *Multimedia and Internet Training Newsletter*, pp. 8–9. A. Hanssen. (1998, July).

Test Questions

A guide to criterion referenced test construction. Baltimore, MD: Johns Hopkins University Press. R. Berk. (1980).

Criterion-referenced test development. Reading, MA: Addison-Wesley. S. Shrock & W. Coscarelli. (1989).

Preparing criterion referenced tests for classroom instruction. New York: Macmillan. N. Gronlund.

Test construction for training evaluation. New York: Van Nostrand Reinhold. C. Denova. (1979).

Tests that work. San Francisco: Pfeiffer. O. Westgaard. (1999).

Using evaluations. Alexandria, VA: ASTD. L. Rae. (1986).

Evaluation of Trainee Learning

Comprehensive open skill test design. *Performance & Instruction*, pp. 16–28. J. Desmedt. (1991, November/December).

Evaluating job-related training. Englewood Cliffs, NJ: Prentice Hall. B. Deming. (1982).

How to measure performance. Thousand Oaks, CA: Sage. L. L. Morris. (1978).

Measuring attitudinal and behavioral change. *Info-Line*, 9110. Alexandria, VA: ASTD.

Measuring instructional intent. Belmont, CA: Ler Siegler & R. Mager. (1973).

Testing for learning outcomes. *Info-Line*, 907. Alexandria, VA: ASTD.

Transfer to the Job

Assuring that learning occurs and transfers to the job. *Performance & Instruction*, pp. 38–43. D. Brethower. (1992, July).

Evaluation techniques that work. *Training & Development*, pp. 52–55. H. Birnbrauer. (1987, July).

The basics: Training transfer. *Technical and Skills Training*, pp. 8–9. A. Reynolds. (1993, February/March).

Transfer of training. Reading, MA: Addison-Wesley. M. Broad. (1992).

Transfer of training: Making training stick. *Info-Line*, 9512. Alexandria, VA: ASTD.

CBA and ROI

Cost-benefit analysis techniques for training investments. *Technical and Skills Training,*
    pp. 18–21. W. Schmidt. (1997, April).

How to measure training results. New York: McGraw-Hill. J. Phillips. (2002).

In action: Implementing training scorecards. Alexandria, VA. ASTD. J. Phillips. (2003).

Measuring return on investment (vol. 1–3). Alexandria, VA: ASTD. J. Phillips (Ed.).
    (1993).

Measuring training's ROI: A case in point. S. B. Parry, in G. M. Piskurich (Ed.), *The
    ASTD handbook of training design and delivery.* Alexandria, VA: ASTD. (1999).

Return on investment in training and performance improvement programs. Houston,
    TX: Gulf. J. Phillips. (1993).

Evaluation (General)

Achieving results from training. San Francisco: Jossey-Bass. R. Brinkerhoff. (1999).

ASTD trainer's tool kit: Evaluation instruments. Alexandria, VA: ASTD.

Evaluating training effectiveness. *Training,* pp. 61–62. C. Eckenboy. (1983, July).

Evaluating training programs: The four levels (2nd ed.). San Francisco: Berrett-
    Koehler. D. Kirkpatrick. (1994).

Handbook of training evaluation and measurement methods. Houston, TX: Gulf.
    J. Phillips. (1983).

In your next class, try this alternative to happiness sheets. *Training,* pp. 77–78. J. B.
    Cornwell. (1978, May).

Why trainees should not evaluate trainers. *Training,* pp. 79–82. M. Broadwell. (1973,
    October).

Shortcuts

Can (and should) instructional design be automated? *Performance & Instruction,*
    27(10), pp. 1–5. D. Gayeski. (1988, November/December).

Development teams for creating technology-based training. J. J. Goldsmith, in G. M.
    Piskurich (Ed.), *The ASTD handbook of training design and delivery.* Alexandria,
    VA: ASTD. (1999).

Knowledge objects. *CBT Solutions,* pp. 1–11. D. Merrill. (1998, March/April).

Rapid instructional design. S. Thiagarajan, in G. M. Piskurich (Ed.), *The ASTD hand-
    book of training design and delivery.* Alexandria, VA: ASTD. (1999).

Rapid prototyping. *Educational Technology Research and Development, 38*(1),
    pp. 31–44. S. D. Tripp. (1990).

Reusable content objectives. *CBT Solutions,* pp. 26–39. A. Hathway. (1998, Janu-
    ary/February).

The ASTD handbook of training design and delivery. Alexandria, VA: ASTD. G. M.
    Piskurich (Ed.). (1999).

Training management systems: How to choose a system your company can live with.
    B. Hall. [www.brandon-hall.com]

Training management systems: The most important development in training since the internet. B. Hall, in G. M. Piskurich (Ed.), Unidentified training objects. *Inside Technology Training*, p. 42. (1999, January).

Using development "shells" for fast and creative multimedia development at American Airlines. *Journal of Instruction Delivery Systems*, 9(3), pp. 3–9. R. Blalock. (1995, February).

Other Resources

Instructional Design (General)

ADDIE Model: www.managersforum.com
ASTD: http://www.astd.org/
Don Clark (alias Big Dog): http://www.nwlink.com/~donclark/hrd.html
International Board of Standards for Training, Performance, and Instruction:
    http://www.ibstpi.org/
International Society for Performance Improvement (ISPI):
    http://www.ispi.org/
Lakewood's Training Supersite: http://www.trainingsupersite.com/
Research Papers: www.gsu.edu/~wwwitr/research.html
Self-Directed Learning: www.sdlglobal.com
The Training Registry: http://www.tregistry.com/
www.Learnativity.com

Activities

10 Ways to Break the Ice Checklist: http://www.susan-boyd.com/training.htm
Caroselli, Marlene: MCCPD@aol.com
Energizers by Training Oasis:
    http://www3.sympatico.ca/thetrainingoasis/mayspice.htm
    Thiagi's Home Page: http://www.thiagi.com/index.html
www.presentersuniversity.com
www.games2train.com

Analysis

Inquisite: www.inquisite.com
Learning Styles Inventory: http://www.howtolearn.com/
Survey Software: www.surveyconnect.com
www.alumnus.caltech.edu/~rouda/T2_NA.html
www.assessmentworks.com
www.bnhexpertsoft.com
Tools: www.mime1.marc.gatech.edu/MM_Tools/analysis.html

Assessment

Advisor 3.0 Computer-Based Assessment and ROI Tool by BNH Software:
www.bnhexpertsoft.com
American Productivity & Quality Center: http://www.apqc.org/
ASTD "Trainer's Toolkit" Needs Assessment Instruments, ASTD, Alexandria, Virginia

Asynchronous E-Learning

Asynchronous Networks: www.aln.org/index.htm
http://www.vnulearning.com/.
David Strom's Web Informant: www.strom.com/pubwork/intra2.html
Distance Learning: http://sunil.umd.edu/dl
Online Training Publication: Learning Without Limits (415) 626-7343
Multimedia and Internet Training Newsletter, Brandon Hall, publisher
(highly recommended!): brandon@brandonhall.com
The Complete Intranet Resource: http://www.intrack.com/intranet/
The Masie Center: www.masie.com
The Web-Based Training Center: http://www.webbasedtraining.com/
www.multimediatraining.com/training.html

CBA and ROI

www.astd.org

CBT and Multimedia

Computer Training Network: http://www.thectn.com/
http://www.allencomm.com
http://www.macromedia.com
http://www.mime1.marc.gatech.edu/MM_Tools/
Kluner Publishers: www.wkap.nl/journalhome.htm/1380–7501
Tom Reeves: http://mime1.marc.gatech.edu/mm_tools/

www.learnativity.con/roi-learning.html
www.school-for-champions.com/training/roi.htm

Evaluation (General)

American Evaluation Association: www.eval.org
LISTSERV list: http://bama.ua.edu/archives/evaltalk.html
LISTSERV list: http://evaluation.wmich.edu/archives
Federal government: www.gao.gov/policy/10 1 4.htm
www.karinrex.com/tc_evals.html

Job Aids and Performance Support Systems

San Diego State University Job Aids:
    http://edweb.sdsu.edu/courses/edtec540/540www/home.html
www2.gsu.edu/~wwwitr/docs/nextgen

Media (Nontechnical)

Comstock: www.comstock.com
Eyewire: www.eyewire.com
PhotoDisc: www.photodisc.com

Pictures and PowerPoint Presentations

http://www.kodak.com/US/en/digital/dlc/book1/chapter7/index.shtml
www.presentersuniversity.com

Objectives

Bloom's Taxonomy: http://mailer.fsu.edu/~jflake/bloom.html
www.adprima.com/objectives.htm
www.web.uct.ac.za/projects/cbe/mcgman/mcqappc.html

Performance Analysis

www.ispi.org
www.partnersinchange.com
www.clarktrainingcomwww.hsa-lps.com

Synchronous E-Learning

American Center for the Study of Distance Learning: http://www.cde.psu.
    edu/acsde
Distance Learning Software: http://ilinc.com

Distance Learning: The Virtual University Gazette: www.geteducated.com/
    vugaz.htm
Online Meeting Center: www.webex.COM
The Distance Education Clearninghouse: www.uwex.edu/disted
USDLA: www.usdla.org
www.distance-educator.com

TBT (Other)

MIT's Research Laboratory of Electronics: http://pellicle.mit.edu/
    VELbIndx.html. This website lists people and projects on the cutting
    edge of research into virtual environments, primarily for training
    applications and haptics (that is, manual sensing and manipulation
    of virtual objects, sensorimotor adaptation, multimodal interactions
    involving visual, auditory, and haptic inputs, and the effects of
    sensorimotor involvement in learning cognitive tasks).
Technical Encyclopedia Online: http://www.webopedia.com
United States Distance Learning Association: http://www.usdla.org
Video conferencing: www.imcca.org

Test Questions

www.thelearningmanager.com/pubdownloads/developing_clear_learning_
    outcomes_and_objectives

Training Settings

Advisor 3.0 (helps analyze training settings): www.bnhexpertsoft.com
Paper on comparison of classroom to CBT to web deliveries:
    www.comet.ucar.edu/presentations/ams96/index.htm

Developing Content

www.infomap.com

About the Author

George M. Piskurich, Ph.D., is an independent consultant based in Macon, Georgia. He provides consulting services and workshops in instructional design, performance improvement, and e-learning to clients throughout the United States. He specializes in performance and training analysis, the design and development of self-directed and individualized learning programs for all levels of the organization, e-learning interventions, multiple-site training systems, telecommuting interventions, and knowledge centers.

Dr. Piskurich has been a presenter and workshop leader at over thirty conferences and symposia, including the International Self-Directed Learning Symposium, the Best of America Conference, and the International Society for Performance Improvement (ISPI) and American Society for Training & Development (ASTD) international conferences. He is an active member of both ISPI and ASTD, where he has held local and national leadership positions. In 1986 he was ASTD's "Instructional Technologist of the Year." He also won the "Best Use of Instructional Technology in Business" award in 1992 for his distributed SDL technical skills training design.

He has edited books on instructional technology, e-learning, human performance technology, and program development; written books on self-directed learning, instructional design, training basics, and telecommuting; and authored many journal articles and book chapters on various topics, including customer service, structured mentoring, and corporate downsizing.

He can be reached at Gpiskurich@cs.com or through his website Gpiskurich.com.

427

Instructor Guide for *Rapid Instructional Design*

*T*he purpose of this guide is to give instructors using *Rapid Instructional Design* as the text for an instructional design course some ideas for activities and exercises that they could use in conjunction with the book.

Because the book follows the basic flow of most instructional design from analysis through evaluation, its text through Chapter Seven should pretty much follow the flow of any basic instructional design class. The activities therefore can build on each other as the class progresses. In the past I've found it works well to have the learners begin with a training needs assessment, even if it is done for a fictitious company, and then, using that as a foundation, follow the process through to the actual creation of a program and its accompanying evaluation measures.

However, I've found that it also works to simply provide the learners with various scenarios that have been created to deal with each step in the design process and have them work each step individually.

Each chapter of the book begins with its own goals, but for a class I would recommend passing out a compilation of objectives based on the goals and combined with any others the instructor feels are needed for a particular class. This will help the learner see the general flow of the class and how the book relates to it. I've included such a list (see Possible Class Objectives); I've also included an outline of what a course based on the book might look like (see Instructional Design Class Outline).

The rest of this instructor guide is divided up according to the chapters in the book, with exhibits, activities, and notes for each chapter. Most of the exhibits and many of the pieces that form the basis of the activities are found in the book as well, thus providing the instructor with some context for them.

As always, if you have any questions or comments on this guide, please feel free to contact me via e-mail (gpiskurich@cs.com) or phone (478-405-8977).

Possible Class Objectives

- Explain the concept of instructional design.
- Discuss the advantages and disadvantages of systematic instructional design.
- State the purpose of analysis.
- Define various types of analysis.
- Describe the process and products of a learning needs analysis.
- Perform a job and task analysis.
- Describe the key parts of a properly written objective.
- Differentiate between knowledge and performance objectives.
- Construct useful behavior-based learner objectives.
- Effectively use the Wachovia Blueprint document to design a course.
- Create a basic instructional plan.
- Explain the concept of criterion-referenced testing.
- Create proper test questions for both knowledge and performance objectives.
- Prepare a well-organized and complete lesson plan.
- Discuss useful techniques for developing participant manuals.
- Choose instructional media that enhance learning.
- Discuss proper methods for performing instructional reviews, beta tests, and pilots.
- Compare the main characteristics of classroom and self-instructional implementations.
- Define Kirkpatrick's four levels of evaluation.
- Discuss the creation of Level 1 and Level 2 evaluation instruments.
- Compare the basic differences between classroom design and technology-based design.

Instructional Design Class Outline

Program Objective: At the end of this program the participants will be able to use effective instructional design techniques to effectively create effective instructional designs

I. Pre-work: Bring to class a training need you are working on, will need to work on, or are just interested in, and any supporting materials you would like to enhance that deal with that need (materials are not necessary if you don't have them).

II. Introduction

    A. Introductions

        1. Facilitator

        2. Class

    B. Overview

        1. Schedule

        2. Participation

            a. Facilitator's training need

            b. Your training need

        3. Mechanics

        4. Book

    C. Class objectives

    D. Your objectives ("At the end of this program I would like to be able to . . .")

III. What is instructional design?

    A. Why do we do it?

    B. Why do we not do it?

    C. Three models

    D. Training versus education

    E. Adult learning

        1. Pedagogy versus andragogy

IV. Analysis

    A. What is analysis?

    B. Common types of analysis

        1. Performance analysis

        2. Training needs analysis

        3. Job and task analysis

            a. Criticality analysis

V. Collecting analysis data

    A. Focus groups

    B. Observation

    C. Interviews

VI. Design

    A. More analyses

        1. Audience analysis

        2. Delivery analysis

    B. Objectives
        1. Mager
        2. Three, four, or five parts to a good objective
        3. Practice
        4. Levels and levels
        5. What to do with objectives
    C. Design documents
        1. Uses of a design document
        2. Parts of a design document
    D. Instructional plan (IP)
        1. Instructional plans versus lesson plans versus scripts
        2. Parts of the IP
    E. Trainee evaluation
        1. Why here?
        2. Criterion referencing
        3. Types of questions and how you know
        4. Creating questions
        5. Question banks
VII. Development
    A. Lesson plan versus facilitator guides
        1. Formats
        2. Parts
    B. Participant's manual
    C. Instructional media
    D. Storyboards
    E. Beta tests and pilots
    E. Reviews
VIII. Implementation
    A. Delivery analysis again
    B. Classroom
    C. Self-instruction
    D. Train the trainer, train the trainee, train the company
IX. Evaluation
    A. Why evaluate?
    B. What to evaluate
    C. How
        1. The four (or five) levels
    D. Who and when
X. Revisions
    A. As needed
    B. Planned

XI. Designing for technology
    A. Asynchronous e-learning
    B. Synchronous e-learning
XII. Summary

CHAPTER ONE

A good icebreaker to introduce learners to the concept of instructional design is to ask them to complete this sentence: "Instructional design is . . ." Compare answers in a group discussion, looking for concepts that are common and key to the process.

A role play can be used when discussing the advantages and disadvantages of ID by having two groups of learners present to the class, which plays the role of a management team, why the company should and should not spend the time and resources to develop a proper ID process for the organization.

Activity: Why We Use ID

This little activity is simply to help summarize the reasons why we do ID. If your learners are not in organizations currently perhaps you can ask them to complete it for a community group they belong to or even for the college they are attending.

Yes	No	I know who my trainees are and what their specific needs are.
Yes	No	I know all the content that the trainees require from my programs.
Yes	No	My trainees always know what is expected of them.
Yes	No	The materials I create are exactly what the content and trainees require.
Yes	No	I always know and use the most effective approach when delivering the required training.
Yes	No	I know whether my trainees learned what they needed to learn.
Yes	No	I know whether my training is being used back on the job.
Yes	No	I always create the most cost-effective training.
Yes	No	The training I create is always the most time effective for me and the trainees.
Yes	No	My training is meeting the needs of my organization.

CHAPTER TWO

ACTIVITY: FORMS OF ANALYSIS

You can start the class out on the road to understanding analysis and save some class time by assigning each form of analysis to a small group and having them report back on the following questions, or something similar:

- What is analyzed?
- What are the best ways to perform this analysis?
- Who needs to be talked to as part of the analysis?
- What needs to be collected as part of the analysis?
- When do you do this analysis?
- What is the product (outcome of the analysis)?

Activity: Root Cause Analysis (RCA)

There are a number of different ways to do root cause analysis. As an activity, assign a different technique to various small groups and ask them to do an RCA on a performance gap that you supply. Have each group report their findings back to the class in a PowerPoint presentation and compare them.

Activity: Nontraining Performance Interventions

As a research activity, have each learner or small groups find a situation in which a performance analysis led to a nontraining intervention and bring it into the class for discussion. Point them in the direction of the Web—particularly the International Society for Performance Improvement (ISPI) website (www.ispi.org)—and the many books and articles that have been written on this process, then let them have at it.

Activity: Fast Performance Analysis

Ask the learners to use the fast performance analysis methodology, using the questions that follow, to do an analysis of a performance problem that they choose from their own lives. This could be at work, with a volunteer organization, or even at home (say, the kids won't pick up their clothes). Have them exchange and critique each other's analysis. It will be hard to get to the final step, but if anyone can, have them report back in later on if the change occurred.

- What is it now?
- Why is it a problem?

- Do we want to fix what is or create something new?

- Either way, what change in performance are we looking for, and from whom or what?

- Did we get the change we were looking for?

Needs Assessment Questions

If your learners are out in the work place, you might ask them to take these questions and interview both a manager and an employee, then come back to the class with their answers for discussion.

Training Needs Assessment Questions for Management

1. Describe the most important business opportunity currently facing your work group.

2. Explain the roadblocks that are keeping you from taking advantage of that opportunity.

3. Describe the most critical business problem currently facing your work group and the roadblocks that may keep you from solving it.

4. In what areas within your work group does there seem to be a gap between expected performance and actual performance?

   Why do you think this is so?

5. Does your work group have any current or anticipated time-critical training needs that you will require assistance in meeting?

6. What training delivery technologies are available for your work group?

7. What is the current training budget for your work group?

8. What training resources do you employ?

   Staff

   Vendors

   Facilities

9. Do you feel the individual contributors in your work group will be capable of and comfortable using computers for their training? Why or why not?

10. What do you consider to be the most important general characteristics of the individual contributors in your work group in relation to training?

    Do they like to attend training? Dislike it?

    Like to learn on their own?

Feel training is important? A necessary evil?

Learn new things slowly? Quickly?

Think that if they don't already know it, they probably don't need it?

11. How do you currently design and deliver training in your work group?

Are you satisfied with this approach? If not, why not?

Training Needs Assessment Questions
for Individual Contributors

- What do you think about the existing training programs?
- How well did the training you received prepare you for the job?
- How could we improve existing training?
- In what way do you like to be trained?
    - Classroom
    - On the job
    - Videotapes
    - Self-instruction
    - Computer instruction
    - Job aids
    - Team training
    - Observing others
    - Working with a mentor
- What are the most common problems you have when doing your job?
- What about your job changes often?
- What about your job always stays the same?
- What do you need to know to excel at your job?
- Who do you think excels at your job now? Why?
- What do you need to have to be more productive?
- When new employees begin working with you, what knowledge or skills do you often find they are missing?

Subject-Matter Expert Selection Form

Name of candidate: _____

Date: _____

Position or title: _____

1. Years of experience in field: _____

2. Years of experience in current position: _____

3. Years of experience with company: _____

4. What do you think makes you an expert in your field?

5. What path did you follow to become an expert?

6. When you find that you do not understand something, where do you go for an answer?

7. What common mistakes do new people make at your job?

8. Could training help them? If so, how?

9. What do you like and dislike about training?

10. What would you change in our current training programs?

11. What advice would you give to someone starting out in your field?

SME Analysis (completed by assessor after reviewing data):

1. Experience	1	2	3	4	5
2. Knowledge of job	1	2	3	4	5
3. Attitude toward helping people	1	2	3	4	5
4. Commitment to training	1	2	3	4	5
5. Assessor's comfort in working with	1	2	3	4	5

Outline Template for an Analysis Report

    I. Overview
        A. General comments
        B. Strategic importance of what was analyzed
        C. Purpose and goals of analysis
    II. Data Collection
        A. Methods employed
        B. Constraints (decisions made on what to do and what not to do)
        C. Instruments used
    III. Sources of Data
        A. Human sources (internal and external)
        B. Data sources (reports, procedures, and the like)
        C. Customer sources
    IV. Conclusions
        A. Performance standards
        B. Performance deficiencies
        C. Causes of deficiencies
        D. Consequences of deficiencies
    V. Recommendations
        A. Training recommendations
          • Goals
          • Target audience
          • Description
          • Benefits
          • Anticipated problems
        B. Nontraining recommendations
          • Rationale
          • Description
          • Audience
          • Benefits
          • Anticipated problems
        C. Other recommendations and commentary

Activity: Cost-Benefit Analysis (CBA)

You can bring CBA into focus here by presenting the learners with a series of scenarios such as those in the book and asking them to perform a CBA. Try to make the scenarios more complicated than the simple ones in the book, and create ones that show both a positive and a negative outcome, then ask why.

....
CHAPTER THREE

ACTIVITY: DATA COLLECTION

To illuminate the differences among the various data collection methods, break the learners into groups and have each group use one of the methods to collect data on the same thing. This might be something related to training or a job and task analysis, or something not related at all, such as marketing for a product or people's opinions of a politician.

Activity: Job and Task Analysis (JTA)

Have the learners use the job and task analysis forms provided, or any other form for this purpose that you wish them to use to perform a job, criticality, and task analysis on a training need that you establish. Make your need relatively simple, such as "Create, print, and file a letter using Microsoft Word for Windows" or any other need that they have the content expertise to analyze and that is small enough for them to logically do.

This activity works best if you allow the learners to critique each other's work at the end of each analysis so they can see how others' thinking processes in the analysis differ from theirs.

If you are going to use this activity as a basis for other activities, be sure to supply the learners with a model JTA at the end of the activity that they can use for this purpose.

Job Analysis Form

Training Need: _____

Job: _____ Date: _____

Date: The date when this form is completed.

Task	Subtasks	Frequency 4 3 2 1	Importance 4 3 2 1	Learning 4 3 2 1	Risk 4 3 2 1

Tasks: The list of tasks is a breakdown of the broad activities to be performed on the job. The task statements should include a concise description of what the employee will do on the job. Begin with an action verb.
Use a noun following the action verb.
Avoid overlap with other tasks.

Subtasks: Any part of a task not at the level of KSA (knowledge, skills, attitude).

Frequency: How frequently is the individual task performed on the job? Each task should be rated as daily, weekly, once a month or less than once a month.
4 = daily
3 = weekly
2 = once a month
1 = less than once a month

Importance: How important is the individual task to overall job effectiveness? Each task should be rated as critical, moderately critical, not critical, or could be omitted.
4 = critical
3 = moderately critical
2 = not critical
1 = could be omitted

Learning: How difficult is the task to learn? Each task should be rated as very difficult, moderately difficult, somewhat difficult, or not difficult.
4 = very difficult
3 = moderately difficult
2 = somewhat difficult
1 = not difficult

Risk: What is the degree of risk associated with performing the task incorrectly? For instance, could the employee be injured or would the mistake cost the company a lot of money? Each task should be rated as high risk, moderate risk, minimal risk, or no risk.
4 = high risk
3 = moderate risk
2 = minimal risk
1 = no risk

Action Verbs

Action verbs are used to describe job tasks and steps. The table presents a list of some action verbs you might use when recording tasks. This list is not all-inclusive. Use the verb that best describes the actual work (performance) on the job. (See more detailed directions following the form.)

If the person's job or task includes the following actions . . .	*. . . then these action verbs are appropriate*
• Appraise conclusions • Compare and contrast • Critique materials • Judge the logical consistency of written material or ideas • Judge the adequacy with which conclusions are supported by data • Judge the value of a work, using internal criteria • Judge the value of a work, using external standards of excellence	Argue Assess Attach Choose Criticize Defend Estimate Evaluate Justify Predict Rate Score Select Support Value
• Assemble parts • Compose or compile a report • Create a new process • Design a new machine • Integrate learning from different areas into a plan for solving problems • Propose a plan for an experiment • Write a computer program or creative story	Arrange Assemble Collect Combine Construct Devise Formulate Generate Manage Modify Organize Plan Prepare Propose Rearrange Reconstruct Set up

If the person's job or task includes the following actions . . .	*. . . then these action verbs are appropriate*
• Assess the relevance of data • Break down a whole into parts • Diagram a workflow • Differentiate functions • Distinguish between facts and inferences • Illustrate relationships • Recognize unstated assumptions • Recognize logical fallacies in reasoning	Analyze Appraise Calculate Categorize Compare Contrast Criticize Discriminate Examine Experiment Question Separate Subdivide Test
• Apply concepts and principles to new situations • Apply laws and theories to practical situations • Compute or solve equations • Demonstrate correct usage of a method, process or procedure • Manipulate objects • Modify a process • Operate equipment • Use in a new situation	Change Choose Construct Dramatize Employ Illustrate Interpret Practice Prepare Produce Relate Schedule Show Sketch Solve Use
• Convert numbers • Estimate future consequences implied in data • Estimate outcomes • Explain concepts, facts and principles • Interpret verbal material • Interpret charts and graphs • Summarize information • Translate verbal material to mathematical formulas	Classify Describe Discuss Distinguish Explain Express Generalize Give examples

If the person's job or task includes the following actions . . .	*. . . then these action verbs are appropriate*
• Translate languages	Identify Indicate Infer Locate Paraphrase Predict Recognize Report Restate Review Rewrite Select Translate
• Define basic terms or concepts • Describe basic processes • Identify methods and procedures • Label parts • List or name key components • Recall specific facts • State principles • Select items from a list	Arrange Duplicate Match Memorize Name Order Recognize Relate Repeat Reproduce State

Task Analysis Form

Task or Subtask: _____

Date: _____

Element	Description
Inputs	
Steps	
Tools	
Standards	
Circumstances	
Outputs	
KSAs	

Inputs: What events, cues, orders, materials, or symptoms indicate that the task must be performed? In other words, what does the employee need to get or receive before he or she can begin subtasks?

Steps: Each task might be broken down into its component steps (processes). The task statements should include a concise description of what the employee will do on the job.
Begin with an action verb.
Use a noun following the action verb.
Refer to the action verb table as needed (see separate sheet).

Tools: What tools, references, equipment, or materials are used to complete the subtasks? Where appropriate, system software (screens and application functions) should be identified.

Standards: How well must the task be performed? Standards such as accuracy, time, quantity, cost, error rate, customer satisfaction.

Circumstances: What circumstances influence task performance? For example, what physical locations, situations, adverse conditions, assistance, level of supervision, obstacles, or barriers exist when the task is being performed?

Outputs: What events, cues, orders, materials, or symptoms indicate that the task has been completed? What has been produced? What is passed on to another group or customer?

Feedback: What feedback does the employee receive when performing the task or after delivering the outputs? Feedback can be informal or formal.

KSAs: The *knowledge, skills,* and *attitudes* that make up this task or subtasks as related to the other information found on this form. These elements are used to write your objectives.

Activity: Learning Analysis

After the learners have completed the JTA and you have discussed the process of learning analysis, ask them to do a learning analysis on the same training need. Compare the products of the two analysis formats and discuss the strengths and weaknesses of each.

Activity: Audience Analysis

Ask the learners to use the information contained in the book, including the various characteristics and the Task Analysis Form template to create their own audience analysis form, then have them use the form to do an audience analysis for a real or simulated training program. Have them create a report, using the data they have gathered and the Audience Analysis Report template, and make copies of it to distribute to all their colleagues for consideration. Discuss the problems they found in taking the data and translating it into a report.

Audience Analysis Report Template

1. How many participants will attend? _____ In each session? _____

2. What are the job responsibilities and functions of the participants?

   _____

   _____

   _____

3. How well do the participants know each other?

   _____

   _____

   _____

4. Are there specific or special potential diversity issues to be aware of within the group?

_____

_____

_____

5. Are there key individuals within the group? (Explain.)

_____

_____

_____

6. Is the training voluntary or mandatory? What have the participants been told?

_____

_____

_____

7. What are the attitudes and beliefs of the participants, sponsor, and managers toward the training topic?

_____

_____

_____

8. What successes and difficulties have the participants encountered with the training topic?

_____

_____

_____

9. What is the skill level of the participants in the training subject matter?

_____

_____

_____

10. What are the barriers the participant might encounter in applying the training back on the job?

_____

_____

_____

11. Have the participants taken other in-house classes?

_____

_____

_____

12. Levels of evaluation to be used: ☐ 1   ☐ 2   ☐ 3

Audience Analysis Report

Number of trainees eligible for this program

Trainee location(s)

Organizational level(s)

Minimum, maximum, and average level of education

Minimum, maximum, and average number of years in position

Minimum, maximum, and average number of years with company

Expected entry-level knowledge and skill background

Previous training related to this training

Average reading level

Language or cultural differences among trainees

Trainee motivation and job satisfaction

Attitude toward training

Special physical characteristics of trainees relevant to training

Special interests of trainees relevant to training

Specific biases of trainees relevant to training

Computer skills and confidence (if applicable)

Activity: Audience Analysis

Your learners should have realized by now that if they had done an audience analysis as they were working on the JTA for the training need you prepared for them, it would have made things easier. Using yourself as the trainee or manager, ask them to do an audience analysis for that need now.

CHAPTER FOUR

DELIVERY CHECKLISTS

Use this checklist to help decide which of the major delivery systems might work best for your training need.

Classroom Training

Use classroom-based training when
- Interaction with the trainer or other participants is important
- Guided discussion will lead to more learning
- Questions will come up that need immediate answers
- You have qualified facilitators in the right numbers to match the training load
- The trainees can afford to be away from their jobs for long periods of time
- You need to have the facilitators do the traveling instead of the trainees
- Individualization is not critical
- You want more control over the training outcome

On-the-Job Training (OJT)

Use OJT when
- Skills need to be mastered in the actual environment
- Training time is limited
- Design time is limited
- Nonmoveable equipment is involved
- Trainee motivation is poor
- The tasks to be learned change frequently
- Qualified classroom trainers are not available
- Work flow needs to be learned as part of the training
- A lot of monitored practice is necessary
- The number of trainees is small

Self-Instruction

Use self-instruction when
- There are a number of highly distributed training sites
- You have a shortage of qualified classroom or OJT trainers
- Turnover is high
- Training must be delivered "just in time"
- Training must be consistent
- The content is relatively stable
- The content is known only by one or a few SMEs

- The training needs to be repeated often
- You want to decrease travel costs
- The training must be done on multiple shifts
- You have the time to develop the programs properly

Technology-Based Training (TBT)

Use TBT when
- Self-instruction is needed (see self-instruction checklist)
- Complex simulations are needed
- The content requires a lot of practice that can be simulated
- The trainees are comfortable or can be made to feel comfortable using computers
- Training is difficult to schedule or classes are hard to fill
- There is plenty of development time and money available
- The hardware is in place or can be bought
- Tracking of the training is critical and time intensive, because of a large number of trainees
- Management is comfortable with TBT or can be sold on the concept
- Updates to the program will be minimal
- The use of multiple media formats will enhance the learning

E-Learning (Instructor-Led or Self-Instructional)

Use e-learning when your environment requires a distributed delivery and
- You need TBT (see TBT checklist) but revisions to content are frequent
- Video is not a critical element in the training
- Live interaction with an instructor is important
- Other content is already available that can be easily linked to
- Content is more soft skill–oriented (instructor-led)
- Heavy feedback (immediate or time sensitive) is required
- Trainees are comfortable with net technology
- Your internal systems can support the usage
- Time and budget are available to produce and implement the training
- You have a large number of training programs that need to be delivered and redelivered at various times

Job Performance Aids

Consider creating job performance aids in lieu of training when
- The tasks are performed infrequently
- It is critical that the tasks be performed exactly
- The tasks are very complex

- Sequencing of the tasks is critical
- Turnover is high
- Training cannot be done in a timely manner
- The consequence of performing the tasks incorrectly is severe
- Tasks change frequently
- The body of knowledge is great
- Practice and feedback are not critical

Activity: Delivery Analysis

Create a series of training scenarios in which only one delivery system stands out as the best approach, and have the learners use delivery analysis to determine the most effective delivery system.

Activity: Blended Delivery Systems

Now create a series of training scenarios in which various blends are the best approach. Give the learners the same instructions as for the previous activity at first, to see if they can recognize the need for a blend. After going over the first example, have them reanalyze for blended solutions. This is the list of behavioral verbs from Chapter Four. It makes an excellent job aid. You may want to make copies of it and pass it out to your learners.

Behavioral Verbs

Knowledge		Comprehension		Application	Analysis	Synthesis	Evaluation
Count	Recall	Associate	Interpret	Apply	Order	Arrange	Appraise
Define	Recite	Compare	Interpolate	Calculate	Group	Combine	Assess
Draw	Read	Compute	Predict	Classify	Translate	Construct	Critique
Identify	Record	Contrast	Translate	Complete	Transform	Create	Determine
Indicate	Repeat	Describe		Demonstrate	Analyze	Design	Evaluate
List	State	Differentiate		Employ	Detect	Develop	Grade
Name	Tabulate	Discuss		Examine	Explain	Formulate	Judge
Point	Trace	Distinguish		Illustrate	Infer	Generalize	Measure
Quote	Write	Estimate		Practice	Separate	Integrate	Rank
Recognize		Extrapolate		Relate	Summarize	Organize	Rate
				Solve	Construct	Plan	Select
				Use		Prepare	Test
				Utilize		Prescribe	Recommend
						Produce	
						Propose	
						Specify	

Activity: Analyzing Objectives

Have the learners analyze the poorly written objectives that follow, to see if they can determine if they are well written and if so, why. Then have them do the same with the well-written objectives.

On the Dim Side . . .

1. Change a light bulb within one minute.
2. Without the use of notes or reference materials, write a two-hundred-word essay on "Why I Hate Emergency Planning."
3. Run the hundred-yard dash (or make a pizza or change a tire).
4. Perform and document a general area radiation survey.
5. Be familiar with safety precautions related to a 16-gauge shotgun.

On The Bright Side . . .

1. Given a ladder of sufficient height and a new light bulb, replace a burned-out ceiling bulb of the same size within one minute and without breaking your neck.
2. Without the use of notes or reference materials, write a two-hundred-word essay on "Why I Like Emergency Planning." Essays must be written in five minutes or less, and must contain no more than two grammatical or spelling errors.
3. Run the hundred-yard dash on a dry track within twenty seconds.
4. In the plant or lab containing radiation check source, perform and document a general area radiation survey in accordance with PNPP procedures and determine any posting requirements.
5. State all of the safety precautions that must be followed when loading a Remington 16-gauge shotgun on an indoor range.

Activity: Critiquing Objectives

Here are two more sets of objectives for the learners to critique. I've left directions for the second group blank to allow you to provide your own, based on how well the learners are doing with this task. These are basically all good objectives under the most basic of writing rules, but by having the learners argue about them they will learn more. In the first group, 1, 5, and 8 are usually determined as good by the majority of learners (though there might be some argument there as well). The rest are usually determined as poor and in need of help by the learners, and you should argue both sides if they don't.

Sample Objectives

Place a checkmark in the box of those objectives that are well written. Rewrite the ones that you feel are lacking.

☐ 1. Write, word for word, the definition of the term *criterion-referenced testing*.

☐ 2. Given a purchase order and the required information for the purchase of a specific item, you will know how to complete the purchase order.

☐ 3. Type a business letter, using the format on page 33 of the Administrative Manual, containing no more than three errors within ten minutes.

☐ 4. Given a forty-minute lecture on the operation of the reactor coolant pump, understanding its operating principles.

☐ 5. The trainee will write from memory the six principles of operating a charging pump as described in Tech Manual pp. 39–85.

☐ 6. When provided with a multimeter and five DC circuits, measure the resistance of each circuit.

☐ 7. Analyze a water sample for pH in accordance with procedure 1-987.

☐ 8. Given a globe valve, rags, Prussian blue, gasket material, packing, and tools, the trainee will be able to disassemble and reassemble a globe valve.

More Objectives

The trainees will be able to . . .

☐ Use their knowledge of the techniques and theory of good management communications to implement an action plan for communicating effectively with fellow employees at all levels of the organization

☐ List the four basic tasks of a router

☐ Differentiate between flat rate and usage lines

☐ Formulate a personal plan for applying the common-knowledge aspects of real estate processes to the practices of their program area

☐ Employ electronic information systems for learning about and dealing with real estate issues

☐ Correctly perform the steps necessary to troubleshoot a failing circuit board so that it passes a Level II inspection

☐ Given a reference manual and template, cut and paste a sentence from one document to another

☐ List the notes of a DC-3 multiswitch without referring to the reference manual

☐ Using the provided job aid properly, send a fax on the FAXator AM-1 machine

☐ Demonstrate interest in staff by talking with them about non-job-related topics

Activity: Creating and Critiquing Objectives

Using the training need and the JTA that they've worked on previously, ask the learners to create well-written objectives for the program. When finished, have them break into pairs and critique each other's objectives.

Another activity here is to have them take their best objective after the critiquing and write it on a transparency, then project the objective for critiquing and discussion by the entire class.

If your learners are out in the business world, you might have them create some objectives for a program they use on the job, then put it through the same critiquing and projection process.

Design Document Template

You may want to have your learners use one or more of these templates to create their own design documents, or have them discuss which template is best in their situation and why.

1. Scope of Project (Focus)

   Goal

   Audience

   Design time and milestones

2. Delivery

   Content

   Method

   Training time

   Problems and opportunities

3. Objectives

4. Materials

5. Who is involved?

6. Topical Outline

7. Administration and Evaluation

8. Links

Simple Design Document Template

1. We need this course because . . .
2. The participants will be . . .
3. The course content will be . . .
4. The course will cost _____ to design and _____ to deliver.
5. Design and implementation staff will include . . .
6. The course will be delivered . . .

Complex Design Document Template

Requesting department:

Requesting supervisor or manager:

Job:

Analyst:

Course title:

Participants:

Identified skills to be taught:

Identified concepts to be taught:

Objectives:

Course description:

Techniques to be used:

☐ Lecture	☐ Discussion	☐ Q and A
☐ Hands-on	☐ Demonstration	☐ Video
☐ CBT	☐ Role Plays	☐ Pre-Work
☐ WBT	☐ Self-Instruction	☐ Games
☐ Other:		

Follow-up activities:

Other departments that might benefit:

Location for training:

Trainers:

Course duration:

Proposed dates:

Number of employees per class:

Development costs:

Delivery costs:

Cost per trainee:

Travel costs:

Cost responsibilities:

Evaluation plan:

Activity: Topic and Expanded Outlines

Using the objectives the learners developed for your training need, now have them create both a topic and an expanded outline for the training program. Ask them to exchange the topic outline and then the expanded version with a partner to discuss differences. Then hold a class discussion concerning the difficulties they found with this process and how these might be overcome. You'll want to provide them with an "official" set of outlines if you are going to carry this threaded activity further.

Course Description Template

   I. Course title

  II. Designer

 III. Scope

  IV. Audience

   V. Training time

  VI. Delivery method

(Up to this point, this model is a lot like our design document, but things change with the next item, as the course description gets into a lot more detail.)

  VII. The task(s) that will be trained on

 VIII. The objectives related to each task

   IX. An overview of how the content of the course fits into the job structure
      A. Where the task is done
      B. Who does it
      C. Why the task is important
      D. Problems associated with poor performance

    X. Prerequisite knowledge necessary before beginning the course

   XI. Lesson overview
      A. Subtasks
      B. Exercises
      C. Practices

XII. Instructional materials

XIII. Visuals or other media

XIV. Reviews

XV. Testing

XVI. Performance monitoring

Activity: Critiquing Test Questions

The ability to create criterion-based test questions is critical to good instructional design. The book presents an activity in which the learner is given questions and objectives and asked to determine if they are criterion referenced. You might want to go over this activity and discuss with the learners the whys and why nots.

You might also want to create another activity just like this from your own objectives and test questions to give the learners even more practice.

Activity: Fairness of Test Questions

The book also presents an activity to determine whether test questions are fairly written based on the criteria given there. Again, you might want to go over this activity with the learners and even supply your own good and bad questions in another series to provide more practice.

Activity: Writing Test Questions

The learners can take the objectives they have written and create criterion-based test questions for them. As with the objectives, have the learners critique each other's questions (for both criterion referencing and fairness) and possibly have them project their best one for class critique and comment.

CHAPTER FIVE

ACTIVITY: LESSON PLANS

Have the learners take their expanded outlines from the common training need that you have had them working through and put them into a lesson plan format. You might allow them to pick the format based on their own needs or the needs of their organization, or you might give them a standard format to use so they can more easily compare what they did. Have them share each other's lesson plans in pairs or groups.

Activity: Parts of the Lesson Plan

Break the class into groups and ask each group to take one part of the lesson plan (pre-activities, introduction, post-activities, and so on) and report back to the group on what it is and how it is used, giving three to five examples of the concept.

Activity: Lesson Plan Job Aid

Ask the learners to complete a lesson plan job aid, using a training need of their own choosing or one that you have supplied.

Lesson Plan Development Job Aid

1. What is the topic? _____

2. Who is the audience? _____

3. How many participants?_____

4. Location of program:_____

5. Who and what are my possible resources?

   _____

   _____

   _____

6. What are the topics to be covered?

   _____

   _____

   _____

7. Program objective: _____

8. Supporting objectives: At the end of this program the trainees will be able to . . .

   _____

   _____

   _____

   _____

   _____

9. Icebreaker: How am I going to capture the audience's attention?

   _____

   _____

10. Motivation: How am I going to create a desire in the trainees to listen and learn?

_____

_____

_____

11. Review and overview: How will I review the previous lesson and give an overview of the next lesson?

_____

_____

_____

_____

_____

12. Learning activities: What activities can I use to involve the trainees?

_____

_____

_____

_____

_____

13. Media requirements: How can I visually enhance the presentation? What handouts and pictures will help me make my points?

_____

_____

_____

_____

_____

14. Summary: How will the main points of the presentation be restated?

_____

_____

15. Questions and answers: What types of question-and-answer processes will I use to make sure the trainees understand the material?

_____

_____

_____

16. Trainee evaluation: How will measurement of trainee mastery be determined?

_____

_____

_____

_____

_____

17. Follow-up: What post-course activities can be useful in ensuring transfer to the job, retention, or both?

_____

_____

Activity: Classroom Activities

Ask the learners to describe on paper and in detail three of their favorite or most useful classroom activities. Now have each learner orally describe one of those activities to the group. Collect the activities and copy them for passing out to all learners as the beginning of their activities tool kit.

Activity: Participant Packages

As an out-of-class assignment, ask the learners to bring in examples of participant packages that they can find, either from their work or from other classes. In small groups, have them critique these packages for completeness and use of good print techniques and then report back on these critiques to the class.

Checklist for Developing Print Material

- Leave plenty of white space (25 percent of the page is not too much)
- Leave space between blocks of content
- Leave space between headings and text
- Use only one or two fonts
- Use 10-point to 14-point type
- Justify the left margin
- Use running headers or footers with page number, unit, course, and revision numbers and course title
- Use simple sentences
- Be sure that the reference for each pronoun is easily understood
- Use illustrations instead of words

- Check readability
  - Have a table of contents
  - Use a new right-hand page for each major subtopic
  - Number the pages
  - Leave wide margins
  - Use "I" and "you"
  - Use the active voice
  - Explain *why* not to do something; don't just say "don't do it"
  - Use short sentences with ten to fifteen words
  - Make paragraphs short, with only three to four sentences
- Beware of
  - Stereotypes
  - Too much repetition
  - Technical jargon (without definition)
  - Acronyms (without explanation)
- Edit, edit, edit

Activity: Media Selection

Ask the learners to add a media component to their lesson plan if they have not already done so. Unless they have a real need, you should not require them to create the media but have them simply note what it should be and look like.

Job Aid for Selecting Media

Media Type	Handouts and Pass-outs	Board	Flip Chart	Overhead	PowerPoint	Video
Uses						
Explain and clarify	1	2	2	1	1	1
Basis for discussion	2	3	2	2	2	1
Organize discussion	1	2	1	2	2	3
Summarize	1	3	3	2	2	2
Education	1	1	1	1	3	1
Size of Audience						
Small	1	2	2	1	3	2
Large	1	3	3	1	1	2

1 = Most desirable; 2 = Alternative; 3 = Least desirable.

Lesson Plan Checklist

☐ Have you listed all the material, tools, equipment, and training aids you will need for the presentation?

☐ Have you checked to be sure that all these things are available and in sufficient quantity?

☐ Has the presentation been developed in a step-by-step sequence?

☐ Are key questions included?

☐ Has consideration been given to taking care of necessary safety precautions?

☐ Have appropriate reminders been included for the use of aids at the proper time?

☐ Has sufficient detail been included to satisfy the needs of the students?

☐ Have provisions been made for individual differences?

☐ Have you decided on the number of students to be used in student participation?

☐ Have you considered the use of some prepared instructional material, such as hand-out sheets?

☐ Will your students spend the greater part of their time learning and applying new information rather than taking notes?

☐ Will the final summary bring out the key points of the lesson?

☐ Do you plan to use an oral or a backboard summary?

☐ Have you considered the assignment of home study?

☐ Have sources of authority for your material been noted?

☐ Have you listed further sources of information relative to the lesson for students' use?

☐ Does your lesson plan show evidence of careful analysis of the topic to be taught?

☐ Could another instructor work from your plan and do a creditable job?

☐ Have you anticipated questions and problems that might arise during your presentation of the lesson?

☐ Does the completed lesson plan present a neat, professional appearance?

☐ Is there space on the plan for revisions?

☐ Have you remembered to include definitions of new and difficult terms?

☐ Have you tried to introduce variety into your teaching of the lesson?

☐ Do you plan to use some of the lesson material for a quiz or test?

☐ Does overall inspection of the lesson reveal a developmental approach using the principles of learning and good organization?

CHAPTER SIX

ACTIVITY: BETA AND PILOT COMPARISON

Ask the learners to take the material they've gathered on pilots and beta tests and create a chart that shows the main differences between the two concepts. It might look something like this:

Beta Test	Pilot
Stop at any point	Must run straight through
Can observe and interact	No direct observation
Questions can be asked during	Questions at end only
Can prepare learners orally	Must be done cold
Program in draft format	Program basically finalized
Different audiences	Target audience only
Time is double	Time is slightly more
Can do all in one room	Must do in learning environment
Tests content	Tests implementation, flow, time

Facilitator Skills Critique Form

Facilitator's Name _____

Directions: For each of the skills listed below, circle the appropriate word to indicate whether the facilitator exhibited each skill. Use the space below each one for any comments or specific suggestions.

1. Presented clearly stated behavioral objectives.   Yes   No

2. Created motivation with a "need to learn."   Yes   No

3. Used instructional media properly.   Yes   No

4. Prepared legible visuals.   Yes   No

5. Exhibited good listening skills.   Yes   No

6. Employed more than one type of learning activity.   Yes   No

7. Nonverbal behaviors were consistent and not distracting. Yes   No

8. Practiced positive verbal techniques.   Yes   No

9. Maintained good eye contact.   Yes   No

10. Provided clear and legible handouts and support materials.   Yes   No

Self-Instruction Facilitator Checklist

Each time a trainee takes a self-instructional package, use this checklist as your guide to help them start properly.

☐ Allow sufficient time for the trainee to complete the package.

☐ Provide quiet space.

☐ Explain that the trainee is responsible for his or her own learning.

☐ Give the trainee an answer sheet from the provided supply.

☐ Explain that all answers are to be recorded on the answer sheet.

☐ Check on the trainee every twenty minutes.

☐ Be available to answer questions.

☐ Record the trainee's name, program title, and completion date on the program completion record.

☐ Have the manager sign the program completion record.

☐ Provide at least one opportunity for guided practice.

CHAPTER SEVEN

ACTIVITY: THE LEVELS OF EVALUATION

Break the learners into five groups and assign an evaluation level to each. Ask them to complete the why, what, who, how, and when questions for their level, and bring in examples of this type of evaluation (hard copy or via the Web) that can be discussed in class. Examples are available through their own experiences and organizations, and ASTD, ISPI, and other websites. This is a good web-hunting exercise to familiarize them with training websites.

Activity: Developing a Multilevel Evaluation

Provide the learners with the rudiments of a training system and ask them to create an evaluation methodology for it that contains all five levels, including a reaction sheet, instructions on the criterion referencing of learner evaluations, a procedure that details ways to do a Level 3 evaluation, and plans for how they will do both Level 4 and Level 5 evaluation.

me

Facilitator Level 1 Evaluation of Self-Instruction

Complete this form by filling in the blanks.

Return the completed form to _____ by _____ .

1. I gave the [title]_____ SDL package to [employee name] _____ .

2. The SDL package was completed in [time] _____ .

3. I had the trainee complete the SDL in the [location] _____ .

4. I checked back with the trainee every _____ minutes or so.

5. I spent [time spent] _____ providing a guided practice session with the trainee.

6. I recorded the trainee's name, SDL title, completion date, and my initials on the _____ form.

7. In general, I feel that the [name of program] will be [impression of program].

   _____

   _____

   _____

Your name: _____

Date: _____

CHAPTER NINE

ACTIVITY: PREPARING FOR ASYNCHRONOUS E-LEARNING

Have the learners use the following Yes or No checklist for either their own or a simulated environment to determine if an organization is ready for e-learning.

Questions to Consider when Analyzing Your Organization's Readiness for E-Learning

Yes No Do the strengths of e-learning match the content we must deliver?

Yes No Do the delivery advantages of e-learning match our learning environment?

Yes No Will e-learning save us design, development, or implementation time?

Yes No Will e-learning be more efficient for our learners?

Yes No Overall, will e-learning provide us with any real cost savings?

Yes No Will our culture support the nonclassroom environment of e-learning?

Yes No Are our trainers and instructors ready to make the shift to asynchronous e-learning?

Yes No Do we have the technology infrastructure in place to support e-learning?

Yes No Do we have the funding to augment the technology as necessary?

Yes No Will we be able to support and maintain the e-learning initiative under current or future conditions?

Yes No Will our learners be ready to become e-learners?

Yes No Is there visible high level support for the process?

Yes No Do we have the right design resources for e-learning?

Yes No Are our learners comfortable with computer operating and e-mail systems?

Activity: Selling E-Learning

Ask the learners to develop a presentation plan for selling their concept of e-learning to the management of an organization, using the selling points in the following list and others that they might feel are valuable. Post these presentation plans for all class members to review and borrow from.

Selling Points for E-Learning

- Cost savings (be careful)
- More effective
- Greater learner choice
- Greater manager control
- Reduced training time
- Geographic implications
- Allows learning 24x7
- Easily updateable
- Provides a consistent message
- Trains large numbers in a short time

Activity: E-Learning Self-Assessment

Ask the learners to complete the e-learning self-assessment for themselves and then discuss its usefulness in initiating an e-learning system and what other items might be added.

E-Learning Self-Assessment

Statement	Yes	No	Comment
I am comfortable using a computer.			
I have little problem learning to use new software.			
I can use a web browser effectively.			
I have used electronic bulletin boards in the past.			
I have engaged in threaded discussions using a computer.			
I participate in chat rooms.			
I'm comfortable interacting on-line with people.			
I'm comfortable using my computer as a learning tool.			
I am self-motivated to learn.			
I feel I can manage my own learning time effectively.			
I feel learning can happen in other places than the classroom.			
I believe I can manage my own learning.			
I have good access to a computer in my work area.			
I have access to a computer and the Internet at home.			

Activity: E-Learning Rollout Plan

Using the following list of ideas and any others you may have discussed, have the learners develop an e-learning rollout plan.

- Use quick start guides to help the learners hit the ground running.
- Run focus groups ahead of time to determine learner needs and build excitement.
- Have a pop-up support function available inside your programs.
- Make sure your start-up phone-in support is 24x7 for the first few weeks.
- Create help screens in your program introduction.
- Have a help desk number available as a menu pop-up.
- Create a major launch event that goes throughout the organization.
- Use giveaways to remind the learners about e-learning.
- Use personal contact where possible.
- Step up your marketing to all levels.
- Use e-mail to announce new programs.
- Communicate learner and departmental successes.
- Write reports and send them to all interested parties.
- Develop rewards and incentives for learners and supervisors.
    - Produce printable completion certificates that can be exchanged for prizes.
    - For management development and other multiprogram processes, create a wall display plaque with spaces for stickers as programs are completed.
    - When a program is completed, have a copy of the completion certificate sent to the learner's boss's printer or computer.
- Create a culture that prizes learning.
- Find incentives for sharing learner learnings with others.
- Develop peer recognition processes.
    - Learner of the month
    - Special events
    - Group e-mails
    - Learner chat rooms or electronic bulletin boards
    - E-newsletters

Self-Directed Learning Plan

Learning Objectives	Learning Process	Resources	Possible Obstacles	Target Dates	Evaluation
What do I need to know or be able to do?	What steps will I need to take?	What resources will I need?	And how to overcome them	When will I complete each step?	I will have succeeded in my learning when . . .

Activity: Asynchronous E-Learning Debate

Hold a debate in which the two debating groups argue the pros and cons of asynchronous e-learning. Two concepts that should be stressed here are (1) this can't be argued outside the environment in which it is being considered, as it is simply a delivery system, and (2) some synchronous advantages and disadvantages will probably sneak in.

Activity: Storyboards

Ask the learners to take everything they have done so far with your common training need and use it to create an asynchronous storyboard for the program, using either any template they feel comfortable with or one that you assign.

Activity: Working with Technical Experts

In a role-play scenario, have the learners work in pairs: one is the instructional designer trying to explain his or her storyboard to the other, who plays the role of the technical expert. After each has tried the instructional designer role, ask them to discuss as a class some of the problems they encountered and then revise their storyboard to make it clearer to the technical expert.

Activity: Learner Interfaces

Ask the learners to do a web search for various types of learner interfaces and bring the URLs in for discussion of good and bad points.

Activity: Evaluating E-Learning Programs

Ask the learners to use the following checklist to evaluate various off-the-shelf e-learning programs.

E-Learning Program Evaluation Checklist

- Indication that a JTA, delivery analysis, and audience analysis were done
- Well-written objectives at various levels
- No need for an instructor
- Directions evident at the start of the program and the start of each chunk as needed
- Proper chunking of content
- Self-tests sprinkled throughout
- Good use, but not abuse, of media
- Plenty of activities and interactions
- Criterion-referenced learner evaluation where needed
- Inclusion of continuing postcourse activities
- Whether the amount and quality of the content is adequate
- Whether the content meets the objectives
- Whether the tone and examples match the needs of the intended audience

E-Learning Design Hints

- List all the materials, tools, equipment, and training aids your learner will need for the program.
- Include a final summary activity.
- Use test-outs where they make sense to decrease learning time.
- Use branching processes for individualization.
- Include a glossary and balloon definitions.
- Include a frequently asked questions screen where possible.
- Design in plenty of examples.
- Use click-and-drag activities to teach sequencing and sorting.

- Label all materials with version numbers.
- Modules should be twelve to fifteen minutes long, maximum.
- All self-tests and other evaluations should have specific directions.
- Make note of your sources of authority for the content.
- Provide sources of further information on topics for clarification or enrichment.
- Chunk, and then chunk again.
- Provide a content help number.
- Use chat and threaded discussion functions to increase interactivity.
- Be sure your scripts are politically correct.
- Be careful that your use of humor is not offensive.
- Reduce scrolling as much as possible; minimize graphics if necessary.
- Provide information with the fewest possible clicks.
- For lots of information use hot links; for small bits use pop-ups and mouseovers.
- Create pop-up and hotlink windows that do not require enlargement or scrolling.

Questions for E-Learning System Development
- Have you performed an analysis of the content you plan to deliver?
    - Does it meet one or more organizational needs?
    - Does it meet individual employee development needs?
    - Is asynchronous e-learning the right delivery for the content?
- Have you created a proper design?
    - Are there enough objectives, are they learner based, are they useable?
    - Is there plenty of interactivity in your programs?
    - Are there both self and formal assessments of the learning?
- Do you have the right user interface or learning site?
    - Has it been tested by your users for ease of use and intuitiveness?
    - Will it meet all your e-learning needs?
    - Are you using it consistently?
- Have you scheduled beta tests and pilots for all your courses?
- Do you know what you need to evaluate and how you plan to do it?

- Do you have the right policies and procedures for your corporate environment?

- Do learners, instructors, designers, and administrators know what their roles are and how they will fulfill them?

- Are there job descriptions for individuals with special roles in your intervention?

- Have the necessary committees been created and populated?

- Is your technology adequate for your implementation?

- Have you chosen the place for the e-learning to occur, and will it be adequate?

- Have all time constraints been considered?

- Has the right help desk function for your intervention been created and staffed?

CHAPTER TEN
ACTIVITY: REPURPOSING FOR SYNCHRONOUS E-LEARNING

Ask the learners to take the classroom program they developed for the common training need—or any other classroom program they might wish to use—and repurpose it for e-learning, using the bullet list that follows as their guide. One item to look for in the repurposing is inclusion of a good number of mini-interactions.

- Objectives are more critical in a synchronous delivery, so review them and tighten them up as needed.

- Planning is more vital, particularly precourse communications.

- Questioning techniques will be different.

- Activities may need to be translated.

- The facilitator guide needs to be more technology specific.

- Watch for areas of the course that contain "talking heads" or "talking PowerPoints."

- Know the hardware and software needs of both the learners and the facilitator and make sure they are met.

- Know the level of computer proficiency of each as well.

- Know what the "need to know" content is.

- Know the time expectations, for both design and in-class time.

- Know the number of learners and where they are located (twelve to fifteen is optimal, twenty is the maximum).

Activity: Chat Activities

Ask the learners to sketch out a simulated plan for using each of the chat activities in the following list as part of their design.

- Learner to instructor
- Learner to learner
- All learners to all learners
- Learner to panel
- Learner group to panel
- Panel to learner
- Panel to learner group

Activity: Synchronous Activities

Have the learners choose two or three synchronous activities from the following list and sketch out a simulated plan for how to use them in a synchronous program.

- Pre-tests
- Knowledge sharing
- Collaborative problem solving
- Team teaching
- Roundtable discussions (via open chat)
- Learner manipulation of facilitator software
- Collaborative writing and editing
- Individual coaching
- Private or group discussions during breaks
- Debates
- Critiquing of information
- Brainstorming
- Individual problem solving with written solutions
- Observation of demonstration
- Games
- Annotative activities: make a list, create a time line, draw a map, draw flow charts, create spreadsheets

- Questioning
- Discussions
- Creating class glossaries
- Application sharing
- Guest experts or panels
- Learners' resource from the Web
- Learners taking over and teaching
- Team competitions
- Using breakout rooms and off line messaging
- Short quizzes to check comprehension and for retention

These quizzes and any Level 2 evaluation questions can be enhanced through the use of graphics and even videos in a synchronous environment.

- Single and multi-user whiteboard activities
- Timed games that increase the excitement and competition, such as Beat the Clock or Ten Thousand Dollar Pyramid

Synchronous Facilitator Guide Template

Time	Content and Notes	Technology	Learner Activity
	Add content outline and any notes to the facilitator here	Place names and numbers of slides of handouts, instructions for other forms of media such as still camera, sound or video, special technology comments, and instructor notes on demonstrations or other technology aspects here	Describe learners' roles and each activity they will be involved in here

Activity: Other Synchronous Instructional Resources

Ask the learners to create a role description for a simulated synchronous program in which each of the following individuals plays a part:

- Panelists

- SMEs, not only for content development but as online or offline experts

- Technical experts who could be available to the learners and to the facilitator before the class and during it

- A cofacilitator who takes on some of the actual teaching aspects

- An assistant, who doesn't share the teaching but handles any necessary support role such as technical help, off line questions and media staging.

- A producer, usually used in a more complex program design to call up media, give cues, and stage panels, experts, or demonstrations.

Activity: Simulated Synchronous Program

Have the learners sketch out the design for using both a message board and a chat room in a simulated synchronous program.

Job Aid: Facilitating Synchronous E-Learning Interactions

Tips for the Facilitator

- Ask provocative questions.
- Work to pull a variety of ideas, answers, and stories from the learners.
- Use open-ended questions to elicit more thoughtful responses.
- Listen to or read the learner comments carefully (don't think ahead).
- Be concise and clear in what you write on the screen or say.
- Validate all replies with positive feedback.
- Debrief.
- Allow the group to exhaust all possibilities before going on.
- Mini-interactions, like a simple hello, are important.
- Take breaks.
- Look for unifying threads during discussions (use them for summaries).
- Encourage learners to assess each other's work.
- Allow learners to help form behavior standards and program goals.
- Encourage; never judge or allow others to judge.
- Be provocative but not argumentative.

- Take time to allow the participants to form answers (dead time is OK).
- Bring in lurkers with nonvolunteer Yes or No questions or by assigning a presentation or question to them in advance.
- Clear response screens periodically.
- Observe breakout rooms and review chat logs.
- Erase whiteboards when needed.
- Talk off line to overly aggressive participants.
- Create special interest groups to work on extraneous issues off line.

Activity: Teaching Learners to Be Synchronous Learners

Ask your learners to create a program for training learners to become synchronous e-learners. Have them share their programs in small groups and then, after making any required changes or additions, post them for other class members to review.

A Self-Assessment of Personal Synchronous E-Learning Characteristics

- Can you accept the responsibility for your own learning?
- Are you comfortable using a computer?
- Are you self-motivated when learning new skills?
- Are you self-disciplined?
- Do you have the desire to learn?
- Are you good at setting goals for yourself and then meeting them?
- Are you able to complete assignments or study for tests without undue procrastination?
- Do you work well in groups?
- Are you comfortable interacting in a chat room or posting to a threaded discussion?
- Do you use e-mail effectively?
- Do you tend to participate in class discussions?
- Are you comfortable working with others when you never see them?
- Can you learn from your fellow students' sharing of their experiences?
- Are you comfortable sharing your experiences and expertise with others to enhance their learning?

Synchronous Class Initiation Checklist

Before the first day of class:

- Send preclass communications:
  - Learner guide and slides (download)
  - Objectives
  - Time and date of class; label time A.M. or P.M. if program is global
  - Evaluation procedures
  - Procedures for logging on: password, dial-in number
  - Contact information for both instructor and participant
  - Posting of bios and pictures
  - Technical problems job aid if available
- Complete software requirements:
  - Schedule session.
  - Create password.
  - Invite attendees.
  - Invite yourself as an attendee.
  - Set up conference call (if needed).
  - Plan for necessary reports.
- Locate proper facilitation environment:
  - No background noise
  - Distraction free
  - Private: use "Do Not Disturb" signs
  - Space for all hardware and note taking
  - Power connection
  - Comfort: seating, heat, and so on
  - Lighting
- Other
  - Create session folder for storing materials.
  - Prepare class roster.
  - Perform final review of program.
  - Coordinate with other resources if they are part of the program.

On class day:

- Set up delivery area.
  - Post "Do Not Disturb" sign.
  - Turn off phone ring and forward calls.
  - Notify colleagues and other key people that you'll be facilitating.
  - Get water.
  - Put clock in view.
  - Set up notes and guides for easy reading.
  - Check in with other resources.
- Set up computer(s).
  - Set up participant machine so you can see what participants are seeing.
  - Close all nonessential applications.
  - Clear browser cache and reboot machine.
  - Set monitor for proper resolution.
  - Check network connections.
  - Check audio and phone.

When class starts:

- Start the session fifteen to thirty minutes early to deal with problems and chat with learners.
- Check for screen resolution problems.
- Begin the program promptly.
- Welcome participants.
- Ask for personal introductions.
- State objectives and ask for feedback.
- Ask for confirmation that everyone is on line and can hear.
- Provide assistance phone number again for emergencies.
- Tour virtual classroom highlights, particularly feedback mechanisms.
- Explain how class will be conducted, particularly aspects such as random nonvolunteer questions, interactions with peers, amount of informality, and special types of activities.
- Be ready with your introductory activity (icebreaker).

Activity: Online Learning

Have two teams debate the pros and cons of online learning. The key concept here is that it must be in terms of the learning environment; if they figure that out early, provide them with a simulated environment or two to help make the debate realistic.

As an offshoot of this, you might provide a number of environments and have small groups debate for each environment, thus showing how the pros and cons are affected by the learning environment.

Online Decision Job Aid

Yes   No   Is the content is mostly knowledge based?

Yes   No   Can any skill-based content be handled in the online environment or by blending?

Yes   No   Can effective activities and exercises be developed?

Yes   No   Are applicable paper-based graphics available, or can they be developed?

Yes   No   Is the need for human interaction during the learning important to its success?

Yes   No   Is there a need for collaborative learning?

Yes   No   Are team-based problem-solving and decision-making activities and practice important?

Yes   No   Is the background knowledge of the learners known?

Yes   No   Is corporate learning discipline strong enough to expect the learners to attend scheduled chat rooms and make posting deadlines?

Yes   No   Are critical content SMEs available often enough to share their expertise during chat room functions or on the discussion boards?

Yes   No   Are the employees who need the content in different locations?

Yes   No   Are competent designers available to create the online program?

Yes   No   Must the content be taught on a periodic basis no matter what the size of the audience?

Yes   No   Is the technology available for online learning?

Yes   No   Are trained online facilitators available?

Yes   No   Can the content be taught in an environment that is not face to face?

Yes   No   Is there a relatively short design window?

Yes   No   Is the content unstable?

Index